WOMEN, MINISTRY AND THE GOSPEL

EXPLORING NEW PARADIGMS

EDITED BY

MARK HUSBANDS AND TIMOTHY LARSEN

IVP Academic

An imprint of InterVarsity Press
Downers Grove, Illinois

InterVarsity Press
P.O. Box 1400, Downers Grove, IL 60515-1426
World Wide Web: www.ivpress.com
E-mail: email@ivpress.com

InterVarsity Press® is the book-publishing division of InterVarsity Christian Fellowship/USA®, a student movement active on campus at hundreds of universities, colleges and schools of nursing in the United States of America, and a member movement of the International Fellowship of Evangelical Students. For information about local and regional activities, write Public Relations Dept., InterVarsity Christian Fellowship/USA, 6400 Schroeder Rd., P.O. Box 7895, Madison, WI 53707-7895, or visit the IVCF website at <www.intervarsity.org>.

Scripture quotations, unless otherwise noted, are from the New Revised Standard Version of the Bible, *copyright 1989 by the Division of Christian Education of the National Council of the Churches of Christ in the USA. Used by permission. All rights reserved.*

The table on p. 109 is from Women, Class and Society in Early Christianity: Models from Luke-Acts *by James M. Arlandson. Copyright © 1997 by Hendrickson Publishers, Inc. Used by permission. All rights reserved.*

Design: Cindy Kiple
Images: preacher: Digital Vision/Getty Images
          woman at lectern: Dave & Les Jacobs/Getty Images

ISBN 978-0-8308-2566-0

Printed in the United States of America ∞

Library of Congress Cataloging-in-Publication Data

Women, ministry and the gospel: exploring new paradigms / edited by
Mark Husbands and Timothy Larsen.
   p. cm.
   Includes bibliographical references and indexes.
   ISBN-13: 978-0-8308-2566-0 (pbk.: alk. paper)
   ISBN-10: 0-8308-2566-5 (pbk.: alk. paper)

1. Women in church work—Congresses. I. Husbands, Mark, 1961- II.
Larsen, Timothy, 1967-
   BV4415.W642   2006
   262'.14082—dc22

                                                                    2006030492

P	16	15	14	13	12	11	10	9	8	7	6	5	4	3	2	1
Y	20	19	18	17	16	15	14	13	12	11	10	09	08	07			

CONTENTS

Abbreviations 7

INTRODUCTION
Mark Husbands and Timothy Larsen 9

PART 1: NEW PERSPECTIVES ON THE BIBLICAL EVIDENCE

1 DEBORAH
A Role Model for Christian Public Ministry
Rebecca G. S. Idestrom 17

2 WHAT WOMEN CAN DO IN MINISTRY
Full Participation Within Biblical Boundaries
James M. Hamilton Jr. 32

3 WOMEN IN MINISTRY
A Further Look at 1 Timothy 2
I. Howard Marshall 53

PART 2: NEW PERSPECTIVES ON THE BODY OF CHRIST

4 PROPHECY, WOMEN IN LEADERSHIP AND THE BODY OF CHRIST
Lynn H. Cohick 81

5 CHRIST'S GIFTED BRIDE
Gendered Members in Ministry in Acts and Paul
Fredrick J. Long 98

PART 3: NEW THEOLOGICAL PERSPECTIVES
ON IDENTITY AND MINISTRY

6 RECONCILIATION AS THE DOGMATIC LOCATION OF HUMANITY
"Your Life Is Hidden with Christ in God"
Mark Husbands 127

7 IDENTITY AND MINISTRY IN LIGHT OF THE GOSPEL
A View from the Kitchen
Margaret Kim Peterson 148

PART 4: NEW PERSPECTIVES FROM THE HUMANITIES
AND SOCIAL SCIENCES

8 OPPOSITE SEXES OR NEIGHBORING SEXES?
What Do the Social Sciences Really Tell Us?
Mary Stewart Van Leeuwen   171

9 HOLY BOLDNESS, HOLY WOMEN
Agents of the Gospel
Cheryl J. Sanders   200

10 WOMEN IN PUBLIC MINISTRY
A Historic Evangelical Distinctive
Timothy Larsen   213

PART 5: BEYOND THE IMPASSE: TOWARD NEW PARADIGMS

11 WOMEN, MINISTRY AND THE GOSPEL
Hints for a New Paradigm?
Henri Blocher   239

12 FORGING A MIDDLE WAY BETWEEN COMPLEMENTARIANS AND
EGALITARIANS
Sarah Sumner   250

13 EGALITARIANS AND COMPLEMENTARIANS TOGETHER?
A Modest Proposal
Timothy George   266

Contributors   289

Name Index   291

Subject Index   294

Scripture Index   301

ABBREVIATIONS

ABCom	Anchor Bible Commentary
BBR	*Bulletin for Biblical Research*
BDAG	*A Greek English Lexicon of the New Testament and Other Early Christian Literature*. By Walter Bauer. Revised and edited by Frederick William Danker. 3rd ed. Chicago and London: University of Chicago Press, 2000.
BECNT	Baker Exegetical Commentary on the New Testament
BJS	*Brown Judaic Studies*
bMeg	*Babylonian Talmud Megilla*
BZNW	*Beihefte zur Zeitschrift für die neutestamentliche Wissenschaft*
CBE	Christians for Biblical Equality. More information on this organization can be found at <www.cbeinternational.org>.
CBMW	The Council on Biblical Manhood and Womanhood. More information and the council can be found at <www.cbmw.org>.
CBQ	*Catholic Biblical Quarterly*
DBE	*Discovering Biblical Equality: Complementarity Without Hierarchy*. Edited by Ronald W. Pierce and Rebecca Merrill Groothuis. Downers Grove: InterVarsity Press, 2005.
EFBT	*Evangelical Feminism and Biblical Truth*. By Wayne Grudem. Sisters, Ore.: Multnomah, 2004.
EvQ	*Evangelical Quarterly*
Int	Interpretation: A Bible Commentary for Teaching and Preaching
JBL	*Journal of Biblical Literature*
JBMW	*Journal for Biblical Manhood and Womanhood*
JETS	*Journal of the Evangelical Theological Society*
JSNT	*Journal for the Study of the New Testament*
JSNTSup	Journal for the Study of the New Testament: Supplement Series
JSOT	*Journal for the Study of the Old Testament*
JSOT	Journal for the Study of the Old Testament: Supplement Series
JTS	*Journal of Theological Studies*

LXX	Septuagint (Greek translation of the Hebrew Bible)
MT	Masoretic Text (of the Hebrew Bible)
NASB	New American Standard Version
NRSV	New Revised Standard Version
NICNT	New International Commentary on the New Testament
NIDOTTE	*New International Dictionary of Old Testament Theology and Exegesis.* By W. A. VanGemeren et al. 5 vols. Grand Rapids: Zondervan, 1997.
NIGTC	New International Greek Testament Commentary
NIV	New International Version
NovT	*Novum Testamentum*
NSBT	New Studies in Biblical Theology
NTS	*New Testament Studies*
RBMW	*Recovering Biblical Manhood and Womanhood: A Response to Evangelical Feminism.* Edited by John Piper and Wayne Grudem. Wheaton, Ill.: Crossway, 1991. The book's full text can be found at <www.cbmw.org/rbmw/>.
SNTSMS	Society for the New Testament Studies Monograph Series
TJ	*Trinity Journal*
TSF Bulletin	*Theological Students Fellowship Bulletin*
TynBul	*Tyndale Bulletin*
WBC	Word Biblical Commentary
WTJ	*Westminster Theological Journal*

INTRODUCTION

The goal of this volume is to present new paradigms and fresh perspectives for evangelicals on an issue that often is prematurely settled with reference to well-entrenched, set-piece arguments. In this book, evangelical scholars think aloud about softer, more nuanced ways to articulate viewpoints on an issue of contemporary significance. Along these lines, it is emblematic that this volume concludes with an essay by Timothy George. Founding dean of Beeson Divinity School and an executive editor of Christianity Today, Dr. George is one of the most trusted evangelical voices in America today. His learned, anchored, irenic and measured spirit is widely respected by evangelicals, including those who self-identify as egalitarians on the question of women in ministry; his Southern Baptist ordination and membership in a congregation in the Southern Baptist Convention locates him in a complementarian context. When we invited him to contribute to this project, Dr. George had never before addressed this issue of women in ministry in print, and we are delighted that a distinctive feature of this volume includes bringing such an important and valuable voice into the conversation. As we had hoped, Dr. George did indeed set the right tone by wisely subtitling his contribution, "A Modest Proposal." Deferring to Dr. George's judicious leadership, we offer this collection as a modest contribution to the ongoing discussions among evangelical Christians regarding the question of women in public ministry. It is certainly not intended to be the last word on the subject or the only book an interested person needs to read in order to grasp the full contours of the debate, but it is, we hope, a valuable counterpart to other works that take a more monolithic and predictable approach to this question.

Committed egalitarians might well be frustrated by the fact that what they view as their best arguments are not aired here. Notably, there is an essay on 1 Timothy 2, perhaps the most important keynote passage for complementarians, but there is no essay on Galatians 3:28, perhaps the keynote passage most often evoked by egalitarians today. Moreover, there is no essay offering a comprehensive biblical and theological case for an egalitarian position, while a faithful and able attempt at a comprehensive view of the complementarian position is presented in the essay by James M. Hamilton Jr., a scholar who has self-identified with that point of view through having an article published in the Council of Biblical Manhood and Womanhood's *Journal for Biblical Manhood and Womanhood*.

Still, committed complementarians might well be frustrated that so many of the essays in this volume, although they only address individual pieces of the puzzle, have an egalitarian drift to them. While Mary Stewart Van Leeuwen's essay is not a holistic biblical and theological case for egalitarianism but rather is confined to questions arising from discussions in the social sciences, she is a prominent self-identified egalitarian serving on the board of reference of Christians for Biblical Equality. Furthermore, a leading New Testament scholar who is a complementarian had promised to provide us with another essay on 1 Timothy 2. The deadline that had been agreed to came and went, and we waited a full year (with a renewed promise that caused us to hope that it would indeed come eventually) before we finally decided, regrettably, that we had to go ahead with this book without that contribution. As the editors of this volume, we would be the first to admit that this collection would have been all the better if it had included a chapter by an eminent biblical scholar expounding this key text of Scripture from a complementarian perspective, as we had planned and been assured that it would. Once again, we can only appeal to those who would have wished for more comprehensive and definitive contributions from one position or the other to allow this book to serve a more modest function.

One might ask, *What then is that function?* As stated, the goal of this volume is to present new paradigms and fresh perspectives for evangelicals on an issue that arguably has an increasing tendency to cover well-worn territory, leaving many with a sense that there must be no substantial way beyond traditional arguments. In this book, evangelical scholars seek to offer less rigid ways of addressing the issue. Henri Blocher and Sarah Sumner make particularly concerted efforts to think outside the standard categories in order to attempt new paradigms. Nevertheless, it would not necessarily be illegitimate for readers to conclude that their offerings can ultimately be categorized as a version of one or the other of the standard options, despite the fact that each author does not want to own the label. However, it is telling indeed that informal discussions with colleagues familiar with these essays quickly revealed that various people had made conflicting judgments about which "camp" the thoughts of these scholars allegedly "ultimately" supported. If these random chats are anything to go by, it would seem that we are quicker to see when someone has appeared to "give ground" and to label them as "on the wrong side" than we are to see how much of our own position they have retained and affirmed.

Also, a variety of scholars work in this volume on specific pieces of the puzzle that might prompt and aid readers who are on their own, wider journey of rethinking or solidifying a stance on this issue. Each piece, however, is far too incomplete to "prove" that one side or the other is the right one on its own. Rebecca Idestrom on Deborah, Fredrick Long on Christ's gifted bride, or Margaret Kim Peterson on "a view from the kitchen"—just to name a few examples—should not be thought of as essays that aim to bear the weight of "deciding" the issue. They are offered as perceptive and temperate contributions that can stimulate the thinking of readers.

The multidisciplinary approach of this volume also strives to refresh the conversation. Evangelicals are Bible people, and many of the chapters presented here are therefore fittingly written by biblical scholars in order to address aspects of the scriptural evidence. Those who are very familiar with biblical arguments, however, might find a new and fruitful way into this conversation by thinking in more formal theological categories and terms—or ecclesial and ministerial ones—or by factoring in the resources offered by the humanities or the social sciences. While it would be arrogant for a historian, for example, to imagine that a contribution from their discipline could "settle" the issue, it would also be arrogant for those outside that field to choose willfully to ignore such God-given resources. More than one essay in this book evokes the apostle Paul's teaching regarding the different members of the body of Christ, and—if we may use that as an analogy—each individual chapter here is not given as if "an eye," as it were, can be the whole argument on women in ministry. Likewise, to continue the analogy, we hope that those who find other disciplines more decisive will not be tempted to assume that because an argument is not "an eye" that it, therefore, has no substantial contribution to make.

Another goal has been to conduct this conversation in a way that is less stri-

dent and heated than is sometimes the case. A tacit assumption of this book is
that fellow brothers and sisters in Christ of good will and deep faith are on
both sides of this issue, and therefore it would behoove us to be concerned
about the moral character of Christian scholarship and witness. In short, under the banner of Christ, we set out to listen to one another and to treat one
another and speak of one another with respect in a spirit of kindness, gracious-
ness and love.

What is it about this conversation that has sometimes made all this so difficult? Both well-defined sides would probably answer that deeper, underlying principles of great import are at stake in this discussion, and it is not at
all our intent to dismiss such claims. Still, it is worth reflecting on another
explanation for the sometimes less than charitable reactions to the theological work of fellow Christians. Whatever ambiguity there might be in theory,
there is no ambiguity about what is happening in practice in any given ecclesial context in terms of gender and ministry. We learn to discern the gender of the people we meet well before we ever start kindergarten. If the new
minister in your church held a heretical doctrine of the Trinity, they might
be able to minister for a long time before this became manifest and was observed, but you would know before they ever said a word if they are a man
or a woman. A church can decide that it is going to leave as an open question, for example, issues that divide Arminians and Calvinists, and their pastor could minister in a way that did not vex either side year upon year, but
the issue of women in ministry can never be set aside as an open question in
this way. Even if the question is pronounced to be formally under review, in
the meantime women are either being allowed to or not being allowed to
preach, teach, serve as elders, be ordained, preside at the Communion table
or otherwise engage in public ministry. It is worth considering the thesis that
church members often fight most aggressively among themselves about issues that are conspicuously visible. This line of thought, incidentally, might
help to explain why the so-called worship wars are often so emotive as well.
In nineteenth-century Britain an entire denomination was once formed as a
result of a dispute regarding whether or not a church should install an organ
for use in corporate worship. There is, of course, merit to thinking about the
visibility of the church as it presses the question of the integrity or coherence
of faith and practice. Accordingly, the visibility of gender offers us a compelling justification for providing a historically and theologically variegated ac-

count of how evangelicals might address the question of women in ministry.

Given the fact that this issue is literally unavoidable, it is a fitting use of the talents of evangelical scholars to endeavor to offer the church new paradigms and perspectives. Although people who join this conversation are perhaps more often assailed than thanked for their pains, we should be grateful to all the scholars who have contributed to this volume for their willingness to use their training, expertise and God-given talents to help the church address this vital issue.

There will always be those who will comment wearily that they thought this issue was settled—or at least decisively argued—long ago, by which they mean that they personally became convinced of a particular position long ago that they see no reason to abandon. We need such people: it would be of little benefit to the church suddenly to find that absolutely everyone was in flux at once! Such people might be tempted to forget, however, that there are always evangelicals who have just at this moment in time had the issue pressed upon them in an inescapable way. We meet them continually: complementarians who are suddenly starting to rethink the issue in the light of a call to ordained ministry that has been discerned by their daughter; egalitarians who have joined a complementarian church and are beginning to see an internal logic and attractiveness to its life, ministry, doctrine and practice; confused young people who have started to see a potential marriage partner in a person with a resolute and decided view on this subject. This book is for them. While we have said that it is not intended as the only book a person needs to read on this issue, we cheerfully recommend this book to anyone who might have just arrived at this issue for the first time, or for someone who has just been stirred to rethink it due to some biblical, theological, ministerial, ecclesial or personal prompt that cannot be ignored.

In the end this book is offered to Christ in the hope that the work of the scholars included in this collection will be blessed, and therefore taken up for genuine consideration and encouragement, as we join with others in seeking to ensure that the visible ministry of the church is a faithful witness to the love, mercy and power of the gospel.

PART ONE

NEW PERSPECTIVES ON THE BIBLICAL EVIDENCE

DEBORAH

A Role Model for Christian Public Ministry

Rebecca G. S. Idestrom

JOHN GOLDINGAY HAS WRITTEN THE FOLLOWING about Deborah: "As someone who combined the role of judge, prophet, leader, and poet, there is no doubt that she is the greatest figure in the book."[1] What leads Goldingay to make such a claim? Is Deborah the greatest figure in the book of Judges? What is it about her and her character that make her stand out? What can we learn from Deborah regarding faithful leadership? In this article, I will explore the leadership role of Deborah in the book of Judges and see how she can become a role model for both men and women in Christian public ministry. In the conclusion, I will consider what we can learn from Deborah and her example as a leader and servant of the Lord.

Deborah was a very gifted, capable and well-respected leader, who served in a number of roles. Her story is told in Judges 4—5. From these two chapters, we learn that as a leader raised up by God, Deborah was a prophet and a judge, who played a major role in bringing deliverance to the people from Canaanite oppression. Besides this, she is also described as a worship leader, a singer, a poet, a wife and mother. Some have also suggested that in the Song of Deborah, she is described as a warrior or military leader. As we can

---

[1]John Goldingay, "Motherhood, Machismo, and the Purpose of Yahweh in Judges 4—5," *Anvil* 12, no. 1 (1995): 24.

see, she had a number of responsibilities as a leader and played an important role in serving the Lord and her people at a critical time in their history. I want to explore these various roles and what we can learn about leadership from her.

There are also a number of things that make her unique within the book of Judges, which make her stand out in many ways. Interestingly, there are a number of similarities and parallels between her and Moses as well as with Samuel. What do these parallels tell us about Deborah and her significance? Deborah is the only judge in the book who is also a prophet. Deborah is the only person who has a song attributed to her. No other narrative about a judge in the book is followed by a poem, a victory song. What is the significance of this? Deborah is also the only judge who is described as doing the work of judging *before* she plays a role in the deliverance of her people from oppression. She is the only woman described as a judge. This makes her unique not only in comparison to the male judges, but also in comparison to the women characters in the book. Deborah stands out among the women in Judges. She is a strong, independent woman who is a person of integrity and faithfulness, whose character is without fault and is seen in a positive light. She is a spiritual leader whose commitment to the Lord is seen in her faithful obedience to be the Lord's messenger and representative to his people.

God raised up Deborah to be a prophet and judge to the people of Israel during the time of the Judges. Let us consider the context in which she ministered. The period of the Judges was a time of crisis for the Israelites, both physically and spiritually. They had entered and settled in the Promised Land under Joshua's leadership. But once Joshua had died (and the elders that followed him also had died; Judg 2:7), the people began a cycle of turning away from the Lord. The book describes a repeated, cyclical pattern in which the people continually did evil in the sight of the Lord by turning to idolatrous worship of other gods. In response, the Lord allowed the Israelites to be oppressed by their enemies. However, when the people cried out to the Lord in their distress, he had mercy on them by raising up judges who governed the people and delivered them from oppression. As long as the judge lived, there was stability and peace in the land, but as soon as the judge died, the people turned away from the Lord and the whole cycle began again (Judg 2:11-23; 3:7-11). As a result the narrator describes this period as a time when the people were doing what seemed right in their own eyes, rather than what was right in the Lord's eyes (Judg 17:6; 21:25). They needed leaders who would remind them that as God's chosen people they were called to faithful love and obedience to the Lord and to the covenant.

What exactly was the role of a judge? Deuteronomy 16:18-20 describes the role of a judge as an arbitrator and dispenser of justice and righteousness. Judges were to be fair and just, and not pervert justice by accepting bribes. Their role was to administer justice according to the law of the Lord. In the book of Judges, we only see Deborah described explicitly in this role (Judg 4:4-5). The other judges are simply described as "judging Israel" without further elaboration. This has led some scholars to suggest that "judging" (*šāpaṭ*) has the broader meaning of governing.[2] Because the Lord used the judges to bring deliverance to the people, they are also referred to as saviors or deliverers (and some argue that this was their primary role).[3] Clinton McCann, following Jon Berquist, suggests that "judge" should be rendered as "bringer of justice." He writes, "This designation suggests that the judges were persons entrusted with the enactment of God's will for the world; this encompassed deliverance from external oppression (2:16, 18), leadership exercised to ensure the exclusive worship and service of God (2:19), and hence the creation of internal conditions to support life as God wills it to be."[4] Thus, the judge was called to bring justice both physically, from external oppression, and spiritually, to instruct and help the Israelites live out their spiritual commitment to the Lord in faithful obedience to the covenant.

Within this group of leaders we find Deborah. How did Deborah fulfill this role as judge? As judge, she both administered justice as well as played a major role in bringing deliverance to her people. Since Deborah is the only one who is described in the role of judge as outlined in Deuteronomy 16:18-20, perhaps her example helps us know what is meant when the narrator simply states that the other judges "judged Israel." She sets the example so there is no need for the narrator to elaborate further. Her example suffices.

There are twelve judges mentioned by name in the book of Judges.[5] Debo-

---

[2]J. Clinton McCann, *Judges*, Int (Louisville, Ky.: John Knox Press, 2002), p. 4.

[3]The Hebrew word for "save/deliver" (*yāsaʿ*) is often used to describe what the judge does (Judg 2:16; 3:31; 6:15; 8:22; 10:1; 13:5).

[4]McCann, *Judges*, p. 4.

[5]McCann argues that the number twelve is significant because the twelve judges represent the twelve tribes. Ibid., p. 5.

rah is the fourth person listed after Othniel, Ehud and Shamgar.[6] How are these twelve judges depicted? The narrative does not tell us much about the six so-called minor or secondary judges, and therefore one can say that they are described in more neutral terms.[7] With the remaining six "major" judges we get a clearer picture of the narrator's evaluation of their leadership. One can argue that the first few judges, including Deborah, are described in more positive terms by the narrator.[8] After that there seems to be a downward spiral during which the failings of the leaders become more and more obvious and tragic. Thus, one of the themes of the book is leadership and/or the lack of leadership that leads to the eventual moral and spiritual decline and disunity among the tribes.[9]

In many ways one can argue that the judges presented in the book are a group of unlikely heroes. In fact, most of these heroes are seen as less than perfect, which has led some to call them "antiheroes."[10] Ehud, an assassin, was probably disabled (unable to use his right hand);[11] Shamgar son of Anat was

---

[6]Most scholars do not include Abimelech in the list of judges, even though he ruled over Israel for three years (Judg 9:22). The words judge or savior are never applied to him. This makes twelve judges in the book of Judges: Othniel, Ehud, Shamgar, Deborah, Gideon, Tola, Jair, Jephthah, Ibzan, Elon, Abdon and Samson. However, not every one of the twelve judges named are explicitly called judges in the book (for example, with Ehud, Shamgar and Gideon, the Hebrew noun or verb for judge (šōpēṭ or šāpaṭ) is never applied to them. But they all played some kind of role in delivering the people from oppression. The noun and verb derived from the Hebrew root "save/deliver" (yāsaʿ) is applied to only six judges: Othniel, Ehud, Shamgar, Gideon, Tola, Samson. Only three judges are described as both judges and saviors (Othniel, Tola and Samson). In 1 Samuel, Eli and Samuel also judged Israel (1 Sam 4:18; 7:15-17). Samuel appointed his two sons Joel and Abijah as judges (1 Sam 8:1-3), but since they perverted justice, the elders of the Israelites complained and demanded a king instead. Thus their time as judges did not last long before Saul was appointed king. Therefore, Samuel is usually remembered as the final judge.

[7]Shamgar, Tola, Jair, Ibzan, Elon and Abdon. These judges are only called minor in that there is not much information given about them in the book.

[8]Dennis T. Olson, "The Book of Judges," in The New Interpreter's Bible, ed. Leander E. Keck, vol. 2 (Nashville: Abingdon, 1998), p. 774. Olson argues that there are three phases that describe the gradual spiritual decline in Israel and its leaders. The first phase (Judg 3:7—5:31) depicts faithful and victorious judges, the second phase (Judg 6:1—10:5) begins the decline into idolatry and disunity, and the third phase (Judg 10:6—16:31) demonstrates the serious deterioration of Israel as reflected in the increasingly tragic and misguided judges.

[9]C. Brown, "Judges," in Joshua, Judges, Ruth, New International Biblical Commentary, ed. J. Harris, C. Brown and M. Moore (Peabody, Mass.: Hendrickson, 2000), pp. 132-33.

[10]Daniel I. Block, "Deborah Among the Judges: The Perspective of the Hebrew Historian," in Faith, Tradition and History: Old Testament Historiography in Its Near Eastern Context, ed. A. R. Millard, James K. Hoffmeier and David W. Baker (Winona Lake, Ind.: Eisenbrauns, 1994), p. 236.

[11]John Goldingay suggests that the fact that Ehud used his left hand indicates that he was disabled not merely left-handed (Goldingay, "Motherhood, Machismo," p. 22). The Hebrew usually translated as left-handed in Judg 3:15 actually reads that he was bound or restricted in his right hand, indicating

probably a Canaanite;[12] Gideon lacked confidence and faith, needing divine assurances in signs; Jephthah, a son of a prostitute, made a foolish vow and ended up sacrificing his daughter; and Samson was a tragic figure whose morality was highly questionable and whose downfall was women and pride.[13] One could argue that when one looks to the book of Judges for examples of leadership that for the most part one gets an ambiguous picture. Many of the judges were part of the problem in Israel's idolatry and apostasy. The morality of some were highly questionable. In many ways, the book illustrates how *not* to be a leader, so that we can learn from the failings and mistakes of the judges. Yet it also demonstrates the grace of God, that the Lord can use less than perfect leaders to do his work. However, not all the judges are described in negative terms. Othniel, the first judge, is not portrayed negatively (Judg 3:7-11), although his story is not elaborated upon but is rather given as an illustration of a judge who follows the paradigm given in Judges 2:16-23.[14] In contrast, the narrator elaborates on the story of Deborah; she is the only judge who is portrayed positively in the narrative. Therefore, when one compares Deborah with this motley crew of judges, she really stands out! In Daniel Block's words, "Deborah is different. She is the only one the narrator cast in an unequivocally positive light."[15]

There are several things that make Deborah stand out from the rest of the judges. First of all, she is the only woman who judges Israel. In a list of leaders where only men are mentioned she stands out in terms of gender.[16] Yet nothing within the biblical record indicates that this was a problem. In fact, Deborah is described as a well-respected authority within the Israelite community.

---

that he could not use his right hand. See also J. Alberto Soggin's support for this interpretation in his commentary, *Judges,* The Old Testament Library (Philadelphia: Westminster Press, 1981), p. 50.

[12]His name seems to indicate that he may have been a foreigner rather than an Israelite, worshiping the warrior goddess Anat, or he may have been an Israelite who may have syncretistically incorporated the worship of Anat into his faith. Or perhaps this syncretism represents the practice of his parents, who named him son of Anat.

[13]Goldingay highlights the unlikely heroes among the judges in his article, "Motherhood, Machismo," p. 22.

[14]Goldingay points out that Othniel is also an unlikely hero. As Caleb's younger brother he is an example of how God uses a younger brother for his purposes, in a culture where the firstborn is the favored one. Ibid., p. 22.

[15]Block, "Deborah Among the Judges," p. 236.

[16]The Hebrew emphasizes her gender in Judges 4:4 by stating "a woman prophetess" (*'iššâ nĕbî'â*) when it is not necessary to say "a woman" before prophetess. The female gender is already indicated in "prophetess."

Ailish Ferguson Eves writes, "The text takes Deborah's status and responsibilities in Israel for granted. She is not introduced as an emergency substitute for the men who have failed to come forward (as some would interpret Judg 4:4; cf. Judg 5:6-7). Her standing in society is a secure and accepted one as a prophet through whom God speaks."[17] In contrast to the other judges, her character stands out as impeccable. The narrator finds no fault in her character; he describes no character flaws. She is highly respected in the community, demonstrated in that the people come to her for advice and counsel, and in how Barak responds to her (Judg 4:4-8). Her authority is never disputed.

There are those who argue that Deborah never really was a judge, although this is a minority view; the majority of scholars do believe that she was a judge. For example, Daniel Block argues that her role was exclusively as a prophet.[18] Block argues that Judges 4:4-5 do not refer to Deborah settling legal disputes for the Israelites as a judge, but rather that the text describes the people coming to her in her role as a prophet, asking God to deliver them from the Canaanite oppression.[19] I do agree with Block that

---

[17]Ailish Ferguson Eves, "Judges," in *The IVP Women's Bible Commentary,* ed. Catherine Clark Kroeger and Mary J. Evans (Downers Grove, Ill.: InterVarsity Press, 2002), p. 133.

[18]Richard Schultz is another scholar who agrees with Block on this matter. See his discussion on *špṭ* in *NIDOTTE,* 4:216.

[19]One of Block's arguments is that in the Hebrew there is a definite article on "judgment" (*lamišpāṭ*), that "the judgment" refers to a particular issue. Block, "Deborah Among the Judges," pp. 238-40; see also his article, "Why Deborah's Different," *Bible Review* 17, no. 3 (2001): 34-40, 49-52. My arguments against Block are the following: the use of the two Qal active participles (*šōpṭâ* and *yôšebet*) seems to indicate continuous action, that this is something she did regularly. The break in the Hebrew narrative sequence to give circumstantial background information also supports this. The fact that she also sits (*yôšebet*) in a certain geographical location under the palm of Deborah and the Israelites know where to find her for advice also supports the view that she served in some "official governmental function," which is something Daniel Block admits: "In fact, her central location between Ramah and Bethel in the highlands of Ephraim made her accessible to the entire nation" (Block, "Deborah Among the Judges," p. 236). The reference to the "palm of Deborah" may refer to Deborah's fame as an important and respected leader. Even if the palm is not named after Deborah but rather after Rebekah's nursemaid Deborah who was buried there (although in Gen 35:8 it is referred to as the Oak of Weeping, rather than as a palm), the narrative still gives the impression that this was the place where Deborah fulfilled her duty as judge. Although Block argues that "judging" can be interpreted in a number of ways, why would the narrator use the word "judge" (*šōpṭâ*) differently from how he used it in the rest of the book? In the larger context of the book, the most natural reading and interpretation of the word *judge* is the one that is used with all the judges. As I have argued above, the example of Deborah actually elaborates on what judging meant in the context of the book. Even if the final clause in verse 5, beginning with the waw consecutive verb, "the people of Israel came up to her for (the) judgment" (*waya'ălû 'ēlêhā bĕnê yiśrā'ēl lamišpāṭ*) refers to a specific incident when the Israelites came to her as a prophet to ask the Lord to deliver them, this does not negate the description in the previous clauses (vv. 4-5a) of her judging the people on a regular basis.

in the larger narrative she is described primarily in her role as prophet and as the Lord's representative. However, this does not negate her other role as judge.[20] The description of Deborah judging the people in Judges 4:4-5 is a circumstantial clause in Hebrew. "At that time Deborah, a prophetess, wife of Lappidoth, was judging Israel. She used to sit under the palm of Deborah between Ramah and Bethel in the hill country of Ephraim, and the Israelites came up to her for judgment." The verses are giving background information about Deborah, who she was and her roles, setting the context for what is about to happen when the Lord brings a prophetic word to her to summon Barak. Deborah was both a judge and prophet according to these verses.

In these two roles, Deborah's ministry has some very interesting parallels with Moses, the great leader, liberator and prophet who also judged the Israelites. In Exodus 18:13-16 we learn that Moses also "sat to judge" the people who came to him to inquire of the Lord and to have their disputes settled. He administered justice by teaching them the statutes and laws of the Lord. Moses' example illustrates what is meant by "judging" (as outlined in Deut 16:18-20). "Sitting in the seat of Moses" so to speak, Deborah, as judge and prophet, also served in this judicial role of administering justice, ministering to the needs of the people by interpreting the Law and speaking the word of the Lord. There are more parallels between Moses and Deborah when one compares Exodus 14—15 with Judges 4—5, where the narrative account of victory over one's enemies is followed by a poem that celebrates the victory in a song. Just as Moses and Miriam sang and celebrated in song after the Israelites crossed the Red Sea and were delivered from the Egyptian army (Ex 15:1-21), Deborah and Barak sing a victory song after the Canaanite enemy is defeated, recorded in the Song of Deborah (Judg 5).[21] The fact that the Song of Deborah in Judges 5 is the only example of a victory song

---

[20]Block and others have noticed that Deborah's name is absent from the list of judges given in 1 Sam 12:9-11 and Heb 11:32, whereas Barak's name is included. In response I must say that these texts do not give comprehensive lists; several judges are left off the list. First Samuel 12:9-11 highlights Barak as one of four people who play a role in bringing deliverance. The writer of the book of Hebrews explicitly says that there is not enough time to tell the stories of all the heroes of faith, highlighting the fact that his list is incomplete (Heb 11:32).

[21]There are a number of interesting parallels between the Song of Deborah and the Song of the Sea, which also strengthen these connections. See Alan J. Hauser, "Two Songs of Victory: A Comparison of Exodus 15 and Judges 5," in *Directions in Biblical Hebrew Poetry*, ed. Elaine R. Follis, JSOTSup 40 (Sheffield: Sheffield Academic Press, 1987), pp. 265-84.

following a deliverance in the book of Judges causes the reader to make the connections between these events and the account of salvation and celebration by the Red Sea even more. This is something that Jewish commentators have noted, even as early as the first century A.D., as demonstrated in Pseudo-Philo's *Biblical Antiquities,* where Deborah is described as a leader like Moses.[22] As did Moses, Deborah leads the people as judge, as prophet, as worship leader.[23]

There are those, however, who argue that Deborah's calling as judge is the exception to the rule. It is true that she was the only female judge, but does that make her the exception? Does that mean that this was only a one-time occurrence, never to be repeated? One can argue that if women were not meant for this role, God would not have raised her up in the first place. The fact that he did speaks volumes! God can raise up wise and capable women, to govern his people, to administer God's justice and to speak his word. Deborah sets the example. But Deborah *was* exceptional in many ways, as we have already seen. She is exceptional when one compares her with the other judges. Deborah is different and stands out in more ways than one.

Most of the judges in the book of Judges became recognized leaders and judges *after* they had defeated the oppressing enemy, whereas Deborah's ministry began *before* the military victory. She was already recognized by the people as a wise and authoritative figure, indicated by the fact that people[24] went to her to have her settle their disputes. Her importance as a leader is acknowledged by the fact that the place where she would give advice and administer justice was named after her as the palm of Deborah (Judg 4:4-5).[25] Moreover, her geographical location, between Ramah and Bethel in the hill country of Ephraim, was accessible to all the tribes, being centrally located. She served the nation as a whole.

Not only was Deborah called to serve the people as a judge, she was also

---

[22]In Cheryl Brown's study of Pseudo-Philo's *Biblical Antiquities,* she finds that Deborah "becomes the feminine counterpart to the greatest leader in all of Israel's history—Moses." Cheryl Anne Brown, *No Longer Silent: First Century Jewish Portraits of Biblical Women,* Gender and the Biblical Tradition (Louisville, Ky.: Westminster John Knox, 1992), p. 40.

[23]Some would argue that Deborah is also a military leader or warrior-like Moses. I will comment more on this below.

[24]The "sons of Israel" (*běnê yiśrā'ēl*) is an expression for the people as a whole.

[25]I think that the palm was named after her rather than after Rebekah's nursemaid because in Gen 35:8 she was buried under an oak tree, not a palm (*tōměr*), and Jacob named it the Oak of Weeping (*'allôn bākût*).

called to be a prophet, raised up to proclaim the word of the Lord in a time of crisis. In the book of Judges, Deborah was the only judge who was also a prophet.[26] In this way, she parallels Samuel, the final judge before the inauguration of the monarchic period (1 Sam 3:19-21; 7:15-17). Samuel was also judge and prophet. Let us consider these parallels and the significance. In 1 Samuel 7:15-17, we learn that Samuel judged Israel all the days of his life and that he would judge the people in a circuit from four locations annually, in Bethel, Gilgal, Mizpah and Ramah (his hometown). Interestingly, Deborah ministered in the same geographical area, although stationed in one place somewhere in the hill country of Ephraim between Bethel and Ramah (Judg 4:5). In Daniel Block's words: "In 1 Samuel, Samuel was obviously presented as a 'judge' after the order of Deborah"[27] (although in his writing, Block emphasizes the parallels between Samuel and Deborah in their prophetic role, rather than in their judicial office). Cheryl Exum has also noted the similar function that Deborah and Samuel play as judge and prophet. Just as Deborah commissions Barak to go into battle, Samuel "anoints Saul king and sends him off to fight the Lord's battles (see esp. 1 Sam 10-15)."[28] Furthermore, Exum points out that Barak is accountable to Deborah as Saul is to Samuel and the Lord.[29] As God's prophet, both Deborah and Samuel represented the Lord and his presence. This is why Barak insisted on having Deborah accompany him into the battle (Judg 4:8) and why the Israelites and Saul sought Samuel's help and presence. Deborah and Samuel symbolized the Lord's divine presence. Daniel Block writes: "Like Samuel in 1 Sam 7:10-11, Deborah clearly functioned as the *alter ego* of Yahweh. Her presence alone was enough to guarantee

---

[26]Besides Deborah, there is only one other prophet mentioned in the whole book of Judges, an anonymous prophet in Judges 6:7-10. As one of only two prophets explicitly mentioned in the book, her role as prophet also stands out and is highlighted.

[27]Block, "Deborah Among the Judges," p. 237. Block points outs similarities and differences between Deborah and Samuel in their role as judge. Because he argues that Deborah was not really a judge in the sense of a savior who delivers the people from oppression, he also asserts that Samuel was not a "deliverer judge." He writes, "As a matter of fact, the view that the narratives of the charismatic judges actually continue through the life of Samuel should be rejected" (Ibid., p. 237 n. 32). But one can also argue that both Deborah and Samuel serve in the role of judge as outlined in Deut 16:18-20, following the example of Moses (Ex 18:13-16), and not as "deliverer judge." As I have already argued above, not all the judges in the book are described explicitly as having delivered the Israelites from oppression (i.e., Jair, Ibzan, Elon and Abdon, Judg 10:3-5; 12:8-15).

[28]J. Cheryl Exum, "'Mother in Israel': A Familiar Figure Reconsidered," in *Feminist Interpretation of the Bible,* ed. Letty M. Russell (Oxford: Basil Blackwell, 1985), p. 84.

[29]Ibid., p. 84.

victory over the enemy."[30] Barak's request that Deborah accompany him into battle on the surface looks like a lack of faith on Barak's part, yet it does not necessarily have to be interpreted as Barak being cowardly or distrusting. Of course, he would be disobedient to the Lord if he did not go! Yet, in Barak's mind, her presence as the Lord's representative would both encourage the troops and guarantee the victory.[31] Perhaps Barak also wanted to consult her for further divine direction as the battle proceeded. In fact, this is exactly what she does. In Judges 4:14, she gives another message from the Lord, assuring him again that the Lord will give him victory. Her prophetic words come true and the enemy is defeated. Just like Samuel (and Moses), she is a true prophet, confirmed in that her prophecies come true (cf. Deut 18:20-22).

In this context I want to highlight that, although Deborah is the only female prophet in the book of Judges, Deborah is not the only female prophet in the Bible. Within the biblical record we have a number of examples of women prophets (both named and unnamed). In fact, there are women prophets mentioned from all the major periods of Israel's history: Miriam (Ex 15:20) and Deborah (from the premonarchic period), Huldah (during the reign of Josiah in the second half of the seventh century B.C.; 2 Kings 22:14-20) and Noadiah (during the postexilic period of Nehemiah's time in the fifth century B.C.; Neh 6:14),[32] as well as unnamed prophetesses like Isaiah's wife (Is 8:3).[33] Not only were there female prophets within Israel, there is evidence that women served as prophets in the other ancient Near Eastern religions. Based on evidence of women proph-

---

[30]Block, "Deborah Among the Judges," p. 249. For the same reason, Block points out, Saul felt relatively secure as long as Samuel was with him, because that meant the Lord's presence was with him (pp. 249-51).

[31]Olson points out that the Hebrew is ambiguous in terms of whether Barak's request for Deborah's accompaniment is seen as wrong and whether her response to him in Judges 4:8-9 is intended as a rebuke or not. The narrator does not explicitly give his evaluation of Barak as either positive or negative. We do not know the tone in which Deborah responds to Barak. Deborah may simply be making a statement of fact, that God will use a woman to bring down the enemy (as the nuance of NRSV). Olson also points out that Barak is never dishonored or shamed in the Song of Deborah but rather is praised along with the rest. Olson makes the interesting observation that Joshua is also not shamed or dishonored for having received help from Rahab, a Canaanite woman and prostitute, in conquering Jericho. Olson believes that the ambiguity in the text is there intentionally to create suspense for the reader. Olson, "Book of Judges," pp. 775-76, 780. I also want to add that in Deborah's prophecy to Barak that God will use Jael, it is *the Lord* who is given the ultimate credit. *He* is the one who will sell Sisera into the hands of a woman (Judg 4:9).

[32]Athalya Brenner, *The Israelite Woman: Social Role and Literary Type in Biblical Narrative*, The Biblical Seminar (Sheffield: JSOT Press, 1985), pp. 57-66.

[33]In the New Testament, besides the Spirit being poured out on both men and women in fulfillment of Joel 2:28-29 in the book of Acts, there is the specific mention of Anna, the temple prophetess in Luke 2:36-38, and Philip's four daughters who prophesy (Acts 21:9).

ets from Mari, Daniel Block points out that Deborah's female gender as a prophet would not have been "surprising in the second-millennium cultural milieu."[34] Even though it was a patriarchal society, the role of prophet was not limited to men; women could also function in this role and be well respected. As God's prophet, Deborah played a significant role in the deliverance of her people from foreign oppression. She was obedient to her calling.

Deborah also stands out in the book of Judges when one compares her with the other women in the book. Interestingly, there are more women characters described in the book of Judges than in any other biblical book.[35] Although Deborah is the only woman judge and prophet, she is not the only woman in the book. The women can be divided into three main categories in terms of their portrayal: valiant women, tragic victims and manipulating villains. Most of the women in the book are portrayed either as victims (Jephthah's daughter, Samson's Philistine wife, the Levite's concubine) or as villains (like Delilah). However, a few women are seen in a more positive light by the narrator; they are strong and courageous women: Achsah, who asks and receives an inheritance (Judg 1:11-15), Manoah's wife, who has a divine encounter with an angel of the Lord and becomes the mother of Samson (Judg 13), and Jael, who played a role in destroying Israel's enemy (Judg 4:17-22; 5:6, 24-27).[36] Among these women, the most valiant one is Deborah, whose character and faithful service stands out.[37] Although there are some who view Deborah with ambivalence because of the role she plays in a war,[38] it is clear that the biblical author

---

[34]Block, "Deborah Among the Judges," p. 247.

[35]Olson finds nineteen women characters altogether in the book. Olson, "Book of Judges," p. 782. Lillian R. Klein finds "eleven fully differentiated females," those who are dramatized as opposed to those women mentioned but undramatized, like the daughters of Jabesh-Gilead and the daughters of Shiloh. Klein categorizes the women further by whether their deeds are active or passive or understood as positive or negative by the reader. See Lillian R. Klein, "A Spectrum of Female Characters in the Book of Judges," in *A Feminist Companion to Judges,* ed. Athalya Brenner (Sheffield: Sheffield Academic Press, 1993), pp. 24-33.

[36]Klein classifies Jael as a woman who is evaluated negatively by the *reader.* But there is nothing in the text that indicates that the *narrator* viewed Jael and her actions in a negative light. In fact, in the Song of Deborah, Jael is celebrated as the "most blessed of women" (Judg 5:24) for her role in conquering the enemy. Jael is often evaluated negatively by those who feel uncomfortable with the notion of women involved in war and violence.

[37]It is important to note that Ruth and Naomi also stand out as positive characters during the period of the Judges, as narrated in the book of Ruth.

[38]Gale A. Yee, "By the Hand of a Woman: The Metaphor of the Woman Warrior in Judges 4," *Semeia* 61 (1993): 125. Of course, for some this ambivalence applies even more to Jael. This ambivalence is rooted in the theological difficulties associated with violence and war in the Bible in general.

views her positively.[39] Through her faithful obedience in proclaiming the word of the Lord, the Israelites were delivered from suffering and oppression.

Together with Barak, she went into battle and proclaimed the Lord's victory (ahead of time) in overthrowing the enemy (Judg 4:6-8, 10, 14). After the enemy was defeated, Deborah and Barak sang a victory song, recorded as the Song of Deborah (Judg 5). Some have suggested that the song depicts Deborah as a warrior and military leader. A number of studies have compared her with the Canaanite warrior goddess Anat.[40] It is true that in this victory song Deborah's role in bringing deliverance is celebrated (Judg 5:1, 7, 12, 15), but she is only one of several participants highlighted who contributed to the victory. In the song, Barak, Jael, the various tribes who participated, the role that nature played, and most importantly, what the Lord did, is emphasized. Furthermore, there is nothing in the narrative account nor in the song to indicate that Deborah actually did any fighting when she accompanied Barak. The woman who does is Jael, not Deborah. Deborah's role in the battle remains the prophet, the messenger of the Lord.[41]

What we do learn from the song is that Deborah is a singer, a poet and a worshiper of the Lord. She is introduced as singing the song together with Barak (Judg 5:1) and then she is admonished to break out in a song (Judg 5:12). Throughout the song, she blesses the Lord (Judg 5:2-3, 9).[42] In the poem, Deborah describes herself as "a mother in Israel" (5:7). This may mean that biologically she was a mother, although the biblical text never mentions

---

[39]Katharine Doob Sakenfeld has written a thought-provoking article on the topic of Deborah and Jael and war, in light of having met women who have experienced the atrocities of war. Katharine Doob Sakenfeld, "Deborah, Jael, and Sisera's Mother: Reading the Scriptures in Cross-Cultural Context," in *Women, Gender, and Christian Community,* ed. Jane Dempsey Douglass and James F. Ka (Louisville, Ky.: Westminster John Knox, 1997), pp. 13-22.

[40]P. C. Craigie, "Deborah and Anat: A Study of Poetic Imagery (Judges 5)," *Zeitschrift für die Alttestamentliche Wissenschaft* 90 (1978): 374-81; J. Glen Taylor, "The Song of Deborah and Two Canaanite Goddesses," *JSOT* 23 (1982): 99-108; Susan Ackerman, *Warrior, Dancer, Seductress, Queen: Women in Judges and Biblical Israel* (New York: Doubleday, 1998), pp. 51-73.

[41]One could argue that the real warrior in the song is the divine warrior, Yahweh (Judg 5).

[42]This poem is one of the oldest Hebrew texts in the Bible. The majority of scholars date it to the mid- or late twelfth century B.C. Although we cannot know for sure who wrote the song, the fact that the song is introduced as having been sung by Deborah and Barak (Judg 5:1) means that the narrator understood it to have been written in that day and perhaps composed by Deborah since she sang it (the Hebrew has the verb "to sing," in feminine singular [watāšar]). The song and the narrative are meant to be read together because the song does not make sense without the narrative filling in the details, where there are gaps in the poem. The song sung by Deborah and Barak "on that day" (bayôm hahû') refers back to the victory described in the narrative account (Judg 4), which concludes with the same phrase "on that day." Olson, "Book of Judges," p. 787.

any of her children. In Judges 4:4, Deborah[43] was introduced as the wife of Lappidoth. But the Hebrew may also be rendered as "a woman of torches" or "a fiery woman" (the meaning of Lappidoth). Therefore, from this introduction it is not completely clear whether she was married or not. However, in the context of ancient Israelite culture, it is most likely that Deborah was married and had children (in a patriarchal world where it was expected for women to marry and have children). Being a judge or prophet did not mean that she had to be single. We know that the prophet Huldah was married, for example (2 Kings 22:14). Yet Deborah's role as wife and mother is not something highlighted in the text; her husband is never mentioned again and no children are named. In Deborah's roles as judge and prophet and in the context of the poem, the phrase "mother in Israel" should probably be understood metaphorically. She was a mother *to* Israel, playing a nurturing, comforting and protective role. The only other time this phrase is used in the Old Testament is in 2 Samuel 20:19, where the wise woman of Abel of Beth-maacah describes the city as a "mother in Israel." Dennis Olson believes that this phrase is more than an endearing title, but instead "may represent the place and office of a wise woman prophet who delivers divine oracles to resolve disputes (see 4:5; 2 Sam 20:16-19)."[44] Deborah has been given an honorific title in Israel in light of her office and authoritative role, as a wise judge and prophet.[45] The phrase "mother *in* Israel" also highlights her role as a national leader, a mother or leader to the whole nation.[46] Cheryl Exum asks the question, "What does it mean to call Deborah a mother in Israel? Her accomplishments described in Judges 4—5 include counsel, inspiration, and leadership. A mother in Israel is one who brings liberation from oppression, provides protection, and ensures the well-being and security of her people."[47]

In conclusion, what can we learn from Deborah about Christian leadership? How can she become a role model for both men and women in public service? Deborah was an influential and prominent leader on the national level, serving

---

[43]The meaning of Deborah's name is "bee." But the root consonants of her name (*dbr*) also form the word "to speak," which relates to her calling as a messenger of the Lord.

[44]Olson, "Book of Judges," p. 787.

[45]Just as "Mother" can be a title of honor, "Father" is also used as an honorific title in the Bible. See Judg 17:10; 1 Sam 24:11; 2 Kings 2:12; 6:21; 13:14.

[46]Linda L. Belleville, "Women Leaders in the Bible," in *DBE*, p. 113.

[47]Exum, "Mother in Israel," p. 85. See also Ackerman, *Warrior, Dancer, Seductress, Queen*, pp. 38-44; Claudia V. Camp, "The Wise Women of 2 Samuel: A Role Model for Women in Early Israel?" *CBQ* 43 (1981): 24-29.

the people as judge and prophet. Today we often make a distinction between serving in the secular sphere, in the marketplace, in the role of governing, and that of being in ministry within the Christian or religious context. This, however, is not how leadership was understood in biblical times. There the two worlds overlapped; the secular and religious spheres were one. All of life was integrated. In biblical times, the judge and king were also spiritual leaders (just as the prophet and priest) called to set an example for the people of faithful living and wholehearted commitment to the Lord. Deborah set this example. Deborah was a respected, trusted leader, a person of integrity, whose commitment to the Lord earned the trust of Barak and of all the people.

As leaders, we too need to gain the trust and respect of the people we serve. This comes with time as we serve and live our lives faithfully within the community. We also need to see all of life as integrated, and not see ministry as something separate from serving in the so-called secular sphere. All service should be seen as ministry.

Deborah was obedient and faithful to her calling as a prophet by giving the word of the Lord in a time of crisis. She was both a woman of faith and of courage. From a human perspective, the odds were against the Israelites. This reality is emphasized by the narrator who twice mentions that Sisera had nine hundred chariots of iron (Judg 4:3, 13). But Deborah had faith and courage. She did not hesitate to accompany Barak into the battle, to be available to give divine direction when needed. We too need to be ready to respond to God's call in the midst of a crisis and fearlessly follow the Lord wherever he may lead us.

Deborah also sets the example of cooperation between leaders, even perhaps between men and women.[48] Deborah and Barak worked together in leading the people to victory over their enemies. Dennis Olson believes that the story of Deborah demonstrates that God works through humans' actions involving "shared leadership, mutual responsibility, and glory that is distributed among several of the main characters (Deborah, Jael, and Barak)."[49] Although many would argue that the book of Judges tends to promote a need for a strictly centralized type of government in the form of the monarchy as a solution to the chaos at the time (see Judg 17:6; 21:25), Olson asserts that Judges

---

[48]Sakenfeld, "Deborah, Jael, and Sisera's Mother," pp. 18-19.
[49]Olson, "Book of Judges," p. 783.

4—5 demonstrate that God also works "effectively through more complex systems where power may be decentralized, duties may be distributed, and no one leader need take all the credit or responsibility."[50] Perhaps the story of Deborah presents a different model of leadership, where leaders cooperate and do not compete with each other. Each share their unique gifts to serve the community as a whole.

Deborah sets the example of a worshiper who leads the people in song and praise to the Lord after he has done a marvelous work. As "mother in Israel" Deborah also played a nurturing role to her people.[51] Ministering in a difficult and chaotic time, she became an instrument of hope and inspiration by speaking the word of the Lord prophetically at a critical time. Deborah is an example of how God raises up leaders to stop oppression and bring justice, freedom and peace.[52] Throughout history, God has always raised up leaders to help his people in times of suffering and oppression. Deborah was such a leader who responded to the divine call. May we learn from her example.

---

[50]Ibid. Olson points out that the Song of Deborah highlights several key players who all "participated in saving Israel: God (5:2-5, 20-21, 31), Deborah (5:7, 12), Jael (5:24-27), some of the Israelite tribes (5:13-18) and Barak (5:9, 12). The praise of God begins and ends the song as an affirmation that God integrates and works across boundaries of gender, tribe, nation and creation within the poem (male/female, Israelite/non-Israelite, some tribes/not other tribes, human/non-human forces of nature)." (Olson, "Book of Judges," p. 776). In his analysis, Olson sees ambiguities in the biblical text in terms of who is the actual judge in the story. He suggests that this is intentional to demonstrate that the role and task of judging is shared between Deborah, Barak and even Jael! (Ibid., p. 774). McCann also suggests that perhaps Deborah, Barak and Jael should be considered as "co-judges" (McCann, *Judges,* p. 49). Although I do agree that all three share in the role of bringing deliverance to Israel, I find it hard to see how the narrator sees Jael as a judge. Barak plays an important role, but the narrator gives the Lord the credit for actually subduing the enemy (Judg 4:7, 9, 14,·15, 23). Deborah is the only one who is explicitly referred to as judge.

[51]Deborah fulfilled many roles as she served the Lord. Today, both men and women juggle several different roles as they fulfill their calling in life. Just as the Lord helped Deborah, he can help us today, as we wear different hats.

[52]As a result, the land had rest and peace for forty years (Judg 5:31).

2

WHAT WOMEN CAN DO IN MINISTRY

Full Participation Within Biblical Boundaries

James M. Hamilton Jr.

IN OUR CULTURE, WE WORSHIP DIVERSITY WITH OUR LIPS, but it seems that our hearts may be set on uniformity. This grows out of a secular understanding of diversity, which results not in variety but in homogeneity. Rather than celebrating diversity in the clothes worn by men and women, we are offered unisex clothing. Rather than celebrating the diversity of sizes and shapes in which people come, many feel pressure to conform their bodies to a cookie-cutter pattern. Rather than celebrating marriages that are diversified by the incorporation of a male and a female, a vocal minority wishes to eliminate the requirement of gender diversity from marriage, and some wish to conduct life as though gender does not exist at all. This attitude is reflected in the recent outcry over some comments made by Larry Summers, president of Harvard University. He reportedly claimed "that the shortage of elite female scientists may stem in part from 'innate' differences between men and women."[1] In a recent editorial in *The Wall Street Journal,* Peggy Noonan comments on where, according to his "open-minded" detractors, Summers went wrong:

---

[1] Michael Dobbs, "Harvard Chief's Comments on Women Assailed," *Washington Post,* January 19, 2005, sec. A, p. 2 <www.washingtonpost.com/wp-dyn/articles/A19181-2005Jan18.html>. I owe this reference to a weblog entered by Prof. Dr. Denny Burk <dennyburk.blogspot.com/2005/01/gender-wars-and-harvard-university.html> (posted January 2005). The saga has continued with no-confidence votes: "Harvard Faculty Gives Summers Thumbs Down," MSNBC.com <www.msnbc.msn.com/id/7201406/>.

His mistake was stepping on the real third rail in American cultural politics. It's not Social Security. It is attempting to reconcile the indisputable equality of all people with their differentness. The left thinks if we're all equal we're all alike. Others say we're all equal but God made us different, too, and maybe he did that to keep things interesting, and maybe he did it because each human group is meant to reflect an aspect of his nature. Our differentness is meant to teach us his infinite variety and complexity. It's all about God.[2]

The issue of gender diversity is also prominent in some sectors of evangelical Christianity, as witnessed by the occasion of this essay. Christians must indulge in the stimulating diversity of God's creation by affirming male and female as *both* being in the image of God, celebrating gender distinctions rather than emasculating men or defeminizing women. No one in this discussion wishes to turn night into day or the sun into the moon, and we dare not turn obedience into rebellion and transgression into piety.

My goal here is to seek a biblical understanding of the phrase "full participation in ministry." If this phrase can be informed by what the Bible says about ministry, the next question to be considered is whether the Bible diversifies the phrase "full participation in ministry" according to gender. In other words, does the Bible give some roles to men and not to women? If we can see "full participation in ministry" through lenses given to us from the Bible, and if the Bible places boundaries on men and women, we must then ask how these statements from an ancient book apply in our contemporary context.

Seeking a Biblical Meaning of "Full Participation in Ministry"

Christians believe in diversity in the body of Christ. We believe that, in the age to come, persons from every tribe and tongue and people and nation will worship the slain lamb who is a lion (Rev 5:6-13). The fact that people from every tribe will worship shows that ethnic distinctions have not been obliterated by the cross, though all races now stand on equal footing before God. In the past God dealt primarily with one race, but now it is not so (Gal 3:28).

We also believe that the Spirit has gifted believers for ministry (1 Cor 12:4-7). We read that not all believers are given the same gifts (1 Cor 12:8-10) and

---

[2]Peggy Noonan, "I'll Link to That: Hunter Thompson, Larry Summers, Hillary, Condi, and the Internet's Patron Saint," *Wall Street Journal*, February 24, 2005 <www.opinionjournal.com/columnists/pnoonan/?id=110006332>.

that all gifts are empowered by the Spirit, who gives as he pleases (1 Cor
12:11). Paul likens the church to a human body, and from his statements
about feet accepting their roles as feet and not wishing to be hands (1 Cor
12:15), ears being ears and not thinking themselves less because they neither
see nor smell (1 Cor 12:16), and each member recognizing the necessity of the
other parts of the body (1 Cor 12:21), we see that Christian ministry is not a
monolithic exercise. In fact, from the catalogue of spiritual gifts in 1 Corinthians 12:28-30 it is clear that not all Christian ministers are apostles, not all
are prophets, not all are teachers (see esp. 1 Cor 12:29).

The first thing that we can say for certain, then, about full participation in
Christian ministry is that it can be likened to the way that one organ or append-
age participates fully in the life of the whole body. Thus, just as we need not see
through our fingertips for our hands to be fully engaged in human life, so also
we need not be exercised in every ministry of the church in order to be fully engaged in the ministry of the church. This frees the feet to walk, the eyes to see,
the teeth to chew and the hands to type. I need not perfect the art of typing with
my toes, nor need I damage myself by trying to walk on my eyeballs. Each member of the body is fully engaged in life as it serves the whole body in the capacity
for which it was designed. And so it is with members of the church. Unfortunately, for many in my own denominational tradition (Southern Baptist), the
perception of a call to serve God vocationally has been automatically equated
with the "call to preach." This has often been so even for those who have not
been gifted to pastor and teach. We will be most happy and effective when we
find the area of service for which we were designed, and we need not fret that
we were not designed for other ministries. Let not the sole of the foot lament the
lack of taste buds, nor the armpit the lack of a sense of smell.

The second thing that may be observed from 1 Corinthians 12 about full
participation in ministry is that the ministries pursued by the members of the
body are assigned to the parts of the body by God. To put this more bluntly,
the members of the body do not select for themselves what role they play in
the life of the body. We see this when Paul writes, "But one and the same Spirit
works all these things, distributing to each individually just as he wills" (1 Cor
12:11).[3] The Spirit is the subject of the verbal action throughout this verse—
he works in all the gifts named in 1 Corinthians 12:8-10, distributing these

---

[3]Unless otherwise noted, all translations of the biblical text are the author's own.

gifts to believers as he, the Spirit, chooses. This concept is restated in verse 18, naming God instead of the Spirit: "But now God has placed the members, each one of them, in the body, just as he desired" (1 Cor 12:18). The same is seen in 1 Corinthians 12:24, "But God composed the body, giving greater honor to the member who lacks," and again in 1 Corinthians 12:28, "And indeed God appointed in the church . . ." The Spirit gives gifts as he wills, God placed members in the body as he desired to do so, and God has blended the members of the body into a whole. The parts of the body do not choose the roles they will play; rather, they receive the gifts the Spirit chooses to give and they take the place in the body assigned to them by God.

Paul apparently writes these things to the Corinthians to promote a unified (1 Cor 12:25-26), loving (1 Cor 13:1-13) and profitable exercise of spiritual gifts in the church (cf. 1 Cor 14:3-5, 12, 19, 26, "Let all things be done for building up"). Full participation in ministry is given by the Spirit, pursued under the lordship of the King Messiah, and empowered by God (1 Cor 12:3, 4-6). So we are safe to conclude that full participation in ministry is for the loving, unified edification of the body to the glory of God (1 Cor 10:31).

We can also conclude that giftings have not been meted out according to gender.[4] This observation is based squarely on Scripture, for Paul explicitly commanded women to teach: "Older women likewise [are to be] . . . teaching what is good, that they might train the younger women to love their husbands, to love children, to be prudent, to be chaste, to be good workers at home, being submissive to their own husbands, in order that the word of God might not be blasphemed" (Tit 2:3-5). My assumption here is that at least some women would be particularly gifted for such teaching ministries, and this assumption is confirmed from observation of gifted women. Thus, it would seem that one of the gifts that is at the center of this discussion—that of teaching—has indeed been given to both males and females. This gift, however, is to be used to unify and edify the body in love.

An important factor in our consideration of full participation in ministry is that Paul's statements regarding spiritual gifts in 1 Corinthians 12—14 reveal that he expects the exercise of gifts to be regulated by his instructions. This can be seen clearly in 1 Corinthians 14:27-40. For example, two or at most three

---

[4]In agreement with Gordon D. Fee, "The Priority of Spirit Gifting for Church Ministry," in *DBE*, p. 241. I wish to express my gratitude to Dr. Robert Phillips of the Roberts Library at Southwestern Baptist Theological Seminary for letting me use his personal copy of this volume.

are to speak in tongues, followed by interpretation. If there is no one to interpret, those gifted with tongues are not to exercise their gift (1 Cor 14:27-28). This indicates that the possession of a gift does not mandate the use of that gift in every circumstance.

What has been observed thus far about full participation in ministry indicates that full participation does not demand that one be engaged in every ministry of the church. Nor does full participation require that one employ one's gift at every available opportunity. Full participation does require loving, edifying exercise of one's gifts according to the purpose for which one has been designed by God.

BIBLICAL BOUNDARIES FOR BOTH MEN AND WOMEN

What limitations does the Bible place upon men who are engaged in Christian ministry? The stipulations for men in ministry mainly have to do with issues of character (1 Tim 3:1-13; Tit 1:5-9; 1 Pet 5:1-4). It is also clear, however, that Paul expects elders to teach the truth and counter falsehood (Tit 1:9), and that recognition in the church requires adherence to his instructions (1 Cor 14:38, "if one does not recognize this, he is not recognized"). Thus, the boundaries placed upon elders have to do with the fruit their lives produce, in that they can be disqualified by either their own actions or the actions of those who belong to their households (1 Tim 3:2-7; Tit 1:6). There is not an explicit command in Scripture that men not disciple younger women in one-on-one settings, but we can observe that while women are told to train younger women, prudence indicates that it would not be wise for men to enter into private, one-on-one mentoring relationships with younger women who are not their daughters.[5] As serious as these boundaries for men in ministry are, they are really not the issue in this discussion, though they are related to the discussion, and I will return to them in my conclusion.

A recent contribution to this debate has asserted, "The *differences between men and women* do not justify granting men unique and perpetual prerogatives of leadership and authority not shared by women."[6] The question to be considered here is whether the *Bible* regulates the use of the gift of teaching ac-

---

[5]The fact that some in our culture are seeking to legalize homosexual "marriage" also makes the observation that men are not equipped to bear and nurse children germane. The president of Harvard may be in hot water for saying so, but there really are biological differences between men and women.
[6]Pierce and Groothuis, Introduction to *DBE*, p. 13 (emphasis added).

cording to gender. If the Bible does this, then perceived differences between men and women (or the lack thereof) may either confirm what the Bible says or be reason to trust God and obey his Word in spite of what we see,[7] depending on how the situation seems to us. Those who, like the president of Harvard, perceive differences between the genders will be confirmed. Those who do not perceive such differences will have occasion to trust God, leaning not on their own understanding.

On the positive side we can affirm that in the Bible there are examples, authorizations and even commands for women to be engaged in some teaching ministries. First, from the *example* of Priscilla and Aquila instructing Apollos (Acts 18:26), it seems legitimate for a husband and wife team to give private[8] instruction to individual men. Perhaps there is even a warrant in this text for a woman to tutor a man in a private setting, but in any case this text does not give us an example of a woman teaching men. Second, from the instructions Paul gives about how women are to pray and prophesy in church in 1 Corinthians 11, we seem to have *authorization* for women to do those things.[9] Third, from Titus 2:3-5, women are *commanded* to teach younger women.

Paul clearly assumes that women pray and prophesy in the context of the gathered congregation in 1 Corinthians 11, and he does not demand that they cease, though he does regulate the practice in significant ways.[10] In this text Paul instructs women who pray and prophesy in church to do so with a head covering (1 Cor 11:5). Since this head covering is referred to as a "sign of au-

---

[7]When we combine the observation that parents were to teach their children the law (Deut 6:7), with the observation that the "teaching" referred to in Prov 3:1 is described with a form of the Hebrew word *tôrâ*, it seems that the oft-cited dictum in Prov 3:5, "trust in Yahweh with all of your heart, and do not lean upon your understanding," is an explicit call to trust Yahweh and obey his word even if it does not make sense (would the command to release one's slaves every seven years [Deut 15:12] have seemed a reasonable thing to do?).

[8]See BDAG on *proslambanō*, 883.3: "Priscilla and Aquila take Apollos aside to teach him undisturbed," and compare the use of the verb in Mt 16:22 and Mk 8:32.

[9]In agreement with Fee, "Priority of Spirit Gifting," p. 249.

[10]Limitations of space and time prevent detailed treatment of this passage. For my view, see "Gender Roles and the Glory of God: A Sermon on 1 Corinthians 11:2-12," *JBMW* 9, no. 2 (2004): 35-39, which is freely available online at <www.cbmw.org/journal/editions/9-2.pdf>. Significant contributions to this discussion include Gordon D. Fee, "Praying and Prophesying in the Assemblies: 1 Corinthians 11:2-16," in *DBE*, pp. 142-60, and Thomas R. Schreiner's response, "A Review of 'Praying and Prophesying in the Assemblies: 1 Corinthians 11:2-16' by Gordon Fee," *JBMW*, forthcoming. See also Schreiner's essay, "Head Coverings, Prophecies, and the Trinity: 1 Corinthians 11:2-16," in *RBMW*, pp. 117-32, which is available free online at <www.cbmw.org/rbmw/rbmw.pdf>.

thority" (1 Cor 11:10),[11] and since the men are not to cover their heads when they pray or prophesy, it seems best to take this as a cultural emblem of femininity. In other words, Paul is instructing the women to cover their heads so that they might be explicitly feminine in the way they pray and prophesy in church. Similarly, the men are to have their heads uncovered in order to be masculine when they pray and prophesy in church (cf. 1 Cor 11:4, 7, 14).

Because men and women are commanded to do opposite things in this passage, it seems that 1 Corinthians 11 allows women to pray and prophesy in church as long as they do so in a way that does not play down gender distinctions. It is clear enough what praying in the gathered congregation entails, but the question of what it means to prophesy is more difficult. In my view, from what we see in 1 Corinthians, prophecy is authoritative, spontaneous, Spirit-inspired utterance in the context of the congregation. Once these Spirit-inspired utterances have been made, Paul writes in 1 Corinthians 14:29 that the others who have not spoken are to evaluate the prophecies. It is of note that in this context Paul makes allowance for a speaking prophet to be interrupted by a *revelation* (*ean . . . apokalyphthē,* "if something is revealed") coming to another prophet who is seated, and in that case the one speaking is to give way to the recipient of the revelation (1 Cor 14:30). The immediate reception of the prophetic word, which allows for one prophet to interrupt another, shows us that prophecy does not consist of prepared remarks growing out of concentrated study of the Scripture. Thus, prophecy seems to be Spirit-inspired, revelatory speech, and the inspired, spontaneous, revelatory character of prophecy distinguishes it from the teaching of the Scriptures.[12] Given the language of "passing on/delivering/depositing" "sound teaching" and "tradi-

---

[11]Rendered directly, the text reads: "On account of this, a woman ought to have authority upon her head." This is taken as a "symbol/sign of authority" by the ASV, ESV, NAB, NAS, NET, NIV, NJB, NKJV and NRSV. Fee argues that the text should be understood as saying "the woman ought to have authority on her head" ("Praying and Prophesying," pp. 155-57), but he fails to refute the seven arguments Schreiner gives in support of the way most English translations render the text (see Schreiner, "Head Coverings, Prophecies, and the Trinity," pp. 126-27, 131).

[12]Contra Fee, "Priority of Spirit Gifting," p. 249: "Likewise 'prophecy' is Paul's preferred form of speech addressed to the rest of the community and as such probably stands for all such forms of speech (teaching, revelation, word of knowledge, word of wisdom, etc.; see 1 Cor 14:6)." In 1 Cor 14:6, Paul asks, "how will I benefit you, unless I speak to you, whether by revelation or by knowledge or by prophecy or by teaching?" This verse does not present "prophecy" in the way that Fee suggests—as a general term that "stands for all such forms of speech." Rather, prophecy is named as one of four kinds of speech, and since it is listed third it does not appear that the other three forms of speech are giving examples of different kinds of "prophecies."

tions" in the New Testament (see, e.g., Lk 1:2; 1 Cor 11:23; 15:1, 3; 2 Thess 2:15; 2 Tim 1:14; 4:2-3; Tit 1:9; 2:1; Jude 1:3), it seems that teaching derives not from a spontaneous revelation but from what the teacher has "received" from the apostolic teaching that has been "passed on"—whether through direct instruction or through the written word (Lk 1:2; Rom 16:25-26 [?]; 2 Thess 2:15; 1 Tim 5:18; 2 Tim 3:16; Heb 2:3; 2 Pet 3:15-16).[13]

Paul permits women to pray and prophesy in the church in 1 Corinthians 11, which indicates that his command that the women be silent in 1 Corinthians 14:34 is to be applied to the evaluation and application of prophecies.[14] Women can utter prophecies, but they are not to sit in judgment on the prophecies delivered by men. When it comes time to judge prophecies, the women are to remain silent. Keener argues that the focus of the silence of the women is on their asking of questions (1 Cor 14:35), but he grants that asking questions is seen in ancient literature to be a means of challenging the authority of a speaker.[15] Keener suggests that the issue is either that "Mediterranean protocol would disapprove of an otherwise honorable woman addressing unrelated men,"[16] or that it was inappropriate for women to reveal their ignorance by asking uninformed questions.[17] Keener also notes that Paul appeals to the law to support this dictum (1 Cor 14:34), but asserts that "the law nowhere specifically commands either women's silence or their submission!"[18] We will re-

---

[13]2 Peter 1:20-21 is a fundamental text for the evangelical doctrine of Scripture, and if evangelicals have interpreted it correctly, the making of Scripture is referred to as "prophecy." The question mark after Rom 16:25-26 points to a question as to whether Rom 16:26 might refer to *New Testament* Scripture, and 1 Tim 5:18 quotes Lk 10:7 as "Scripture," thus the reference to the written Word.

[14]Craig S. Keener ("Learning in the Assemblies: 1 Corinthians 14:34-35," in *DBE*, p. 163) rejects this view. He suggests that "one cannot simply assume that Paul's claim that it is 'shameful' for a woman to speak in the assembly (1 Cor 14:35) is meant to be transcultural, any more than his earlier injunction to cover their heads (related to shame in 1 Cor 11:5-6) or his later one to greet with a holy kiss" (p. 167). This is both problematic and unpersuasive. The particular manifestation of a principle—head covering for women or a holy kiss in greeting—may be culturally bound, but the principle can nevertheless be obeyed in culturally appropriate ways. Since head coverings could be interpreted as nothing more than fashion statements in our culture, women should be explicit about their femininity and submissive hearts in ways that speak to our culture. Also, though we do not kiss each other in modern western culture, we still need to greet one another warmly. I am more inclined to the view that women should cover their heads when praying and prophesying and that we should cultivate the practice of greeting one another with holy kisses than I am to the position that we can simply bracket these commands out as not normative for us today. See the helpful treatment of this issue by D. A. Carson, "Silent in the Churches: On the Role of Women in 1 Corinthians 14:33b-36," in *RBMW.*

[15]Keener, "Learning in the Assemblies," pp. 164-65, citing Plutarch's essay *On Lectures* 11.

[16]Ibid., p. 166.

[17]Ibid., p. 168.

[18]Ibid., pp. 169-70.

turn to the question of this appeal to "the law" in 1 Corinthians 14:34 in the next section. For now it is enough to notice that Keener's observation that by asking questions an interpolator might "compete intellectually with an inadequately prepared lecturer"[19] is in harmony with the view that women are not to evaluate prophecies lest they exercise authority over men.

Nowhere in the Bible are women instructed as to how they are to go about teaching or shepherding men. Where this is addressed Paul writes, "I do not permit a woman to teach or to have authority over a man" (1 Tim 2:12).[20] We will consider Paul's appeal to the created order in 1 Timothy 2:13-14 in the next section, but here the following contextual observations are pertinent. First, though this is a letter to Timothy, it was almost surely meant to be read to the church in Ephesus: "The epistle's conclusion (6:21) makes this dual nature obvious when it says, 'Grace be with you [plural].'"[21] Second, 1 Timothy 2 appears to provide instructions for worship, addressing prayers in 1 Timothy 2:1-8 and the adornment and roles of women in 2:9-15. Each section is introduced by instructions (1 Tim 2:1-2; 2:9-12) and followed by theological considerations which provide the basis for the commands and instructions Paul has set forth (1 Tim 2:3-7, 13-15). Paul states in verse 8 that he intends his instructions to apply "in every place," and then the instructions regarding women are introduced with *hōsautōs*, "likewise" (v. 9). This seems to indicate at least that Paul wants these instructions to apply in all the house churches of Ephesus. If Paul intended 1 Timothy to be read in more places than Ephesus, as he expected his other letters to be read in other churches (cf. Col 4:16; 1 Thess 5:27), then it would seem that Paul intends these instructions to apply everywhere. As Mounce puts it, "The context suggests that Paul is thinking of

---

[19]Ibid., p. 165.

[20]The clearest and most convincing treatment of this passage is the one presented by Thomas R. Schreiner, "An Interpretation of 1 Timothy 2:9-15: A Dialogue with Scholarship," in *Women in the Church: A Fresh Analysis of 1 Timothy 2:9-15*, ed. Andreas J. Köstenberger, Thomas R. Schreiner and H. Scott Baldwin (Grand Rapids: Baker, 1995), pp. 105-54. A second edition of this volume is now available. See below for discussion of whether this text is an "ad hoc word to a very case-specific issue in the churches of Ephesus" (as Fee argues, "Priority of Spirit Gifting," p. 252). To suggest regarding 1 Timothy that "Paul's posture throughout is corrective rather than didactic" (so Linda L. Belleville, "Teaching and Usurping Authority: 1 Timothy 2:11-15," in *DBE*, p. 206) is a false dichotomy. Paul is everywhere corrective precisely by being didactic—what people believe and think is reflected in what they do.

[21]William D. Mounce, *Pastoral Epistles*, WBC (Nashville: Thomas Nelson, 2000), p. 4: "The letter is private in that it is written to Timothy, but public in that Paul is writing through Timothy to the church." Bracketed note original to Mounce.

every place in the world where Christians worship."[22] Paul's statements about the roles of men and women in his other letters comport well with the perspective articulated in 1 Timothy 2 (1 Cor 11:2-16; 14:34-35; Eph 5:21-33; Col 3:18-19).

Linda Belleville has argued that 1 Timothy 2:12, when properly interpreted, means "I do not permit a woman to teach a man in a dominating way."[23] When we compare this translation, however, to the syntax of the Greek it purports to represent, it is no exaggeration to say that this is a very interpretive translation. The negated verb *epitrepō*, "I do not permit," takes the dative direct object *gynaiki*, "for a woman," and the verbal idea is clarified by two complementary infinitives, *didaskein*, "to teach," and *authentein*, "to exercise authority"; both of these infinitives have *andros*, "over a man," as their object. Belleville's translation takes the first infinitive as complementing the verb but transforms the second infinitive into an adverbial modifier of the first. Paul is perfectly capable of modifying infinitives, often doing so with prepositional phrases (see 1 Tim 2:4, 8, 9, 12). If he had intended the second infinitive as an adverbial modifier of the first, it is doubtful that his grammar would be what it is. As it is, the text reads, "But I do not permit for a woman to teach [a man][24] or to exercise authority over a man" (1 Tim 2:12). Paul's grammatical structure indicates that it is not merely exercising authority over men that is prohibited but also the teaching of men by women.[25]

It is probably not coincidental that the two things Paul says that women

---

[22]Ibid., p. 107. See esp. 1 Tim 2:13-15; 3:15.

[23]Belleville, "Teaching and Usurping Authority," p. 219.

[24]Bracketed words showing that both infinitives are modified by ἀνδρός. So also Mounce, *Pastoral Epistles*, p. 123. Mounce cites D. J. Moo, "The Interpretation of 1 Timothy 2:11-15: A Rejoinder," *TJ* 2 (1981): 202, and both also cite Herbert Weir Smyth, *Greek Grammar* (Cambridge, Mass.: Harvard University Press, 1984), §1634, in explanation of the genitive case of ἀνδρός (αὐθεντέω takes a genitive direct object, and when two verbs share an object, as here, the case of the object is determined by the nearer verb).

[25]The most convincing treatment of the grammar of this text is Andreas J. Köstenberger, "A Complex Sentence Structure in 1 Timothy 2:12," in *Women in the Church: A Fresh Analysis of 1 Timothy 2:9-15*, ed. Andreas J. Köstenberger, Thomas R. Schreiner and H. Scott Baldwin (Grand Rapids: Baker, 1995), pp. 81-103. We have noted that Fee regards this as an "ad hoc word to a very case-specific issue in the churches of Ephesus" ("Priority of Spirit Gifting," p. 252). Similarly, Belleville suggests that this was a problem specific to the women in Ephesus ("Teaching and Usurping Authority," pp. 206, 209, 219, 223). The main problem with this view is that Paul does not explicitly address a particular issue confined only to the women in Ephesus, nor does he indicate that what he says here is not a stipulation to be followed "in every place" (1 Tim 2:8). As will be discussed below, Paul does not explain 1 Tim 2:12 by recourse to the situation in Ephesus but by appeal to Genesis 1—3.

are not to do in 1 Timothy 2:12 are the two things for which elders are to be rewarded in 1 Timothy 5:17, "The elders who rule well must be considered worthy of double honor, especially those who labor in preaching and teaching." The very ministries that Paul says that women are not to do, teaching and exercising authority, are the ministries for which elders are to be honored. When we combine this with the observation that when Paul describes the qualifications for the office of elder he mentions teaching and ruling and speaks only with reference to men (1 Tim 3:1-7; Tit 1:5-9)—whereas with the office of deacon he addresses women who might be deacons—it seems reasonable to conclude that Paul does not expect women to serve as elders.[26] That the elder/overseer must be qualified for the task of "holding fast the faithful word according to the teaching, in order that he might be able to exhort in healthy teaching and to refute those who speak against it" (Tit 1:9) is difficult to square with Fee's claim that "in no instance in Paul's letters does he mention leader(s) who are to be in charge of what takes place."[27]

From what Paul says about deacons, again, it seems that women can serve as deacons (1 Tim 3:8-13, esp. v. 11), and this appears more likely when we consider Phoebe (Rom 16:1). It is important to note, however, that whereas Paul calls for an elder to be "apt to teach" (1 Tim 3:2), and regularly refers to the elders serving as stewards of God's house (1 Tim 3:5; Tit 1:7), there are no parallel teaching and governing qualifications for deacons.

Luke Timothy Johnson has suggested that 1 Timothy 2:12 is in "sharp

---

[26]I want to register an objection to a caricature at this point. Fee writes concerning 1 Tim 2:12, "Whatever else, it does not seem to be dealing with 'offices' in the church; at least that certainly cannot be demonstrated, even if one were to wish desperately for it to be so" ("Priority of Spirit Gifting," p. 252). I disagree with Fee on this point because I am compelled by the biblical evidence—as articulated above. I want to embrace whatever the Bible teaches, and so if the Bible did not contain the texts discussed here, I would gladly join the egalitarian cause. Therefore, suggesting that those who take the view I have articulated "wish desperately for it to be so" is unhelpful. I only wish desperately to obey everything the Bible says for the glory of God. Even if Fee were correct that there is no connection to the "offices," a woman regularly teaching men would almost certainly be excluded by 1 Tim 2:12.

[27]Fee, "Priority of Spirit Gifting," p. 251. This text also stands against Belleville's claim that "teaching in the New Testament period was an activity and not an office" ("Teaching and Usurping Authority," p. 221). Fee also minimizes what the NT says about "officers" in the churches earlier, suggesting that elders "eventually came to be called *episkopoi* (overseers)" (p. 243). The problem with this assertion is that the NT uses "elders" interchangeably with "overseers" in several places. See Acts 20:17, where the Ephesian elders meet with Paul and are then referred to as "overseers" in Acts 20:28. Cf. also Tit 1:5, 7; 1 Pet 5:1-2.

tension with other Pauline declarations of a more egalitarian character, above all Gal 3:28."[28] Judith M. Gundry-Volf, however, has convincingly shown that what Paul presents here is "a model of thought in which equality does not presuppose all-out sameness (dissolution of femininity or/and masculinity) but sameness *in some respects*—with respect to sin and with respect to the way of salvation."[29] The challenge for evangelicals will be holding 1 Timothy 2:12 together with Galatians 3:28. Both males and females participate in baptism—unlike circumcision,[30] and in Christian churches we do not separate the women from the men in worship. But we dare not follow Robert Schuller's advice and read the Bible the way we eat fish—avoiding the parts we find disagreeable.[31] We who submit ourselves to the authority of Scripture must do all we can to live as though "*all* Scripture is God-breathed" (2 Tim 3:16) not just the parts we like. Indeed, we must do all we can to like it all (cf. Ps 119:103).

What follows, then, is a summary of the ministries the Bible authorizes women to pursue in New Testament churches. This list focuses on teaching ministries and offices that might be held by women in the church, so it is not exhaustive.[32] Nor is it arranged in a manner that intends to rank these ministries in a perceived order of importance. First, women can serve the church as deacons (Rom 16:1; 1 Tim 3:8). Second, women can stand before the gathered congregation and pray or prophesy (1 Cor 11:5). Third, women can partner with their husbands to instruct other men in private situations (Acts 18:26).

---

[28]Luke Timothy Johnson, *The First and Second Letters to Timothy,* ABCom (New York: Doubleday, 2001), p. 208, cf. also p. 211.

[29]Judith M. Gundry-Volf, "Christ and Gender: A Study of Difference and Equality in Gal 3,28," in *Jesus Christus als die Mitte der Schrift,* ed. C. Landmesser et al., BZNW 86 (New York: Walter de Gruyter, 1997), p. 476 (emphasis hers). Similarly E. Earle Ellis, *Pauline Theology: Ministry and Society* (Grand Rapids: Eerdmans, 1989), pp. 84-85.

[30]Gundry-Volf, "Christ and Gender," p. 458.

[31]Transcript of "Politically Incorrect with Bill Maher (November 23, 2001)" available online at <www.geocities.com/~dvadi/pi/pi_11232001.html> (accessed March 9, 2005). The transcript of Schuller's full comment reads as follows: "First of all, you can find things in any holy book. I'm a Christian. I believe the Bible. I can find things in the Bible that I don't like, that I don't agree with, that I think are not—what do I do? I tell people who become Christians, the Bible is our holy book, but read the Bible the way you eat fish—carefully. [Light laughter] Don't choke on a bone. [Laughter] Pick the food that serves you well." I owe this reference to Nathan Lino.

[32]For lists of ministries relating to authority, teaching and public visibility ranked from greatest influence to least, see Grudem, *EFBT,* pp. 85-90. Grudem points out that these lists are not meant to rank activities according to "value or importance" (p. 85), and he identifies on pages 93-97 which ministries from these lists, in his view, are open to women. I am in general agreement with his thoughtful assessment.

Fourth, women can teach other women (Tit 2:3-5). And fifth, women can teach young males who are not considered "men" by the culture (cf. 2 Tim 1:5; 3:15).[33]

The boundaries the Bible places upon the ministries women pursue may also be summarized as follows. Again, this list is not exhaustive, as it focuses on the exercise of teaching ministries and offices and does not address the character qualities required of all who minister in the church. First, since Paul says that women are not to exercise authority over men, if women serve as deacons there should not be men under their authority. Second, since Paul says that women are not to teach men, women who are gifted to teach should exercise their gift in the service of children, young males who are not men, and other women, but they are not to teach men.[34]

Summarizing the first two parts of this essay, we have seen that full participation in ministry is not the free exercise of any and every ministerial role or function. Rather, full participation in ministry is realized when a member of the body takes up the ministry assigned by God under the lordship of Christ as empowered by the Spirit. We have also seen that 1 Corinthians 11 urges that when women pray and prophesy in church they are to do so in an explicitly feminine way, and that when prophecies are judged women are to remain silent (1 Cor 14:34-35). Finally, we have seen that 1 Timothy 2:12 states that

---

[33]Mounce rightly notes that though Paul never says Timothy's mother and grandmother taught him, this is nevertheless "the apparent meaning of the text" (*Pastoral Epistles*, p. 123).

[34]Fee ("Priority of Spirit Gifting," p. 251) suggests that "the two well-known and much-debated texts, 1 Corinthians 14:34-35 and 1 Timothy 2:11-12, seem to stand in open contradiction to the rest of the evidence." He then proceeds to reassert his view that 1 Cor 14:34-35 was not original to Paul, leaving only 1 Tim 2:11-12, which he claims was "an ad hoc word to a very case-specific issue in the churches of Ephesus" (pp. 251-52). When we list the texts that *DBE* wrestles with, however, it does not appear that 1 Cor 14:34-35 and 1 Tim 2:11-12 stand alone. On the contrary, there are other texts in the New Testament which explicitly treat gender in a manner that harmonizes with the two texts Fee isolates. Some come from Paul (1 Cor 11:2-16; Col 3:18-19 and Eph 5:21-33; then there is Paul's treatment of Gen 1—3, but *DBE* does not deal with Tit 2:1-6), and one comes from Peter, 1 Pet 3:1-7. Suddenly the gender statements in 1 Cor 14:34-35 and 1 Tim 2:11-12 are standing with at least five other passages which offer clear statements on how men and women are to conduct themselves. What is troubling about the essays in *DBE* is that once the authors have sifted the data, nothing can have a clear meaning. What the texts appear to say, according to these authors, is not what they mean. Or, in the case of I. Howard Marshall's essay ("Mutual Love and Submission in Marriage: Colossians 3:18-19 and Ephesians 5:21-33" in *DBE*), the Bible clearly means what it says but it no longer applies: "some culturally specific scriptural teaching and commands are no longer mandatory" (p. 202). Those who submit themselves to the authority of Scripture will seek to conform Christian culture to the commands of the NT, resisting the temptation to transform the Bible into a book the world will approve of.

women are neither to teach nor to exercise authority over men.[35] Thus, whereas women serve the church in many capacities in the New Testament—they partner with their husbands to give private instruction, they pray and prophesy in church, they teach younger women and young males who are not men—they neither serve in the capacity of elder nor function as regular teachers of men. This means that women are not the authoritative leaders and teachers of the church. In the third and final section of this essay, we turn to the question of how these biblical boundaries the New Testament articulates are to be applied in the twenty-first century.

FULL PARTICIPATION, BIBLICAL BOUNDARIES AND THE CHURCH TODAY

Christians affirm that the Bible is inspired by God, useful to his people and to be embraced in its entirety. The Bible, for us, is not an oppressor from which we need be liberated. It is liberating to learn from the Bible where freedom from bondage may be found—in obedience. Further, affirming that God created all things good, Christians believe that gender, too, is good, not something to be ignored, minimized or even obliterated.

When Paul explains why women who pray and prophesy in church should do so with their heads covered, he seems to base his argument on what it means to be male and female. The conjunction *gar,* "for," in 1 Corinthians 11:7 indicates that in this verse Paul is offering an explanation that justifies what he has said in the previous verses, and he writes, "For indeed a man ought not to cover his head, being the image and glory of God; but the woman is the glory of man" (1 Cor 11:7). Here Paul explains his call for women to cover their heads by proclaiming that "woman is the glory of man." By contrast, men are not to cover their heads because they are the "image and glory of God." This points to a *fundamental difference between the genders.*

If one were hoping to find indications in 1 Corinthians 11 that these verses are not transcultural, the situation gets worse in 1 Corinthians 11:8-9. Another *gar,* "for," indicates that Paul is explaining his appeal to the nature of gender

---

[35]In the brief compass of this essay it is impossible to deal with all of the exegetical issues regarding this text raised in Professor Howard Marshall's presentation. It does not seem to me that Marshall has raised new considerations, but he has summarized those that egalitarians generally raise. All of these are convincingly treated in Schreiner's updated essay on the passage, which is now available in the second edition of *Women in the Church.* I am thankful to have seen a prepublication draft of Schreiner's essay.

in verse 7 with the words in I Corinthians 11:8, "For man is not from woman, but woman from man." Paul seems to be pointing to the fact that Adam was not made from Eve, but Eve from Adam. The possible significance of the order will be considered below, but aside from that consideration, in verse 9 yet another *gar*, "for," indicates that this verse is explaining at least part of the significance of the fact that the man did not come from the woman but the woman from man: "for also the man was not created on account of the woman but the woman on account of the man" (1 Cor 11:9). Paul's understanding derives from the words of Genesis 2, where we read that God put Adam in the garden to work it and keep it (Gen 2:15) and Eve in the garden to help Adam (Gen 2:18). Having given these three reasons—man is the image and glory of God and woman is the glory of man (1 Cor 11:7); woman was created from man, not man from woman (1 Cor 11:8); and woman was made for man, not man for woman (1 Cor 11:9)—Paul concludes in 1 Corinthians 11:10, "On account of this a woman ought to have a sign of authority upon her head on account of the angels." Thus, Paul's argument in 1 Corinthians 11 is not based upon Greco-Roman cultural convention, but on the nature of gender and on the pre-Fall (Gen 2) created order. These considerations indicate that what Paul calls for here is transcultural.[36]

Does this mean that women in our society should wear head coverings? In my judgment, the issue is not head coverings. Paul's transcultural appeal is not to a particular form of adornment. Paul's transcultural appeal is to the reality that "Christ is the head of every man, man is the head of woman, and God is the head of Christ" (1 Cor 11:3),[37] which is reflected in man being the "image and glory of God" and woman being "the glory of man" (1 Cor 11:7). Thus, the issue is *gender* and what gender portrays. Peggy Noonan got it right: "It's all about God." The issue in this passage is not the external head covering but

---

[36]I find William J. Webb's recent suggestion that our understanding of what Paul wrote should be influenced by our estimation of what Paul would have written if he were alive today unconvincing. He writes, "if Paul were alive, he would update his procreation point to argue. . . . This updated argument requires those within a modern context to rethink their understanding of biblical anthropology and readjust the relative weighting of male-and-female status accordingly." W. J. Webb, "Balancing Paul's Original-Creation and Pro-Creation Arguments: 1 Corinthians 11:11-12 in Light of Modern Embryology," *WTJ* 66 (2004): 282-83. The authority of Scripture constrains us to what Paul wrote, and we are not free to decide what he would have written. The danger of such an approach lies in the tendency of the modern scholar to remake Jesus and Paul into his or her own image, as Schweitzer taught us.

[37]Wayne Grudem's work on the word *kephalē*, "head," remains unrefuted and is now conveniently gathered in one place in his *EFBT*, pp. 201-11, 544-51, 552-99.

what that head covering represents. For this reason, it does not seem to me that the church in the twenty-first century has a responsibility to make sure that when women pray and prophesy in church they do so with their heads covered. But the church does have a responsibility to make sure that when women pray and prophesy they do so in a way that proclaims to the culture their submission to male headship and their glad embrace of feminine identity. In other words, it needs to be clear to anyone watching that this female is praying or prophesying as a female. She is not trying to take on the role of a man. So, in my judgment, the *expression* of gender roles—the head covering—is not transcultural. Gender roles themselves, however, are transcultural. The appeal to the nature of gender in 1 Corinthians 11:7, to the order of creation in 1 Corinthians 11:8, and to the created purpose of the male and female in 1 Corinthians 11:9 demands that the church reflect the structure of authority outlined in 1 Corinthians 11:3—God-Christ-Man-Woman.[38]

The call for women to remain silent when prophecies are judged in 1 Corinthians 14:34 is supported by the statement "as the law also says." Paul does not exegete the created order here as he did in 1 Corinthians 11:7-9, but it seems most plausible that he is referring to the considerations enumerated there. An analogous reference back to previously cited Old Testament material can be seen in 1 Corinthians 4:6. There Paul expresses his desire that his audience will "learn not to go beyond what has been written," and the reference to "what has been written" appears to point back to the Old Testament texts cited earlier in 1 Corinthians pertaining to boasting and introduced by "it has been written" (1 Cor 1:19, 31; 2:9; 3:19-20).[39] Paul's reference in 1 Corinthians 4:6 to "what has been written," on this understanding, would parallel the words "as the law also says" in 14:34. Both are pointing back to related interpretation of the OT that has appeared earlier in the letter. Thus, the call for women to be silent when prophecies are evaluated in 14:34 is based on the same transcultural considerations about gender Paul articulated from Genesis 1—2 in 1 Corinthians 11:7-9.[40]

Paul's teaching on gender roles is notably consistent.[41] His explanation as to

---

[38]See comments in n. 13 above.

[39]So David E. Garland, *1 Corinthians*, BECNT (Grand Rapids: Baker, 2003), p. 135.

[40]So also Carson, "Silent in the Churches," p. 152. Contra Garland, *1 Corinthians*, p. 673; Keener, "Learning in the Assemblies," pp. 165-71.

[41]So also Johnson, *The First and Second Letters to Timothy,* p. 206.

why women are not to teach or exercise authority over men in 1 Timothy 2:13-15 is conceptually equivalent to the explanation seen in 1 Corinthians 11. Having stated that women are not to teach men or exercise authority over them in 1 Timothy 2:12, Paul introduces his explanation in 1 Timothy 2:13 with, no surprise here, the word *gar*, "for." Just as Paul had explained that Adam was created first in 1 Corinthians 11:8, in 1 Timothy 2:13 he writes, "For Adam was formed first, then Eve." He continues in 1 Timothy 2:14, "And Adam was not deceived, but the woman, being deceived, fell into transgression." By introducing this consideration as an explanation of why he does not permit a woman to teach or exercise authority over a man, Paul implies that there is some significance to both the order in which the genders were created and the reality that Eve, not Adam, was deceived and fell into transgression.

Several observations about Genesis 1—3 shed light on why these considerations are significant for Paul. Here I can only enumerate them in the order they appear in Genesis. First, male and female are *both* in the image of God (Gen 1:27). Second, the creation of the male and the female is presented as having taken place at different points (first the man, Gen 2:7, then the woman, Gen 2:22), they are made from different material (the man from dirt, 2:7, the woman from the man's rib, Gen 2:22), the making of each is described with different verbs (the man is "formed" in 2:7, *yāṣar*, the woman is "built" in 2:22, *bānâ*), and they are made for different purposes (the man to work and keep the garden, Gen 2:15, the woman to help the man, Gen 2:18, 20). Third, the command not to eat from the tree of the knowledge of good and evil is given to the man in Genesis 2:17 before the creation of the woman is described. Then it is the man to whom God calls, even though it was the woman who ate first, which indicates that it was the man's responsibility to teach and enforce the commandment.[42] This understanding finds support in Romans 5:12, "through one man sin entered the world and death through sin." Fourth, just as God exercised dominion over his creation in Genesis 1 by naming it (e.g., Gen 1:5, "God called the light Day"), the male is exercising his authority over God's creation by naming the animals (Gen 2:19). The male is thus ruling (Gen 1:28) as God's image-bearing vice-regent. In Genesis 2:23 the male exercises his authority over the female by naming her just as he has been naming the

---

[42]G. K. Beale suggests that part of Adam's work of keeping the garden included protecting it from unclean influences such as the serpent. G. K. Beale, *The Temple and the Church's Mission: A Biblical Theology of the Dwelling Place of God*, NSBT 17 (Downers Grove, Ill.: InterVarsity Press, 2004), p. 69.

animals. He does not give her the personal name Eve until Genesis 3:20; in Genesis 2:23 he is probably "classifying" her, as he has presumably done with the animals.[43] Fifth, the characters in the narrative appear in the following order in Genesis 2: God (Gen 2:2-5), man (Gen 2:7), the animals (Gen 2:19), then the woman (Gen 2:22), with the solidarity of man and woman stressed in Genesis 2:23. This order is upended in Genesis 3, with the characters coming on the scene as follows: the snake (Gen 3:1a), the woman (Gen 3:1b), the man (Gen 3:6) and finally God (Gen 3:8). This structure lends itself to the conclusion that by approaching the woman the snake is subverting the created order,[44] an order reflected in 1 Corinthians 11:3: God-Christ-man-woman. Based on what we have seen from Genesis, complementary gender roles are not introduced as part of the curse on humanity. Rather, what seems to be introduced in Genesis 3:16 is feminine rebellion against the structure of authority that God has built into his creation.

If the attempt to deceive the woman is in fact a subversion of the created order, this would explain the appeal to the sequence in which the man and woman were made both in 1 Timothy 2:13 and in 1 Corinthians 11:8, with 1 Timothy 2:14 elaborating upon the situation in order to clarify Paul's point.[45]

---

[43]The man's naming of the woman, however, should not be construed as an impersonal exercise of duty, rude superiority or abstract patriarchy, for the man's statement upon his receipt of God's gift of the woman is humanity's first poem. The man's spontaneous overflow of powerful emotion communicates tender solidarity, the woman's origin, his role as her leader (naming her) and her essential equality with him ("flesh of flesh"). Here we see *ontological equality* ("bone of bone," "flesh of flesh") and *functional subordination* ("she shall be called woman").

[44]Similarly Schreiner, "An Interpretation of 1 Timothy 2:9-15," p. 145. For a thorough review of the positions taken on 1 Tim 2:13-14, see Mounce, *Pastoral Epistles,* pp. 130-43. The explanation above seeks to take Paul's exegesis seriously, and I find it more plausible than Johnson's. He suggests that Paul's "logic is flawed," and that "Paul was not in this case engaging in sober exegesis of Genesis, but supporting his culturally conservative position on the basis of texts that in his eyes demonstrate the greater dignity and intelligence of men and, therefore, the need for women to be silent and subordinate to men" (Johnson, *First and Second Letters to Timothy,* p. 208). Against the suggestion that Paul's logic was flawed, it seems to me that Johnson has not appreciated Paul's understanding of Genesis 1—3. Johnson continues, "I agree that our growth in understanding . . . makes it impossible to regard the statements disqualifying women from public speech and roles of leadership as either true or normative" (ibid., pp. 208-9). We can be grateful to Johnson for his honesty. He is an egalitarian because he thinks that Paul's judgment was both wrong and untrue.

[45]We read in 1 Timothy 2:15: "But she shall be saved through childbearing, if they remain in faith and in love and in sanctification with self control." The singular "she shall be saved" may be a nod to the "seed of the woman" who will crush the head of the "seed of the serpent" (Gen 3:15). But the switch to the plural in the words, "if they remain," broadens the application of this verse out to all women. By making this conditional upon remaining "in faith," Paul safeguards against the false conclusion that he is endorsing child-bearing as a meritorious work that earns salvation. He seems to have selected the most feminine thing a woman can do—something men are not equipped for—and stated

Richard Hess argues that "the view that the man's creation before the woman's implies his authority over her cannot be sustained by study of the text of Genesis 2, the context of Genesis 1—3, the comparative literature of the ancient Near East or the invocation of putative customs of primogeniture in ancient Israel."[46] But Paul cites the fact that man was made first, along with the facts that woman was made from man and for man, as reasons for the ordering of ministry according to gender in the church. Paul bases his understanding of male headship and authority on these features of Genesis 1—3. For evangelicals, the relevant question is, Whose interpretation of Genesis 1—3 is deemed authoritative—that of the modern scholar or that of the apostle Paul?[47] For my part, I agree with the conclusion of Douglas Moo: "We must conclude that the restrictions imposed by Paul in 1 Timothy 2:12 are valid for Christians in all places and all times."[48]

CONCLUSION

I have argued that a biblical understanding of full participation in ministry does not mean that one exercises one's gifts in any and every circumstance. Rather, full participation in ministry means exercising one's gifts under the lordship of Christ by the power of the Spirit in accordance with one's role in the body as assigned by the Father. God has also assigned gender to human

---

that women will be saved if they continue in faith and do this, bear children. So what Paul points to here is that women must embrace their feminine identity. Embracing one's role as a woman is a way to demonstrate faith in God, give evidence of salvation, and honor the Creator who alone has power to determine gender. Here again, Paul is insisting that gender is important. Those who believe are to embrace the role as male or as female that has been assigned to them by God. Similarly, in more detail, Mounce, *Pastoral Epistles*, p. 148, and Schreiner, "An Interpretation of 1 Timothy 2:9-15," pp. 146-53.

[46]Richard S. Hess, "Equality With and Without Innocence: Genesis 1—3," in *DBE*, p. 86. By arguing that the citation of "1 Timothy 2:13 as evidence that Paul understood the sequential creation of humanity to imply an intended hierarchy of man over woman" is "problematic" (p. 84), Hess appears to be calling Paul's own argument into question. It is very difficult to see 1 Tim 2:13-14 as something other than an explanation of 2:12, so to argue against this explanation is not to argue against complementarians but against Paul.

[47]This question arises from my experience with not a few evangelicals who seem willing to say that OT texts do not mean what NT authors say they mean. This is of course a wider issue, which needs careful discussion on a case-by-case basis. I merely note the point here to register my view that we should start from the assumption that NT exegesis of OT texts is not atomistic, irrational and illegitimate, but reasonable and hermeneutically sound—once we understand their presuppositions about the OT and what has taken place in Messiah Jesus.

[48]Douglas Moo, "What Does It Mean Not to Teach or Have Authority over Men: 1 Timothy 2:11-15," in *RBMW*, p. 188.

beings, and the Bible sets parameters on what one may do in ministry according to gender. These boundaries should be understood not as oppressive constraints but as signposts on the way to the broad place in which to roam (Ps 119:45). The way of happiness is the way of holiness, and the way of obedience is the way of freedom. Thus, whether it seems right to us or not, the Bible promises good to us if we hold firm to its commands. This includes Paul's words in 1 Timothy 2:12, 1 Corinthians 11:2-16 and 1 Corinthians 14:29-35. What can women do in ministry? Many, many things, but they may not teach men or exercise authority over them.

I promised earlier that I would return to boundaries the Bible provides for men in ministry. The words of Titus 1:9 were cited above, and I revisit them here. Paul writes that an elder/overseer must be one who is "holding fast the faithful word according to the teaching, in order that he might be able to exhort in healthy teaching and to refute those who speak against it" (Tit 1:9). If men do not hold fast to Paul's teaching, they do not meet the "necessary" (*dei*, Tit 1:7) qualifications for elders. If men are not able to exhort in sound doctrine, they do not meet the necessary qualifications. If men are not able to rebuke those who speak against sound teaching, they do not meet the qualifications. In view of the New Testament canon, men who wish to minister in the church as elders must hold fast to Paul's teaching, and this includes Paul's teaching on gender in 1 Corinthians 11; 14; and 1 Timothy 2. May the Lord raise up men who meet all the qualifications for ministry, both those that pertain to character and those that relate to holding fast to sound teaching, exhorting others in it and refuting those who contradict. The boundaries the Lord has given to his people may at times seem restrictive, but life and freedom and joy are found in glad-hearted obedience. May he make us those for whom his commands are not burdensome (1 Jn 5:3).[49]

POSTSCRIPT

Against the better judgment of some, who showed their love for me by taking time to suggest other ways of improving this essay, I have chosen to leave it

---

[49]I wish to express my gratitude to those who helped me think about this issue at the 2005 Wheaton Theology Conference, especially Drs. Stephen Spencer and Bruce Winter. I would also like to thank two of my students, Mrs. Rhenae Abrams and Mr. Brad Smith, and Drs. Stefana Dan Laing, Jay E. Smith and Thomas R. Schreiner for reading earlier drafts of this essay and making many helpful suggestions.

largely as presented (though seeking to soften its tone at points). This decision was made largely in the hope that readers might experience something of the atmosphere of the 2005 Wheaton Theology Conference, where most of the other presentations came to conclusions different from mine. Being in the minority at the conference gave to me the sense of being an outsider who had wandered into an assemblage of people speaking unknown languages (cf. 1 Cor 14:22-23). From comments made by other presenters, it is also clear that where those who hold my perspective are in the majority, the same sense of being an outsider among people speaking unknown tongues is felt by egalitarians, and thus it seems that many who participate in this conversation are *unable to hear* what concerns those with whom they disagree. Of course we all hear each other, but we all weigh respective considerations differently. I am in hearty agreement with those at the conference—chiefly Timothy George and Sarah Sumner—who called for renewed attempts by the respective sides to listen to one another. Perhaps we could add to this the prayer that God might once again reverse the effects of Babel, as he did on the day of Pentecost long ago, and once again cause the Spirit from on high to fall on us with power that those who speak in different mother tongues might hear and understand one another (Acts 2:7-11). Unless the Lord gives both sides ears to hear and hearts to understand, we will remain those to whom one of the secrets of the kingdom of heaven (unity on this issue) has not been given (Mt 13:11).

3

WOMEN IN MINISTRY

A Further Look at 1 Timothy 2

I. Howard Marshall

FORTY YEARS AGO THE BRITISH METHODIST CHURCH, of which I am a member, already accepted the ministry of women as lay preachers but not as ordained ministers. Before her marriage my wife had belonged to the Christian Brethren, a Christian group in which the biblical requirements (as they saw them) regarding women were extended to the exclusion of them from taking any spoken part in a mixed company, and especially in a Sunday "breaking of bread" service. In that service they might not pray, nor even request the singing of a particular hymn,[1] nor even read the Scriptures, still less comment on them, and they were required to wear head-coverings—which, you might have thought, in the light of 1 Corinthians 11 should surely have legitimized their praying. Understanding all this as obedience to what Scripture required, the Brethren adhered to this position and in whole or part some of them still do.[2] Then I found myself appointed to serve on a working group of the Church of Scotland's Panel on Doctrine, which was looking at the question of ordination of women, and I had to try to come to terms with the issue. Not long afterward the Methodist Church experienced a breakdown in its discussions to-

---

[1] But they were allowed to join in the singing!
[2] I recently attended a morning "breaking of bread" meeting where the women present were expressly told that they could not take part verbally, although no dress requirements were imposed.

ward organic union with the Church of England, which at that time was strongly against women in ordained ministry, and, since the Methodist Church no longer felt under pressure not to do so in the interest of unity, it began to accept women into the ministry. So I was now a member of a church with ordained women ministers. Subsequently I served for a period as a member of the church's selection committee for candidates for the ministry and had to assess the qualities of applicants regardless of whether they were male or female. Throughout this process I faced the dilemma of whether I could reconcile the practice of the church and my own involvement in it with my acceptance of the authority of Scripture, and I confess that I did not find it easy to do so at that time. You will observe, for I'm trying to be honest, that I was looking for a reconciliation of church practice with Scripture rather than necessarily for a direct encouragement and legitimation of church practice by Scripture.[3]

Many Christians have moved some way since those days, and today the position is rather different. Nevertheless, there is still very considerable disagreement among us on this issue, both from evangelicals and from upholders of traditional positions in the Roman Catholic Church and some other denominations.[4]

CONTEMPORARY PROS AND CONS OF WOMEN'S MINISTRY

Why is it that the possibility of women in certain forms of ministry[5] is rejected by fellow evangelicals?[6]

---

[3]This could be regarded as going by something akin to the normative principle, by which no practice directly condemned by the Bible should be allowed in the church, rather than the regulative principle, by which only what is practiced or commanded in the Bible is lawful. I say "akin" because it could be argued that prima facie the ministry of women is condemned by Scripture, and my question was whether this was the correct interpretation of Scripture. There are many things that Christians today believe are part of their Christian duty although they are not expressly commanded in Scripture, like promoting democracy instead of dictatorship (by whatever other name it may be called). See I. Howard Marshall, *Beyond the Bible: Moving from Scripture to Theology* (Grand Rapids: Baker, 2004), pp. 40-42.

[4]Most recently see Grudem, *EFBT*. Cf. Wayne Grudem, *Systematic Theology: An Introduction to Biblical Doctrine* (Grand Rapids: Zondervan, 1994), pp. 937-45.

[5]I shall use the term "women's ministry" in this paper to refer narrowly to the types of ministry by women that are forbidden by its opponents, while recognizing that there are many forms of wider ministry that were open to women in Scripture and are fully recognized by most evangelical Christians today. We are concerned with women teaching and exercising leadership in the kind of roles generally recognized by ordination in the United Kingdom (I cannot speak for North America). I firmly believe that many of our problems regarding ministry generally would be mitigated by a less rigid understanding of ordination and by getting rid of the unbiblical distinction between clergy and laity.

[6]I leave aside the problems faced by Roman Catholics and others with their (in my opinion) flawed understanding of ordained ministers as priests.

1. The first and obvious reason is a claim that their position is supported by what is thought to be the plain sense of Scripture. First Timothy 2:8-15 appears to rule out women teaching and exercising authority over men for all time and to do so on the basis of the personal authority of the author of this passage,[7] which is then backed up by an argument from Scripture.

2. A second reason is that some of the proponents of women's ministry are associated with a strident feminism that treats Scripture and evangelical doctrine lightly, and there is the fear that the movement for women's ministry comes from this stable and brings with it other runners who may be less welcome as they gallop on without restraint.[8]

3. A third reason is that the introduction of women's ministry in some churches has not always been accompanied by adequate attention to the difficulties that may be caused by putting women into positions traditionally held by men without considering how those positions may need some modification. Women and men are different from one another! I know of a small number of cases where marriages of ordained women have run onto the rocks, and I think that this is because the implications of ordination and the conditions of ministerial life had not been properly considered.[9] But some might want to argue that such undesirable consequences are the inevitable result of following a practice which (in their eyes) is not scripturally based.

None of these are compelling arguments for rejecting the possibility of women's ministry. But within the limits of this chapter I shall have to concentrate my attention on the first point.

On the other side, the proponents of women's ministry can draw attention to various pragmatic arguments that have to do with the decline in the number of men seeking ordination, the manifest competence and godliness of many women pastors, and the casuistry that comes in when we try to draw fine lines between, for example, senior pastors, pastors, occasional preachers in church,

---

[7]The author is Paul or somebody who claims to write on his behalf. Either way the text is part of canonical Scripture and is authoritative. I shall refer to its author as "Paul."

[8]This is a major motive underlying the campaign led by Grudem, cf. *EFBT*, p. 17.

[9]It is an interesting speculation whether the opposition to women's ministry reflects not only a particular understanding of authoritative Scripture but also a cultural setting in which the dominance of men (both as men and as husbands) is felt to be under threat and there is strong pressure to maintain the status quo.

missionaries on the field, lay workers and so on. We also have the fact that in society at large women now exercise the kind of roles that consistent opponents of women in ministry must regard as inappropriate for them to have.[10] These points, like the secondary ones on the other side, are relevant, and we cannot altogether ignore them while dealing with the primary point: how do we interpret Scripture? For an important part of interpretation lies in recognizing where our cultural and specific situations differ from those in which Scripture was composed and asking whether the Scriptural teaching that was given in a way that was suited to the ancient situation needs to be reinterpreted for a different situation.

An Exegesis of 1 Timothy 2:8-15

In 1999 I published a commentary in which detailed attention was given to 1 Timothy 2:8-15.[11] It preceded half-a-dozen or so further commentaries by R. F. Collins, L. T. Johnson, W. L. Liefeld, W. D. Mounce, J. D. Quinn and W. C. Wacker,[12] alongside which must be placed a number of monographs and articles that discuss the passage.[13] To assess these subsequent contributions in de-

---

[10]Grudem (*EFBT*, pp. 140, 392-93) holds that male leadership applies only in the home and the church, but this would seem to be a failure to take 1 Timothy 2:12 in the literal and serious way that he commends; compare how the regulations on women's dress in verse 9 clearly do not apply only to what is worn in church but to life generally. Presumably complementarians would have to extend the scope of the prohibition to those situations where a woman might exercise authority in a secular business or organization in which her husband was on a lower level.

[11]I. Howard Marshall, *The Pastoral Epistles: A Critical and Exegetical Commentary*, International Critical Commentary Series (Edinburgh: T & T Clark, 2004).

[12]Raymond F. Collins, *1 & 2 Timothy and Titus: A Commentary*, The New Testament Library (Louisville, Ky.: Westminster John Knox, 2002). Luke Timothy Johnson, *The First and Second Letters to Timothy: A New Translation with Introduction and Commentary*, ABCom (New York: Doubleday, 2001). However, Johnson had earlier published a shorter commentary in which the substance of his understanding was already clearly presented. See Luke Timothy Johnson, *Letters to Paul's Delegates: 1 Timothy, 2 Timothy, Titus* (Valley Forge, Penn.: Trinity Press International, 1996). Walter L. Liefeld, *1 and 2 Timothy, Titus*, The NIV Application Commentary (Grand Rapids: Zondervan, 1999). William D. Mounce, *Pastoral Epistles*, WBC (Nashville: Thomas Nelson, 2000). Jerome D. Quinn and William C. Wacker, *The First and Second Letters to Timothy*, Eerdmans Critical Commentary (Grand Rapids: Eerdmans, 2000), p. 239, hold that the pericope includes 1 Tim 3:1 which refers backwards to the Christian message in 1 Tim 2:15. They then regard the whole section from 1 Tim 2:11 as a piece of Jewish Christian parenesis used in Christian liturgy and originally "a Christian, perhaps Roman, liturgy of marriage in the latter part of the first century." The former interpretation is possible, but nothing vital for our present purpose hangs upon a decision one way or the other. The latter is speculation without any positive evidence in its favor.

[13]J. M. Holmes, *Text in a Whirlwind: A Critique of Four Exegetical Devices at 1 Timothy 2.9-15* (Sheffield: Sheffield Academic Press, 2000), questions the assumption that 1 Tim 2:1-2, 8-12 deals with activities taking place in the congregation and holds that the whole of 1 Tim 2:1—3:13 deals with the

tail is impossible.[14] But it may be helpful if I outline the position that I defended and then consider how it stands in the light of continuing scholarship.[15]

First, the situation into which the passage was written was one in which the congregation(s) for which Timothy had responsibility were evidently failing in their duty of prayer and had to be reminded of God's desire to save all people, a purpose which is evidently forwarded by the prayers of his people. One obstacle to prayer was the contentiousness of (some of) the men; another was the attitude of (some of) the women who were wearing costly clothing and jewelry, which was both showy and extravagant and probably also sexually enticing. Paul shares in the critique of this kind of deportment, which is found both elsewhere in Scripture and also in the secular world. The proper adornment of believers (a point applied to the women in particular but manifestly of broader application) is good deeds. It is appropriate at this juncture to mention the important and to my mind essentially convincing contribution of Bruce Winter, but there is no need for me to elaborate on it in the present context.[16]

---

character of believers (and leaders) and not with what they do in the congregational meeting. Verses 11-12 do not necessarily deal with learning in the congregation. The aspect of the verbs is significant, and yields the translation "I also permit a woman neither constantly to direct, nor to dominate a man. She should be tranquil." The primary background is not false teaching (it is rather the foolish chatter and controversy from which heresy emerges). There is no convincing evidence that the women were deserting traditional female roles. It follows that the teaching in 1 Tim 2:9-15 is of universal and not just local application. Verses 13-15 are concerned purely with Eve's entry into a state of transgression. She (Eve) could expect to be saved through the (ongoing process of) childbearing (culminating in the coming of the Messiah) set in train by her union with her husband, provided that they (Adam and Eve) were to live appropriately in faith.

Holmes tends to assume some points that are important to his thesis without much discussion and to assume that some interpretations have been refuted by other scholars again without discussing the relative strengths of the arguments. The stress that he lays on the aspect of the verb ("constantly to direct") seems most unnatural. To say that "the Author has chosen to prohibit the *continual* practice of those actions, not the actions themselves" (p. 94) is casuistic and unconvincing. And to suggest that the concern is the foolish chatter arising from heresy rather than the false teaching itself (p. 108) is splitting hairs and does no t do justice to the amount of space spent on the latter. See my review in *Evangel* 20, no. 2 (2002): 60-61.

It has not been possible within the confines of this article to engage with A. Merz, *Die fiktive Selbstauslegung des Paulus: Intertextuelle Studien zur Intention und Rezeption der Pastoralbriefe* (Göttingen: Vandenhoeck & Ruprecht, 2004).

[14]I did a survey of what was then available in my article "The Pastoral Epistles in (Very) Recent Study," *Midwestern Journal of Theology* 2 (2003): 3-37.

[15]I am grateful to Philip H. Towner for letting me preview the treatment of this passage in his recently published major commentary *The Letters to Timothy and Titus*, NICNT (Grand Rapids: Eerdmans, 2006).

[16]See Bruce W. Winter, *Roman Wives, Roman Widows: The Appearance of New Women and the Pauline*

Second, alongside this, but no doubt related to it, is an insistence that the women should learn in a quiet and submissive manner. This must reflect at least the possibility of something different taking place. Three things could be involved here. The first is some kind of vocal reaction to the teaching in a way that would have been unacceptable in mixed company at that time. Elsewhere in the Pastoral Epistles what is in effect a similar curb is put upon persons (only men?) who were vociferously propagating unorthodox opinions in the congregation and causing dissensions and arguments (Tit 1:10-14; 3:9-11; 2 Tim 2:14-26). Hence the second thing involved here is likely to have been the acceptance of these dubious teachings by the women (2 Tim 3:6-7), a point that is probably reflected in 1 Timothy 2:15. Information from 1 Corinthians may suggest a third factor: the women there were told to ask questions of their husbands at home (1 Cor 14:35). This may reflect the undoubted fact that by and large the women were poorly educated in comparison with the men, with a far higher level of illiteracy, and this lack of education may have been apparent in the general standard of their contribution to the discussion. So the women were encouraged to learn but to do so in an appropriate spirit.

But then, third, Paul goes further and states that he does not allow a woman to teach nor to exercise authority over a man. It is generally assumed by traditionalists that, since elsewhere older women are encouraged to be good teachers (Tit 2:3) and the young Timothy was taught by his mother and grandmother (2 Tim 1:5; 3:15),[17] the prohibition is of women teaching adult men, perhaps thinking especially of their husbands, and/or that the prohibition is of public teaching in a congregational meeting rather than in the privacy of a home,[18] and/or that the reference is thus to what might be regarded as the "of-

---

Communities (Grand Rapids: Eerdmans, 2003); Bruce W. Winter, "The 'New' Roman Wife and 1 Timothy 2:9-15: The Search for a *Sitz im Leben*," *TynBul* 51 (2000): 285-94. The kind of reconstruction of the background advocated by Winter is rejected by R. W. Wall, "1 Timothy 2:9-15 Reconsidered (Again)," *BBR* 14, no. 1 (2004): 81-103, on the grounds that there is no evidence within the text itself to support it. Wall's view appears to be that the writer is simply expressing a general concern for the development of Christian character "differentiated according to standard caricatures," i.e., the place of a woman in the society of the time as choosing a teacher "from whom she can then learn quietly, and to whose gospel teaching she could then submit" (p. 91).

[17]This is the clear implication of these verses taken together.

[18]It is important to observe that the point appears to be concerned not just with the subordination of the individual woman to her husband (or other responsible male) but also with a general prohibition of women taking part in the public areas of life that were reserved for men. Even if the teaching in Genesis might be thought to offer a basis for the former, it is hard to extend it to the latter.

ficial, authoritative" setting forth of Christian doctrine rather than something less formal. In such ways the prohibition here might be harmonized with indications of their teaching functions elsewhere. As for the exercise of authority, the proponents of the traditional position argue that the very rare word used here simply means "to exercise authority" with no negative nuances regarding the kind or manner of authority. However, the unusual word usage, which conveys ideas of exercising domination,[19] strongly suggests that the authority in question was of an unacceptable character in the social context. Hence the prohibition of teaching here is probably of a particular kind of teaching which was unacceptable in mixed company. The background to all of this was the contemporary understanding of marriage that required the subordination of the wife to her husband, for which there is plenty of evidence,[20] and the general prohibition of public roles to women.[21] Consequently, the behavior of the women would have been an impediment to the evangelization of men who held that the Christians were rejecting both Jewish and Hellenistic ideals regarding married life and the place of women.[22]

Further, in view of the reference to Eve's being deceived, it is difficult to avoid the impression that false teaching is in mind and that it was accompanied by a domineering and argumentative kind of approach; more specifically, it does look as though some kind of assertion of women's dominance over men was being made, and this may have been linked with speculative teaching based on Genesis to advance the claims of the women.[23]

Consequently, it is a wrong kind of authority that is being condemned rather than a proper use of authority.

Fourth, this point is then backed up or illustrated by reference to Eve. It seems more probable that the latter is the case. The readers are reminded

---

[19]See below.

[20]See, for example, Collins, *1 & 2 Timothy*, pp. 69-70.

[21]Jerome H. Neyrey, "'Teaching You in Public and from House to House' (Acts 20.20): Unpacking a Cultural Stereotype," *JSNT* 26 (2003): 69-102. See now Brian J. Capper, "To Keep Silent, Ask Husbands at Home, and Not to Have Authority over Men. (1 Corinthians 14:33-36 and 1 Timothy 2:11-12) The Transition from Gathering in Private to Meeting in Public Space in Second Generation Christianity and the Exclusion of Women from Leadership of the Public Assembly," *TZ* 61 (2005): 113-31, 301-19.

[22]Another factor to which Philip H. Towner draws attention is the possibility of an over-realized eschatology coupled with a "Spirit-enthusiasm" which was leading to exaggerated forms of behavior. Philip H. Towner, *The Goal of Our Instruction: The Structure of Theology and Ethics in the Pastoral Epistles* (Sheffield: JSOT Press, 1989), pp. 28-42.

[23]Whether it was expressed in the manner of the women's behavior or a specifically claimed dominance may be left open.

that Adam was created first, with the implication that therefore Eve was not superior to him. Further, they are reminded that she was deceived and so became a transgressor. Therefore, the contemporary women should beware lest they be deceived and are warned not to think themselves superior to men.

Finally, the women are told that "she" will be saved through the bearing of children, a phrase that must include the actual physical act of bearing children but also may refer to the concomitant task of bringing them up.[24] The singular term "she" is thought by many to refer in the first place to Eve, but the rest of the verse makes it clear to me that the primary thought is of the writer's contemporaries. "Saved" refers to the full attainment of salvation, and the explanation that makes sense of the situation is that some women thought that they had to be teachers in order to achieve their full salvation. This was associated with a reaction against childbearing and (perhaps) the carrying out of domestic duties. It fits in with the rejection of marriage by some teachers in the congregation, which may well have included abstention from sexual relationships within existing marriages (1 Tim 4:1-3). Paul is telling them that they serve God equally well and indeed appropriately and necessarily in fulfilling the function assigned to them and not to men, namely, the bearing and upbringing of children. Yet, to avoid any suggestion that they are saved by what could easily become the performance of a particular duty (like some religious ritual), he insists that they must show the Christian qualities of faith, love, holiness and the self-control or "propriety" (TNIV) that was commended to them in 1 Timothy 2:9. Thus the thought of propriety forms a kind of bracket round the passage.

Putting all this together, we must envisage a complicated background situation[25] involving various factors that combined to necessitate a ban on women behaving in unseemly ways (including ostentatious dress and inappropriate forms of teaching activity). The overriding factor seems to be the social situation in which the Jewish and Hellenistic understanding of the place of women in society and marriage was being threatened by the activities of some women who were acting in a disruptive manner in the congregational meeting and teaching in a domineering manner. This was probably

---

[24]The view that the specific childbearing is the birth of the Messiah to Mary continues to find supporters, but it is an extraordinary way to refer to it.

[25]I would emphasize that historical situations are seldom simple, and that we must allow for the complexity of human motivation rather than seek for easy explanations in terms of single factors.

also connected with a rejection of marriage and childbearing by "emanci-
pated" women. This went against the expectations of the time and was
bringing the gospel into discredit, just as Titus 2:5 clearly indicates in a related piece of teaching.[26] It was this situation that motivated the prohibition
here. And it was necessary to refute the wrong ideas that appear to have
been drawn from Genesis by offering a different understanding of the creation and Fall narrative.

1 TIMOTHY 2:8-15 AND THE CHURCH TODAY

All of this provides a plausible setting for a strong prohibition of women teaching and exercising an unacceptable authority over the men. The question that
then arises is the one of application to readers other than the original audience
in the congregations supervised by Timothy. Was this intended as a rule for all
situations and for all time? How is it to be applied today?

1. The starting point must be the fact that salvation is available equally to
   women and men. All of Paul's readers in Galatia have been baptized into
   Christ and have put on Christ; it does not matter whether they are Jews or
   Greeks, slaves or free, male or female: they are all one in and through their
   new relationship with Jesus (Gal 3:28).[27] Since they are all one in Christ,
   they are all one in the church. But how far does the breaking down of the
   barriers extend? Free people and slaves worked side by side in the gospel.
   Jews and Greeks worked together. We do not know of any restrictions on
   their participation and service. But were women excluded in principle from
   some kinds of participation and service?[28] And were restrictions that might

---

[26]Thomas R. Schreiner's claim that this point was not in Paul's mind because it is not explicitly mentioned here is not convincing. Thomas R. Schreiner, "Women in Ministry," in *Two Views on Women in
Ministry*, ed. James R. Beck and Craig L. Blomberg (Grand Rapids: Zondervan, 2001), p. 223 n. 86.
The motive of not doing things that cause stumbling blocks for evangelism is sufficiently widespread
in the New Testament to be taken for granted generally.

[27]The construction is not easy to understand: does Paul mean that they become one corporate person
in Christ, hence united with one another, or does he mean that they are all the same (a Jew is no
different from a Greek)? Either way, he is saying that the differences between people do not matter
in the case of all who are in Christ.

[28]There is, of course, nothing in the text of Galatians to suggest that this issue was in Paul's mind at this
juncture. To be sure, if women did not take part in public life (or their doing so was frowned upon
by traditionalists), it might be assumed that the text implied nothing different. But even so it would
still be fair to ask whether the text contains implications for their place in a different ordering of society, just as the church eventually asked about the position of slaves and came to repudiate the social
understanding that first-century Christians had scarcely begun to question.

be taken for granted in the social situations of first-century society intended to be perpetuated forever?

2. The participation of women in many kinds of Christian service in New Testament congregations is attested. Certainly, it is often argued that we do not have unequivocal evidence for them acting as leaders of groups that may have included men (husbands? slaves?),[29] but this position is hard to sustain in the light of the apostle Junia (Rom 16:7).[30] In any case, we have to bear in mind that the lack of evidence for this function is probably due to the social constraints of the time rather than to doctrinal objections.

3. The presence or risk of heresy must always be taken seriously, but it does not constitute a basis for the silencing only of women; in fact the Pastoral Epistles take equally strong if not stronger action against the heretical men by banning them from the meeting.

4. Domineering and assertions of gender superiority are wrong in any situation. But leadership can and must be exercised in a different kind of way. Most of the problems about women's ministry would have been avoided if the concept of ministry as humble service (both of God and to the congregation) had been recognized from the outset over against the concepts of authority, hierarchy and worldly position that have overlaid it in much of the church.

5. The situation of women today is very different from that in Paul's days. Women are generally educated to the same level as men and are able to hold similar positions in the secular world. Families are no longer as large as they were in the first century, domestic life has been revolutionized by technology, and the average expectation of life is much longer, so that a woman's life and activity are not

---

[29]The recognition that women took part in most kinds of service except those involving ultimate responsibility and public teaching is found in Andreas J. Köstenberger, "Women in the Pauline Mission," in The Gospel to the Nations: Perspectives on Paul's Mission, ed. Peter Bolt and Mark Thompson (Downers Grove, Ill.: InterVarsity Press, 2000), pp. 221-47. The article fails to take into account the way in which the culture of the time imposed restrictions on what women might do, so that the absence of examples of them taking ultimate responsibility and doing public teaching is not remarkable and is not necessarily due to theological principles. Compare how the lack of women among the twelve apostles chosen by Jesus was inevitable under the constraints of the social situation of the time and cannot be assumed to be the expression of a theological principle that excluded them.

[30]The view that Junia was an apostle is disputed on syntactical grounds by Michael H. Burer and Daniel B. Wallace, "Was Junia Really an Apostle? A Reexamination of Romans 16:7," NTS 47 (2001): 76-91, followed by Grudem, EFBT, pp. 223-27, who calls it "a highly speculative and flimsy foundation." However, the reexamination has not established its point. See Linda Belleville, "A Re-examination of Romans 16:7 in Light of Primary Source Materials," NTS 51 (2005): 231-49.

restricted to the years when a young family has to be cared for. There is emphatically a place, however, for reminding some couples of the need to bear children and to bring them up "in the nurture and admonition of the Lord," and 1 Timothy 2:15 is a verse that has something positive to say in this regard.

6. People today in the Western world do not find any impropriety in women taking part in secular life, in contributing to Christian meetings, in writing Christian books (whether novels, devotional books, commentaries on Scripture or doctrinal disquisitions) or composing Christian hymns. In so doing they undoubtedly teach men! The casuistry that has to be resorted to in order to make the prohibition workable is a clear demonstration that the principle cannot be consistently maintained. How can it be right for complementarians to read and cite books on Bible and theology written by women and disallow them from saying the same things in a church meeting?

7. Pragmatically, if the cause of the gospel is our chief concern, then the vast contribution that women can make and feel called to make to it could make a tremendous difference to our effectiveness in evangelism and building up the church. In other words, the gospel is hindered by an unnecessary prohibition on women's ministry, since nobody (apart from complementarians) finds it in any way strange or off-putting, whereas it would in fact be helped by encouraging it.[31]

8. The argument from Scripture that is used here by Paul seems to be directed against particular misunderstandings. It needs careful examination:[32]

   a. The argument from priority in creation was one that is found in Jewish sources. The creation story is assumed to be paradigmatic for people subsequently. Its force here is to deny the superiority of Eve over Adam and hence of a wife over her husband. No doubt for first-century Jews it established the superiority of Adam over Eve. But two points can be made. The one is that the passage is used for a negative function, and it does not necessarily function positively to assert that

---

[31]Grudem, *EFBT*, p. 496, replies that complementarianism does not deprive the church of workers, provided the women engage in the ministries proper to them. But that does not answer the need for pastors and teachers.

[32]It is sometimes objected that the animals were created before Adam, so (if the argument from priority is upheld) that should make them superior to him. The objection ignores the facts that Genesis presents the creation of man as the apex of creation and that the argument was accepted within Judaism.

the husband is superior to his wife. There is a third position, which is that they are equal to each other. This is an insight that is not reached in the New Testament, but there are hints pointing in that direction, specifically in Galatians 3:28; 1 Peter 3:7 and Ephesians 5:21. It is the implication or application of the biblical teaching that demands the fullest possible love by a husband for his wife.[33]

The other point is that, whereas in first-century society, it was presumably thought that teaching by a wife was inconsistent with his authority over her, this is not so in contemporary Western culture. If my wife is better than me at cooking, I follow her instructions and submit to her authority when I am assisting to prepare a meal. If she has a superior knowledge of New Testament Greek than I, then I submit to her authority in regard to how the subjunctive mood is used. If she has done a course on the exegesis and theology of Romans and I have not, then it is appropriate for me to submit to being taught by her in this matter, and nobody would think that this was improper, whether it was in a so-called public or a private setting. In short, the command not to teach or exercise authority over a man is a cultural application of a principle regarding how a wife is to behave toward her husband, and the application is not timeless. The argument from priority in creation does not lead to a timeless prohibition on wives teaching their husbands (or other men). Paul, it should be noted, does not *command* the dominance of man over woman or of husband over wife in this passage, and it is my firm belief that he would have rejected any domination by men over women just as vigorously.

b. It is splitting hairs to say that Adam was not deceived. He fell to the temptation posed by his wife, just as she fell to the temptation by the serpent.[34] The point is simply that Eve was not immune to temptation; in fact she sinned before her husband![35] The fact that Eve was de-

---

[33]I. Howard Marshall, "Mutual Love and Submission in Marriage: Colossians 3:18-19 and Ephesians 5:21-33," in *DBE*, pp. 186-204; esp. 195-98.

[34]Genesis makes no reference to Adam being deceived by the serpent, but he is condemned for listening to the voice of his wife. Since Adam knew that he must not eat the fruit (Gen 2:17), either he ignored this command when Eve gave him the fruit or he was told the story of the conversation with the serpent and still chose to disobey the command; to say that he was not deceived is pedantic.

[35]To understand the statement to mean "Eve was not created before Adam, but she sinned before him" is the best way of avoiding the contradiction with the fact that Adam also sinned.

ceived can hardly imply that all her descendants would be deceived or at least be deceived more than men are. It is simply a warning that all of us, including women, are open to temptation and fall to it. If Eve and all subsequent women were inevitably deceived in a way that men are not deceived, this would render them incapable of teaching anybody and not just men.[36] Certainly the mention of Eve being deceived is unmotivated if the particular women in mind here were not teaching falsely, but against this we have the positive references to women teaching in the wider context of 2 Timothy and Titus. The prohibition here is directed against a particular situation, which was not a problem when the other two letters were written.[37]

This situation may well be that the women in question were teaching in a way that asserted or expressed their superiority to men rather than teaching sound doctrine in an acceptable manner. There is the strong likelihood that they were drawing false conclusions out of Genesis by following the "Jewish myths and genealogies" (1 Tim 1:4; cf. Tit 3:9), and this is what triggers Paul's interpretation of the story of the creation and Fall. In 1 Timothy 4:1 false teaching is traced to deceitful spirits and demonic teachings, and in 1 Timothy 5:15 we hear of young widows who have gone after Satan. The women are reminded that Eve fell in the same kind of way.

9. So long as we understand church leadership as meaning "he told her what to do and she had to obey," then we shall go down wrong routes. What kind of things do church leaders tell the others to do? How far do pastors have an authority that cannot be challenged, when most church constitutions with which I am familiar rest authority and responsibility in church councils at different levels, and in many church constitutions ultimately in the congregation as a whole? Why should pastoral counseling and oversight be understood as an exercise of authority and so unacceptable? Even if we accept some kind of priority of husbands over wives (or of men over women) for the sake of the argument, the question must be posed as to how the

---

[36]Consequently, some defenders of the traditional position argue that the women whose teaching was forbidden in 1 Tim 2 were not in fact teaching any false doctrine. This seems most unlikely in view of the reference to Eve being deceived.

[37]To be sure, the danger is mentioned in 2 Tim 3:6-7, but the stress here is more on the activity of the male false teachers who victimized the women.

teaching function of a woman or her pastoral care for others in the congregation can be construed as being incompatible with a subordinate position.
In other words, the prohibitions imposed here are to be understood as a
particular application of an understanding of subordination and not as a
basic principle applicable for all time. And if we agree that the teaching
given here involved some kind of error, possibly error regarding the role of
women, then the prohibition expressed here is limited in scope and does
not apply to sound teaching by women.

In the light of these considerations, it seems to me that the basic points are
exegetical ones, concerning what the passage is teaching in its original context,
rather than attempts to shift its meaning, but the exegesis is inevitably affected
by the perspectives of the interpreter. Exegesis and application are both involved in this assessment of the passage, but I would claim that what I have
been arguing is essentially exegetical.

ASSESSING THE COMPLEMENTARIAN INTERPRETATION

How has the passage fared in subsequent study? Over against my interpretation must be placed the kind of interpretation offered by such scholars as
W. Grudem, A. Köstenberger, W. D. Mounce and T. R. Schreiner. What are the
significant points of difference? Here I focus the discussion on the work of
Schreiner and Grudem.

The complementarian view is presented by Schreiner in what is a helpful
summary and revision of his previously published views.[38] He has moved from
his earlier position in that he no longer suggests that women are temperamen-
tally unsuited to leadership in the church. Indeed, he admits that some "un-
questionably have the spiritual gift of teaching" and should exercise it, but then
insists that this is not the same thing as functioning "as regular teachers of the
congregation."[39] I find such distinctions artificial and quite unpersuasive.

1. Schreiner accepts that Paul is concerned here with principles that can and
   must still be applied today, while allowing for cultural differences, just as
   the principle that women should dress modestly can and should be applied
   today with appropriate application in a different culture. However, his rec-

---

[38]James R. Beck and Craig L. Blomberg, eds., *Two Views on Women in Ministry* (Grand Rapids: Zondervan, 2001), pp. 177-232; pp. 218-26 are specifically on this passage.
[39]Schreiner, "Women in Ministry," pp. 191-92.

ognition that the dress code may be applied differently does not affect his acceptance of the subordination code since, in his view, this apparently is not affected by a different cultural situation.

The important concession that is made here is that the principles should be applied in a manner appropriate to the culture, and this means that the blanket rejection of elaborate hairstyles, expensive jewelry and clothing and dressing (or lack of dress)[40] in sexually explicit ways can be replaced by something more adapted to our culture. But that then raises the question whether the command about women not teaching or having authority over (domineering) men is to be understood differently today where teaching by a woman is not considered by most people to constitute exercising authority (or domineering),[41] and in this article Schreiner does not discuss this question.

2. Schreiner claims that the teaching that is forbidden is not forbidden because it was heretical and that the issue is not domineering over men but simply exercising authority; this is coupled with the argument that the syntax requires that both activities, teaching and exercising authority, are to be understood positively and that neither of them is to be understood pejoratively.

    Each of these points is questionable exegetically.

    a. The use of the verb *teach* rather than "teach false doctrine" does not rule out the possibility that false teaching may have been the issue. Certainly, elsewhere in the Pastoral Epistles there are examples of teaching by women of one another and of their children that is assumed to be free from error. These, however, are in the other epistles, and they do not rule out the possibility that there was a specific case of error in the context of 1 Timothy. They certainly make it clear that elsewhere in the letters there is no rejection of teaching by women on the grounds that it is intrinsically unsound.[42] To repeat what I have

---

[40]The point is sometimes muddied by the curious literal interpretation that since 1 Pet 3:3 cannot be forbidding the wearing of all clothes, therefore it cannot be forbidding the wearing of all jewelry. But it is surely clear from the context that it is the wearing of expensive clothing that is in mind; Grudem (*EFBT*, p. 331 n. 4) is wrong to say that the correct translation is "clothes" and that "fine" is an interpretive addition; it is expensive dress and adornment of whatever kind that is here prohibited.

[41]The point will stand whatever view we take of the meaning of *authenteō*.

[42]It is argued that the fact that some women were teaching unsound material would not be a ground for imposing a blanket ban on all women teaching, just as there is no ban on all men teaching because some were false teachers. But it does seem from the combination of "teach" and "domineer/have authority over a man" that it is a particular kind of woman teaching in an unacceptable way that is the problem, and that teaching by a woman that was not characterized by this attitude was permitted.

written earlier: "Although, then, the prohibition may appear to be universally applicable to women, it is in fact meant for a specific group of women among the recipients of the letter."[43]

b. The proposed "neutral" meaning of the verb *authenteō* as simply to exercise authority is very uncertain, and I do not see how it can be understood otherwise than in a strong or even pejorative sense.[44]

c. The syntactical argument that the two activities must both be understood in the same sense (whether good or bad)[45] is not entirely compelling,[46] although if the second verb refers to an unacceptable activity, this requires that the former be understood also in the same way.

If the traditionalist argument fails at this point, then the question of the underlying principle is opened up.[47]

3. It is claimed that the disallowing of women to act in these ways is primarily based on a so-called creation ordinance: God's intention at creation would be contravened. This establishes the priority of man over woman, or husband over wife.

There is some ambiguity here, in that it is not clear whether the alleged ordinance places any woman under any man or simply a wife under her

---

[43]Marshall, *Pastoral Epistles*, p. 455.

[44]Grudem (*EFBT*, pp. 317-18) appeals to what he regards as a conclusive survey by Al Wolters, "A Semantic Study of *authentēs* and Its Derivatives," *Journal of Graeco-Roman Christianity* 1 (2000): 145-75, which surveys the material and argues for a positive or neutral understanding; see, however, Linda Belleville, "Teaching and Usurping Authority: 1 Timothy 2:11-15," in *DBE*, pp. 205-23 (esp. pp. 209-17). The verb *authenteō* does not refer to the ordinary exercise of authority but to domination or gaining the upper hand, and what is condemned is not ordinary teaching but teaching in which women were trying to dominate men. The women were being deceived by the false teachers (hence the reference to Eve's deception by the serpent). In my opinion Belleville has the better of the debate. See further Winter, *Roman Wives*, pp. 116-19. Liefeld (*1 and 2 Timothy, Titus*, p. 99) helpfully suggests that the word may have a strong sense rather than a negative one. Even if this particular word could be shown to have a neutral sense in itself, it would still be the case that the problem was the culturally unacceptable nature of teaching by women in a mixed group at that time.

[45]I took this view in Marshall, *Pastoral Epistles*, pp. 458-60.

[46]Belleville, "Teaching and Usurping Authority," pp. 217-19.

[47]Grudem (*EFBT*, p. 316) says that my argument (*Pastoral Epistles*, p. 458 n. 157) that for Paul to have said, "I do not permit women to teach falsely" would entail the unexpressed and unintended consequence "But I do permit men to do so" if so, then to say "I do not permit women to exercise autocratic power over men" would have the corollary "But I do permit men to do so over women." Hence, he argues that *authenteō* cannot have a negative meaning. But Paul's prohibition is against the particular teaching given by these particular women because it was false; and the second part of the prohibition indicates why it was unacceptable in that it was an expression of a wrong attitude toward men; there is no indication whatever that this same attitude by men toward women would have been acceptable.

husband (and unmarried daughters under their father).[48] If the latter, presumably any wife could teach when her husband was not present, and we are in danger of descending into casuistry. If the former, then we are in real trouble with the structures of modern society, and even of ancient, where the rule of a queen was rare but certainly not unknown. More importantly, the Genesis story has nothing to say that would make all women (or any woman) subject to all men (or any man). One cannot deduce a general subordination of women to men from the position of the wife in relation to her husband. The appeal to Genesis surely has to do with the marriage relationship and is invoked here to remind the wife that she is not to dominate her husband. But if so, is it really the case that a husband is subjected to domination by the activity of his wife in teaching?

4. Schreiner disallows the argument that women generally were less educated than men, since it is not mentioned in the passage and it did not apply to all women; Priscilla, it is argued, was educated but was included in the ban.

But the fact that Paul does not explicitly appeal to this point does not mean that it is irrelevant, and in the case of Priscilla it is significant that elsewhere she was active as a teacher (whether alongside her husband or independently does not affect the issue[49]). Philo commented on the ease with which women were deceived and on their lack of education.[50] The point is simply the statistical one that women were less likely to be competent at teaching.[51] Indeed, Bruce Winter notes that evidence for the existence of women as professional teachers in the Hellenistic world is hard to find. It would, therefore, have been very unusual and perhaps unacceptable in the culture of the time for women to teach.

5. Schreiner rejects the argument that the women were teaching heresy. (a) Men

---

[48]Grudem (*EFBT*, pp. 296-99) argues for the former view. Cf. Marshall, *Pastoral Epistles*, p. 444.

[49]Presumably if Grudem holds that a senior pastor cannot authorize a woman to disobey Scripture by teaching, neither can a husband (*EFBT*, p. 382), in which case Aquila should not have allowed Priscilla to teach Apollos even when he himself was present.

[50]Collins, *1 & 2 Timothy*, pp. 69-70, citing Plutarch *Moralia* 142.

[51]The point is contested by Grudem (*EFBT*, pp. 288-95) but the fact that he can produce examples of some educated women (a point that nobody denies) does not invalidate the basic assertion regarding the general situation. Esther Yue L. Ng, *"Acts of Paul and Thecla*: Women's Stories and Precedent?" *JTS*, n.s. 55, no. 1 (2004): 1-29, states categorically that "the consensus among scholars is that ancient women generally received less education than their male contemporaries and were therefore less likely to be authors or readers of literary works" (p. 27). Nobody denies that there were some well-educated women; the point is that in general women were less well-educated.

were also teaching false doctrine and they are not forbidden to teach here. (b) Not all the women were teaching heresy, so why forbid them all? (c) The attempts to identify the false teaching by some scholars have been speculative and unpersuasive.

In the case of point (c) I would be the first to grant that some of the proposals regarding the nature of the false teaching have done the egalitarian case far more harm than good. But I would also point out that *all* the proponents of false teaching are silenced in the Pastoral Epistles (2 Tim 2:16, 25-26; 3:5; Tit 1:10-11; 3:10-11; cf. 1 Tim 1:19-20; 5:19-20; 6:20-21). Some of the false teaching in the situation involved the forbidding of marriage, which inevitably affected the women if they went along with it, and we know that there were young widows whose sexual morality left something to be desired.

Further, we have the fact that Eve was deceived by the serpent. Temptation and false teaching ("You shall not surely die") belong inseparably together. Schreiner admits the difficulty of this verse, and suggests that the point is not that Eve was deceived but that the serpent was "subverting male headship by tempting Eve rather than Adam"; the serpent should have respected male headship by tempting the male and not the woman, or at least attacking the male first. This is ingenious, but surely its appearance of ingenuity is its undoing. It is not the sense of the passage in Genesis, and it has no basis in the text of 1 Timothy where all the stress lies on the transgression of Eve and the serpent is not actually mentioned. This interpretation is a counsel of despair.

Grudem, who tends to argue mostly on the basis of "this is simply what God commanded," holds that the deception of Eve by the serpent points toward an inherent character in women generally that makes them less fitted than men to preserving the doctrinal purity of the church. Here he is in line with the position of D. Doriani and the earlier position of Schreiner.[52] But surely simply to state this position is to refute it. Grudem uses it to argue that no exceptions can be allowed: the principle applies "to all women as they are representatives of womanhood as well." On the contrary, one might have thought that the existence of exceptions was an indication that

---

[52]Grudem, *EFBT,* pp. 69-73. Cf. Daniel Doriani, "A History of the Interpretation of 1 Timothy 2," in *Women in the Church: A Fresh Analysis of 1 Timothy 2:9-15,* ed. Andreas J. Köstenberger et al. (Grand Rapids: Baker, 1995), pp. 213-67 (264-65); Schreiner, "Women in Ministry," pp. 105-54 (145-46).

there was something wrong with the interpretation of 1 Timothy 2:14 and with the weight that is being put on it.

6. Interpretations of 1 Timothy 2:15 vary. Schreiner's interpretation is much in line with my own. Köstenberger holds that it teaches that women will escape ("be saved") from Satan by way of procreation. Presumably, if they devote themselves to God's creation purpose for them by having children and thus avoid the temptation to teach, they will be safe from the wiles of Satan. In church they should learn submissively, and not teach or rule.[53] Traditionalists agree that the precise interpretation of this verse does not alter the main thrust of the passage which rests upon the authoritative command in 1 Timothy 2:12 that forbids women from teaching and exercising authority in the church and is backed up by the appeal to the priority of Adam in creation.[54]

I personally find the interpretation of 1 Timothy 2:15 in terms of the spiritual salvation of women more persuasive, but in the end there is not a lot of difference between being saved from Satan and being spiritually saved at the last judgment, and I have no difficulty in insisting on the God-given role of childbearing and rearing. But where I differ is on the conclusion that teaching and ministering are incompatible claims on a woman's attention, particularly if she is unmarried, unable to have children, or at a stage in life where the care of children is no longer a responsibility.

ROLES AND COMPLEMENTARITY

The argument of the complementarians is quite simply that teaching and hav-

---

[53]Andreas J. Köstenberger, "Ascertaining Women's God-Ordained Roles: An Interpretation of 1 Timothy 2:15," *BBR* 7 (1997): 107-44.

[54]A fresh view is offered by Wall, "1 Timothy 2:9-15," who holds that the writer is describing how Eve is created by God, then deceived by the serpent, but finally her renewed relationship with God is envisaged when she bears her first child "with the help of the Lord" (Gen 4:1); Eve is then seen as typological of Christian women. This gives a theological and missionary motive for the writer's instructions. Thus the woman who practices virtue by her modesty in dress and demeanor, her good works and her acceptance of teaching from her male colleagues is an example to outsiders and serves the cause of the gospel. On this view, it would seem that the writer is simply accepting the social mores of the time regarding the place of women, and the reference to Eve serves not to back up the call for submission but to emphasize typologically God's concern for the salvation of women. Wall's article is not easy to follow, and the future tense in verse 15 seems to me to create an obstacle to interpreting it of Eve. Another view is offered by Kenneth L. Waters Sr., "Saved Through Childbearing: Virtues as Children in 1 Timothy 2:11-15," *JBL* 123, no. 4 (2004): 703-35, who argues that the childbearing is allegorical of the bearing of virtues (in a Philonic kind of way). Since the virtues stand alongside the bearing of children, this view is not convincing.

ing authority over men by women is forbidden by 1 Timothy 2 itself and is based on the implied ordinance in the creation story. No other considerations are relevant. And no rationale for the divine command can or need be given. Nevertheless, the question of rationale cannot be avoided. The older rationale lay in the inferiority of women to men, their lack of equality. This is now rightly abandoned. A different kind of rationale lies in postulating that in God's plan men and women have different roles and that teaching and leadership in church are a male role. K. Giles has argued that this postulate is a comparatively recent one and was unknown in earlier centuries. It has been invented to try to find some rational ground for the divine prohibition, since (we may assume) God has good reasons for his rulings.[55]

In his response Köstenberger essentially grants the point by stating that the complementarian case does not rest on role theory[56] and arguing that, whether the case is "historic" or not, the real question is whether it accurately interprets Scripture.

An important point that I do not recollect having seen in the literature but that is quite significant is that the list of congregational activities forbidden to women because they are the prerogative of men is not balanced by any list of activities forbidden to men because they are the prerogative of women. This is a further indication that the role theory of Paul's prohibition breaks down: it gives purely a list of activities prohibited to women because they have a different role from men, but men apparently do not have a different role from women except in that they are permitted to do not only all that women do but also more in the church. This is a consideration that demonstrates that the complementarians would be wise not to speak about *different* roles for men and women. It makes nonsense of any attempt to depict specific characteristics of women, not shared by men, which make them more appropriate functionaries in some areas than the men.

A corollary of this point may be drawn. The upholders of this position prefer to be known as complementarians in that they assert that God has given complementary roles to men and women that are both needed in order that the church may have the fullness of God's blessing. But if we have a situation in

---

[55]Kevin Giles, "A Critique of the 'Novel' Contemporary Interpretation of 1 Timothy 2:9-15 Given in the Book, *Women in the Church*," *EvQ* 72 (2000): 151-67, 195-215; see Andreas J. Köstenberger, "Women in the Church: A Response to Kevin Giles," *EvQ* 73 (2001): 205-24.

[56]Köstenberger, "Response to Giles," p. 219.

which the men can do all that the women do and more in the church, then it is surely the case that the women are not doing anything complementary to what the men do. In that case the self-description of supporters of this position as "complementarians" is misleading since the women are not complementing the men by doing things that the latter are forbidden or unable to do. And there is, of course, nothing in 1 Timothy 2 that the women can do by way of ministry except what the men can also do.[57] The only difference apparently is the bearing and nurture of children in the household, which is a different sphere of activity.

Grudem has next to no mention of roles, and he clearly restricts his tight prohibition on women teaching and exercising leadership purely to the church situation and not to the situation in secular employment where he accepts male-female equality.[58] He further argues that the teaching in 1 Timothy 2 is the actual principle that is unchangeable and is not the cultural or situation-related expression of a principle that might be interpreted otherwise. Strangely he doesn't apply this to the principle of not wearing expensive clothing and jewelry. What he does is to say that it is ostentation that is wrong, and that you can wear jewelry if it is not ostentatious. But what is the difference between jewelry in the ancient world and jewelry in the modern? Why do complementarians avoid the issue of whether 1 Timothy 2:11 is also expressed in cultural terms and not look for an underlying principle that may require it to be differently instantiated in the contemporary world?

When he does refer to roles, Grudem suggests that there are differences in abilities and preferences (the old Schreiner argument), but he insists that God's prohibition is not based on them:

> It seems to be the case that God ordinarily gives to men some abilities and preferences that are appropriate to leadership (such as a more aggressive disposition and a sense of responsibility and rightness in leadership), and ordinarily gives to women some abilities and preferences that are appropriate to support that leadership (such as a more nurturing and caring disposition and a sense of rightness in fulfilling a supporting role for their husbands).[59]

Whatever we might think of this statement, it is not used as an argument but is simply a broad generalization that may or may not be true and is irrele-

---

[57]The activity of the older women in teaching the younger ones (Tit 2:3-4) would seem to be the only exception. But is this one exception an adequate basis for the concept of complementarity?

[58]Grudem, *EFBT*, pp. 392-93, 445.

[59]Ibid., p. 440.

vant.[60] It is also perhaps simply wrong in that it does not hinder Grudem's recognition of the leadership roles of women in secular life.

In short, we are dealing with a case that depends solely upon an *ipse dixit* by God's messenger that is assumed to be a principle to be applied literally for all time. Consequently Grudem can argue that the debate is between people who accept the authority of Scripture and people who don't.

AN UNSUPPORTED PROHIBITION

The results of this discussion are to show (a) that we are left with no rationale for the prohibition beyond the simple "God said so" (and we cannot even guess at his reasons),[61] and (b) that the prohibition applies only in one area of life and not elsewhere, which makes it all the more extraordinary.[62] But if what we have is a prohibition by God for which no rationale exists except that he issued it and for which all arguments based on its beneficial or detrimental effects are deemed irrelevant, then this does raise enormous doubts as to whether the prohibition has been correctly understood. This is the point that complementarians refuse to grant. For Grudem in particular the prohibition is ultimately a matter of "accept what God has said because he said it; and no other consideration is relevant."

Therefore, the question at issue is whether the passage is correctly exegeted and interpreted as a timeless prohibition that admits of no exceptions.

Let us be clear what the prohibition excludes:

- All teaching by women to groups that include men.[63] This applies not just

---

[60]This does not prevent Grudem (Ibid., p. 496) from claiming that feminism "works in destructive ways in women's lives" and using this as an argument in favor of complementarianism.

[61]The proponents of the complementarian view have in effect lifted it out of the realm of theological discussion by denying the relevance of any consideration except their conviction that God has said it, and we cannot question or disobey his word (or, we must add, their interpretation of it).

[62]The matter of subordination within the home is of course closely connected with it, so that the two are almost one issue. My point is that secular life is apparently untouched by the prohibition (so, clearly, Grudem, *EFBT*, p. 445).

[63]There are, of course, situations in other cultures where some forms of Christian witness by men to women are not possible and where only women can approach women, and equally there are some situations (e.g., in Muslim cultures) where it would be inappropriate for women to minister to men. Such tactical matters do not affect the basic issue. Hence Towner can comment: "Experimentation with greater freedom in women's ministry activities might, for the sake of the church's mission, need to move in concert with cultural trends. What this means for Christianity in traditional Asian or Muslim contexts is that too much too fast could endanger the church's witness and credibility. But in much of the Western world, too little too slow could neutralize the church's impact in society just as effectively" (*Timothy and Titus,* p. 239).

to congregational meetings but also to other Christian contexts (except for house groups and the like).[64]

- Supervision of male employees in a Christian organization.

- Activities of teaching and pastoring that have been delegated by a male leader who retains overall control.

- Teaching in theological institutions. (This must be a reference to mixed ones, not to exclusively female ones.)[65]

Along the same lines is Grudem's rejection of the suggestion that a woman may teach or exercise leadership as a subordinate member of a team led by a man, so that she has no inherent authority as a woman but delegated authority. (This would have forbidden Priscilla teaching alongside Aquila, unless we are being casuistical and saying that he forbade her to do so only when he was not present, or that the instruction of Apollos was "private": is a modern house-group "private" as opposed to a "public" service?[66]) That too is disallowed because what 1 Timothy 2 is forbidding is teaching by women, and senior pastors must not tell women to break God's prohibition.

I suggest that this detailed listing of what women may and may not do in minute detail is the reductio ad absurdum of the complementarian case. It reminds one rather too clearly of the thirty-nine things forbidden on the sabbath in the Mishnah.[67]

Grudem feels strongly about the issue because he sees it as an example of the church giving in to liberalism. He argues illogically that, since liberalism and women's ordination go together, so women's ordination by

---

[64]Grudem (*EFBT,* p. 75) is happy to let women contribute in home Bible studies, since apparently the "teaching" that they give to their husbands is different from what is given "in church" where it carries some kind of endorsement by the leadership; but they should not "teach" in a home Bible study (ibid., p. 95). If the original creation "ordinance" was that a woman should be subject to her husband, it does look as though this has now been widened out to make all women subject to all men. And, as I noted above, some Christian groups have enlarged the prohibition to prevent women from taking any vocal part in a meeting for the breaking of bread.

[65]Ibid., pp. 381-83, 389-91.

[66]Grudem (ibid., p. 75) adopts this line. But surely the reason why Apollos was corrected "privately" was not because it would have been improper for Priscilla to have done it publicly (Aquila could have done it where she was not allowed to) but because it would not have been seemly to show up the shortcomings of a teacher in the presence of other people (cf. the analogy—it is nothing more—of Mt 18:15-17).

[67]Cf. Liefeld, *1 and 2 Timothy, Titus,* p. 112.

evangelicals is a step toward liberalism, and accuses scholars like R. T. France of liberal attitudes.[68] He also claims that egalitarianism will have massive bad effects on the church since we are on the path that will lead eventually to acceptance of the moral validity of homosexual practice.[69] Further, it has a destructive effect on women's lives by no longer allowing them to be uniquely feminine. I do not understand how egalitarianism takes away from women the ability, not possessed by men, to bear children and to nurse them and to give them a kind of love and nurture that is not the same as that of a father, even if I would find it hard to express just how it differs.

CONCLUSION

What, then, do we do with this passage? I have argued that in the light of exegesis we can see that the complementarian understanding of it as a prohibition of women teaching and exercising authority is mistaken: the passage deals with a specific kind of situation and does so by way of application rather than by a statement of unchangeable principle. It is important to avoid any impression that egalitarians ignore it or refuse to take it seriously and to insist that we can and must use it positively as authoritative instruction for believers today along such lines as these:

1. It requires all people in church to behave with decorum and to avoid sinful behavior that prevents prayer being effective.

2. It demands the avoidance of all secular display of wealth and position and of an immodest and enticing expression of sexuality in the congregation (not just in formal congregational meetings).[70]

3. It reminds us of the need for sound doctrinal teaching in the church, of the need for people to teach it, and of the need for congregations to accept it and live by it.

---

[68]Grudem, *EFBT*, p. 505.

[69]Ibid., p. 513. Such a conclusion is strongly resisted by William J. Webb, *Slaves, Women & Homosexuals: Exploring the Hermeneutics of Cultural Analysis* (Downers Grove, Ill.: InterVarsity Press, 2001), and R. T. France, *A Slippery Slope? The Ordination of Women and Homosexual Practice—A Case Study in Biblical Interpretation* (Cambridge: Grove Books, 2000).

[70]Of course, what counts as improper may vary from one society and culture to another. What might be regarded as a modest lifestyle in Menlo Park or Wheaton could be embarrassingly lavish in Burkina Faso. And what is sexually improper in Saudi Arabia would not be so in Tunbridge Wells.

4. It emphasizes the need for godliness and good deeds as the appropriate outward expression of Christian character.

5. It inculcates an ethic of humility and courtesy that still needs emphasis today.

6. If it tells women not to domineer, the same lesson can equally be applied to men who may consciously or unconsciously also domineer over women. Similarly, if it tells men not to engage in anger and disputation, it also says the same to women.

7. It warns of the danger of being deceived regardless of the source.

8. It warns against denigrating the importance of marriage, bearing children and the development of family life in favor of other pursuits. And this most definitely includes fathers who refuse to accept their parental and other domestic responsibilities.

9. It begins and ends with the need for cultivation of Christian character.

10. It has an ultimate purpose of not putting obstacles in the way of the gospel and adding luster to the message.[71]

I think that the issue raised by the debate is one of grave significance. At various points in his book Grudem castigates egalitarians for silencing complementarians and not giving them an opportunity to teach their position. Yet he looks forward to a time when complementarians will gain the upper hand and reword the constitutions of churches, denominations and institutions to forbid egalitarian practices, in other words precisely the kind of muzzling that he complains about when it is practiced against complementarians. Grudem takes this inconsistent position because he is so convinced that egalitarianism is an evil in itself and an inevitable staging point on the way to worse doctrines and practices, rejection of the supreme authority of Scripture and acceptance of homosexual practice. It is hard for egalitarians to respond to this criticism; no matter how much they protest, they will be told that they do not really accept the authority of Scripture and that to give way on one issue is to open the floodgates to many.

---

[71]Hence Liefeld argues that "the application should facilitate the fulfilment of Paul's missionary purpose in our own social context rather than repeat the same restrictions that were appropriate then but can be a hindrance to conversions now" (Liefeld, *1 and 2 Timothy, Titus*, p. 114).

Nevertheless, for our part, we must insist that we do hold to the authority of Scripture, and that the issue is one of the correct exegesis and interpretation of Scripture.[72] In a situation where responsible evangelical interpreters who share the same belief in the authority of Scripture differ in interpretation, we maybe need to recognize that this is an issue where differences of opinion exist and must be tolerated. And we certainly need to appeal to our complementarian brothers and sisters in Christ, saying in the words of Oliver Cromwell to the General Assembly of the Church of Scotland: "I beseech you in the bowels of Christ: think it possible that you may be mistaken."

---

[72]One cannot do everything in one presentation, and I have not taken up the question of ongoing trajectories of liberation so strongly rejected by Grudem, *EFBT*, pp. 600-645.

PART TWO

New Perspectives
on the Body
of Christ

PROPHECY, WOMEN IN LEADERSHIP AND THE BODY OF CHRIST

Lynn H. Cohick

WHEN I LIVED IN KENYA, THE WOMAN WHO CLEANED our rented house wore a scarf covering her hair. I never saw her or any of the other local Kenyan women bareheaded. One day, I asked her why she wore the scarf on her head, and she said so she could pray at any time, because the Bible said that women could pray only with their heads covered. Thanking her for her answer, I turned away wondering if she thought my prayers were ever heard!

In another conversation, this time with students at the seminary where I taught, I was asked what Paul meant in 1 Corinthians 11 about women's hair. A pastor asked me why it was that "God had not created 'their' women with hair that grew down long." Why had God made the black Africans' hair to be kinky, not straight and thus able to cover?

Interpretations and questions surrounding 1 Corinthians 11:2-16 have permeated the church globally, and I'm not sure always to good effect. Grave misunderstandings about male/female and masculine/feminine hinder a solid interpretation of Paul's admittedly enigmatic comments. Overlooked in this discussion is the depiction and role of prophecy in the church and the larger Greco-Roman society. For a full appreciation of Paul's intentions, the common cultural assumptions surrounding femaleness and gender must be accounted for. When these factors are considered, the passage speaks favorably to women speaking publicly and with authority in the church.

To make my case, I'll look briefly at the concerns raised in feminist studies about the social construct of gender and the difficulty of re-creating historical women's lives. Next, I'll examine representative typologies offered to explain 1 Corinthians 11:2-16, specifically noting their anthropology—how they explain the place of women and men and the construction of gender in the passage. Gender assumptions underpinning prophecy in the Greco-Roman world will be underscored. Finally, a careful examination of Paul's focus on the creation story will help unpack his intentions.

SOCIAL CONSTRUCTION OF GENDER

Feminist scholars have been chastised for focusing myopically on the admittedly significant gender issues raised in this passage. However, this complaint is registered without a clear appreciation that real men and women lived within a matrix of Greco-Roman social and gender constructs that guided and limited their movements. These norms were often understood as simply natural or common sense and thus in no need of substantiation or defense. Approaching the passage without recognizing the powerful force that gender constructs play in describing real people is to risk misunderstanding or falsely recreating the historical world of the text. We cannot know real women (or men) unmediated—we see them through the grid of gender constructs. Once acknowledged, the reader can be alert to ways in which *typoi* and standard images (such as virgin and whore) work in the historical retelling of events, including biblical events.[1]

Gender distinction, feminine and masculine, involves a cultural enterprise (though I am not suggesting that sex is a cultural creation). Sherry Ortner has persuasively argued that culture is a male domain, while women are circumscribed to the realm of nature.[2] It is not simply that men and women are different, but that men are better. Men have explained women as the Other and have placed negative value on that otherness.[3] In a variety of ways, the Greco-

---

[1]Miriam Peskowitz, "Spinning Tales: On Reading Gender and Otherness in Tannaitic Texts," in *The Other in Jewish Thought and History,* ed. Laurence J. Silberstein and Robert L. Cohn (New York: New York University Press, 1994), pp. 91-120. Peskowitz explores the trope of spinning and weaving as these tasks were used as encoded messages of gendered chastity and modesty.

[2]Sherry Ortner, "Is Nature to Culture as Female is to Male?" in *Woman, Culture, and Society,* ed. Michelle Rosaldo and Louise Lamphere (Stanford: Stanford University Press, 1974), pp. 67-88.

[3]The classic discussion of this is Simone de Beauvoir, *The Second Sex,* trans. and ed. H. M. Parshley (New York: Knopf, 1974). Ross Kraemer discusses the issue of Other in the Greco-Roman world, Ross Kraemer, "The Other as Woman: An Aspect of Polemic among Pagans, Jews and Christians in the Greco-Roman World," in *The Other in Jewish Thought and History,* ed. Laurence J. Silberstein and Robert L. Cohn (New York: New York University Press, 1994), pp. 121-44.

Roman world conveyed that "natural truth" in literature, social customs, legal practices and religious rites. Paul swam in the same sea—as did his churches. They saw the world through their gendered constructs that minimized female participation in culture (public life) and relegated the value of private life as the women's sphere.

The question of gender can be raised in another way. Feminist theologians have rightly drawn attention to scholars' perspectives as they interact with the text. In assessing this, Anthony Thiselton comments that "it is therefore right that feminist hermeneutics *begins* by letting the horizons of biblical texts interact with horizons of *women's experience.*"[4] Mary Aquin O'Neill builds on this claim, adding that "feminist theologians did not begin with method, but with theological anthropology."[5] It is precisely the question of anthropology that engages debate in 1 Corinthians 11:2-16—what is man, what is woman, within society and before God?

If I thought that Paul was trapped in his cultural milieu, I could stop my argument right now. But Paul's own words reflect not only his times, but also the redemptive history of God's salvation plan for his people. I suggest that while Paul offers a nod to common public opinion about women's bodies and gender constructs, he ultimately overturns cultural valuations in light of the redemptive work of God through Christ in the life of the Spirit-led believer and within the Spirit-led church.

INTERPRETIVE TYPOLOGIES

To persuade you of my case, I will examine several typologies used to interpret 1 Corinthians 11:2-16. The first typology might be called a doctrinal approach or what William Webb calls a "static hermeneutic."[6] This view understands the Bible predominately in ahistorical terms and looks to apply isolated biblical texts to parallel or equivalent situations today. A second typology is the socio-historical model, represented, for example, by Bruce Winter, who examines

---

[4]Anthony C. Thiselton, *New Horizons in Hermeneutics: The Theory and Practice of Transforming Biblical Reading* (Grand Rapids: Zondervan, 1992), p. 462.

[5]Mary Aquin O'Neill, "The Nature of Women and the Method of Theology," *Theological Studies* 56 (1995): 730. I do not agree with O'Neill's declaration that Jesus alone cannot accomplish redemption, and her subsequent turning to Mariological tradition.

[6]William J. Webb, *Slaves, Women & Homosexuals* (Downers Grove, Ill.: InterVarsity Press, 2001), pp. 31-35. For an example of this method, see Robert W. Yarbrough, "The Hermeneutics of 1 Timothy 2:9-15," in *Women in the Church*, ed. Andreas J. Köstenberger, Thomas R. Schreiner and H. Scott Baldwin (Grand Rapids: Baker, 1995), pp. 155-96.

the social and cultural norms governing Greco-Roman society and compares them with Paul's argument and the inferred case brought by "the strong" in Corinth.[7] A third typology is William Webb's redemptive movement hermeneutic.[8] Webb argues that the biblical text is best understood as reflecting a redemptive spirit pointing toward goals often only hinted at in the original context. A fourth position, the medical/biological typology, looks at the ideological weight given to women's bodies, especially as they are described through medical or biological lenses. Dale Martin uses this tool in deciphering Paul's claims about the human body in 1 Corinthians.[9] A fifth typology, the rhetorical method, examines the text's polemic and rhetoric. This approach is arguably ahistorical, but for reasons altogether different from the doctrinal model. This typology suggests that any rhetorical work, including 1 Corinthians, does not offer direct (and perhaps not even indirect) historical material. A careful analysis of the work's polemic, however, will yield the opponent's view, and from there, decisions can be made about the historical situation underlying the debate. Antoinette Wire's work on the Corinthian women prophets offers intriguing suggestions into their theology and resulting behaviors.

In applying these typologies to 1 Corinthians, I argue that the Greco-Roman view of the female body illumines several aspects of Paul's argument, including Paul's qualified acceptance of his culture's understanding of male and female bodies and the concept of pollution as it relates to men and women prophesying. Moreover, based on rhetorical analysis, I suggest that the Corinthians misunderstood their baptism and new life in Christ. This led Paul to emphasize two concepts particularly relevant to 1 Corinthians 11:2-16: (1) the order and process of salvation history, including the relationship between God the Father and God the Son, and between God and humanity; (2) the importance of differentiation and of mutuality.

STATIC/DOCTRINAL TYPOLOGY

Turning to our first typology, the static or doctrinal model, Robert Yarbrough

---

[7]Bruce W. Winter, *Roman Wives, Roman Widows* (Grand Rapids: Eerdmans, 2003).

[8]Francis Watson might call Webb's approach a hermeneutic of recovery. Francis Watson, "Strategies of Recovery and Resistance: Hermeneutical Reflections on Genesis 1—3 and its Pauline Reception," *JSNT* 45 (1992): 79-103.

[9]Dale B. Martin, *The Corinthian Body* (New Haven: Yale University Press, 1995).

uses what he calls the "historic position"[10] to explain 1 Timothy 2:9-15. In labeling his typology "historic" he declares that his answers fit with the historic position of the church in its understanding of men and women. Yarbrough points to changes in our modern culture, leading away from an undefined ancient world culture to the lamented liberalism and individualism of our twenty-first century. He warns the church against following secular culture's path to moral destruction, maintaining that only "weighty hermeneutical considerations"[11] should constrain us to change the form (but never the essence) of the biblical text. For instance, he concludes that the injunction to greet others with a holy kiss is fulfilled within some modern cultures with an equivalent custom. He accepts that women can go without a head covering, but cautions that "it is definitely not the case that if women go without head coverings now, they are also free to set aside 1 Tim. 2:11-12"[12] as interpreted by Yarbrough.

Yarbrough's argument takes aim at Krister Stendahl, F. F. Bruce and Kevin Giles for succumbing to the Enlightenment's humanism, which puts the interpreter in the center of the discussion, rather than the biblical text. Assumed in his argument is the ahistorical nature of the biblical text—it seems to float above the peculiarities of its own day. He also assumes the reader can stand objectively outside Scripture's story and draw unbiased, universal conclusions. Yarbrough offers no rationale, however, for why a holy kiss or a veil is optional, but female subordination is not. His method does not help distinguish the form (kiss/veil) from the substance (female subordination). Moreover, he accuses Bruce and Giles of failing to follow God with their whole hearts, "the interpreter's own life and soul are integral to the blessedness of the message. . . . this means rightly applying [the passage] is not only . . . about exegetical rigor and conceptual sophistication . . . it has everything to do with how the Lord regards the state of our hearts."[13] Rejection of traditional interpretation indicates a lack of spirituality, according to Yarbrough's thesis.

SOCIOHISTORICAL TYPOLOGY

Turning to our next typology, Bruce Winter, in his *Roman Wives, Roman Widows,* draws on the sociohistorical model to reconstruct the author's ancient

---

[10]Yarbrough, "Hermeneutics of 1 Timothy 2:9-15," pp. 190-91.
[11]Ibid., p. 192
[12]Ibid., p. 192 n. 169.
[13]Ibid., pp. 193-94.

milieu, recognizing the interplay between Paul, his church community and the wider Greco-Roman community. However, Winter might not give adequate attention to the possibility of gender construction in analyzing his literary data. He assumes for the most part that what a (male) author writes about women's behavior is basically factual, if perhaps given to hyperbole. After collecting the historical data, Winter then draws judgments about Paul's purpose in writing.

Specifically, Winter reconstructs a group of renegade women and their "loose" customs as the instigators of problems among the Corinthians. These strong women took their cue from none other than members of the emperor's own family and other elites who flaunted social propriety. The influence of this small but powerful group of women rippled out into the Roman world and challenged the status quo in cities like Corinth. The problem addressed by Paul in 1 Corinthians 11:2-16 was rooted in wives' social rebellion against prescribed marriage norms and laws of modesty. Winter suggests the veil or mantle (palla) was society's way of portraying and enforcing a wife's submission to her husband. For the sake of the church's missionary witness, Paul stands with the status quo and requires that married female prophets dress in socially acceptable ways. Moreover, Paul wants to avoid the risk that the church might be accused of unlawful behavior if married women flaunt social conventions.[14]

Following Winter's argument, we can understand why Paul would want to restrict wives in Corinth, for they were mimicking behavior deemed fast and loose in their culture. But how do we understand the passage's meaning for today? Winter critiques those hermeneutics that merely apply simplistically a passage to a contemporary situation without clearly stating "criteria for selectivity" in determining how and why to apply it.[15] He also cautions those who would dismiss all cultural references, for "some aspects of New Testament teaching were distinct and consciously ran counter to the cultural norms of the day."[16] Winter offers extensive material on Roman views of women, especially in its legal code, to help make astute judgments on the social world of Paul's churches. But I did not find in Winter's Roman Wives, Roman Widows an explicit hermeneutic for the contemporary church.

---

[14]Winter, Roman Wives, pp. 77-96.
[15]Ibid., pp. xiii-xiv.
[16]Ibid., p. xiv.

REDEMPTIVE MOVEMENT TYPOLOGY

Perhaps Webb's redemptive movement hermeneutic would help interpret Winter's argument. Webb's typology looks for the "redemptive spirit" of the text. So, for example, Paul speaks specifically about slavery, and never once calls for its abolition. Yet Webb maintains that within the biblical text's conversation about slavery, seeds are planted for that institution's destruction. The Bible undercuts the very premises upon which that social institution was founded, paving the way for its ultimate demise.

Yet Webb's model might not bring complete clarity. Applied to Winter's findings, Webb's typology could be used to suggest that, as Paul is moving in a socially conservative direction, therefore the church should permit only minimal participation of women in its public life today. And Kevin Vanhoozer expresses concern over the logic of Webb's thesis, specifically that "spirit" might be too vague and undefined a term, allowing for a movement above or outside the text.[17] Yet Webb is at pains to stay within the biblical texts, pointing to "seed" passages that guide the movement's trajectory.

Webb might argue that his redemptive movement typology would relate well with Winter's findings. Webb accepts that 1 Corinthians 11:2-16 is laden with cultural limitations, but finds in verse 11's claim of interdependence between men and women, the "'seed idea,' setting up the potential for further movement that would be mostly unrealized in Paul's ministry setting."[18] He concludes that "in his own day Paul merely uses mutuality in Christ (1 Cor 11:11) to take the edge off of patriarchy," but adds, "the fuller implications of gender equality and mutuality in Christ are only starting to be realized."[19] Webb maintains that the Spirit's movement is toward full participation, however slowly realized. He concludes that Paul moves in the direction of women's wide-ranging participation; my point is that Winter's findings need not *necessarily* support Webb's conclusions.

MEDICAL/BIOLOGICAL TYPOLOGY

Winter's argument supplies necessary and helpful historical background for

---

[17]Kevin Vanhoozer, "Into the Great Beyond: A Theologian's Response to the Marshall Plan," in I. Howard Marshall, *Beyond the Bible: Moving from Scripture to Theology* (Grand Rapids: Baker, 2004), pp. 90-91. Vanhoozer suggests looking for *"patterns of judgment"* rooted in the "gospel of Jesus Christ" (p. 93).

[18]Webb, *Slaves, Women & Homosexuals,* p. 276.

[19]Ibid.

our quest, but ultimately fails to answer my concerns, and so I turn to a final typology that looks at the medical and biological assumptions about the female body as a way into Paul's argument. While Bruce Winter notes the legal and social turmoil caused by Augustus's daughter, Julia's, behavior (and those who followed her), he does not speculate on why such behavior would be unacceptable. Dale Martin, in his work *The Corinthian Body*, seeks to reach behind the social norms to the gender ideology that informs them.[20]

Martin contends that many ancient Greeks and Romans believed the female was altogether different from the male. The female body was composed of different, more porous and moister material.[21] Philosophers and physicians concluded that a female had an increased risk of pollution, because her body was more permeable.[22] Yet alongside this view of women as made of dissimilar, more permeable material, there existed another view of the human body. In this view, the body did not risk defilement from without, but rather sought to maintain its health by keeping equilibrium among the numerous fluids. Martin believes "the strong" in Corinth held this view, which explains why some men did not worry about visiting a prostitute. They would have concluded that sex merely depleted the sperm fluid a bit, and as long as sexual activity was regulated, the various bodily fluids could be maintained in a balance.[23] There was little danger to the spiritual or physical health of the body. In Martin's analysis, Paul rejects the strong's configuration of the body and insists that both men and women can be infected or polluted by uncleanness from the outside.

. Martin suggests that Paul is interested here in two things, order and sexu-

---

[20]Martin understands ideology as the "relationship between language and social structures of power. . . . ideological analysis examines language as rhetoric—that is, as the attempt to persuade" (Martin, *Corinthian Body*, p. xiv).

[21]Ibid., p. 249. He quotes Soranus (2nd c. C.E.) "The female is by nature different from the male, so much so that Aristotle and Zenon the Epicurean say that the female is imperfect, the male, however is perfect." *Gynecology*, trans. Temkin 3 prooemium 3.

[22]Moreover, the hair on men and women's bodies was understood as hollow, and thus acted as a vacuum, potentially drawing body fluids in particular directions. A woman's long head hair served to draw up into her uterus the male's semen. Short hair on women could limit fecundity. Depilatory of women's pubic hairs, a common practice, was thought to increase the suction pull from the hair on her head. Thus, a woman's head hair was seen as part of her sexual organs, integral to the sexual act. Martin argues these assumptions are present in Paul's discussion in 1 Cor 11:2-16. Martin, *Corinthian Body*, pp. 222-28, 237-39. See also Troy W. Martin, "Paul's Argument from Nature for the Veil in 1 Corinthians 11:13-15: A Testicle Instead of a Head Covering," *JBL* 123, no. 1 (2004): 75-84.

[23]Martin, *Corinthian Body*, pp. 200-205.

ality, both which involve controlling the female body.[24] He maintains that Paul holds the typical Greco-Roman hierchical view of men and women, as seen in 1 Corinthians 11:3.[25] This view of women as inherently physically substandard necessitates precautions when prophesying. The woman herself is in danger of being polluted because her body is less resistant to outside forces so she must cover her head to minimize the danger. Using the social categories of shame/honor, Paul asserts that what the Corinthian women prophets were doing with their head, exposing it in some way, was tantamount to exposing their "private parts,"[26] which Paul declares shameful.[27]

According to Martin, not only did Paul worry about the vulnerability of women prophets, but even more, he was anxious about the church's exposure to pollution when women prophesy. The female body was the chink in the church's armor, the "devil's gateway" to borrow Tertullian's term (*Apparel* 1.1). It allowed for foreign matter, alien spirits and cosmic pollution to enter into the body of Christ, the church.[28] Martin argues that 1 Corinthians 11:2-16 "addresses not an individualistic issue of piety, respect, or subordination. Rather the issue is a communal one, affecting each member of the body."[29]

Martin concludes that Paul upheld the male-female hierarchy of the Roman world. Paul did so because of his ideological convictions that women were of a different, weaker constitution than men. Not until the resurrection of the

---

[24]Ibid., p. 242.

[25]Ibid., p. 232. "The implication of hierarchy that is obvious in the first pair (God-man) cannot be denied to the second pair (man-woman)." Christopher Mount argues that 1 Cor 11:3-16 is an interpolation because the locus of authority in chapter 11 is based on ecclesiastical consensus of the churches, while the center of authority in chapters 12—14 is Paul's own as one possessed by the spirit. Christopher Mount, "1 Corinthians 11:3-16: Spirit Possession and Authority in a non-Pauline Interpolation," *JBL* 124, no. 2 (2005): 313-40.

[26]Troy W. Martin writes, "Paul appropriately instructs women in the service of God to cover their hair since it is a part of the female genitalia" ("Paul's Argument from Nature," p. 84).

[27]Martin, *Corinthian Body*, pp. 242-47. Martin suggests that ideology of gender is behind Paul's statement that nature itself teaches that women should have long hair (1 Cor 11:14). Martin imagines that Paul and his audience share an understanding about what is naturally female and naturally male, specifically that a woman's long hair is part of her sexuality and reproductive system. Modesty requires it to be covered or knotted up at the neck, even as her genitals are covered. Nature is interpreted to have created for women a veil, which is her long hair. Human culture manufactures veils to cover the head and hair (but not face) in accordance with the teaching of nature.

[28]Ibid., p. 244-45. As an example of these cosmic forces endangering the church body, Martin suggests that Paul's reference to angels in 1 Cor 11:10 might reflect an apocalyptic belief that angels were active in the spiritual world of the church. He points to 1 Cor 6:2-3 where Paul admits that the Corinthians will judge angels, thus implying that angels are fallible (see also 2 Cor 12:7 and Rom 8:38).

[29]Ibid., p. 248.

body would women be free from this hierarchy. And even then, the promise was not of equality, for "even after the resurrection femininity will not be any less inferior; it will simply be subsumed into the superior strength and density of masculinity."[30]

CRITIQUE OF MARTIN'S TYPOLOGY

Is pollution of and from the female body a key perception to unlock 1 Corinthians 11:2-16? As intriguing as his study of Corinthian correspondence is, Martin's analysis of this passage is ultimately unconvincing. Martin does not establish whether the medical and biological presuppositions he finds prevalent in the Greco-Roman world were formative in Paul's message to the Corinthians. This failure arises out of his conviction that the prevailing ideology and the related power structures defining gender in the Greco-Roman period "diffuse themselves throughout societies and classes even when they are not recognized."[31] As such, Martin contends that "although Paul's authorial intentions (insofar as they may be constructed) are not entirely irrelevant, they are not decisive for establishing the correctness of my interpretation."[32] Though Martin has Paul a prisoner of Greco-Roman gender ideology, he argues (correctly, I think) that Paul in 1 Corinthians 12—14 overturns social hierarchy (status and class categories). In this, Martin appears to suggest that Paul was conscious of his social environment's ideology; how else could he critique it?

Martin nowhere explains why Paul would want such a reversal of status, why Paul taught that tongues were secondary to prophecy or why Paul would be "liberated" in one area of his social worldview (status) and trapped in another (gender). The answers lie, I suggest, in Paul's discourse about creation in 1 Corinthians 11:7-12. Paul's intellectual setting included conscious reflection on Israel's Scripture and Jewish practices. With his church in Corinth, Paul sought to shift the center of gravity from the social ideology pervasive in their pagan world, to one organized around the story of Israel and its God, what Richard Hays calls the "conversion of the imagination."[33] Martin's omission of

---

[30]Ibid., p. 249.

[31]Martin, p. xiv.

[32]Ibid.

[33]Richard B. Hays, "The Conversion of the Imagination: Scripture and Eschatology in 1 Corinthians," *New Testament Studies* 45.3 (1999): 391-412. He writes on page 395 that Paul "was calling Gentiles to understand their identity anew in light of the gospel of Jesus Christ—a gospel message comprehensible only in relation to the larger narrative of God's dealing with Israel."

Paul's discourse on creation leads both to his conclusion that Paul is confined to the gender ideology of his day and to his inability to suggest why Paul would desire that the body of Christ be unified.

MARTIN'S DISCUSSION OF 1 CORINTHIANS 12—14

Martin suggests that Paul's acceptance of gender hierarchical norms stands over against his rejection of other social divisions that stratified Roman society. Pointing to Paul's use of body as a metaphor for the church, he notes that Paul overturns the metaphor's customary meaning. The prevailing connotation supported the status quo and was a defense of the naturalness of social hierarchy. Paul throws a spanner in the works by questioning this cultural truism.

Two particular points raised by Martin are germane to our agenda. First, he points out that 1 Corinthians 12:23 reads "and what we judge (or suppose) to be the less honorable of the body, to these we accord more honor, and our least beautiful (presentable) have more beauty (presentableness), whereas our beautiful parts do not need it."[34] Within an honor/shame culture, bestowing honor was acknowledging status. To honor "the weak" was to give them status. Thus Martin postulates that Paul reinterprets honor within the church to include each member. He writes "his [Paul's] rhetoric pushes for an actual reversal of the normal, 'this-worldly' attribution of honor and status."[35] In Paul's culture, women would be included in the "weak" category. Martin's conclusion that Paul overturns social hierarchies and gives status to the weak therefore would seem to include women. As I'm sure Martin would agree, women are not a discrete class, but women were (and are) part of all levels of social hierarchy. Wealthy women would have more status than male slaves. Martin cannot erase the gender component from his claims about class and status.

Second, Martin examines 1 Corinthians 14:14-17, which contrasts mind (*nous*) and spirit (*pneuma*). He suggests that ancient common opinion would have spirit always trumping mind, believing that mind is inactive when the spirit speaks. Arranged on a hierarchy, spirit is of higher status than mind. But Paul disrupts this picture. He mandates that the mind and spirit work together; the latter must accede to the former. As this is played out in the church,

---

[34]Martin, *Corinthian Body*, p. 94.
[35]Ibid., p. 96.

it had radical implications. Martin notes "to say that a slave and a master should work in tandem or that a patron should not expect his client to give way to him would have sounded revolutionary. At the very least, it would have been perceived as overturning traditional status expectations."[36]

If Paul saw prophecy as an outside force penetrating the body,[37] he might offer some protection to the women, such as head covering. But Paul ultimately undercuts this social Band-Aid in his assertion that mind and spirit work together. Both male and female prophets have power or "mind" to control the spirit speaking through them. If Paul overturns the status hierarchy of spirit over mind, then Paul's encouragement of female prophets ultimately undercuts the gender hierarchy present in his cultural milieu. Ultimately, prophecy done in the church levels all social and gender hierarchies.

One last point concerning the context of 1 Corinthians 11:2-16, Martin fails to appreciate the thrust of Paul's use of "glory" in 1 Corinthians 11:7-10 (NIV; NRSV n. s). Paul's discussion of glory belonging only to God looks back to chapter 10 and the Corinthians' laissez faire attitude toward pagan festivals and idols. Antoinette Wire comments, "the exclusive right of God to glory is the foundation of Paul's theology, so no other argument is more authoritative to him than the dissociation of human from divine."[38] Wire argues that Paul is concerned about two competing "glories": one human and one divine.[39] This statement has several implications for our study of Paul's arguments about the Godhead and humanity, and it merits further examination.[40]

---

[36]Martin, *Corinthian Body,* p. 102.

[37]Karen King, "Prophetic Power and Women's Authority," in *Women Preachers and Prophets Through Two Millennia of Christianity,* ed. Beverly Mayne Kienzle and Pamela J. Walker (Los Angeles: University of California Press, 1998), p. 28. King observes that in both Christian and non-Christian sources a prophetess's sexual status is noted frequently, while almost no mention is made about a prophet's sexual status. Plutarch did not personally believe a prophet would be possessed by a spirit/god, but does attest to this belief's widespread influence (*Moralia* 414E).

[38]Antoinette Wire, *The Corinthian Women Prophets: A Reconstruction Through Paul's Rhetoric* (Minneapolis: Fortress, 1990), p. 120.

[39]See also Linda Belleville, "Κεφαλή and the Thorny Issue of Headcovering in 1 Corinthians 11:2-16," in *Paul and the Corinthians, Studies on a Community in Conflict: Essays in Honour of Margaret Thrall,* ed. Trevor J. Burke and J. Keith Elliott (Leiden: Brill, 2003), pp. 215-31.

[40]An additional benefit of Wire's comments is that they take seriously Paul's comments directed to men in the passage. Commentators have long noted, but not discussed, the parity between injunctions to men and women in the passage, steadfastly maintaining that the passage is primarily about women. For an important corrective to this, see Linda Belleville, "Κεφαλή and the Thorny Issue of Headcovering," and Jerome Murphy-O'Connor, "Sex and Logic in 1 Cor 11:2-16," *CBQ* 40, no. 4 (1980): 483.

ARGUMENT FROM CREATION AND THE GODHEAD

Martin does not address Paul's statement in 1 Corinthians 11:3 that "the head of Christ is God," except to maintain that verse three speaks of hierarchy. Yet because Paul links the two, the conversation about male and female must be accompanied by a discussion of Paul's understanding of the Godhead. Three particular instances concern us wherein Paul speaks of Christ in relation to God—"Christ is of God" (1 Cor 3:23 NIV); "the head of Christ is God" (1 Cor 11:3 NIV); and "the Son himself will be made subject to him who put everything under him, so that God may be all in all" (1 Cor 15:28 NIV). In each case, I suggest the context speaks to order and mutuality within a discussion of difference and soteriology.[41]

I' Corinthians 3:21-23, Paul stresses the futility of human wisdom and the folly of exalting human leaders. Paul declares that the Lord assigns each believer his or her task (1 Cor 3:5); for example, Paul planted and Apollos watered. Paul expands the Corinthians' vision beyond the wisdom of this world to the future eschatological triumph that is theirs in Christ, who is, with God, reconciling the world. Thiselton remarks, "Even Christ does not choose exemption from the principle that God assigns to each his or her calling, even if at the same time this is the Christ-like God who gives 'all things' to his people."[42]

In 1 Corinthians 15:24-28, Paul exclaims that Christ will accomplish all of his redemptive tasks, defeating death completely, and will establish his kingdom. The Father gives the kingdom to the Son, and the Son gives it back to the Father, so that "God may be all in all" (15:28). The differentiation noted by Paul (1) does not supersede the singleness of purpose to which the Father and the Son are committed and (2) is not timelessly essential. The differentiation between the Son and Father is at the level of agency and the means by which God in Christ intends to redeem the world.[43] Christ taking on human flesh, the incarnation, is central to God's redemptive plan. In discussing Christ's humanity, Paul makes statements that suggest Christ's subordination to God the Father, but this seems natural as humans *are* subordinate to God. Paul is not suggesting any essential or constant (incarnation aside) subordination of the second person of the Trinity.

---

[41]Gordon Fee, *The First Epistle to the Corinthians*, NICNT (Grand Rapids: Eerdmans, 1987), p. 155.

[42]Anthony Thiselton, *The First Epistle to the Corinthians*, NIGTC (Grand Rapids: Eerdmans, 2000), p. 329.

[43]Ibid., p. 1237.

Concerning 1 Corinthians 11:3, the definition of *kephalē* dominates the evangelical church's discussion. The argument seems to stall over whether *kephalē* refers to something like "source" or "authority." Thiselton's choice of "preeminent" is helpful because it recognizes that Paul might have chosen *kephalē* precisely because it carried multiple meanings. I think Paul uses the term "body" in a polyvalent manner in 1 Corinthians 11:17-34, which opens up the possibility that *kephalē* in 1 Corinthians 11:3-4 serves more than a single purpose. Not only does it represent the part of the physical body from which hair grows (and according to Paul, needs to be covered on women) but it also, I suggest, represents a synecdoche whereby the specific part (head) stands for the whole.[44] Following this suggestion, Paul would be stating that Christ represents humanity as the "head" of man, and represents God to humanity as God is his "head." In Philippians 2:5, Paul speaks of Christ in the "form" of God, suggesting that difference is united in mutuality. In terms of man as *kephalē* of woman, this seems to fit with Paul's discussion in 1 Corinthians 11:8-9 that man was in order of creation the first or preeminent.

The principle of order and differentiation is found in 1 Corinthians 11:7-12 wherein Paul speaks of man/male as the image and glory of God and woman as the glory of man.[45] Usually in the New Testament, Christ is identified as the image of God (Jn 1:1-3; 1 Cor 8:6; Col 1:15-18; Heb 1:1-3). Only in 1 Corinthians 11:7 is the male identified as the image of God.[46] Paul is reflecting on the eschatological implications of the gospel grounded in the Genesis account of creation. He is making a case for order (not hierarchy) and mutuality, which exists only when difference is present.[47] Fee notes that woman "is thus man's glory because she 'came from man' and was created 'for him.' She is not thereby subordinate to him, but necessary for him. She exists to his honor . . . so that he might be complete and that together they might form humanity."[48]

Furthermore, a careful reading of Paul's use of the creation narrative reveals that Paul is undercutting the social assumptions of his day. Martin believes that

---

[44]Ibid., p. 816.

[45]Ibid., p. 836.

[46]Ephesians 4:24 and Col 3:10 speak of believers being renewed in the image of the Creator God.

[47]Judith Gundry-Volf notes, "Paul's main point is that man and woman are both the *glory of another* and therefore both have an obligation not to cause shame to their 'heads.'" Gundry-Volf, "Gender and Creation in 1 Cor. 11:2-16: A Study in Paul's Theological Method," in *Evangelium, Schriftauslegung, Kirche: Festschrift für Peter Stuhlmacher,* ed. J. Adna, S. J. Hafemann and O. Hofius (Göttingen: Vandenhoeck & Ruprecht, 1997), p. 157

[48]Fee, *First Epistle to the Corinthians,* p. 517.

Paul's statement in 1 Corinthians 11:11 about the interdependence of man and woman does not suggest equality. I acknowledge his point—just because men need women, that does not make women equal to men any more than the fact that slave owners need slaves does not make slaves equal to their owners. The Genesis story, however, makes clear that men and women are of the same material. Woman is taken from man. So even if we grant Martin his claim that Paul was influenced by the ancient ideology of gender and pollution, Paul's reference to the Genesis story would suggest that, for Paul, the female body is *no more* susceptible to pollution than the male's body. Paul advocates precautions for both men and women. Men must not visit prostitutes and thereby risk pollution from a non-Christian in an illicit relationship (1 Cor 6:12-20). And women must be cautious when prophesying. However, the dangers do not outweigh the benefits, for Paul insists that prophecy is critical to the health of the body/church.

Instead of prophecy, the Corinthians emphasized tongues. The theological stance underlying their behaviors as described or insinuated by Paul in 1 Corinthians 11:2-16 was pieced together by Antoinette Wire using rhetorical analysis.[49] She finds in Paul's baptismal formula (1 Cor 12:13) a polemic against their views. Paul declares "for we were all baptized by one Spirit so as to form one body, whether Jews or Gentiles, slave or free" (1 Cor 12:13). Paul uses a similar formula in Galatians 3:27-28 (see also Col 3:9-11), but the difference between the Corinthians' formula and the one used for the Galatians is instructive. The pair "male and female" is found only in Galatians. Wire argues that this was the first or earliest pair, and that the baptismal creed grew from reflection on the creation account in Genesis. Wire suggests that the Corinthian women prophets believed their new creation in Christ overturned the old creation described in Genesis. In Christ, then, the male/female divide has been torn down; Christ did not affirm sex distinctions. The Corinthians saw Christ as the image of God, *not* male and female, and going beyond original creation. Thus Paul reasserts that the gospel does not overturn the good-

---

[49]Wire, *Corinthian Women Prophets*. Antoinette Wire's rhetorical typology reflects anything but confidence in the possibility of unmediated historical evidence within 1 Corinthians. She is skeptical of Paul's descriptions of the Corinthians, for example, "not many of you were wise, powerful, prominent," because Paul is engaged in an argument, not in making historical descriptions. Her approach theorizes that Paul's rhetoric would be effective only if he was accurate about his opponent's views. Paul's letter can reveal history, therefore, but only if and when he properly understood his opponent's position and faithfully argued against it. Wire inserts another caveat; she believes this history happens within Paul's rhetorical world.

ness of creation, wherein God declared "it was very good" (Gen 1:31). Paul is at pains to express that difference is necessary for unity and mutuality, both among social classes and ethic groups as well as between male and female.

Interestingly, in the baptismal formula in 1 Corinthians 12:13, Paul does not say (as he does to the Galatians) *neither* Jew nor Greek, but *whether* Jew or Greek. Paul's overarching point in chapter 12 is the need for diversity within the body of Christ.[50] Wire concludes "social distinctions are not overcome in Christ but are accepted and integrated into Christ."[51] Building on this need for difference, Thiselton remarks that "Paul insists that true human relationality entails *otherness* and indeed *respect for the otherness of the other* as a necessary basis for true reciprocity, mutuality and relationality that constitutes what it is to be human."[52]

Wire suggests that the female prophets in Corinth concluded that being new creatures in Christ, with Christ as the image of God—*not* male and female—meant rejection of sex-specific practices and designated gender roles. Wire contends that Paul is reasserting patriarchy in 1 Corinthians 11:2-16.[53] I take issue with Wire's conclusion. Paul's point is that they are to prophesy as females within their culture, not behaving disrespectfully to males. Paul calls on these female prophets to follow the semiotic codes of gender differentiation for their culture. Thiselton notes that Paul affirms that the female prophets "**keep control** *of* (how people perceive) **their heads,** because the issue here . . . remains that of assertive autonomy *versus self-control*."[54]

CONCLUSION

How does this information impact our understanding of the text's role in the church today? Though Martin is not interested in what the church should do today, his approach to chapters 12—14 shares some of the same concerns raised in Webb's hermeneutic. Martin explains the Greco-Roman setting, particularly its honor/shame and status categories and then argues that Paul overturns those social norms. Martin, however, does not address *why* Paul might do so, and this is where Webb might come in. Webb's redemptive-movement hermeneutic suggests that the gospel can (though it does not always) critique

---

[50]For discussion about diversity see Fee, *First Epistle to the Corinthians*, pp. 582-83.
[51]Wire, *The Corinthian Women Prophets*, p. 138.
[52]Thiselton, *The First Epistle to the Corinthians*, pp. 842-43. Emphasis in original.
[53]Wire, *Corinthian Women Prophets*, pp. 126-34.
[54]Thiselton, *First Epistle to the Corinthians*, p. 839. Emphasis in original.

culture. The spirit of the text moves in a redemptive way, shaping the culture of the church to match the gospel. Webb's attention to the redemptive aspect of Scripture could be helpfully applied to Martin's work by highlighting the important place of the creation story in Paul's argument.

I appreciate Vanhoozer's concerns that Webb's phrasing "the spirit of the text" might be at times too ephemeral and imprecise.[55] Perhaps it would be better to argue that the redemptive light of Christ shines full on the social and gender hierarchies, exposing their inadequacies. Webb's theory also helps us deal with the antiquated science and worldviews under which the biblical writers labored. We no longer understand women to be made of biologically inferior material, though we too have our gender constructs. We are not concerned about pollution in the way that Paul perhaps was. Webb's hermeneutic allows for the gospel message to move comfortably from that setting to our modern or postmodern and scientific paradigms, and to future ones as well.

In sum, Paul encourages women to prophesy, based on 1 Corinthians 11, though he wants this activity done with full recognition of gender distinctiveness. Chapters 12—14 show Paul's desire for more prophecy and less speaking in tongues. Women are part of the group to which Paul speaks in 1 Corinthians 12—14. Paul continues the discussion of prophecy from chapter 11 to chapter 12, thus his more obvious social critique also contains a gender critique. Martin did not push his findings far enough because he did not link the prophecy in chapter 11 with the same discussion in 12—14. Paul views the church body as ultimately censuring status norms which govern social interactions. The church, in the power and gifting of the Holy Spirit, elevates the weak, displaying mutuality among its different members.

The Corinthians' faulty view of God's redemptive plan through Christ skewed their view of human relationships and the relationship between humans and God. This false assessment was rooted in their deficient view of the Father and the Son. Paul took on the unenviable task of declaring both differentiation and mutuality. He notes that there are different gifts, different parts of Christ's body and differences represented in male and female. Yet he is at pains to advocate mutuality of gifts, the oneness of the body and the goodness of God's creation—male and female.

---

[55]Vanhoozer, "Into the Great Beyond," pp. 90-95.

CHRIST'S GIFTED BRIDE

Gendered Members in Ministry in Acts and Paul

Fredrick J. Long

THE QUESTION OF WOMEN IN MINISTRY IS AN exegetical and cultural one, both in Paul's day and in our own.[1] Although Paul encouraged (married) women to pray and to prophesy with their heads covered (signifying their married status) (1 Cor 11:5),[2] he three chapters later tells certain women to "keep silent" in the assemblies (*en tais ekklēsiais*) "as the law says" (1 Cor 14:34), "for it is shameful for a woman to speak in an assembly" (1 Cor 14:35).[3] These two sets

---

[1] E. Earle Ellis, *Pauline Theology: Ministry and Society* (Grand Rapids: Eerdmans, 1989) is right to locate Paul's thoughts on women in ministry culturally; and Ellis's conclusion in "Silenced Wives of Corinth (1 Cor. 14:34-5)," in *New Testament Textual Criticism: Its Significance for Exegesis: Essays in Honour of Bruce M. Metzger,* ed. E. J. Epp and G. D. Fee (New York: Oxford University Press, 1981), p. 218, that I Cor 14:35-36 is an application of principles in cultural context is instructive.

[2] See Bruce W. Winter, *Roman Wives, Roman Widows: The Appearance of New Women and the Pauline Communities* (Grand Rapids: Eerdmans, 2003).

[3] The translation of biblical texts will be mine, unless otherwise noted. Winter, *Roman Wives,* p. 93, suggests that since no OT law prohibiting women from speaking in public can be found, that the law Paul refers to may be Roman law in which "Women were not to intervene (*intercede*) in public settings or come between two parties, and an imperial ban had already existed from the time of Augustus on women intervening on behalf of their husbands in the context of legal argument." Winter rightly points to Paul's description of having outsiders present during prophesying (1 Cor 14:22-25), who would observe how the Christian wives behaved in relation to their husbands. Also, throughout 1 Corinthians Paul was at pains to educate the Corinthian community properly how to relate socially, morally and politically within the broader Roman world: concerning wisdom (1 Cor 1:18-20; 3:18-23)

of perspectives in 1 Corinthians are so difficult to reconcile that many notable and conservative interpreters conclude that 1 Corinthians 14:34-36 is not originally from Paul.[4] It is easy, too, for scholars to dismiss as non-Pauline the injunctions of 1 Timothy 2:12 that "a woman not teach or have authority over a man."[5] However, clearly in 1 Corinthians 14:34-36 Paul has wives in view ("let them ask their own husbands at home," v. 35) and there are very substantial reasons to think that in 1 Timothy 2:12 Paul is restricting a wife's (public) role in relation to her husband.[6]

In both these passages, one needs to understand the Greco-Roman expectations and constraints for how a married woman should relate to her husband, and how suspicious Roman officials were of "corrupting" influences of new religions (such as Christianity) on Roman women (see discussion below).[7] At the same time, there is another exegetical observation that illuminates this topic, namely, the fact that *the New Testament gift lists in context are completely gender neutral*, an observation that is not sufficiently em-

---

and speech (1 Cor 2:5-8), Paul's ministry (1 Cor 2:1-5; 4:8-13), sexual immorality (1 Cor 5:1, 9-13; 6:9-13), lawsuits (1 Cor 6:1-3), marriage (1 Cor 7:12-16) and one's general calling (1 Cor 7:17, 20-24, 29-31), idolatry (1 Cor 8, 10), outreach to win all types of people (1 Cor 9:19-23), worship and head coverings (1 Cor 11:5-6, 10), spiritual gifts (1 Cor 12:2, 13) and outsiders in relation to spiritual gifts (1 Cor 14:12, 22-25), and even beliefs about the resurrection (1 Cor 15:19, 31-33).

[4]See Gordon D. Fee, *The First Epistle to the Corinthians*, NICNT (Grand Rapids: Eerdmans, 1987), pp. 699-705. More recently, see Richard B. Hays, *First Corinthians*, Int (Louisville, Ky.: John Knox Press, 1997). For a more conservative alternative, Ellis, "Silenced Wives," p. 219, suggests that Paul added these comments in the autograph as marginal notes.

[5]See, e.g., William Klassen, "Musonius Rufus, Jesus and Paul: Three First-Century Feminists," in *From Jesus to Paul: Studies in Honour of Francis Wright Beare*, ed. J. C. Hurd and G. P. Richardson (Waterloo, Ont.: Wilfrid Laurier University Press, 1984), p. 204. Also, it is easy for scholars to dismiss Paul's injunctions in 1 Tim 2:12, because the letter is considered by them to be deutero-Pauline.

[6]See Ellis, *Pauline Theology*, pp. 67-78; for Ellis's earlier treatment of 1 Cor 14:35-36 and why wives are in view, see "Silenced Wives," pp. 216-18. For 1 Tim 2:12-15, there is the correspondence of "submission" language with the household codes where wives and husbands are addressed (1 Cor 14:34-35; Eph 5:21-33; Col 3:18; 1 Pet 3:1-7), the change from plural (*women* generally) to singular (a *wife*) at 1 Tim 2:11, Paul's appeal to the creation order and the first married couple (Adam and Eve, the first husband and wife) in 1 Tim 2:13-14, and the matter of "childbearing" in 1 Tim 2:15.

[7]For a review of women in ministry with Paul, see Wendy Cotter, "Women's Authority Roles in Paul's Churches: Countercultural or Conventional?" *NovT* 36 (1994): 350-72. Also helpful is the work of James G. Sigountos and Myron Shanks, "Public Roles for Women in the Pauline Church: A Reappraisal of the Evidence," *JETS* 26, no. 3 (1983): 283-95, who argue that Paul's "cultural" injunctions about women speaking/teaching should be understood against Greek aversions of women (in general) teaching (as opposed to prophesying, praying or functioning as priestesses). However, not taken sufficiently into account in their work is the relevance of the NT gift lists, the view that Paul is restricting the public role of wives in relation to their husbands, the Roman government's fear of the influences of Eastern religions on married women, and the broader considerations of women's participation in voluntary associations. See below.

phasized.[8] Thus, much more work is needed to locate Paul's theology of giftedness within the broader Greco-Roman religious, philosophical and social milieu and to consider the implications of this for a biblical theology of women in ministry today.[9]

In this chapter, then, I explore the foundational event of Pentecost in Acts 2 and Joel's prophecy as it relates to gendered giftedness and Christian ministry. In Acts, Luke shows great concern to present the Christian movement as a *legitimate* and *legal* social movement with respect to basic Roman mores. Women are not featured in the narrative as speakers in public, although their involvement in ministry is evident, as one would expect given women's active participation in religious Greco-Roman and Jewish voluntary associations. Then I look at gift lists in the rest of the New Testament, especially in Paul. At the same time, research and evidence concerning the Mediterranean voluntary associations will be brought to bear on Acts and the gift lists and the topic of women in ministry. Arguably, theological principles derived from God's fulfillment of prophecy in Acts 2 and Paul's general discussions of gifts must be our foundation for a theology of women in ministry, rather than Paul's application of such principles to women/wives in his social and cultural context (as in 1 Cor 14:34-35; 1 Tim 2:11-15). So, contemporary theologians need to evaluate which New Testament passages reflect general transcultural principles for ministry as the proper basis for a biblical theology of women in ministry today.[10]

GIFTS FOR CHRIST'S BRIDE

The bride of Christ is presently a *gifted* church prepared for ministry in the world.[11] This gifting is from the risen and exalted Christ who intends to fill all

---

[8]Roger W. Gehring, *House Church and Mission: The Importance of Household Structures in Early Christianity* (Peabody, Mass.: Hendrickson, 2004), p. 221 n. 575, briefly makes this observation regarding the gift lists in 1 Cor 12:8-10, 28-30 and Rom 12:6-8.

[9]See the innovative work of Elisabeth Schüssler-Fiorenza, *In Memory of Her: A Feminist Theological Reconstruction of Christian Origins* (New York: Crossroad, 1986), pp. 295-309; and Carolyn Osiek and David L. Balch, *Families in the New Testament World: Households and House Churches* (Louisville, Ky.: Westminster John Knox, 1997), chap. 6.

[10]David M. Scholer, "Hermeneutical Gerrymandering: Hurley on Women and Authority," *TSF Bulletin* 6, no. 5 (1983): 12, rightly critiques James B. Hurley, *Man and Woman in Biblical Perspective*, Contemporary Evangelical Perspectives: Contemporary Issues (Grand Rapids: Zondervan, 1981), for building a biblical theology of women in ministry with 1 Tim 2:11-15 as the "control" text, when it is clear that Paul's statements are made within a particular polemical and cultural context.

[11]In the NT, the church is depicted as the current bride of Christ (Eph 5:25-27; Rev 22:17) or possibly awaiting marriage to Christ (2 Cor 11:2; Rev 21:2, 9; cf. Rev 19:7).

things (Eph 4:10-11; cf. Eph 1:10). The writings of the apostles Paul and Peter contain multiple descriptions of gifts: Romans 12:6-8; 1 Corinthians 12:8-10, 28-30; 13:1-3; Ephesians 4:11; 1 Peter 4:10-11. Axiomatic is the observation that *nowhere in these texts is there the suggestion that these gifts have a restricted distribution or role according to gender.* And given women's active role in the Greco-Roman voluntary associations (see extensive discussion below), one cannot claim that Paul assumes a gender restriction—quite the opposite would have been true. Additionally, in Acts 2, the apostle Peter quotes Joel 2:28-32 (MT 3:1-5) to explain the outpouring of the Spirit. Joel's prophecy indicates clearly that prophetic ministry will be carried out by both men and women. Although such passages as these are affirmed as having relevance for the issue of women in ministry, this foundation is not often adequately built upon.[12] In this section of the chapter, I will explore the relation of Joel's prophecy of God's outpouring of his Spirit to Christian ministry as described in Acts. Then I will focus on giftedness in Paul and Peter, looking closely at 1 Corinthians 11—14.

JOEL 2:28-32 IN ACTS

The Septuagint text of Joel 2:28-32 is cited by Peter on Pentecost in Acts 2:16-21 at the founding of the ministry of the church. The group on which the Spirit was poured included both men and women, since the word "all" in Acts 2:1 includes the women mentioned in Acts 1:14-15. Otherwise, the fulfillment of the prophecy of Joel would be in question.[13] Properly understanding Joel's prophecy in Acts 2:16-18 is critical:

> But this is what has been spoken through the prophet Joel, "And it will be in the last days," says God, "I will pour out from my Spirit upon all flesh, and your sons will prophesy, and your daughters will prophesy and your young men will see visions and your older men will dream dreams. And indeed upon my [*mou*] male servants and my [*mou*] female servants in those days I will pour out from

---

[12]R. T. France, *Women in the Church's Ministry: A Test-Case for Biblical Hermeneutics* (Carlisle, U.K.: Paternoster, 1995), p. 53; Stanley Grenz and Denise Muir Kjesbo, *Women in the Church: A Biblical Theology of Women in Ministry* (Downers Grove, Ill.: InterVarsity Press, 1995), pp. 190-98; Ben Witherington III, *Women in the Earliest Churches* (Cambridge: Cambridge University Press, 1988), p. 152; Schüssler-Fiorenza, *In Memory of Her*, p. 185. An exception is the excellent treatment of Turid Karlsen Seim, *The Double Message: Patterns of Gender in Luke-Acts*, Studies of the New Testament and Its World (Edinburgh: T & T Clark, 1994), chap. 5, esp. pp. 170-71.

[13]Seim, *Double Message*, pp. 164-68, 171.

my Spirit, and they will prophesy *[kai prophēteusousin]*."

Most notable is the fact that Joel's original prophecy radically cuts across gender (sons and daughters; male and female servants), age (young and old men), social status (free and slave) and ethnicity (all flesh).[14] However, in the context of Luke, Joel's prophecy is interpreted to elevate the role of women in ministry. Turid Seim argues that the dimension of social status in Joel's prophecy ("male and female *servants*") is transformed in Acts to roles of ministry by the Lukan verbal additions of "my" *(mou)* to "male and female servants" and "they will prophesy" *(prophēteusousin)*, making these male and females *servants of the Lord* and indicating their role to function *prophetically*.[15] What is stressed here is God's prerogative of ownership over these male and female servants *and* their continuous activity of prophesying.[16] Finally, Peter ends his sermon by relating that this promise of the Spirit is "for you, and your children *[tois teknois]*, and to all *[pasin]* who are far away" (Acts 2:38-39). Such language indicates the gender-inclusive nature of the outpouring; the use of the word "children" *(tekna)* as opposed to "sons" *(huioi)* is gender inclusive, and so is "all" *(pantes)*.[17]

In addition to speaking prophetically *(prophēteuō)*, Joel describes "seeing visions" and "dreaming dreams." However, the Hebrew conception of a prophet included receiving dreams and visions, as is made clear in Numbers 12:6 (cf. Deut 13:1-5; Jer 23:28).[18] This location in Numbers also provides the framework for a more complete understanding of Joel's prophecy. Although setting forth a new and unexpected vision of the bestowal of the Spirit "without regard

---

[14]C. F. Keil and F. Delitzsch, *Commentary on the Old Testament: Minor Prophets,* trans. J. Martin, vol. 10 (Grand Rapids: Eerdmans, 1982), pp. 210-11, rightly argue that the inclusive scope of humanity is in view (all flesh) and correlate this with the Lord's previous statement to restrict his Spirit among human flesh in Gen 5:3. However, Jewish contemporaries took this to mean that the Spirit and accompanying gift of prophesying would be given only to Israelites; see Seim, *Double Message,* p. 169.

[15]Seim, *Double Message,* pp. 170-71.

[16]To be servants of the Lord is to be counted among God's faithful people (Ezra 5:11), especially during times of persecution (2 Kings 10:23; Dan 3:26) and the Lord will vindicate his servants (Is 54:17). The title "Servant of the Lord" in the OT is reserved almost exclusively for Moses (Deut 34:5; Josh 1:1, 13, 15; 2 Kings 18:12; although it is used also of David in Ps 18:1; 36:1) and is transferred to Joshua only at Joshua's death (Josh 24:29). Seim (*Double Message,* p. 175) also finds that "On the few occasions when Luke employs *doulos /doulē* to designate the relationship of human persons to God, it is always connected to the Spirit: Lk. 1.38, 48; 2.29; Acts 2.18; 4.29 and 16.17 (?). The Spirit marks out God's total right of disposal over persons and history, as it is expressed through the series of directives given by the Spirit steering the course of events in Acts."

[17]Seim, *Double Message,* p. 166.

[18]Keil and Delitzsch, *Minor Prophets,* p. 211.

to sex, age, or rank,"[19] Joel builds upon Numbers 11:16-29, which relates a critical incident at the beginning of the national life of Israel after the Exodus. The sequence of events in Numbers is as follows: The Lord told Moses to select seventy elders to give him assistance in leading the people (Num 11:16-17). Moses obeyed (Num 11:24), and the Spirit was given to the seventy elders and they consequently prophesied (Num 11:25). Two elders continued to prophesy, and when this fact was reported to Moses by Joshua, Moses declared: "Are you jealous for my sake? Would that all the LORD's people were prophets, that the LORD would put His Spirit upon them!" (Num 11:29 NASB 95).

Prophets in Israel occupied a vital position of authority, merging human leadership and divine representation (cf. Ex 7:1). Pivotal and central persons are designated "a prophet" (*nābî'; prophētēs*): Abraham (Gen 20:7); Moses (Deut 18:15; 34:10); Aaron (Ex 7:1); Samuel (1 Sam 3:20); Saul (1 Sam 10:10-12); Elijah (1 Kings 18:22); Elisha (1 Kings 19:16) and so forth. But, also one finds five women who are called "prophetesses" (*něbî'â; prophētis*): Miriam (Ex 15:20); Deborah (Judg 4:4); Huldah (2 Kings 22:14); Noadiah (Neh 6:14, using *prophētēs*); and an unnamed mother (Is 8:3). The rabbinic tradition adds four others: Sarah, Hannah, Abigail and Esther (*bMeg* 14a), although some of these women are critiqued as being proud.[20] Again, it is critical to emphasize that being a prophet in Israel was associated with leading and speaking God's authoritative word to God's people.

The prophet Joel, many centuries after Moses, was inspired to recast Moses' hope of God's Spirit empowering individuals for prophetic ministry in such a way as to transcend gender, age and social status. Then many centuries later, Peter applies Joel's prophecy to the beginning of the life of the Christian community. The implication is that God's Spirit in the new covenant will distribute *leadership* gifts, such as prophesying, to women as well as to men.[21]

How does Joel's prophecy regarding prophetic ministry play out in the rest of the book of Acts? And how are women portrayed as exhibiting prophetic leadership roles? To answer the first question, E. Earle Ellis surveys the role of prophet in Acts, and concludes that "Luke restricts the term or title *prophētēs*, as it is used of his contemporaries, to a select number of 'leading men' (cf. Acts 15:22) who exercise considerable influence in the Christian

---

[19]Ibid.

[20]The reference and discussion is found in Seim, *Double Message,* pp. 168-69.

[21]Witherington, *Women in the Earliest Churches,* p. 152. See also below.

Community."[22] Ellis then lists these male prophets and leaders: "Agabus (Acts 11:27-28; cf. 21:10); a group resident in Antioch, including Barnabas and Paul (Acts 13:1); and the two prophets who accompanied the Jerusalem decree to Antioch, Judas Barsabbas and Silas (Acts 15:22, 32)"; and Peter, who although not deemed a prophet by name, nevertheless has visions and dreams (Acts 10:10-16) and acts as a prophet, when knowing the motivations of one's heart (Acts 5:3-4; 8:21-23). Ellis admits that it is possible to add to this group the four daughters of Philip "who prophesied."[23] Such a possibility is likely, given that the Greek construction emphasizes both the verbal action of prophesying as an attribute of the daughters (periphrastic/predicate participle) and the continuation of their prophesying (present tense). Furthermore, Luke's highlighting of these women as "daughters" (*thygatēr*) correlates back to Joel's prophecy.[24]

Ellis also considers the ways in which this prophetic ministry is exercised: prediction (Acts 11:28; 20:23, 25, 29; 21:11), leadership in decision making in the community (Acts 13:1; 15:27), exposition of Scripture and teaching by exhortation.[25] In the end, Ellis concludes that "Although prophecy is a possibility for any Christian, it is primarily identified with certain leaders who exercise it as a ministry."[26] In this light, it is erroneous to think that prophecy (as opposed to teaching) is a mindless activity (since one is given inspired thoughts by God) or that prophecy works with God's authority (rather than with one's own authority as in teaching), and, from either basis, to argue that only prophecy is suitable for women (since it is mindless and based upon God's authority), whereas teaching is not (since it requires thought and one's own authority).[27] If one were working strictly with a Greco-Roman cultural view of women and model of prophecy in which mind and spirit were separated, this may be argued. However, the New Testament authors Luke and Paul are grounded in Hebrew spirituality in which the *whole* person is engaged with God. For example, in 1 Corinthians 12—14, Paul argues against the Corinthians' Hellenistic *misunderstandings* of Christian

---

[22]E. Earle Ellis, "The Role of the Christian Prophet in Acts," in *Apostolic History and the Gospel: Biblical and Historical Essays Presented to F. F. Bruce on His 60th Birthday*, ed. W. W. Gasque and R. P. Martin (Grand Rapids: Eerdmans, 1970), p. 55.

[23]Ibid., pp. 55-56.

[24]Seim, *Double Message*, pp. 180-81.

[25]See the discussion in Ellis, "Role of the Christian Prophet," pp. 56-62.

[26]Ibid., p. 56.

[27]For an excellent examination of these issues, see Sigountos and Shanks, "Public Roles."

giftedness (see 1 Cor 12:2) that was unintelligible, ecstatic, unedifying and "immature" with regard to their "thinking" (1 Cor 14:20). Instead, Paul urged the Corinthians to a mindful and intelligible exercise of spiritual gifts, with one's mind fully engaged in coordination with one's spirit (1 Cor 14:13-15) and with one fully in control of the prophetic experience (1 Cor 14:32). Paul was working within and urging a biblical model of prophesying, and he lists prophets second only to apostles (1 Cor 12:28).

To answer the second question (How are women portrayed as prophets in Acts?), indeed, women's roles as prophets are minor, even though they do exist, as Philip's daughters demonstrate. Seim rightly argues that "The prophesying daughters are themselves the guarantee that the eschatological outpouring of the Spirit has actually taken place, in keeping with the promise of Joel's prophecy."[28] She concludes generally that Luke has "silenced" women. The "daughter" prophetesses in Luke (Anna, daughter of Phanuel; Lk 2:36-38) and Acts (Philip's four virgin daughters; Acts 21:9) have no voice, whereas their male counterparts do (Simon in Lk 2:25-35; and Agabus in Acts 21:10-11; cf. Lk 11:28). This leads Seim naturally to consider why this is the case: "Luke draws up quite strict boundaries for women's activity in relation to the Jewish and Greco-Roman public world. In this way, he is in accord with the apologetic considerations that also colour the epistles in questions dealing with women."[29] And again Seim argues:

> The silence imposed on women is connected with the public character of the proclamation in Luke, in societies where and at a time when the distance between the world of men and the world of women very largely coincided with the difference between a public sphere and private sphere. Women's lives were determined by the domestic routines and responsibilities, and even well-off and aristocratic women were seldom direct participants in a public context.[30]

This last point—"that aristocratic women were seldom direct participants in a public context"—needs some modification.[31] For, while women in the Greco-

---

[28]Seim, *Double Message,* p. 168.

[29]Ibid., p. 259.

[30]Ibid., p. 255.

[31]Kathleen E. Corley, in her review of Turid Karlsen Seim, *The Double Message: Patterns of Gender in Luke-Acts,* in *Review of Biblical Literature* (June 26, 2006): p. 3, offers a correction of Seim's point: "Furthermore, that Luke limits women from public proclamations in his narrative is best understood as a reflection of a common Greco-Roman ideal shared by Jews and Romans alike; it is not simply due to limitations on Jewish women as witnesses (pp. 12-13; 23-24; 137; 156)."

Roman world played a significantly less public role than that of men, they still did play a role, especially well-to-do women. In addition, Carolyn Osiek argues that such "social invisibility is conceptual: it exists in the minds of those who articulate the ideal and may bear no resemblance to what is really going on."[32]

CHRISTIAN WOMEN IN ACTS IN THE GRECO-ROMAN MILIEU

James M. Arlandson's recent work on *Women, Class, and Society in Early Christianity* (1997) summarizes the inscriptional and numismatic (from coins) evidence that shows conclusively that women held a variety of political positions in a variety of locations in the Roman Empire.[33] These positions were not at the highest city levels—the local council (or *boulē*) made up of wealthy male landowners and the popular assembly (or *ekklēsia*) made up of enrolled adult male citizens—but included lesser officials, political retainers (clerks, magistrates, judges) and religious leaders.[34] Although it is true that the percentage of women holding these positions is much less then men, it is also true that women occupied them not simply as honorific titles (i.e., with no real power or authority involved) nor only because of one's husband's positions.[35] Indeed, they likely fulfilled functionary roles, as even was the case with women leaders in Jewish synagogues.[36]

The greater social freedom of Roman women was increasing in the first century,[37] and would have affected the Roman East (i.e., Greece, Asia Minor and Judea) more sporadically, since Greek customs of dining, veiling and domestic structure were more conservative than Roman.[38] Instrumental was the wealth of the women, as Arlandson argues: "More money meant more freedom, which resulted in social boundaries becoming a little more porous. Social boundaries usually manifested physical boundaries—women were typified as being do-

---

[32]Carolyn Osiek, "Women in House Churches," in *Common Life in the Early Church: Essays Honoring Graydon F. Snyder,* ed. J. Hills (Harrisburg, Penn.: Trinity International, 1998), p. 302.

[33]James M. Arlandson, *Women, Class, and Society in Early Christianity: Models from Luke-Acts* (Peabody, Mass.: Hendrickson, 1997), pp. 31-33; contra Osiek, who limits women to occupying patron status and not any leadership role ("Women in House Churches," p. 309).

[34]Arlandson, *Women, Class,* pp. 25-52; and Ramsay MacMullen, "Women in Public in the Roman Empire," *Historia* 29 (1980): 208-18.

[35]Arlandson, *Women, Class,* pp. 33-35.

[36]See Bernadette J. Brooten, *Women Leaders in the Ancient Synagogue: Inscriptional Evidence and Background Issues,* BJS 36 (Chico, Calif.: Scholars Press, 1982).

[37]See Osiek and Balch, *Families in the New Testament World,* pp. 57-60; and the summary of such trends in Osiek "Women," p. 302.

[38]On the veiling, see Osiek, "Women in House Churches," p. 307.

mestic—but wealth purchased for them access into the outside world, often without a male guardian."[39]

However, essentially Seim's basic observation seems sound to me: Although Luke tips his hat to women prophets as a sign of the fulfillment of Joel's proph-

Table 5.1. Summary of Witherington's Discussion of Women in Acts[40]

Incidental References to Male-Female Parallelism	Ananias and Sapphira (5:1-11) Priscilla and Aquila (chap. 18) Felix and Drusilla (24:24) Agrippa and Bernice (3x; 25:13—26:12) Men and women converts (5:14) Men and women Christians persecuted (9:2; cf. 8:3) Lydia (16:12-15, 40) and the male jailer (16:23-39) Dionysius and Damaris are converted at Athens (17:34)
Male-Female Role Reversal	Males become servants for widows (6:1-7)
Female Prominence	Women converts (17:4) Prominent women converts mentioned before men (17:12)
Women as Prominent Converts or *mēteres synagōgēs*	Women who supply home and hospitality; house churches and the only two such places mentioned in Acts are owned by women: the widow Mary, Mother of John Mark (12:12-17; note also the servant Rhoda's prominent role in this context), and the first Macedonian convert, Lydia, whose house becomes a church (16:12-40).
Women as Deaconesses	Possibly in 9:36-42, where the "female disciple" (*mathētria*) Tabitha, whom Peter raised back to life, apparently was ministering to the widows, who took great interest in her healing and to whom Peter carefully presents her alive (9:39, 41).
Women as Prophetesses	Philip's four virgin daughters who were prophesying (*ēsan . . . prophēteuousai*), that is, holding an office of prophesying (21:9).
Women as Teachers	Priscilla and Aquila, who taught Apollos more accurately, with Priscilla mentioned first (18:26). Also, Paul deliberately leaves them in Ephesus for the purpose of teaching (18:19).

---

[39]Arlandson, *Women, Class*, p. 37.
[40]This table is my summary of material from Witherington, *Women in the Earliest Churches*, pp. 143-54.

ecy, he is otherwise constrained not to have them speak publicly.[41] This is evident when one observes how present women are in Acts and yet how silent they are. Ben Witherington III's survey, which centers on particular aspects of women in ministry, helps to demonstrate this point (see table 5.1).[42]

Women are participants of the gospel and its spread; they are talking, teaching and leading, but we as readers must usually infer these activities from Luke's narrative descriptions in Acts, with two notable exceptions: Priscilla and Aquila teaching Apollos, and Philip's prophesying daughters. But we do not actually hear these women speaking.

Compare the chart of Witherington's survey (table 5.1) to Arlandson's chart (table 5.2) describing women and their response to and participation in the gospel in Luke-Acts. Arlandson's research shows that the theme of reversal of fortunes spoken about prophetically in Luke 1—2 (the low are exalted and the powerful are brought down) is not equally applied in Luke-Acts—lowly women are raised up, but wealthy women tend to remain exalted and actively participate in household ministries of the church (whereas wealthy and powerful men are shown to be brought low).[43]

This does not mean that women are always responsive to the gospel in Luke-Acts.[44] Nevertheless, it is evident that Luke affirmed the leadership of women in house churches (Mary in Acts 12:12; Lydia in Acts 16:14-15, 40).[45] Also, a prominent woman is engaged in a teaching setting (Priscilla and Aquila

---

[41]For her cautions about making too rigid a distinction between public versus private spheres in relation to household structures, see Osiek, "Women in House Churches," pp. 302-3.

[42]Witherington, *Women in the Earliest Churches*, pp. 143-54.

[43]Arlandson, *Women, Class*, pp. 191-93.

[44]Arlandson's opposite list ("Women Resistant to or Not Favored by the Kingdom of God") is as follows (p. 123):

Luke	Acts
Herodias 3:19	Sapphira 5:1-11
Woman from crowd 11:27-28	Candace 8:27
Servant accusing Peter 22:55-62	Prominent Antiochenes of Pisidia 13:50
	Philippians 16:13
Women in Sayings	Drusilla 24:24
Newlywed 14:20	Bernice 25:23
Prostitutes 15:30	
Women in Noah's days 17:27	
Lot's wife 17:32	
One grinding grain 17:35	

[45]Rosalie Beck, "The Women of Acts: Foremothers of the Christian Church," in *With Steadfast Purpose: Essays on Acts*, ed. N. H. Keathley (Waco, Tex.: Baylor University Press, 1990), pp. 294-96.

Table 5.2. Arlandson's Summary of "Women Receptive to or Favored by the Kingdom of God" in Luke-Acts[46]

LUKE	ACTS
Elizabeth 1:5-7, 24-25, 39-80	Mary 1:14
Mary 1:27-36; 1:26-56; 2:5-7, 16-19, 22-27,	Praying disciples 1:14
33-34, 39, 41-51; 8:19-21	At Pentecost 2:4
Anna 2:36-38	Jerusalem disciples 5:14
Simon's mother-in-law 4:38-39	Hellenistic widows 6:1-7
Grieving widow 7:11-17	Hebrew widows 6:1-7
"Sinful" woman 7:36-50	Persecuted 8:8; 9:2
Healed and delivered disciples 8:2	Samaritans 8:12
Mary Magdalene 8:2; 24:10	Tabitha 9:36-42
Joanna 8:3; 24:10	Widows 9:89-41
Susanna 8:3	Mary, the mother of John 12:12
Financial contributors 8:3	Rhoda 12:13-15
Jairus's daughter 8:41-42, 49-56	Timothy's mother 16:1
Hemorrhaging woman 8:43-48	Lydia 16:14-15, 40
Mary 10:38-42	Pythoness slave 16:16-24
Martha 10:38-42	Prominent Thessalonians 17:4
"Daughter of Abraham" 13:10-17	Prominent Bereans 17:12
Poor-generous widow 21:1-4	Damaris 17:34
At crucifixion 23:27-31, 49	Prisca 18:2-3, 18, 26
At burial 23:55	Tyrian disciples 21:5
At resurrection 24:1-8	Philip's daughters 21:9
Mary, mother of James 24:10	Paul's sister 23:16
Reporters of resurrection 24:9-11; cf.	
24:22-24	**Women in Speeches**
	Prophetic disciples 2:17-18
Women in Sayings	Persecuted disciples 22:4 (cf. 8:3; 9:2)
Widow of Zarephath 4:25-26	
Doers of the word 8:21	
Queen of the South 11:31	
Beaten slaves 12:45	
Oikos divided 12:52-53	
Baker 13:21	
Oikos divided 14:26	
Woman and lost coin 15:8-10	
Divorcees 16:18	
One grinding grain 17:35	
Persistent widow 18:1-8	
Honor your mother 18:20	
Oikos divided 18:29	
Widow in levirate marriages 20:28-40	
Widows 20:47	
Oikos divided 21:16	
Persecuted 21:23	
Reporters of resurrection 24:22-24;	
cf. 24:9-1	

---

[46]This chart is primarily taken from Arlandson, *Women, Class*, pp. 121-22.

with Apollos, Acts 18:26).[47] Again, however, these women are not depicted as actually speaking in the narrative. Luke reflects the common Roman value, as Ramsay MacMullen has said about "Women in Public in the Roman Empire": "They are to be seen . . . but not heard."[48]

Taking a step back from these observations, we need to consider Luke's larger goals in writing. Vernon K. Robbins has recently argued that one of Luke's primary intentions is to show that "Roman law, correctly applied, grants Christians the right to pursue the project started by Jesus, and the goals of Christianity, rightly understood, work congruently with the goals of the Roman empire." Additionally, the "two-volume narrative presupposes that the eastern Roman empire is an appropriate work place for the emissaries of God who are carrying out the project inaugurated by Jesus of Nazareth."[49] It is also relevant to our discussion here that Robbins locates the Christian leaders, especially in the second half of Acts, as occupying the social status of "independent artisans or above" throughout the eastern Mediterranean and that their place of work are synagogues or households.[50] Although Robbins's study does not specifically treat the social location of women in the Roman world, Roman laws and mores affected perceptions about appropriate women's roles. What would have been socially acceptable public work for women to be engaged in, especially in religious contexts?

WOMEN IN GRECO-ROMAN VOLUNTARY ASSOCIATIONS

As indicted above, the legal freedom of Roman women was increasing during the first century, so that women could obtain legal rights over their own property (if they bore three or more children), participate in banquets with their husbands, and less and less were required to wear marriage veils in the Roman West.[51] However, one social location where legality, social roles and public mores converged was religious groups and their meetings, generally classified under the voluntary associations or *collegia* (among several other names). The

---

[47]Arlandson, *Women, Class,* p. 193.

[48]MacMullen, "Women in Public," p. 216.

[49]Vernon K. Robbins, "Luke-Acts: A Mixed Population Seeks a Home in the Roman Empire," in *Images of Empire,* ed. L. Alexander (Sheffield, U.K.: JSOT Press, 1991), p. 202, available online:<www.religion.emory.edu/faculty/robbins/Pdfs/MixedPopulation.pdf>.

[50]Ibid., p. 213. Robbins directs readers to the study of Loveday C. A. Alexander, "Luke's Preface in the Context of Greek Preface Writing," *NovT* 28 (1986): 48-76, in which she argues that Luke's preface was composed along the lines of the manuals for artisans.

[51]Osiek, "Women in House Churches," p. 302; on the loosening of veiling more, see p. 307.

growing Roman freedom of women also "was responsible for greater and more 'equal' participation" of women in voluntary associations.[52]

Although the suggestion that early Christian churches would have been perceived as and functioned as a type of voluntary association is not a recent one, current, detailed scholarly work has greatly advanced our understanding of these groups in relation to Pauline Christianity.[53] The early Christians were just one of many groups active in the Mediterranean basin. Such organizations included the Jewish synagogues, trade guilds or societies, athletic clubs, funerary associations, religious groups and philosophical communities—all of which may be classified as voluntary associations. Indeed, there was considerable fluidity in these types of groups and in the nomenclature used to describe them, with non-Christian Gentile groups referring to themselves as synagogues, and many other seemingly odd transpositions.[54]

Scholars have recently begun to correlate research on voluntary associations with the early Christians' communities, investigating the extent of comparisons, the nature of voluntary associations, and their membership across social status and gender. Women played active roles—even leadership roles—in various types of voluntary associations. Of course, it depended on the type of association, some of which excluded women altogether. Religiously, women served in a variety of capacities.[55] These included torch bearers in processions, divine expositors (lit. "theologians," *theologoi*—Demeter Cult 1st-2nd cen-

---

[52]John S. Kloppenborg, "Edwin Hatch, Churches, and *Collegia*," in *Origins and Method: Towards a New Understanding of Judaism and Christianity: Essays in Honour of John C. Hurd,* ed. B. H. McLean, JSNT-Sup 86, no.1 (Sheffield, U.K.: JSOT Press, 1993), p. 234. Arlandson (*Women, Class,* p. 91) concludes one of his book sections by summarizing: "Women were active members of *collegia* in Rome, and this probably reflects the situation in the East, since the East was undergoing prosperity and therefore social freedom for women."

[53]For the history of interpretation see Kloppenborg, "Edwin Hatch," pp. 212-38. A major monograph on the subject is by Philip A. Harland, *Associations, Synagogues, and Congregations: Claiming a Place in Ancient Mediterranean Society* (Minneapolis: Fortress, 2003). See also the erudite collection of essays edited by John S. Kloppenborg and Stephen G. Wilson, eds., *Voluntary Associations in the Graeco-Roman World* (New York: Routledge, 1996), and the essay by B. Hudson McLean, "The Agrippinilla Inscription: Religious Associations and Early Church Formation," in *Origins and Method: Towards a New Understanding of Judaism and Christianity,* ed. B. H. McLean, JSNTSup 86, no.1 (Sheffield, U.K.: JSOT Press, 1993), pp. 239-70.

[54]See Kloppenborg, "Edwin Hatch," p. 231; and Harland, *Associations, Synagogues,* pp. 3, 49-50. See also Wayne O. McCready, "*EKKLĒSIA* and Voluntary Associations," in Kloppenborg and Wilson, *Voluntary Associations,* pp. 59-73.

[55]For primary texts, see the compilation of Ross Shepard Kraemer, *Women's Religions in the Greco-Roman World: A Sourcebook* (New York: Oxford University Press, 2004).

tury),[56] high priestesses, patronesses or benefactors (cf. Phoebe in Rom 16:2), prophetesses[57] and synagogue leaders.[58] At the turn of the first century, the names of two women are found even among the traditionally male-exclusive "dancing cowherds of Pergamum," who would recite prayers, sing hymns and dance in reenactments of the foundation story of Dionysius, in which the god inspired his maenads to rip apart the herds as the herders watched stupefied.[59]

The Roman authorities were particularly touchy with foreign religious groups or superstitions.[60] There was a history of Roman concern for the influence of foreign religion on the social order, *especially as it affected married women*. David Balch has surveyed the agitated Roman response to the devotees to the god Dionysius and the devotees to the goddess Isis.[61] These associations enjoyed broad distribution in the early first century. But they had become socially mollified, having been transformed from the initially wild bacchanals outlawed in Rome in 186 B.C. to acceptable activities inclusive of men, although still featuring women prominently as high priestesses.[62]

What makes this so relevant is that Jews, and later Christians, were "named" with these same religious groups and were accused of the same corrupting influences on women. As foreign cults, the Romans feared the perversion of the household—and the empire: "As goes the household, so goes the state."[63] The focus of concern was both *the perversion of married women sexually* and the general slander *that the particular group was seditious or revolutionary.*

---

[56]Harland, *Associations, Synagogues*, p. 71.

[57]For selected texts in translation, see Antoinette C. Wire, *The Corinthian Women Prophets: A Reconstruction through Paul's Rhetoric* (Minneapolis: Fortress, 1995), pp. 237-69.

[58]For ancient references, see Harland, *Associations, Synagogues*, pp. 44-49, 59, 288 n. 20. For women as leaders in synagogues, see McLean, "Agrippinilla Inscription," pp. 259-66, and Brooten, *Women Leaders*, although the Jewish inscriptions that Brooten studies are from the second century and later.

[59]See Harland, *Associations, Synagogues*, p. 48.

[60]See the survey of Roman law in relation to these associations by Wendy Cotter, "The Collegia and Roman Law: State Restrictions on Voluntary Associations, 64 BCE-200 CE," in Kloppenborg and Wilson, *Voluntary Associations*, pp. 74-89.

[61]David L. Balch, *Let Wives Be Submissive: The Domestic Code in 1 Peter*, Society of Biblical Literature Monograph Series 26 (Chico, Calif.: Scholars Press, 1981), chap. 5.

[62]McLean, "Agrippinilla Inscription," pp. 259-61. For an ancient text that describes the measures taken in 186 B.C. to firmly regulate the Dionysian cult, see Mary R. Lefkowitz and Maureen B. Fant, eds., *Women's Life in Greece & Rome: A Source Book in Translation* (Baltimore: Johns Hopkins University Press, 1982), pp. 250-52.

[63]Osiek, "Women in House Churches," p. 303. Among the many conclusions, Balch (*Let Wives Be Submissive*, pp. 23-62) demonstrates the common analogy between managing households and managing cities, as well as the recognition that proper management of the household relationships would impact the governance of the city/empire.

And, in the case of the Isis cult, the concern was that *the roles of male and female were reversed.*[64] This reversal was completely unacceptable to Roman sensibilities, which held that its founder "Romulus brought the women to great prudence and orderly conduct" in subordination to their husbands.[65]

APOLOGETICS AND HERMENEUTICS OF ACTS

Returning to Luke-Acts, it seems likely, given the book's generally accepted apologetic presentation, that Luke was sensitive to portray the early Christians as nonsubversive to Roman authority, and especially Roman mores about women in public. It is significant, as Witherington notes, that "most of the women we find in Acts playing a significant role were either single or widowed."[66] The implication is that Luke was cautious and conservative in his representation of the first Christians in the Roman world, acknowledging the dictum that *married* women should neither be too visible nor vocal. At the same time, John S. Kloppenborg is correct to note that Luke "implicitly characterizes churches as extensions of the synagogue. . . . The apologetic purpose of Luke is clear."[67] This allowed early Christians protection under Judaism's legal status of *religio licita.* So both the conservative presentation of married women and the association of Christians with the synagogue make historical and apologetic sense, given the constant tension and threat the Roman authorities had for any new "superstition" and their perversion of (married) women.[68]

Hermeneutically, the question for us is this: As Scripture, is Acts to be read *descriptively* as a historical account of the earliest church or *prescriptively* as model and paradigm for today? (I grant that this dichotomy is too simplistic.) If

---

[64]For the perversions associated with the Dionysian cult and Roman laws and admonitions by public figures in their writings against it, see Balch, *Let Wives Be Submissive,* pp. 65-69; for the Isis cult, see pp. 69-73, and for Judaism, see pp. 73-74.

[65]Lefkowitz and Fant, *Women's Life,* p. 173; Balch, *Let Wives Be Submissive,* p. 72.

[66]Witherington, *Women in the Earliest Churches,* p. 152; so also Seim, *Double Message,* pp. 179-84; see especially chap. 6. Seim (p. 257) comments on asceticism in women: "It offered them an opportunity to move outside the limiting constraints of the conventional gender-determined roles of daughter, wife and mother. By withdrawing their sexuality from control by others and by controlling it themselves, they gained the possibility of exercising a power and an authority from which they were otherwise excluded."

[67]Kloppenborg, "Edwin Hatch," p. 212.

[68]A fascinating study on this subject, which describes the social relationships at the end of the first century, is by Robert Wilken, *The Christian as the Romans Saw Them* (New Haven, Conn.: Yale University Press, 1984).

understood prescriptively, then we have an obligation to develop models of ministry based on precedents set in the text. New Testament introductions and biblical interpretation textbooks commonly address the descriptive/prescriptive issue, with the conclusion offered that Acts is primarily descriptive, although containing prescription as well, which one must derive cautiously from the text.[69] Speaking to this question from a biblical theological perspective is I. Howard Marshall, whose view is sound that Acts presents "essentially a theology of mission" and that Luke "is not interested in church organization and office" but rather "with the progress of the Word rather than with the church."[70] I would add that the Christian mode of ministry, continued from and inspired by Jesus, is fundamentally incarnational: being in the world, but not of it; meeting people where they are, and yet moving them into kingdom values, lifestyles and communities (see Paul's articulation of this model in 1 Cor 9:19-22).[71]

So then, it is crucial for us to discern the transcultural values portrayed in Act's narrative as distinct from their particular incarnational accommodation within the Mediterranean world.[72] Arguably, the most secure place to begin to study those values is *through God's own initiative throughout the narrative description in Acts*. And I would argue that the bestowal of the Holy Spirit and Peter's inspired correlation of this event to Joel's prophecy in Acts 2 is foundational.[73] From this we surmise that it remains God's prerogative to give gifts to persons, and God will do so as he pleases, to both women and men (Joel 2:28-32; Acts 2:16-21). This general principle, as well as the Med-

---

[69]See, e.g., Walter A. Elwell and Robert W. Yarbrough, *Encountering the New Testament* (Grand Rapids: Baker, 1998), pp. 212-13.

[70]I. Howard Marshall, *New Testament Theology: Many Witnesses, One Gospel* (Downers Grove, Ill.: Inter-Varsity Press, 2004), p. 186.

[71]For a discussion of Paul's incarnational ministry practices in his adaptation of ancient rhetorical conventions, see the final chapter of Fredrick J. Long, *Ancient Rhetoric and Paul's Apology: The Compositional Unity of 2 Corinthians*, SNTSMS 131 (Cambridge: Cambridge University Press, 2004).

[72]I was first introduced to the need for evaluation of cultural versus transcultural principles in the process of biblical interpretation when learning the inductive Bible study approach of Robert A. Traina, *Methodical Bible Study* (New York: Gains and Harris, 1952; reprint, Grand Rapids: Zondervan, 2002), and taught by his student, David Bauer, at Asbury Theological Seminary. They currently are writing a sequel/revision to this seminal work.

[73]Examples of other values include delegation of shared ministry to Spirit-filled individuals (Acts 7), the inclusion of Gentiles into God's salvation plan (Acts 10), and the formation of multicultural churches who send out missionaries (Acts 11, 13). This leads, then, to obedient human responses to preach exegetically (Acts 2, 13), to have fellowship (Acts 2:41-47; 4:32-35), to pray during times of persecution (Acts 4:23-31; 12:12), to send out missionaries to the nations (Acts 13—28), and to establish networks of house churches, even in the homes of women (Acts 12:12; 16:14-15, 40).

Table 5.3. The Gift Lists: A Comprehensive Comparison of Ordering

1 Cor 12:8-10	1 Cor 12:28	1 Cor 12:29-30	1 Cor 13:1-3*	Rom 12:6-8*	Eph 4:11	1 Pet 4:10-11
	apostles	apostles			apostles	
word of wisdom	prophets	prophecy	2-prophecy	1-prophecy	prophets	speaking
word of knowledge	teachers	teaching	3-knowledge	3-teaching	evangelists	
faith	miracles	miracles	4-faith		pastor-teacher	
gifts of healings	gifts of healings	gifts of healings				
working miracles						
prophecy				4-exhortation		
discerning of spirits						
				2-serving		serving
	helping		5-giving (?)	5-giving		
	governing			6-ruling		
				7-showing mercy		
kinds of tongues	diverse tongues	tongues	1-tongues			
interpreting tongues		interpreting (tongues)		*The order in 1 Cor 13:1-3 and Rom 12:6-8 has been altered. The numbers show the original order in context.		

iterranean context of religious associations, should be brought to bear on locating Paul's specific admonitions about women/wives speaking or not speaking (1 Cor 14:34-35; but cf. 1 Cor 11:5) and teaching or not teaching (1 Tim 2:11-12).

But this brings us to other pressing questions: Do the New Testament gift lists delimit their distribution according to gender? Did Acts 2 and Joel's prophecy have any influence on Paul? And how would Paul's general principles of giftedness have been understood and have functioned socially within the Mediterranean context of women's participation in the various types of voluntary associations?

THE GIFT LISTS IN PAUL AND PETER

Paul's and Peter's presentations contain general statements about God's and Christ's and the Spirit's distribution of gifts, services and ministries that are entirely gender neutral. This is not surprising, since one-quarter of Paul's known ministry companions are women.[74] The selection, ordering and description of each gift list in Paul and Peter have been shaped by the theological perspective and rhetorical needs of each discourse. But the gift ordering is strikingly similar (see table 5.3).

There is a diversity of gifts, and we must conclude that each gift list was not intended to be comprehensive. Also, the variability of nomenclature for the description of the various religious functions, offices and leadership roles was typical in voluntary associations.[75]

I take it as axiomatic that any particular listing is determined by the situations that Paul and Peter are addressing in each instance and the perceived theological needs of the audience. For example, notice how broadly Peter casts the scope and purpose of gifts as constituting serving (*diakoneō*) one another (1 Pet 4:10). He seems to be aware of more gifts when he mentions "manifold grace of God" (*poikilēs charitos theou*) (NASB 95). Yet Peter essentially limits his discussion of the gifts to "speaking" (*laleō*) as speaking "the oracles of God" (*logia theou*)[76] and "serving" (*diakoneō*) (1 Pet 4:11). These two areas represent the classic depiction of word and deed (see Lk 24:19; Rom 15:18; Col 3:17; 1 Jn 3:18).[77]

Likewise, in Ephesians Paul describes in broad categories the ministry of the church. The church is to grow numerically (Eph 3:1-9; 4:4), morally especially in terms of love, holiness and truth (Eph 4:1-3, 12-15, 17, 24; 4:25—5:1; 5:9; 6:14), and in the knowledge of Jesus Christ (Eph 1:17; 3:14-19; 4:13). How this

---

[74]Gehring, *House Church*, p. 211.

[75]Explicit comparison to the NT gift lists (1 Cor 12:27-31) and other places in the NT passages using leadership titles (e.g., Phil 1:1; Rom 16:1; Eph 2:19-21) is made by McLean, "Agrippinilla Inscription," p. 259, and Kloppenborg, "Edwin Hatch," pp. 231-34.

[76]In the only occurrences in the NT, *logia theou* refers to Mosaic law (Acts 7:38) or Hebrew Scriptures more generally (Rom 3:2; Heb 5:12).

[77]Peter's brevity and focus on speaking may be due to his emphasis on the word of the gospel (1 Pet 1:22-25), which, when accepted, gives birth to new believers (1 Pet 1:23). Indeed, this word is the gospel proclamation (1 Pet 1:25). Peter is writing to new believers who need to be fed by the "pure milk of the word" (1 Pet 2:2). In 2 Peter, he understands clearly that young believers can be exploited by people speaking false words (2 Pet 2:3). As far as serving, Peter understood that the core trait of discipleship is serving as Christ served us (cf. Mk 10:45).

growth takes place is through the exalted Christ, who "gave gifts to persons *[anthrōpois]*" (Eph 4:8). Note that Paul (and the LXX) used the gender-inclusive noun *anthrōpois*. So, what kinds of gifted speaking leaders contribute to the growth of the church in this way? In Ephesians 4:11 these include apostles, prophets, evangelists and pastor-teachers (possibly one position because of the shared definite article). These titles would not suggest any gender restrictions, despite the fact that they are masculine forms, since masculine forms are regularly used inclusively (e.g., "brethren," *adelphoi,* or "saints," *hagioi*).[78] It is significant, too, that Paul considers the church's goal to attain to the knowledge and understanding of the Son of God, "to the mature man" (*eis andra teleion,* Eph 4:13), because the church is to grow into him since he is the head of the body (Eph 4:15), the body being the church, Christ's bride (Eph 5:23).[79]

In Romans 12:3-8, Paul describes seven gifts and the manner of their use. Although similar to the other gift lists, this particular listing is influenced by themes that Paul has emphasized in Romans (exhortation, giving, ruling and mercy—the last four gifts)[80] and the general nature of giftedness (prophecy, serving and teaching—the first three gifts). We must note the primary position of prophecy; apostleship is omitted altogether, probably because of

---

[78]Osiek ("Women in House Churches," pp. 305-6) stresses this point, but is mistaken in citing *diakonos* as an example of a masculine gendered term applied to a women, since *diakonos* in form is both masculine and feminine (BDAG s.v.), and there is no corresponding female equivalent. Of these positions of giftedness used in Eph 4:11, only *prophet* (*prophētēs*) has a feminine role counterpart *prophetess* (*prophētis*). The fact that only the masculine *prophet* (*prophētēs*) is used here and not additionally *prophetess* (*prophētis*) is due to the gender-inclusive nature of the masculine noun. In Eph 2:20 and Eph 3:5 Paul had already used the plural forms of both *apostles* and *prophets,* to indicate the foundation laid in the preaching of the gospel. It is unlikely that Paul would have necessarily meant to exclude women from these groups, since he refers to a woman as an apostle in Rom 16:7 (Junias), probably knew of Philip's daughters as prophetesses (Acts 21:9), affirmed the prophesying of women (1 Cor 11:5), and was likely aware of the implication of Joel's prophecy for the ongoing ministry of the church. See discussion of Joel 2 in 1 Cor below.

[79]I understand the prepositional phrase as functioning appositionally to the Son of God (*tou huiou tou theou*) as a restatement of the purpose to what the church is to attain.

[80]During the course of the letter, Paul exhorted them (*parakaleō,* Rom 12:1; 15:30; 16:17) speaking boldly on certain matters (Rom 15:15). Paul's inclusion of giving (*metadidōmi*) relates to his example of giving (Rom 1:11) which is in turn related to receiving fruit (*karpos*) from the Romans (Rom 1:13), by which Paul probably has in mind their financial gift of support (cf. Phil 4:17; Rom 15:28) for his future missionary work to Spain (Rom 15:24). Ruling (*proistēmi*) would relate to Paul's discussion of submitting to the governing authorities in Rom 13. Finally, Paul's inclusion of giving mercy (*eleeō*) fits quite naturally, since he has elaborated extensively on God's acting mercifully (*eleeō,* Rom 9:15, 18; 11:30-32) and bestowing mercy (*eleos,* Rom 9:23; 11:31; 15:9; cf. *oiktirmos,* "compassion," Rom 12:1). This may have the added benefit of bringing healing between those strong and weak in faith (Rom 14—15).

Paul's sensitivity to the issue of missionary turf (see Rom 15:20-23). As in Ephesians and 1 Peter, there are no gender restrictions whatsoever, here or throughout Romans.[81] Paul speaks to *everyone* (*panti*, Rom 12:3); God allotted a measure of faith to *each person* (*hekastō*, Rom 12:3); there are *many members* in one body (*en heni sōmati polla melē*, Rom 12:4); all members (*ta . . . melē panta*, Rom 12:4) do not function the same; but the many are one body (*hoi polloi hen sōma*, Rom 12:5) and members of one another (*heis allēlōn*, Rom 12:5).

GIFTS IN 1 CORINTHIANS

These first gift lists treated above really serve to accentuate the uniqueness of Paul's extensive treatment of gifts and gifted individuals in 1 Corinthians 12—14. Although chapters 12—14 cohere around the inclusion of "spiritual" (*pneumatikos*) and "to be ignorant" (*agnoeō*) at the beginning and ending of the unit (1 Cor 12:1; 14:37-38), there is some reason thematically and structurally to include chapter 11 with chapters 12—14, since the corporate worship setting is in view.[82]

Looking at the beginning of 1 Corinthians 11, some interpreters are puzzled why Paul should begin to praise the Corinthians for remembering him "in everything" (*panta*) and for holding on to the traditions, when he quickly began to correct their behavior in the successive two units (1 Cor 11:3-16, 17-32). In the first section, Paul admonished married women to be properly veiled; and even more harshly, in 1 Corinthians 11:17-32 he confronted the Corinthians concerning improprieties of drunkenness and social segregation during the Lord's Supper.[83] So what tradition was in Paul's mind? And what was the basis for Paul's praise of the Corinthians?

To begin then, Anthony C. Thiselton rightly summarizes to what tradi-

---

[81]In Romans an analogy is made of a woman, who, after bereaved of her husband (the Law) in death, is now able to marry another man. This speaks to believers who are able to be joined to Christ (7:2-4).

[82]See Kenneth E. Bailey, "The Structure of 1 Corinthians and Paul's Theological Method with Special Reference to 4:17," *NovT* 25 (1983): 170-73.

[83]Fee, *Corinthians*, 499 n.29, is less certain about the contents of the traditions, admitting that traditions (*paradoseis*) more than likely refers to "'traditions' that have to do with worship." But, oddly, Fee does not consider that the Corinthians are observing any tradition successfully: "although he commends them for 'keeping the traditions,' nonetheless in what follows in chaps. 11-14 there does not seem to be a single instance of their doing so; indeed, in 11:17-34 they are doing anything but" (p. 500).

tions Paul refers: "*Many commentators believe that the tradition for which Paul commends the readers is the eschatological inclusion of men and women as active participants in prayer and prophetic speech*" (italics are Thiselton's).[84] This eschatological tradition is none other than the Pentecost tradition of Acts 2 and Joel's prophecy. Such a view garners support from three considerations. First, Paul uniquely needed to address speaking in tongues/languages as a problem in the Corinthian worship. In no other place in the New Testament is tongue-speaking treated; yet it is featured primarily in Acts 2. Second, within 1 Corinthians Paul has alluded to Joel's prophecy (Joel 2:32 [MT 3:5]; found also in Acts 2:21; Rom 10:13): "with all those calling upon the name of our Lord Jesus Christ in every place, theirs and ours" (1 Cor 1:2b).[85] Thiselton observes that the reference to "the day of the Lord" in 1 Corinthians 1:7-8 makes the allusion more probable.[86] Additionally, Thiselton sees a relationship with 1 Corinthians 12:3 where calling on the name of the Lord is equivalent to confessing "Jesus is Lord."[87] These correlations increase the likelihood that Paul has Joel's prophecy in mind in 1 Corinthians 11—14. Third, it is likely that the Corinthians were inspired with renewed enthusiasm by the visit of some missionary teacher after Paul left Corinth, either Cephas or Apollos or both (cf. 1 Cor 1:12; 3:22), and this enthusiasm may very well have prompted them to reenact in worship the Pentecost experience in order to legitimate their own spiritual status.[88] Paul's task, then, was to remind the Corinthians that the purpose of giftedness, especially speaking in languages, is to build up the church, both in terms of eliciting confession

---

[84]So, Anthony C. Thiselton, *The First Epistle to the Corinthians*, NIGTC (Grand Rapids; Eerdmans, 2000), p. 811.

[85]So the Eberhard Nestle and Kurt Aland, ed., *Novum Testamentum Graece*, 26th ed. (Stuttgart: Deutsche Bibelgesellschaft, 1979), pp. 440, 767, lists Joel 3:5 as an allusion; so too Seim, *Double Message*, p. 170.

[86]Thiselton, *First Corinthians*, p. 78.

[87]Ibid., p. 79.

[88]If Peter was the inspiration, this was because he was present at Pentecost. If Apollos, then it was because of his recent education about matters of the Spirit before coming to Corinth (Acts 18:25-26, "knowing only the baptism of John"), bringing also his rhetorical expertise and his baptismal fervor to Corinth (Acts 18:24-25), perhaps successfully baptizing a number of the Corinthians (1 Cor 3:4-8, "Paul planted and Apollos watered"), resulting in Paul's need to defend his baptismal record (1 Cor 1:14-17) and relatively poor speech (1 Cor 2:1-4). In either case, the Corinthians may have been rather enamored with Peter or Apollos as teachers resulting in the devaluing of their esteem of Paul, thus requiring Paul to defend himself in 1 Corinthians 1—4 and 9. For a reconstruction of the Corinthians criticism of Paul as contained in the Corinthian correspondences, see Long, *Ancient Rhetoric*, chap. 7.

and conversion (resulting in one saying "Jesus is Lord," 1 Cor 12:3; or worshiping God, 1 Cor 14:24-25) and in terms of moral growth and fortification (1 Cor 14:3, 5, 26). Paul argued that the intelligible gift of prophecy best supported these ends, rather than unintelligible speaking in tongues (1 Cor 14:1-25).

So, why did Paul praise the Corinthians? *Because they rightly held to the tradition and allowed for women to be active participants as ones who pray and prophesy in Christian worship.* Returning to 1 Corinthians 11, let me offer a partial reconstruction of the situation. Paul praised the Corinthians for following the tradition (Joel's prophecy and Peter's sermon in Acts 2) that he had already passed along about men and women prophesying. And the women in turn had quite appropriately prophesied in the Corinthian church. In this Paul praised them, because they remembered him "in everything." Paul, thus, completely affirmed the prophetic gifting of women in the Corinthian church (1 Cor 11:5). So important is prophecy that Paul placed it second only to apostleship in the ordering of the gifts (1 Cor 12:28), and Paul urged them all to seek to prophesy (1 Cor 14:1, 5, 24).[89]

To place this scenario within the milieu of Greco-Roman religious associations becomes even more suggestive. It was common for pagan devotees to perform reenactments of the foundational story associated with their deity (e.g., Dionysius, Aphrodite, Prometheus, Serapis).[90] I would argue that the Corinthians may have understood Joel's prophecy and the events of Pentecost as the foundation story of the emerging Christian assembly. However, their attempts at reenactment went amiss, because of an overemphasis on speaking in (ecstatic) tongues at the expense of intelligible speech. To rectify this, Paul reminded the Corinthians of being "led astray" in their past pagan involvement in idol worship, in which Paul specifies that the idols were "mute" (1 Cor 12:2), thus pointing to the fact that humans spoke for these "mute" (*aphōna*) idols, often in ecstatic utterances either as enigmatic riddles or unintelligible speech. The pagan religious philosopher Iamblichus explained how various religious "signs" (*sēmeia*) were sought after in order to legitimate one's spiritual experience. One sign was ecstatic utterances of var-

---

[89]That Paul should order the gifts is not accidental, and that he puts apostles first is quite strategic given the Corinthian disesteem toward him such that he needed to defend his apostleship in 1 Cor 4; 9.

[90]See Harland, *Associations, Synagogues*, pp. 46, 60, 71, 73; McLean, "Agrippinilla Inscription," p. 259.

ious kinds.[91] So, given the Corinthians' prior involvement in idol worship, to which Paul drew their attention in 1 Corinthians 12:2, it is likely that the Corinthians were mixing pagan worship practices (ecstatic religious vocalizations) with their Christian worship and the intelligible languages gift described in Acts 2.

In response to this confusion, Paul established a proper theology of the various types of gifts, services and manifestations as originating from the same triune God (1 Cor 12:4-6, rather than from diverse spirits or gods) and their relative and mutually interdependent functioning in the church body (1 Cor 12). At the same time, Paul sought to redirect the Corinthians' "zealousness for spirits" (*zēlōtai este pneumatōn*, 1 Cor 14:12a) to the pursuit of love (1 Cor 13) and to prophesying, because prophesying is intelligible speech that can lead to edification (1 Cor 14:3, 5, 12b, 24-26). All of this is to say, that for Paul to praise the Corinthian women for prophesying is no small thing. This was exactly what he would have preferred all the Corinthians to be doing (1 Cor 14:1, 5, 24, 31, 39).

Finally, as with the other gift lists in the New Testament, in 1 Corinthians 12—14 Paul places no gender restriction on the distribution and operation of the gifts. The gifts are given to each one (*hekastos*) as the Spirit wills (1 Cor 12:7-11); all are members (*panta ta melē*) baptized into one body (1 Cor 12:12-13) and individually members (*melē ek merous*) of the body of Christ (1 Cor 12:27). The members, each one of them (*ta melē, hen hekaston*

---

[91]Iamblichus's description of pagan divine possession in *On the Mysteries* 3.5 (late 3rd century) uses significantly similar terminology and provides an analogy to what the Corinthians probably had considered typical religious expression prior to converting to Christianity.

There are many different kinds [*eidē*] of divine possession, and there are different ways of awakening the divine spirit; consequently there are many different signs [*ta polla sēmeia*] of this state. For one thing, there are different gods [*hoi theoi*] from whom we receive the spirit [i.e., are inspired = *epipneometha*] and this results in a variety of forms in which the inspiration manifests itself; further, the kinds of influence exerted are different, and so there are various ways in which the divine seizure takes place. . . .

Hence the signs of possession [*ta sēmeia tōn epipneomenōn*] are manifold: either movement of the body and its parts, or complete relaxation; (either) singing choirs, round dances, and harmonious voices, or the opposite of these. (The) bodies have been seen to rise up, grow, or move freely in the air, and the opposite has also been observed. They have been heard to utter (different) voices of equal strength, or with great diversity and inequality, in tones that alternated with silence; and again in other cases harmonious crescendo or diminuendo of tone, and in still other cases other kinds of utterance.

This translation is from Frederick C. Grant, *Hellenistic Religions: The Age of Syncretism,* The Library of Liberal Arts (Indianapolis: Bobbs-Merrill, 1953), p. 174.

autōn), are arranged as God wills (1 Cor 12:18); and, one and all (*kath' hena pantes*) offer gifts of ministry to unbelievers and to one another (1 Cor 14:24, 26, 31).[92]

CONCLUSION

I have attempted to provide a biblical theological basis for understanding women in ministry within the context of spiritual gifts as described in Joel, Acts, Paul and Peter. Joel's prophecy about women receiving the Spirit and prophesying is quoted foundationally at the initial outpouring of the Holy Spirit at Pentecost. The event is the foundation story of the new Christian community. Joel's prophecy builds upon Moses' desire and vision that all of God's people receive his Spirit and prophesy. In the context of the book of Numbers, Moses was directed by God to select *leaders* on whom he would send his Spirit. This Old Testament event is transformed by Joel's prophecy to involve gifted women in leadership. The prophecy's fulfillment at Pentecost in the book of Acts demonstrates that gifted women are now in ministry in the new covenant. However, Luke was reticent to record these women speaking, even though the narrative depicts them conducting ministry, being persecuted along with men (Acts 8:3; 9:2; 22:4), and fulfilling various levels of leadership roles (prophesying, running house churches, teaching). Luke's reluctance is to be understood as an accommodation to Roman mores about new foreign superstitions and religious movements.

Turning to the New Testament gift lists in Peter and Paul revealed no gender restrictions whatsoever. Considered in light of the Greco-Roman milieu of increased Roman women's freedom and participation in voluntary associations, one cannot argue that Paul assumed gender restrictions on the use of gifts or the roles associated with them. Men and women then certainly would not have. Rather, the principles of God's distribution of gifts and the leadership roles of Christian ministry derived exegetically from these passages (1 Pet 4; Rom 12; Eph 4; 1 Cor 12; Acts 2) should provide the theological basis for constructing a biblical theology of women in ministry.

---

[92] It is of no consequence that Paul omits "male and female" from the baptismal formula in 1 Cor 12:13, because it is readily assumed from the context of 1 Cor 11:11. Thiselton (*First Corinthians*, p. 998) commenting on 1 Cor 12:13, apparently mistakenly includes the pairing of male and female in his discussion, so accustomed is Thiselton to Paul's phraseology and thinking: "The **all** and the reference to transcending the Jew-Gentile, male-female, slave-free divisions of Paul's day reflect the reference to baptism in Gal. 3:27-28" (emphasis Thiselton's).

I have intentionally avoided mentioning Paul's own ministry practice of encouraging his women coworkers to function as leaders within the *ekklēsia*,[93] which Cotter considers to have been "countercultural activity."[94] Indeed, philosophically Paul's liberating stance toward woman ranks along with Jesus' and one of Paul's contemporaries, the eclectic Stoic philosopher Musonius Rufus, the Roman Socrates.[95] Paul understood that such women had received gifts from "one and the same Spirit, who allots to each one individually just as the Spirit chooses" (1 Cor 12:11). He along with Moses would agree: Would that all God's people were full of his Spirit and prophesy!

---

[93]Paul repeatedly affirmed the giftedness and ministry of a dozen women as deaconesses (Phoebe, Rom 16:1), leaders of home churches (Lydia, Acts 16:14-15, 40; Chloe, 1 Cor 1:11; Nympha, Col 4:15), coworkers (Priscilla, Rom 16:3; Euodia and Syntyche, Phil 4:2-3), one as a patroness (Phoebe, Rom 16:2) and one even as an apostle (Junia, Rom 16:7).

[94]Cotter, "Women's Authority Roles." See also E. A. Judge, "Paul as a Radical Critic of Society," *Interchange* 16 (1974): 191-203.

[95]See Klassen, "Musonius Rufus," and E. A. Judge, "Paul as a Radical Critic," pp. 198-203.

PART THREE

NEW THEOLOGICAL PERSPECTIVES ON IDENTITY AND MINISTRY

RECONCILIATION AS THE DOGMATIC LOCATION OF HUMANITY

"Your Life Is Hidden with Christ in God"

Mark Husbands

CHRISTIAN DOGMATICS IS HUMAN ACTION TAKEN up in glad obedience to the living God of the gospel. Dogmatics glorifies God by setting this gospel before the church in such a way as to promote judgments that conform to the pattern and freedom of divine self-revelation. In order to do this, dogmatics takes up both a critical and constructive posture in relation to the church. It aids the well-being and life of the church by setting forth in her midst patterns of disciplined and faithful reflection on Holy Scripture. Confessing that Jesus Christ is the proper and definitive subject matter of the whole of Scripture, dogmatic theology seeks first and foremost to draw the church's speech, worship and ministry into faithful correspondence to the living and prophetic action of the risen Lord. As an instance of dogmatic theology, this chapter seeks to direct our attention to the gospel's claim on us in Scripture's language of the renewal of human personhood in divine reconciliation.

Christian dogmatics, however, serves a necessarily critical role when the church resists the discipline of the Word, when patterns of judgment and practice emerge that demonstrate an unwillingness to abide disciplined obedience to the Word. As a faith rooted in history, we must openly acknowledge the fact that growth in wisdom and faithfulness is often a painful and extended process: seldom do we ever reach clarity on issues of great importance quickly and with ease. To speak of our history as a history of redemption, however, is to signal an awareness that we are, like Israel, a people whose history is not imposed on it by existing norms, but are a people whose history is still being written. We properly regard ourselves as being caught up in the judgment and reconciliation of.God.

At the very beginning of the struggle between the German church and the rise of National Socialism, Dietrich Bonhoeffer saw that in this conflict, the gospel is the only real weapon given to the church by which she might defend herself. Not incidentally, the question of ecumenical unity is given considerable prominence in Bonhoeffer's work, as it directly pertains to the possibility of the church speaking with one voice against forces of evil. Bonhoeffer's investment in this question is patently on display in his warning that we can and must only speak as the church. To do so is to herald the truth of the gospel, to bear the moral obligation of truthfulness. As Bonhoeffer expressed it, "we may not play with the truth, or else it will destroy us," for "here we are on the edge of the abyss."[1]

While I will return to this 1932 lecture on the theological basis of ecumenical confession, I want to turn our attention, however briefly, to a rather different comment by Bonhoeffer—one that bears directly on the concerns of this volume and the broader question of the church's stance with respect to the full participation of the ministry of women in the church:

> The church must be able to say the Word of God, the word of authority, here and now, in the most concrete way possible, from knowledge of the situation. The church may not therefore preach timeless principles however true, but only commandments which are true today. God is "always" *God* to us "*today*."[2]

This passage shows Bonhoeffer's eagerness to push the church toward the recognition that theology is "the church's self-understanding of its own nature on the basis of its understanding of the revelation of God in Christ," to which he adds, "this self-understanding of necessity always begins where there is a new trend in the church's understanding of itself."[3] Although the church must always stand under such judgment, in order to speak the Word of God now, the question of the public ministry of women is not in fact a new question for

---

[1] Dietrich Bonhoeffer, *No Rusty Swords; Letters, Lectures, and Notes, 1928-1936, from the Collected Works of Dietrich Bonhoeffer* (London: Collins, 1965), p. 172.
[2] Ibid., p. 162.
[3] Ibid., p. 158.

evangelical Christians, as the work of my colleague Timothy Larsen has ably demonstrated.[4] However, the fact that much of our positive history on the question of women in ministry stands in the shadow of contemporary debate suggests how important it is to set this issue within a larger frame.

The issue that stands before us is one of obedience and faithfulness to the witness of God. Put differently, the existence of conflict on the question of women in ministry presents us with an occasion to reflect on and derive a renewed sense of our identity as God's people. This chapter provides a self-critically *dogmatic* reading of holy Scripture in which the command of God is heard within a particular context. Discernment, accordingly, does not occur apart from the task of seeking to attend to patterns of judgment that emerge out of the church's reading of holy Scripture as she faithfully seeks to engage in a critical and ongoing assessment of the history of the church and the corresponding history of her reception and interpretation of the meaning of Scripture. Likewise, dogmatics must also demonstrate attention not only to the development of doctrine, but also to the contemporary question of Does the church hear and live out the gospel *today*? I say this if only to indicate the tall order that stands before us in our shared attempt to better understand God's command for the church with respect to women in ministry. This chapter, as such, is no more than a modest contribution to the task of offering a dogmatic reflection upon the nature of ministry and human personhood. In short, I am seeking to do no more than cast a tiny bit of light on the question of how the identity of human personhood bears upon Christian ministry and witness, in full knowledge of the fact that so much more needs to be done.

The following argument begins with a brief reflection on the topic of ordained, or as I will put it, "ordered" ministry. I shall then proceed to offer an account of human personhood as "being-in-encounter," where I introduce the subject of a relational or covenant ontology of grace. The third section of this chapter is dedicated to the task of showing the problematic nature of the appeal to "orders of creation." In the penultimate section of the argument, I take up a discussion of the relationship between reconciliation, baptism and Christ, leaving me to draw things together with a brief comment on Paul's assertion in Colossians 3:3 that our life is "hidden in Christ." We shall argue that entrance

---

[4]Cf. Timothy Larsen's contribution to this volume, chap. 10 "Women in Public Ministry: A Historic Evangelical Distinctive."

into the public ministry of the church rests on the prior and constitutive activity of God: the culturally and religiously transgressive nature of the gospel is patently on display in the recognition that baptism is an event that sets women in relation to Christ in precisely the same way that it does for men. This chapter argues the thesis that when the question of human identity is set within the dogmatic location of the reconciliation, the commitment to the full public ministry of women in the church properly follows from their common entrance into the covenant of grace through God's constitutive and redemptive action in Christ.

THE QUESTION OF "ORDERED" MINISTRY

If Oliver O'Donovan is correct in his belief that "epochs are characterized not by positions but by debates" such that "it is the way they state their disagreements . . . that binds the thinkers of any age together,"[5] then we need to ask whether the debate among complementarians and egalitarians is truly worth having. It is not that the debate in question fails to bring our attention to matters of consequence, but rather, the problem lies in the fact that the terms of reference have been so misplaced. How often in the course of this debate are we reminded of the really basic questions? How central to the question of "ordered" ministry is the affirmation that Christ is the head of the church? Is ministry understood to be service and witness to the gospel by those who have been born of Word and Spirit? Put differently, does this controversy truly cast light on the fact that it is the living Word, not creaturely self-assertion, who constitutes the being of the church? Is Christ the center and ground of Christian proclamation and witness or has this question been displaced in our consideration of exegetical, historical or dogmatic concerns?

As I seek to demonstrate, the question of the full participation and service of women in the ministry of the church deserves great care, if for no other reason than the fact that Christianity breaks with Judaism on the question of circumcision. The issue of gender stands near the beginning of the Christian life because women and men enter into relation with Christ on precisely the same grounds. Picking up the thread of an earlier remark, if the task of dogmatic theology is one of seeking to glorify God by setting forth the gospel in a man-

---

[5]Oliver O'Donovan, *The Desire of the Nations: Rediscovering the Roots of Political Theology* (New York: Cambridge University Press, 1996), p. 9.

ner that promotes judgments that conform to the command of God, then we need clarity vis-à-vis the constitutive basis on which the church founds her doctrine of ministry.

In the New Testament, for instance, the apostolate is a collection of followers of Christ who have been empowered to exercise disciplinary power and judgment, calling the church to faithfulness.[6] Along such lines, we need to be reminded of the fact that when ministry is understood as being something far more than teaching, but as creaturely and ordered work in the service of public worship and liturgy, the "ordered" minister occupies much more than a simply administrative or exegetical post; he or she lives under the burden of having to address the church in the name of the Lord. The proclamation of the divine Word is a task that lies strictly beyond the innate capacity of any human creature, male or female. The only true basis of a life of service in the ministry of Word and sacrament lies in the order and freedom of God alone.

Hans Urs von Balthasar captures the sense of all this when he points out that the church does not exist by virtue of her *charism,* but only exists on the basis of having been accosted by the divine Word. Drawing out the implications of this dogmatic claim for an understanding of ordered ministry, von Balthasar states:

> This is the first quality that the priest I am looking for would have to have; for he would have to be a priest, or at any rate he would have to have been commissioned and authorized from above, by Christ, to confront me with God's incarnate word in such a manner that I can be sure that it is not I who am making use of it; I have to know that I have not from the very outset emasculated it by psychologizing, interpreting, demythologizing it away to such an extent that it can no longer create in me what it wills.[7]

How often do we set before the church the claim that ordered ministry is first and foremost a matter of *divine* commission? By extension, we must recognize that Christian ministry is neither a matter of self-appointment, nor is it strictly a function of the church's sacramental or charismatic office. The church may aspire to do no more than petition the Spirit to descend on and anoint the candidate for ministry, knowing all along that her work is no more than that of

---

[6]Rowan Williams, "Women and the Ministry: A Case for Theological Seriousness," in *Feminine in the Church,* ed. Monica Furlong (London: SPCK, 1984), p. 13.

[7]Hans Urs von Balthasar, *Elucidations* (London, SPCK, 1975), p. 107, cited in Williams, "Women and the Ministry," pp. 12-13.

acknowledgment, petition and thanksgiving. This view corresponds to von Balthasar's judgment that one of the most important qualifications for ministry is an openness to serve rather than master holy Scripture. Ordered ministry, as such, is not a matter of providing singularly direct and assertive leadership or judgment concerning the meaning of the text. Rather, it is a matter of modesty and faithfulness in the wake of a commission to proclaim the gospel. In all of this, we ought to remember that women rather than men were the first to receive the epiphany and were subsequently commissioned by the risen Lord to proclaim the good news of the resurrection. This alone ought to leave an indelible mark on our understanding of ministry: God first appointed women to proclaim the gospel to the apostles.

HUMAN PERSONHOOD AS "BEING-IN-ENCOUNTER"

I want us to take up the question of human personhood as "being-in-encounter" with the following claim: for the Christian, self-knowledge must be an act of discipleship.[8] The term *discipleship* is employed here in order to draw attention to the fact that when it comes to the question of personhood, we must be willing to set aside any confidence we might have in the belief that we accurately know ourselves and the world apart from Christ. It is not insignificant that Paul declares it is Jesus Christ who stands as the one in whom "all things in heaven and on earth were created, things visible and invisible, whether thrones or dominions or rulers or powers—all things have been created through him and for him. He himself is before all things, and in him all things hold together" (Col 1:16-17). Far from diminishing the importance of created reality, the essential point of Paul's teaching here is to point us toward recognizing the preeminence of Christ in all things. In following Paul's lead, we are able to draw together two related claims: (1) creation and redemption are fulfilled in Christ, with the result that (2) we may read the Genesis narrative in anticipation of the full disclosure of humanity in Jesus Christ, the true Adam. With this in view, let us first turn to the work Irenaeus, and then to the creation narrative in Genesis.

Irenaeus, bishop of Lyons, is one of the earliest and most remarkable figures in the history of Christianity. The significance of his work, in part, lies in the way he resolves the apparent tension between creation and redemption by focusing his attention on the person and work of Christ. In what is both the first

---

[8]Karl Barth, *Church Dogmatics,* 3/2:53.

theological textbook of the church and at the same time a commanding account of divine reconciliation, *Adversus omnes haereses (Against Heresies)*, we find an extended theological treatise on the opening chapter of Ephesians. In book 3.18 of *Against Heresies* we are given a concise statement of Irenaeus's classic doctrine of recapitulation. Here he presents the significance of the incarnation and the work of Christ in the following manner: "but when he became incarnate, and was made man, he commenced afresh the long line of human beings, and furnished us, in a brief comprehensive manner, with salvation; so that what we had lost in Adam—namely, to be according to the image and likeness of God—that we might recover in Christ Jesus."[9] Insisting on the coherence of all of reality in the incarnate Word, Irenaeus not only secures the integrity of Jesus, but he also establishes the ground of human flourishing in Christ.[10] According to Irenaeus, not only does the incarnate Word furnish us with salvation, but in doing so, he restores to us the possibility of human existence—human existence, that is, "according to the image and likeness of God." The significance of all of this for our understanding of the *imago Dei* is spelled out with some care by Douglas Farrow, who maintains that "here is a noteworthy treatment of the *imago Dei* which eschews the rationalism of the Greek tradition for a relational ontology based on the gift of the Spirit."[11] In a piece of remarkably perceptive analysis, Farrow draws out the implications of Irenaeus's account of the economic work of the "two hands" of God, Word and Spirit:

> We are not surprised, then, to find that Irenaeus also provided a pneumatological exposition of recapitulation. If Jesus is head of the human race from Adam to the last generation, if indeed he is lord of all creation, it is as and because the Spirit lends to that creation a perichoretic form of existence which is centered on him. Conversely, if creation becomes fruitful and fecund, flourishing in all its particulars as God intended it to, it is because through Christ the waters of the Spirit flow upon it.[12]

It is evident that one of the most important contributions Irenaeus makes to our present argument stems from his claim that communion and fellowship

---

[9]Irenaeus *Against Heresies* 3.18.1 (*Ante-Nicene Fathers* 1).

[10]Douglas Farrow, *Ascension and Ecclesia: On the Significance of the Doctrine of the Ascension for Ecclesiology and Christian Cosmology* (Edinburgh: T & T Clark, 1999), p. 55.

[11]Ibid., p. 59.

[12]Ibid., p. 60.

with God is only possible on the basis of the prior and constitutive work of the triune God. The way to capture all of this is to speak of human existence and flourishing in terms of a "relational ontology." Doing so, however, requires that we turn our backs on an essentialist ontology where existence is thought to be an essential property of the human person. A relational ontology, on the other hand, is one that comprehends existence in terms of the ongoing creative and sustaining work of the triune God. To "exist" in this sense is to find oneself already drawn into a living encounter with Christ, the one in whom, according to Luke, "we live and move and have our being" (Acts 17:28).

With all of this in place, let us turn our attention to the second creation narrative in the book of Genesis in order to better comprehend the way in which holy Scripture fractures anew our grasp and language of creaturely life as a life of fellowship and relation. As we shall see, the creation narratives in the book of Genesis represent the way in which the basic form of humanity is that of "being-in-encounter" or, put more simply, human life as "co-humanity."

I have chosen to concentrate my attention on the second of the two creation narratives in Genesis given the fact that feminist scholars often find this account to be most problematic. It is generally held that this material is harmful to women for three basic reasons. First, it appears to accord metaphysical priority to the male gender on the grounds that man is created first. Second, a distinction is usually drawn on the basis of the constitutive matter out of which they are created: where man is created out of the dust, woman is fashioned out of the side of man. And finally, woman is called a "helper" of Adam, a term that has customarily been interpreted to mean that Eve is Adam's subordinate, adjunct or mere assistant, and certainly not his equal. Although a thorough response to all three of these objections would be profitable, let us simply take this third issue and see if sufficient light can be brought to bear on the meaning of the term *helper* in order to better understand the meaning of a relational ontology. For if woman does not in fact genuinely correspond to man, then the overall force of our thesis would be severely threatened.

Our positive anthropology would flounder if the creation narrative of Genesis 2:4-25 required the affirmation of a substantial and ontological difference between man and woman. I will show that a close reading of this biblical text does not in fact support the argument for an essential difference between male and female. To do so I have entered into conversation with the work of Charlotte von

Kirschbaum, who correctly argues that when the text declares that "It is not good that the man should be alone; I will make him a helper as his partner" (Gen 2:18), a window is thrown open on the question of woman. Far from speaking of the priority and privilege of man, von Kirschbaum wisely underscores the way in which the biblical text presses us to recognize that it is Adam who, alone, fails to recognize his own identity and is placed into a sleep only to awaken with the very possibility of his human identity standing before him.

As von Kirschbaum indicates, Eve is the one in whom Adam comes to recognize the meaning of human identity and fellowship: "God created not a solitary human being," she writes, "but human beings in relationship, that is, in a manner corresponding to his own nonsolitariness. He placed human beings in a mode of existence similar to his own. Existing then as male and female together, human beings are made in the image of God."[13] The meaning of divine intention rests in part on the full meaning of the Hebrew word ʿ*ēzer* a term often rendered into English as "helper" or "partner." To call Eve ʿ*ēzer* does not convey the sense that she was ordained to be nothing more than a mere adjunct, subordinate or aide. We know, for instance, that the term ʿ*ēzer* is generally employed to speak of God. In effect, this term captures the way in which, out of one's abundance, one has the capacity to turn and meet the needs of someone else. In the biblical text, this "other" or corresponding partner is Israel; one who, in a condition of weakness or brokenness, desperately needs the care and love of her ʿ*ēzer*, God. In the Old Testament, time and time again God exercises divine mercy and strength for the sake of Israel. Perhaps one of the most poignant examples of this appears in Psalm 72:12 where as the ʿ*ēzer* of God's people, God acts on behalf of the broken and oppressed in order to restore justice, life and freedom:

> For he delivers the needy when they call,
>   the poor and those who have no helper.
> He has pity on the weak and the needy,
>   and saves the lives of the needy.
> From oppression and violence he redeems their life;
>   and precious is their blood in his sight. (Ps 72:12-14)

---

[13]Charlotte von Kirschbaum, *The Question of Woman: The Collected Writings of Charlotte von Kirschbaum*, trans. John Shepherd, edited and with an introduction by Eleanor Jackson (Grand Rapids: Eerdmans, 1999), p. 56.

When we allow the broader canonical depiction of this term to shape our understanding of this second creation narrative, we are better able to reconsider a passage of Scripture that has been customarily read in ways that accord privilege, status and authority to men over against women. The force of the term ʿēzer is even more provocative once you consider the addition of the Hebrew word kĕnegdô. Charlotte von Kirschbaum was aided in coming to see the full sense of this phrase by reading the German translation of Genesis 2:18 in the Zurich Bible. Here the Hebrew phrase ʾeʿĕśeh-lô ʿēzer kĕnegdô (I will make a helper as his partner) is rendered in German as *eine Gehilfe schaffen, die ihm ein Gegenüber sei*. In translating the Hebrew text in this way, the Zurich Bible has captured what is often missed in English. The German word *Gegenüber,* which is roughly equivalent to the English word "helper" or "partner," conveys the rich sense of the Hebrew phrase ʿēzer kĕnegdô and suggests that Eve is to Adam something on the order of a "protagonist," "counterpart," "sparring partner" or even "sounding board."[14] The phrase ʿēzer kĕnegdô, therefore, conveys a sense of the fundamental equality, correspondence and reciprocity of Eve with Adam. For this reason, von Kirschbaum properly claims that apart from his encounter with Eve, Adam does not possess self-understanding or identity; in the midst of all that God has provided for him in creation; apart from Eve, Adam is alone. Von Kirschbaum writes:

> Adam . . . is thus only a passive participant: the "helper" is not his doing. He does not awaken until she is already standing there before him, a human being like himself, but not himself, in whom he recognizes himself, not as a replica of himself, but as a mysterious yet infinitely intimate "other," someone whom he can recognize only as a "helper" God brought to him, whom he cannot continue to view as an object in his surroundings, whom he can encounter only as a "Thou," as a fellow human being in the closest, most intimate, form. This is what woman means for man. And man "recognizes" her. . . . In the encounter with woman he becomes man.[15]

It ought to be recognized that in the course of seeking to provide a more accurate understanding of the phrase ʿēzer kĕnegdô, von Kirschbaum has effectively subverted the traditional reading of this narrative. In this second creation narrative, Eve is not regarded as a being subordinate to Adam, but rather

---

[14]Cf. the discussion of the issues pertaining to the German translation of ʿēzer in Eleanor Jackson's introduction to von Kirschbaum's *Collected Writings*, pp. 23-24.

[15]Ibid., pp. 58-59.

is a full and genuine partner to Adam. Alone, he lacks a complete sense of his own being. His identity as a human person rests entirely on the creative work and gracious provision of God. In short, for Adam to be properly human, he must encounter and recognize Eve as his *ʿēzer kĕnegdô*—a fitting counterpart, sounding-board or sparing partner.

Given our earlier consideration of the theological significance of a relational ontology, our present exegesis of this creation narrative ought to be seen as providing further biblical warrant for the claim that the meaning of human personhood does not lie in the affirmation of an ontological asymmetry between male and female. Rather, we have seen that in his encounter with Eve, Adam comes to recognize that human identity is manifest in relation to another. It is instructive to note, underscore and remember that in this being-in-encounter, Eve is much more than simply the passive subordinate to Adam. Eve stands before Adam and only in her presence does he come to understand the full meaning and possibility of his own human existence. *Together* they represent the actuality of human fellowship, life and correspondence. Far from being an occasion for the common reduction of human identity to gender, von Kirschbaum's reading of this material enables us to construct an account of human identity in which the broader meaning and possibility of human existence is revealed. This is precisely the realization that the language of a relational ontology or covenant ontology of grace is seeking to recover. In this precise sense, human flourishing requires fellowship or relation with another person, given to us by God. As such, Adam only comes to *self*-understanding in the recognition that before him exists one with whom he can properly live as a human person.

Having established that the relationship between Eve and Adam follows the gracious provision of God, rather than a function of a natural human capacity, let us now turn to the problematic question of the appeal to the "orders of creation."

THE PROBLEMATIC NATURE OF THE APPEAL TO "ORDERS OF CREATION"

Here I suggest that a number of rhetorical strategies and arguments are employed by those who wish to exclude women from public ministry. Roughly three types of argument are commonly offered in defense of this traditional exclusion of women. The decision to exclude women from ordered ministry is

often based on an appeal to (1) particular biblical texts including 1 Timothy
2:11-15; 1 Corinthians 14:33-38; and 1 Corinthians 11:2-16; or (2) the claim
that the participation of women would transgress cultural norms of propriety
and therefore cause offense to the gospel; or finally, (3) reference is occasionally made to the "order of creation." This third line of argument will occupy
our attention in this section.

A telling example of the way in which the appeal to the order of creation is
made in order to substantiate what is deemed to be a normative understanding
of the gender difference between man and woman can be found in the volume
by John Piper titled *What's the Difference? Manhood and Womanhood Defined According to the Bible*. Early on in this work we encounter the claim that "the tendency today is to stress the equality of men and women by minimizing the
unique significance of our maleness or femaleness. But this depreciation of
male and female personhood is a great loss."[16] No evidence, however, is entered into the record in support of this claim. In its place, we are offered an
unequivocal appeal to the order of creation. Piper expresses the point in the
following:

> When the Bible teaches that men and women fulfill different roles in relation to
> each other, charging man with a unique leadership role, it bases this differenti-
> ation not on temporary cultural norms but on permanent facts of creation. . . .
> In the Bible, differentiated roles for men and women are never traced back to
> the fall of man and woman into sin. Rather, the foundation of this differentiation
> is traced back to the way things were in Eden before sin warped our relation-
> ships. Differentiated roles were corrupted, not created, by the fall. They were
> created by God.[17]

At one level, John Piper is to be commended for his effort of seeking to determine the consequences of his position for relations among men and women in
the workplace. His overall proposal, however, is taken up with considerable
problems. While granting the fact that under very particular circumstances a
woman may be in a position where she bears some influence on a man in the
workplace, Piper maintains that if this relationship is to be personal, it must
also be nondirective, otherwise the male's own sense of masculinity is violated.
As Piper puts it, "to the degree that a woman's influence over man is personal

---

[16]John Piper, *What's the Difference?* (Wheaton, Ill.: Crossway, 1990), p. 14.
[17]Ibid., p. 17.

and directive it will generally offend a man's good, God-given sense of responsibility and leadership, and thus controvert God's created order."[18] The fact that no substantial evidence is put forward to support the extrapolation from a particular experience to some general norm appears to suggest that, for Piper, the universality of this "one man's experience" is self-evident. It bears noting that Piper is not alone in this appeal to the order of creation.

A classic instance of this appeal to the created order is to be found in Emil Brunner's theological anthropology, *Man in Revolt*. On the basis of an appeal to the order of creation Brunner limns the distinct character of men and women with such transparency and confidence that he is worth quoting in full:

> The man is the one who produces, he is the leader; the woman is receptive, and she preserves life; it is the man's duty to shape the new; it is the woman's duty to write it and adapt it to that which already exists. The man has to go forth and make the earth subject to him, the woman looks within and guards the hidden unity. The man must be objective and universalize, woman must be subjective and individualise; the man must build, the woman adorns; the man must conquer, the woman must tend; the man must comprehend all with his mind, the woman must impregnate all with the life of her soul. It is the duty of man to plan and to master, of the woman to understand and to unite.[19]

Quite apart from the question of how it is that Brunner came to possess this list of gender distinctives, it is crucial to see how readily he moves from *is* to *ought*.[20] The indicative, "man is the one who produces, he is the leader," migrates very quickly into the imperative, "man must conquer" or "must comprehend all with his mind." Concomitantly, the woman, who is perceived to be "receptive" and to be one who "preserves life," must "be subjective and individualise," "adorn" and "impregnate all with the life of her soul."

In light of our two examples, the fundamental problem with the appeal to creation orders does not lie in the relative arbitrariness of what is perceived to be divinely ordained as a natural order of human existence. Rather, the crucial problem lies in the fact that once something has been accorded the status of an "order of creation" then the command of God has been locked up in a static order that cannot be revised. Lying behind all of this is the awareness that such

---

[18]Ibid., p. 44.
[19]Emil Brunner, *Man in Revolt, a Christian Anthropology*, trans. Olive Wyon (New York: Scribner's Sons, 1939), p. 358.
[20]Cf. Barth, *Church Dogmatics* 3/4:152-53.

an appeal has immense potential to encode an ideology, leaving the church with no alternative but to blindly obey a given prescription as if God himself had commanded it.

To his immense credit, Bonhoeffer rejects the possibility that we might find God's commandment in the orders of creation. "There is a special danger in this argument," Bonhoeffer writes, for "just about everything can be defended by it."[21] The full force of Bonhoeffer's judgment extends to the reality of the Fall. No order of creation, Bonhoeffer maintains, has escaped the effects of sin with the result that "there is no longer any possibility of regarding any features *per se* as orders of creation and of perceiving the will of God *directly* in them."[22] The consequence of Bonhoeffer's attack on the appeal to the order of creation is that it enables him to clear away a false alternative in order to set before us the following positive assertion: "the commandment cannot stem from anywhere but the origin of promise and fulfillment, from Christ."[23] Set within the context of the shameful and bewildering submission of the German church to the ideology of "blood, race and soil," Bonhoeffer insists on the claim that "*any order*—however ancient and sacred it may be—*can be dissolved,* and must be dissolved when it closes itself up in itself, grows rigid and no longer permits the proclamation of revelation."[24] On the strength of this remark, it ought now to be clear that the church must resist the language of orders of creation, for within this appeal lies the possibility of ideology and oppression.

Let me summarize what we have accomplished thus far. If the decision to exclude women from public ministry is deemed to be less than entirely compelling given I. Howard Marshall's exegesis of 1 Timothy 2:11-15,[25] and if reference to propriety has been subverted by showing how ruinous it is to accommodate one's understanding of ministry on the grounds of ecclesial and clerical respectability,[26] and finally, if the appeal to orders of creation has been deemed problematic in light of its ideological capacity to deafen our hearing

---

[21]Bonhoeffer, *No Rusty Swords,* p. 165.

[22]Ibid., p. 166 (italics in original).

[23]Ibid.

[24]Ibid., p. 167 (italics in original).

[25]Cf. Marshall's contribution to this volume, "Women in Ministry: A Further Look at 1 Timothy 2," chapter 3.

[26]Cf. the discussion of the development and rationale for the exclusion of women from public ministry in both the African American church and fundamentalist/early evangelical traditions in Cheryl J. Sanders's "Holy Boldness, Holy Women: Agents of the Gospel" and Timothy Larsen's "Women in Public Ministry: A Historic Evangelical Distinctive" (chapters 9 and 10 of this volume).

of the divine command made known in Jesus Christ, then we find ourselves in the position of having to recast the question of human identity. Given this, we are now in a position to consider the dogmatic argument that warrants the church's acceptance of the full participation of women in public ministry. In the final section of this chapter, we shall turn yet to Scripture with a view toward understanding the way in which Christianity breaks with Judaism in its understanding of the equality of women and men.

RECONCILIATION, BAPTISM AND CHRIST

Given the overall aim of this chapter to draw the church's reflection and ministry into faithful conformity to the prophetic witness of her risen Lord, it is singularly important that when we turn to Paul's declaration in Galatians 3:28 that we do so with careful attention to the presiding issues. What problems lie behind Paul's remarkable affirmation that "there is no longer Jew or Greek, there is no longer slave or free, there is no longer male and female"? And what does it mean for Paul to say "all of you are *one* in Christ Jesus"? I want to argue that the full significance of Paul's teaching here is readily missed if we fail to see that Paul is setting in place a remarkable claim: a properly Christian doctrine of salvation is one that secures the basis on which we enter into the covenant of grace and therefore become the true family of Abraham. From Paul's day forward, Christians have properly argued that entrance into the people of God does not strictly follow from obedience to Jewish law, but is obtained in the redemptive and substitutionary atonement of Jesus Christ. This distinction follows from Paul's judgment that the natural differences between Jew and Gentile are not *decisive* when it comes to being identified as the people of God. How then does he arrive at this position, and what significance does his teaching have for our understanding of theological anthropology and the place of women in ministry? On these matters I wish to say two things.

First, it is crucial to see that Paul is astonished by the fact that the churches in Galatia have so eagerly traded away the freedom of the gospel. They have traded this away, moreover, for the putative security of another gospel. Under the influence of Jewish Christians, Gentile churches had come to believe that their right standing before God required obedience to aspects of Jewish law, including circumcision. Profoundly vexed, Paul asks "You foolish Galatians! Who has bewitched you? It was before your eyes that Jesus Christ was publicly exhibited as crucified! . . . Did you receive the Spirit by doing the works of the law or by believing what you heard? Are you so foolish? Having started with the Spirit, are you now ending with the flesh?" (Gal 3:1-3). Note here the significance of three aspects of Paul's teaching: (1) the gospel proclamation of Jesus Christ *crucified*; (2) the necessity of the gift and ongoing presence of the Spirit; and finally, (3) Paul's opposition to those who set aside life in the Spirit for life in the flesh. All of this requires Paul to oppose the efforts of those who have sought to impose on Gentile Christians the requirement to observe Jewish customs and religious practice. As I have indicated, Paul opposes this effort for a number of reasons, but among his chief concern lies the question of privileging Jewish ethnicity. A few verses later in Galatians Paul asserts with considerable force: "those who believe are the descendants of Abraham . . . those who believe are blessed with Abraham, who believed" (Gal 3:7, 9). The blessing of covenantal faithfulness and life with God comes not through obedience to the law but through Christ, so that we might be justified and receive the promise of the Spirit through faith (cf. Gal 3:7-14). On this basis, Paul ostensibly commands Gentile Christians not to rely on "the flesh" but to continue to live in the *freedom* of the gospel.

Second, Paul draws a careful parallel between two concomitant sets of categories. The opposition of flesh and Spirit mirrors the contrast that Paul draws between circumcision and baptism. In the postscript to the letter, for instance, Paul observes that "it is those who want to make a good showing in the flesh that try to compel you to be circumcised" (Gal 6:12). By way of contrast, he adds, "May I never boast of anything except the cross of our Lord Jesus Christ" (Gal 6:14). Paul is evidently placing considerable pressure on these churches to remember that true confidence before God rests entirely on the gospel of Christ. This claim is then underscored by Paul's return, yet again, to the question of circumcision, where he writes, "For neither circumcision nor uncircumcision is anything; but a new creation is everything!" (Gal 6:15). If there is any place for boasting here for Paul, it is boasting in the redemptive work of Jesus Christ. Paul's language of "new creation" is crucial as it brings into sharp relief the significance of his earlier remarks in Galatians 3:27 where we encounter the statement: "As many of you as were baptized into Christ have clothed yourselves with Christ."[27] Where

---

[27] Cf. Paul's comments in Col 2:11-12, where a contrast is drawn between circumcision in the flesh and circumcision by the Spirit and where the latter is connected to baptism.

reconciliation is tied to union with Christ, the connection between baptism and new creation is unmistakable. Accordingly, baptism and union with Christ constitute the essential backdrop against which Paul offers the staggering claim of Galatians 3:28: "There is no longer Jew or Greek, there is no longer slave or free, there is no longer male and female; for all of you are one in Christ Jesus."

It is vital to remember that the presiding issue in Paul's letter to the Galatians is circumcision. Paul counters the effort to secure a right standing before God on the basis of circumcision by admonishing the Galatian churches with the truth that only those who have been baptized into the death of Christ may be true children of the family of Abraham. As N. T. Wright comments on this material, Paul opposed the rite of circumcision not only because it accorded privilege and status to Jewish ethnicity, but because it "marked out Jews from Gentiles in a way which automatically privileges males."[28] In light of this, Paul's reference to baptism in verse 27 is immediately granted a fresh hearing. Whereas circumcision sets Jews against Gentiles and accords to Jewish *men* prestige and privilege unavailable to women, Christian baptism is a rite that grants entrance into the life and ministry of the church, to women and men alike.

The consummate force of Paul's grasp of the disruptive nature of the gospel is patently on display in the stark contrast that is drawn between Christian baptism and Jewish circumcision in the flesh. In light of the gospel, Paul is no longer willing to countenance the view that the differences between Jew and Gentile, slave or free, or even our identity as "male and female" constitute valid grounds on which to distinguish who may enter into the covenant of grace. In baptism we are all marked, equally, and in the same way, by the sign of the cross and in the name of the holy Trinity, because it is the Spirit who works to unite us to the death and resurrection of Jesus. In quite stark opposition to the practice of circumcision, baptism is the work of God, and for this reason it represents the order of reconciliation in which divine action precedes and is constitutive of human correspondence and faithfulness. The significance of baptism for Paul does not appear to rest on the candidate's own subjective experience or commitment, but rather lies in the objective work of the triune

---

[28]N. T. Wright, "Biblical Basis for Women's Service in the Church," presentation delivered at the 2004 International Symposium on Men, Women and the Church: A Biblical Approach to Relationships, held at St. John's College in Durham, England.

God, for baptism is not a matter of "the flesh" but of the Spirit.[29]

As Paul's instruction in Romans 6:4 reminds us, "we have been buried with him by baptism into death, so that, just as Christ was raised from the dead by the glory of the Father, so we too might walk in newness of life." Christian baptism, therefore, sets us in an almost irrevocable relation to Christ and his church. Baptism, in and through the work of the Spirit, places women and men alike on a new path and relation to God in Christ. What does this mean for the identity and ministry of women?

The culturally and religiously transgressive nature of the gospel is patently on display in Paul's affirmation that women and men *alike* are baptized into Christ. Given the objective nature and force of baptism as the work of God, it is clear that baptism is an event that sets women in relation to Christ in precisely the same way that it does for men. Baptism, if you will, marks a sinner as one who has been washed clean by the blood of the Lamb of God. This fact alone has immense implications for how we ought to speak of the proper ground on which women and men alike may enter into the service of the church. In baptism, women and men are made the object of divine grace. On a slightly different note, whereas Judaism openly sanctioned a hierarchy and distinction between male and female, with privilege and honor being granted to the former, Paul regards Christian baptism as an event that not only affirms the equal status and dignity of women and men alike, but more importantly, demonstrates their common identity *in Christ*. Reconciliation in Christ is granted to women and men on precisely the same terms, for all are by the Spirit, joined to Christ. Far from perpetuating a "created order" in which men are given privilege and entrance into ministry, and women, by virtue of their bodies, are excluded from the common task of bearing witness to the gospel through the proclamation and ministry of the Word, Christian baptism marks us all as those who have been born of water and Spirit, and so share a common identity as "new creation," as members of his body, the body of Christ.

A genuine commitment to women's service and full participation in the public ministry of the church follows from our common participation in the

---

[29]Now of course the church is right to accord a place for the confession of faith alongside the act of baptism, but it is vital to recognize that such confession is itself no more than a response or faithful attestation to the prior, constitutive and gracious work of God. For it is only on this basis that it is possible to draw a clear line between flesh and Spirit, circumcision and baptism, and this, it seems, is precisely what Paul is seeking to accomplish.

covenant of grace, for we confess that in Christ, as "male and female," we have been drawn into a living fellowship and participation in the work of God's people. The church's confession of the activity of God in baptism serves to remind us that true personhood lies in being joined to the death and resurrection of Christ. And now I conclude with a brief comment on the significance of Paul's language in Colossians 3:3, where he reminds us that our life is hidden with Christ in God.

OUR LIFE IS "HIDDEN WITH CHRIST" (COL 3:3)

Christ's work of reconciliation constitutes the sole ground on which we might begin to speak of human personhood. This remarkable passage in Colossians 3:1-3 makes the following affirmation:

> So if you have been raised with Christ, seek the things that are above, where Christ is, seated at the right hand of God. Set your minds on things that are above, not on things that are on earth, for you have died, and your life is hidden with Christ in God.

While the text is often read in ways that inspire quietistic and personal devotion to Christ, we need to remember the political force of the language pertaining to the ascension of the One who is now "seated at the right hand of God." In point of fact, this passage sends us back into the world with confidence that we live under the rule and lordship of the true God. In the midst of the various challenges of creaturely life, we are reminded of the fact that we have been drawn into the kingdom and reign of Christ.

It is here that our earlier language of being-in-encounter—or put differently, our reference to a relational ontology—can be brought into its proper service. Paul directs the churches of Galatia to no longer consider Christian identity and service in light of distinction between "male and female" precisely because of the fact that in Christ they now share a common life. To confess that our life is "hidden" with Christ is to be reminded of the fact that our current anxiety regarding identity and gender cannot be resolved on strictly natural or political levels. The demand for the full participation of women in ministry is not, at its root, an Enlightenment question reflected in the need to secure the democratic and political rights of an individual *qua* human person. To the contrary, if our life is truly hidden with Christ in God, then we must affirm a principled modesty regarding the meaning and identity of human persons. However unsettling it might be to hear that our proper identity lies beyond our grasp, this is precisely what has been accomplished for us in Christ. Being-in-encounter in this sense is a way of speaking of the kind of fellowship and correspondence we have with the One who has elected us for himself in Christ, as a "fitting partner." The source, telos and ratio of our lives rest outside of ourselves in Christ, and only in this relation may we be said to truly live. We are not so completely overpowered by this relationship as to no longer have a proper identity. Rather, personhood and identity follow from the gracious activity of the triune God. Through God's act of reconciliation, we have been set free for a life of genuine covenantal fellowship and creaturely correspondence.

Conclusion

There are, as I have sought to demonstrate, remarkable dogmatic sources and patterns of judgment that can and must be marshaled in the service of helping the church to recover a genuine sense of her identity as the people of God. If self-knowledge must be an act of discipleship, then here, on the question of women in ministry, the strongest arguments that may be put forward in defense of the full participation of women in public ministry will be ones that demonstrate faithfulness both to Scripture and to God's reconciliation of the world in Christ. As our consideration of a relational ontology of grace has indicated, to live as followers of Christ is to find ourselves in the position of having to confess that we are those who have been marked by an event that stands prior to and outside of ourselves. Namely, with Christ, we have already been set within the order of reconciliation.

As the people of God we are those who openly confess that "we live and move and have our being" in Christ (Acts 17:28). To return to Bonhoeffer, "The church must be able to say the Word of God, the word of authority, here and now, in the most concrete way possible, from knowledge of the situation. The church may not therefore preach timeless principles however true, but only commandments which are true today. God is 'always' God to us 'today.'"[30] In recognition of this grand claim of the gospel, we ought to live in such a manner as to bear witness to fact that God grants his people the full confidence to hear the proclamation of the good news from those "ordered" by

---

[30]Bonhoeffer, No Rusty Swords, p. 162.

Christ and anointed by the Spirit. May we give honor and glory to the God of the gospel as we receive from his hand the proclamation of the Word, and may God richly bless the public and common ministry of women and men in the service of his Word.

Identity and Ministry in Light of the Gospel

A View from the Kitchen

Margaret Kim Peterson

FOR THE PAST COUPLE OF YEARS, I HAVE BEEN WORKING on a book about house-keeping as a spiritual practice. I first started thinking about housekeeping in these terms shortly after I graduated from my doctoral program and moved to the other side of the podium as a college professor of theology. At that time, there were a couple of publishers who were launching new book series having to do with the "Christian practice of everyday life" (as one of these series was titled).[1] The idea was to think about Christian faith not simply as a matter of "things Christians believe" ("Jesus is Lord," for example) and then "apply" to their daily lives (a typically conservative or evangelical tack), nor simply a matter of "things Christians do" (pursue justice, for example) and then reflect on them theologically (a typically activist or progressive tack); but rather to reflect on the interaction between believing and doing and the way that believing and doing, particularly in community, issue in "Christian practices" that are more than the sum of their parts and that embody Christian faith more fully than can one-sided emphases on individual efforts at believing Christian doctrine or doing Christian things.

---

[1]Books in The Christian Practice of Everyday Life series are published by Brazos Press; books in the Practices of Faith series are published by Jossey-Bass.

I thought this sounded like a great way to approach doing theology and to express the integral relationships that do in fact exist between what we as Christians believe to be true about God and humans and the world we live in, and what we actually do with our lives and bodies and relationships in the course of our daily lives. But the more I listened to the movers and shakers behind these book series (a number of whom were my former graduate-school classmates), the more it seemed to me that something was missing. All the proposed topics seemed to be about things like politics and economics and ecological protection; and as important as all these subjects are, none of them seemed really to touch what had long been the primary substance of my everyday life, namely, housework.

I had spent most of my life rather happily doing housework in one setting or another, aware that this was not very fashionable, but not really caring, since, after all, I did like it and on some level sensed the value of it, even if I didn't think about it very deeply. My adventures in housework became rather more intense, however, during the years that I was in graduate school. I married my first husband at the end of the first year of my doctoral program and buried him at the beginning of my sixth year. Over the years his worsening illness absorbed more and more of my energy, until in the last few months of his life I could do little more than moan to my therapist, "I can't cope; I can't cope; I can hardly get to the grocery store."

I understood then, with a clarity that I have experienced at few other times in my life, that getting to the grocery store was one of the things that Really Mattered. The dissertation could wait; dinner could not. Forget all the abstruse theological ideas that my classmates and teachers seemed to debate with such verve in the graduate seminars I was attending. Forget fantasies of "accomplishing something." Perhaps somewhere in the world there were people who measured their days by how much they got done—at work, in class, wherever. I measured my days by whether, at the end of them, the members of my household had been dressed and fed and bathed and put to bed. If we had been, then that was a good day. I had done what mattered most. Everything else was gravy.

As I moved in subsequent years through widowhood into a second marriage and then into motherhood, my practice of housekeeping changed to accommodate the changes in my household. But I retained the long-held sense, of which I had been made so consciously aware during those difficult years of illness, that housekeeping—cooking, cleaning, laundry, all the large and small tasks that go into keeping a household humming along—was not a trivial matter but a serious one. People need to eat, to sleep, to have clothes to wear, a place to read, a place to play, a place into which to welcome guests and from which to go forth into the world. Where was the theological book that would describe and unpack and explore the nature and significance of the work that makes all those things possible? I finally realized that if there was going to be such a book, I was going to have to write it myself.

I'm still working on it. But in the course of my work on the book—which is, again, about housekeeping as spiritual practice, not about women and public ministry—I have nonetheless trodden on some ground that has struck the organizers of this conference as possibly relevant to the subject of women and public ministry. So, for what they are worth, here are some of my thoughts on the subject. I'm going to start by talking about two stories in the Gospel of Luke, and about the interpretation of these stories in a number of standard modern biblical commentaries. I would like then to go on to unpack some aspects of three nouns in my main title—*identity, ministry* and *gospel*—particularly as these bear on the subjects of women and ministry, and then at the end return to the Gospel of Luke and its interpretation and to the implications of that interpretation for the practice of both housekeeping and ministry.

TWO STORIES

In chapters 9 and 10 of his Gospel, the evangelist Luke tells two stories about interactions between Jesus and followers or would-be followers of Jesus. In Luke 9:59-60, Jesus says to a man, "Follow me," to which the man replies, "Lord, let me first go and bury my father." Jesus says to him, "Let the dead bury their own dead; but as for you, go and proclaim the kingdom of God." In Luke 10:38-42, Jesus and his entourage are received at the house of Mary and Martha. Mary sits at Jesus' feet and listens to him, and Martha goes to Jesus and says, "Lord, do you not care that my sister has left me to do all the work by myself? Tell her then to help me." Jesus replies, "Martha, Martha, you are worried and distracted by many things; there is need of only one thing. Mary has chosen the better part, which will not be taken away from her."

Form critics characterize both of these pericopes as pronouncement stories, and there are obvious similarities between them. In both stories, a follower or potential follower of Jesus makes a request of him, and in both stories Jesus

gives an apparently negative answer. It is therefore interesting that modern ex-
egetes treat the two stories in significantly different ways. In short, they are
sympathetic with the man who wants to bury his father and unsympathetic
with Martha. When modern biblical commentators[2] look at Martha, they see
a frazzled, overextended woman with too many pots on the stove. Martha
wants to be the perfect hostess, they explain. She is trying to prepare an elaborate meal, when something simple would have done just as well—better, in
fact, since serving something simple would leave time left over to sit at Jesus'
feet, like Mary. The only remarkable thing these commentators see in this story
is that Jesus commends Mary, a woman, for her devotion. That Jesus rebukes
Martha is utterly unsurprising. Martha is wasting her time on unnecessary
things and needs to be redirected.

When these same commentators look, however, at Jesus' would-be follower
in Luke 9:59, the man who wants to bury his father, they see not a woman asking for help with the housework, but a man requesting permission to perform
the most sacred of filial duties. This is a serious request, not a frivolous one,
and Jesus' answer thus seems shockingly harsh and in no way readily explica-
ble. Interpretive suggestions vary, but the shared bottom line is this: not for a
moment does any commentator imagine that Jesus is instructing the follower
to stop wasting his time on unnecessary things like burial. The follower has a
filial obligation that may not be neglected; the point of Jesus' paradoxical and
obscure words must therefore lie elsewhere.

It is my suspicion that the different treatment accorded these two followers
or would-be followers of Jesus is strongly correlated with the fact that the follower in Luke 9 is a man requesting permission to perform labor that is gendered male ("men's work," in other words), and that moreover is heavily
freighted with religious and moral significance, whereas the follower in
Luke 10 is a woman involved in labor that is gendered female ("women's
work"), and that in modern society is generally considered secular or utilitar-
ian rather than religious or moral in nature.

But must we really read these stories this way? Must we agree with the ap-

---

[2]Cf., for example, C. F. Evans, *Saint Luke*, Trinity Press International New Testament Commentaries
(Philadelphia: Trinity Press International, 1990); Luke Timothy Johnson, *The Gospel of Luke*, Sacra
Pagina (Collegeville, Minn.: Liturgical Press, 1991); Joel B. Green, *The Gospel of Luke*, NICNT (Grand
Rapids: Eerdmans, 1997); Joseph A. Fitzmyer, *The Gospel According to Luke*, 2 vols. ABCom 28-28a
(New York: Doubleday, 1981, 1985). For a somewhat more sympathetic treatment of Martha, cf.
Fred B. Craddock, *Luke*, Int (Louisville, Ky.: John Knox Press, 1990).

parent conclusion (or assumption) that cooking (or "women's work" more generally) is of no particular value in light of the gospel, whereas burial (or "men's work") is of significant value in light of the gospel? Or is there good reason to take Martha and her concerns just as seriously as the man and his concerns, to see Jesus' words to her as just as paradoxical and mysterious as his words to the man, to see "women's work" as just as spiritually significant as "men's work"—to see it, in fact, as significant in a way that calls into question the whole distinction between "men's" and "women's" work? I think there is. I think there are good reasons to read these stories in ways that call into question a number of commonly held assumptions about the identity of men and women and their involvement in the worlds of work and ministry, and that press us away from bifurcated notions of "men's" and "women's" work (in either the sacred or the secular realm) and toward a unified vision of "the Lord's work," to be undertaken by women and men together across a variety of continua—from "public" to "private" and "ministerial" to "secular."

MALE AND FEMALE IDENTITY

To look first at the question of "identity": who people are is always intimately tied up, both in perception and in reality, with what they do. It is thus difficult to talk about the identity of human beings as men or women without talking about men's and women's work. This is surely the reason why so much evangelical conversation about men and women revolves around the subject of men's and women's "roles." The idea that a real man or woman knows his or her "role" and is prepared to play it has always struck me as a rather artificial construct, rather like the Sabellian notion of the doctrine of the Trinity. In a Sabellian view of things, the names "Father," "Son" and "Holy Spirit" do not refer to any distinct persons subsisting in the one being of God; instead, these are roles played by God as he holds up first one mask, then another, before him as he plays out the drama of redemption on his cosmic stage. "Father," "Son" and "Holy Spirit" are not God as God is in himself; they are ways God chooses to appear and to act. They conceal, rather than reveal, who God is in God's own self. The Nicene Fathers rejected Sabellian theories as inadequate to the reality of God in Christ, and I am similarly skeptical of the identification and description of men's and women's "roles," as if it were either possible or desirable to conceal the identity of individual women and men behind the mask of women's and men's roles. But the fact remains: who people are is intimately related to what people do, and not all people do the same thing. In particular, gendered divisions of labor exist in every culture. These divisions are not the same in every culture—what is men's work in one culture (farming, for example) may be women's work in another culture. But every culture has its ideas about what properly constitutes men's and women's work, and it strikes me that the contemporary American evangelical discussion about women and public ministry has at its heart a discussion about the gendered division of labor. Perhaps there are other things going on as well, but there is at least this: a conversation about whether, and to what degree, "public ministry" may be construed as women's work.

This qualifier "public" is a significant one, in that the separation of work into "public" and "private" spheres and the assignment of "men's work" to the public sphere and "women's work" to the private sphere is one that in this country occurred over the course of the later nineteenth and early twentieth centuries, with the advent of industrialization. It has long been common to suppose that industrialization took place in the public sphere, thus affecting the work of men who came to labor there, and left untouched the private sphere, thus also leaving untouched the work of women, whose place was and remained in the home. As the historian of household technology Ruth Schwartz Cowan[3] has pointed out, however, industrialization affected the home just as surely as it did the factories and gristmills and railroads that tend to come more quickly to mind when we think of the industrial revolution.

Most notably for our purposes, industrialization virtually created that species of human activity that we call "housework." Before the mid-nineteenth century, the English word *housework* did not exist. What did exist were the words *housewifery* and *husbandry,* which since the Middle Ages had described the women's work and the men's work, respectively, that was required to run an agrarian household of the kind that became typical of the middle classes—people who were not aristocrats governing large households employing and sheltering dozens or hundreds of individuals, nor people laboring in the homes and on the farms of others, but married couples working their own land and supporting their own (relatively) small households. As Cowan observes, the word *housework* would probably have made no sense to anyone

---

[3]Ruth Schwartz Cowan, *More Work for Mother: The Ironies of Household Technology from the Open Hearth to the Microwave* (New York: Basic Books, 1983).

prior to industrialization, "since—with the exception of seamen, miners, soldiers, and peddlers—almost all people worked in or on the grounds of a house, their own, or someone else's."[4]

The process of industrialization in separating work places from home places, and identifying the former as a man's place and the latter as a woman's place, so altered the work of women that a new word was required to describe it: housework. No longer did women work together in the home with men in performing tasks that while differentiated by gender were equally and together necessary for the flourishing and even the survival of the household. Before industrialization, men grew grain, and women baked it into bread; men made lye, and women made the soap and scrubbed the floors; men made and mended clothing made of leather, and women made and mended clothing made of cloth. After industrialization, many tasks traditionally accorded to men were performed in factories, leaving the men who had been doing that work at home free to seek employment in those same factories.

Some tasks traditionally accorded to women also moved to factories—the making of clothes, for example, and the baking of bread—but many of them remained in the home, where they were nonetheless transformed by changes in household technology. Running water, refrigeration, gas and electric stoves, washing machines—all these dramatically changed "women's work" by, among other things, making an individual housewife able, at least if she worked hard and fast enough, to perform for her household as much or more work as had previously required the labor of two or three adult women (that is, the preindustrial housewife and her hired help). Hence Cowan's title: *More Work for Mother*. Industrialization did not eliminate, or even reduce, women's work; what it did was vastly to increase the productivity of women working at home. At the same time it changed women's work from an activity that was inextricably enmeshed with men's work, both of which were located in and around the home, to an activity that took place in a separate sphere from men's work. Women's work was located in the privacy of the home; men's work in the public sphere of the factory and the marketplace.

But if the whole notion of private and public spheres, with the assignment of women's work to the private sphere and of men's work to the public sphere, is a cultural artifact arising from the processes of industrialization, it

---

[4]Ibid., p. 18.

seems to me very problematic to assume these distinctions as the starting place for discussions of women and men and Christian ministry. The stated topic here today is women and "public ministry." It sounds like a distinction is being made between "public" ministry and some other kind of ministry, presumably "private," with the assumption that we all know what the public and private realms are, and the further assumption that women's involvement in the private sphere (whether "ministerial" or not) and men's involvement in the public sphere (including that slice of it designated as "ministry") are not at issue. What is at issue is a boundary-crossing kind of activity, that of women's involvement in a particular aspect of the public sphere, namely, public ministry.

It is my impression that not all persons who would oppose the involvement of women in public ministry would oppose the involvement of women in other areas of the public sphere, although there certainly are some who would do so. I had a seminary professor who thought there was something fundamentally unnatural about a woman being a man's boss and who believed therefore that no woman should hold a position higher than any man in a given organization's hierarchy. I doubt that he had ever given much thought to the real-world implications of this, but then again, maybe he had. Perhaps he envisioned not the wholesale subordination of women in public life, but their segregation in women-only corporations and institutions. I suspect, though, that he wasn't really thinking about details; he was thinking about the grand scheme of things, and in the grand scheme to which he subscribed, a woman's place was in the home, period, and if women stayed in the home, the problem of women being men's bosses anywhere else would simply never arise.

A view like this simply gives far too much God-given weight to the existence of separate public and private spheres and to the exclusive assignment of men and men's work to the public sphere and women and women's work to the private sphere. And there are few people I know who would wish to defend such a view. Most people I know take for granted the existence of separate or semi-separate public and private spheres, but at the same time think that a certain degree, at least, of boundary-crossing is a positive good. They think it is a good thing for women to participate in the public sphere (although they may prefer to see women as school principals, for example, than as chief executives of Fortune 500 companies), and they think it is a good thing for men to participate in the private sphere (although they may prefer that husbands "help" their wives around the house than that men assume primary responsibility for the house and the children).

The real disagreements about boundary-crossing come up when one particular aspect of the public sphere is in view, namely, "public *ministry*." But what is "public ministry," and what is the "private ministry" from which the adjective *public* presumably distinguishes it? And how coherent and defensible are these categories anyway?

WHAT IS "PUBLIC MINISTRY"?

What is "ministry"? Presbyterians, of whom I am one, tend in addressing this question to turn to the fourfold pattern of ministry established in sixteenth-century Geneva by the reformer John Calvin (who himself adapted this fourfold pattern from an earlier one set in place in Strasbourg by Martin Bucer). According to Calvin, the ministerial offices of the church include pastors, teachers, elders and deacons.[5] Pastors were responsible for the proclamation of the gospel and the administration of the sacraments, teachers for public and private instruction in Christian doctrine, elders for the exercise of moral discipline, and deacons for the care of the poor. The offices of deacon and elder were understood as lay offices (that is, they were unpaid), and the offices of pastor and teacher were professional offices (that is, paid). And in Calvin's day, it perhaps goes without saying, all four offices were restricted exclusively to men.

Bucer and Calvin's fourfold pattern of ministry was never universal among Protestants, and it has not survived intact even among most Presbyterians. The PC(USA), for example, of which I am a member, ordains deacons, elders and "ministers of word and sacrament," but not teachers per se. This is why I am not ordained (that is, to the professional ministry). I hold lay office as a deacon, but I am not ordained to professional office. I am a seminary- and university-trained theologian working as a college professor of theology, but in the PC(USA) that is not an ordainable call. (Calvin would be astonished.) But even if we restrict our view to the three offices of deacon, elder and pastor, there is among the heirs of the Reformation nothing approaching universal agreement that these offices comprehend the range of activities that may be designated as

---

[5]John Calvin *Institutes of the Christian Religion* 4.3.4-9. This fourfold pattern is set in contrast to the older (Catholic) threefold pattern of bishops, priests and deacons.

"ministerial," let alone what specific responsibilities these offices involve or to whom they should be open.

To give, again, a personal example: over the course of the past twenty years or so, I have been a member of three congregations, all of them heir to the Reformed tradition in one way or another. These congregations all employ professional pastoral staff, and all have boards of deacons. What the deacons are responsible for varies from church to church: in one, the deacons are responsible for spiritual oversight, in another they are responsible for the building, in another they visit the sick. Two of the churches also have boards of elders, and two have boards of trustees (not, we might note, one of Calvin's categories). In addition, all of these churches have on staff paid professional women and men who are not ordained to any office but who function in a variety of capacities—as choir directors, organists, youth leaders, counselors, directors of Christian education. And in each church there are many women and men who serve as nonordained, unpaid volunteers in a range of capacities: as Sunday school teachers, as youth workers, as participants in mission projects.

Which of all of these people are engaged in "public ministry"? The simple answer would seem to be "the ordained ones. The rest of them are doing things that are 'not ministry.'" But are the ordained people—the pastors, the elders, the deacons, the trustees (well, mostly they get installed rather than ordained, but still)—really doing more properly "ministerial" work—at least in the sense of Calvin's fourfold model of ministry—than are all the other folks on the paid and unpaid rolls of the church? Are the ordained people busy preaching, teaching, exercising discipline and caring for the poor, and is everybody else doing other ancillary tasks?

It doesn't look that way to me. Deacons who take care of the building are ordained, and Sunday school teachers who instruct the children are not. Trustees who look after the money are officeholders, and youth ministers who look after the young people are not. Pastors who preach and teach and evangelize at home are ordained, and laypeople who preach and teach and evangelize on mission trips or as career missionaries are not. And virtually no one who cares for the poor is ordained to do so. You can volunteer to run the local food pantry, but no one is going to ordain you to do it.

It is this lack of correspondence between theoretical schemes of what constitutes ministry, and what officeholders and nonofficeholders in the church actually do, that renders a nonsensical question like "What should be the nature of women's involvement in public ministry?" What *is* public ministry? All too often, "ministry" gets equated with "officeholding," and then arguments are had over whether women should be admitted to or barred from particular offices, on the apparent assumption that if they are admitted to or barred from these offices then they will have been admitted to or barred from "ministry." Meanwhile, the deacons are looking after the building, and no one is looking after the poor—except, perhaps, the women who have been barred from serving in any office and who have therefore turned their energies to volunteering at the food pantry.

To put this another way: all too often I hear the word *ministry* being used formally rather than materially. It refers to a certain kind of status, with the power and the visibility and the decision-making authority that go along with that status. It does not refer to any particular kind of activity—preaching, for example, or the administration of the sacraments—that is seen as irreducibly "ministerial" and thus closed in principle to any nonordained person, male or female. In my experience, in fact, it is often the churches that guard most zealously the notion of an all-male pastorate who are also the most willing to open their pulpits to nonordained people like missionaries (including, on occasion, women missionaries) and to play fast and loose with the administration of the sacraments—allowing Bible study groups to celebrate the Lord's Supper in the absence of a pastor and in isolation from the rest of the congregation, for example, or encouraging pilgrims to the Holy Land to be baptized (or worse, rebaptized) there by whoever happens to be handy.

This emphasis on ministerial office rather than on ministerial activity is ironic, given that Protestants have traditionally placed the emphasis the other way around. Protestants have conceived of ministry as concerned primarily with doing rather than with being. In a Catholic understanding, a priest is ontologically different from a layperson, and it is that ontological difference, brought about through the episcopal laying-on of hands in ordination, that makes the priest able to do what no layperson, no matter how pious, can do, namely, confect a valid Eucharist. But in a Protestant understanding, every Christian is a priest unto God by virtue of his or her baptism, and all ordination does is to identify some person or persons who, for the sake of good order, are going to do publicly and officially what any one of us could theoretically do and ought already to be doing privately and unofficially: testify to the truth of the gospel, confess our sins and hear others' confessions, move our fellow

Christians by word and example to faith and good works, and so forth.

What too many Protestants do, I think, is to emphasize the category of "public ministry" in such a way that the category becomes far more important than anything it contains. In contrast to a Catholic position, which sees the priest as special because he can do something special (namely, confect a valid Eucharist), too many Protestants see the pastor as special because, well, just because he's special. There is nothing the pastor does that can't be done by someone else when push comes to shove; but the pastor is the pastor, and that is what is important—important enough to insist on excluding women from the pastorate, or important enough to insist that women be admitted to the pastorate, depending on where you're coming from.

I'm just not sure this is a fruitful argument to pursue. I wonder if it might be better to come at the question of ministry, and what constitutes ministry, from another angle entirely, one that will make it less likely that we all begin the conversation assuming that we already know the end from the beginning. Perhaps it could be helpful to think less in terms of categories of church office and more in terms of Christian activity or Christian practice. One possible starting place might be the ancient pattern of Christian life called the "works of mercy." The works of mercy have traditionally been enumerated in two lists, the spiritual and the corporeal works of mercy. The spiritual works of mercy are to instruct the ignorant, to counsel the doubtful, to admonish sinners, to bear wrongs patiently, to forgive offenses, to comfort the afflicted and to pray for the living and the dead. The corporeal works of mercy are to feed the hungry, to give drink to the thirsty, to clothe the naked, to shelter the homeless, to visit the sick, to ransom the captive and to bury the dead.

One of the interesting things about these lists is the way they blur many of the distinctions that modern evangelical Protestants, at least, tend to take as given: distinctions between ministerial and nonministerial activities, between the public and private realms, and between men's and women's work. The emphasis here is on continuity, not on discontinuity. Feeding the hungry, instructing the ignorant, sheltering the homeless, comforting the afflicted—all of these are works of mercy, all are expressions of Christian charity, all are ways that Christians can live out their lives in love and service to others. Most of us would find it patently silly if someone were to take out a red pencil and start circling things on these lists that are "ministry" and crossing out things that are not for the sake of being able then to argue about who gets to do ministry and who doesn't. All of these are things Christians are called to do as expressions of faith and charity in the context of their individual and corporate lives.

This is part of the reason that housekeeping matters, theologically and morally as well as practically. Jesus has a good deal to say in the Gospels about the Christian duty to feed the hungry, clothe the naked and shelter the homeless (in fact, it is Jesus' articulation of these duties in his parable of the last judgment [Mt 25:34-40] that forms the basis for the corporeal works of mercy). There is a tendency, I think, on the part of those of us who are well-fed, clothed and housed to imagine that the needy people to whom Jesus refers are people we don't know—the sort of people who are served at homeless shelters and soup kitchens, at which we ought therefore to volunteer at least occasionally. But housework is all about feeding and clothing and sheltering people who, in the absence of that daily work, would otherwise be hungry and ill-clad and ill-housed.

Just how different is this from Christian ministry? In my judgment, Christian ministry consists precisely (if not necessarily exhaustively) in meeting the everyday needs of others, whether those others be our fellow household members, our near neighbors, or people more sociologically or geographically distant from ourselves. I have a friend who spent a number of years as a missionary in Indonesia. She was that species of missionary known as a missionary wife, and she and several other missionary wives noticed, after they had all spent some years on the field, that their husbands spent a great deal of time in meetings, strategizing about ways to evangelize various parts of the world by certain dates. Meanwhile, the wives were busy feeding the hungry, clothing the naked, visiting the sick, not to mention keeping their own houses and rearing their own children (my friend had five). My friend said she and her friends asked each other, "Just who is doing ministry here, anyway?"

THE GOSPEL

We have talked a little about identity and a little about ministry, and now I would like to turn briefly to the gospel, in particular to some aspects of trinitarian and christological doctrine that I think may be helpful as we sort through the relationships of men and women to each other and to their activities in the world and in the church. I should confess that in my discussion of this topic, I am drawing less on my work on housekeeping than on a class on Christian marriage that I teach with my husband, a New Testament scholar who is also my faculty colleague. The subject of housekeeping does inevitably involve reflection on men and women and their relationships and interactions. The subject of marriage does so to an even greater extent. The students in our Christian marriage class arrive already thinking about gender issues and already exceedingly familiar with arguments for and against what appear to be the two stock positions, that of male headship on the one hand and of gender egalitarianism on the other.

We find that, for the most part, our students are very put off by the concept of gender egalitarianism. These young people are heirs both to the feminist·movement and to the culture of divorce. They have been formed by a culture in which it is explicitly affirmed that boys and girls can (and ought) to have exactly the same aspirations and opportunities in life, and in which conflict between spouses seems to lead almost inevitably to marital shipwreck. And yet our students long to find their identities, not as generic human beings, but as women and as men; and they long for peaceable, stable marital relationships. This is not the vision that arises before them when they hear the phrase "gender egalitarianism." They appear rather to see a vision of sexless beings locked in irreconcilable conflict. They see androgyny and anarchy, and they don't want either one. They think gender egalitarianism is the problem, not the solution.

So they turn to traditionalist constructions of gender relationships. They appear to find these attractive for two reasons. First, they hold out the promise of clearly defined gender identities, of women as homemakers and men as breadwinners. Such gender identities are not particularly Christian, in my judgment, in that they owe far more to the cultural phenomenon of industrialization than to anything the Bible does or does not say about men and women, but our students find them very attractive nonetheless. They feel sure that the Bible teaches that men and women are different in significant ways, so when their industrialized culture offers them a ready-made typology of difference—men/public sphere/men's work; women/private sphere/women's work— they are ready to embrace this as equivalent to whatever it is the Bible says about men and women.

The second thing these traditionalist constructions of gender relationships seem to promise is relationships in which conflict is resolved instantaneously and automatically, because the status of the husband as "head" of the wife means that he makes all decisions in contested matters. It is remarkable how

widespread is the equation of "headship" with decision-making power. If I've
heard it once, I've heard it a thousand times: "Sooner or later a husband and a
wife are going to disagree about something, and someone has to make the
call." My students are at pains to point out that of course husbands and wives
should discuss things and try to agree, but they are sure that irreconcilable
conflict is inevitable, and they want a strategy in place to deal with it. That is
what headship is for. Headship is a trump card, and the husband holds it.

Among the problems with this is the assumption that headship is intrin-
sically rooted in conflict. Husbands and wives are never more truly themselves—husband acting as head and deciding, wife acting as not-head and
submitting—than when they find it impossible to reach agreement in any
other way. So it is not only headship, but marriage itself, that is organized
around the supposed inevitability of intractable disagreement. Friendship
doesn't require an advance arrangement as to who will win the inevitable arguments. Only marriage is founded on the assumption that somebody has
to be in charge, because otherwise intractable disagreements will scuttle the
relationship. Frankly, I don't think this is a very attractive brief in favor of
marriage.

It is also fundamentally at odds with the model of headship presented in
Scripture by the apostle Paul. According to Paul, God the Father and God the
Son are the model for husbands and wives in this regard (1 Cor 11:3), and it
is most emphatically not the case that God the Father and God the Son are
most truly themselves when God the Father is strong-arming the Son into doing something that the Son fundamentally disagrees with. On the contrary: the
relationship of the Father and the Son is one that everywhere in Scripture is
portrayed as characterized by perfect peace and mutuality. Whatever "headship" means in the context of the Holy Trinity, it cannot have its basis in conflict, real or potential, between the persons of the Godhead.

It follows, I think, that whatever "headship" means in the context of Christian marriage, and in the context of the relationship of men and women more
generally (if indeed it applies more generally, which is not clear), it cannot
have its basis in conflict there either. Construing headship as "decision-
making authority" is likewise questionable, and for the same reason: the assumption is that "someone has to make the decisions," since, after all, consensus is going to be impossible to arrive at, at least some of the time and possibly
lots of the time. This is not the example shown to us by Jesus and the Father.

When Jesus says, "I do the will of him who sent me," his point surely is not that God the Father calls the shots, and he (Jesus) is an honorary godlet who does as he is told. That is what Arius thought. The Nicene fathers disagreed. The point is that God the Father and God the Son are on the same page; they are a team; they've talked it over and made a plan. They have different parts to play—the Father sends, the Son is sent—but they are coauthors (with the Holy Spirit) of the drama. This, I think, is the kind of mutuality that we should be striving for in our relationships to one another as men and women, as husbands and wives, in work, in ministry, in marriage—not a pseudocooperation in which one sex issues orders and the other sex hastens to comply, but a real cooperation in which there are real conversations and the kind of real give-and-take that is essential for true mutuality.

I am not persuaded that either traditionalist or egalitarian constructions of gender relationships tend, either logically or practically, to issue in this kind of mutuality. It seems to me that both egalitarianism and traditionalism, as commonly construed, are much more about the distribution of power than they are about cooperation. The traditionalists want to see power concentrated in the hands of one spouse or one sex (the male one); the egalitarians want to see power distributed evenly between both spouses and both sexes. But both see relationships between the sexes as a zero-sum game, in which power held by one spouse can only come at the expense of power held by the other. The egalitarians think power should be shared fifty-fifty; the traditionalists think the distribution should be, in the memorable phrase of one of my husband's first-year Bible students, "sixty-forty in favor of the guy."

For the record, I think it is a good idea, on prudential grounds related to the fallenness of all human beings, to have power—marital, ecclesial, political—distributed broadly rather than concentrated narrowly; but the mere distribution of power does not in itself address the question of how true relationship is to be fostered between spouses, between men and women, among human beings generally. Are there ways to think about men and women and their differences and commonalities that can help us to think of human relationships less as a zero-sum game, in which the victory of one person or group is always purchased at the price of the loss of another person or group, and more as an art, in which the whole is more than the sum of its parts?

Early Christian theologians faced a question at least formally similar to this one as they considered the second of two really big questions addressed by the church in its first few centuries. The first question was, What does it mean to say that Jesus is divine? That question was addressed at the Council of Nicea in 325, which affirmed that Jesus is divine, not in some honorary sense ("Jesus is really really really exalted, so we say he is divine, but he is a creature, unlike the most high God, who is not a creature"), but really and truly divine ("Jesus is God in himself, in the sense that he, like God the Father, is the creator and is not a creature").

The second question was, What does it mean to say that this Jesus is a human being, given that he is divine in the sense that he is not a creature? That question was addressed at the Council of Chalcedon in 451, which affirmed that Jesus, the one divine Son of the Father, was incarnate as a human being in such a way that according to his divine nature he was God as God is God, and according to his human nature he was a human being as any human being is a human being. He was, and remains, one divine person in two natures, a divine nature and a human nature, in which two natures are united in his one divine person "without confusion, without change, without division, without separation."

As the theologians of the early church wrestled with these issues, both before and after the Council of Chalcedon, two schools of christological thought emerged, one centered in Antioch and one in Alexandria. The school of Alexandria emphasized the subordination of Jesus' human nature to his deity. The school of Antioch emphasized the integrity of each nature, the human as well as the divine. Each school discovered that its chosen emphasis could be taken too far. The Alexandrines learned to steer clear of monophysitism, the erroneous affirmation that Jesus' human nature was completely subsumed by his deity. The Antiochenes learned to steer clear of Nestorianism, the erroneous affirmation that Jesus' human and divine natures were so fundamentally independent of one another as to constitute two persons. But neither school of thought was ever abandoned in favor of unanimous adherence to the other, because, in fact, both were necessary. Each school of thought pointed to important aspects of biblical and theological truth about who Jesus is, and each served as a helpful corrective to the potential pitfalls of the other.

I wonder if it is possible—and, more than that, if it might be helpful—to think about conversations in the church today about men and women and their relationship to one another as broadly analogous to early church conversations about the divine and the human natures of Christ and their relationship to one another. I think there is room in the church for the traditionalist emphasis on what is, after all, the biblical concept of headship, and for the egalitarian emphasis on the equally biblical concept of mutuality ("submit to *one another*," St. Paul said). I don't think that for the conversation to move forward one of these emphases has to be identified as the only right one.

I do think that there needs to be attention given to how these emphases are expressed and to the directions they are taken. And I think there needs to be a recognition that if we play men and women against one another, everybody loses. The theologians of the early church recognized early on that emphasizing the integrity of Christ's natures at the expense of their union, or the other way around, issued in truncated, unhelpful and fundamentally untrue theological formulations. It seems to me that an awful lot of what gets written and said about women and men and their relationship to one another in the church and in the world is similarly truncated, unhelpful and fundamentally untrue. I think we can do better. I think the very nature of the gospel itself calls and empowers us to do better.

ANOTHER LOOK AT OUR TWO STORIES

We have traveled a long way in these considerations of identity, ministry and the gospel from the two stories in the Gospel of Luke with which we began. In closing I turn once more to these two stories, the one about the man who wanted to bury his father and the other about Martha of Bethany. What would happen if in reading these stories we were to keep in mind what I think is a proper skepticism about the existence of hard and fast boundaries between public and private spheres, between men's and women's work, between religious and secular and ministerial and nonministerial activities? I think that the first thing that would happen is that we would see these stories as more similar than dissimilar, and we would see Jesus' words to each of his questioners as difficult words, words that call into question deeply held human convictions about what is important. In the man's case, Jesus is apparently challenging the performance of the sacred duty to bury one's parents; in Martha's case, Jesus is apparently challenging the performance of the sacred duty of hospitality.

In modern American culture, hospitality tends to be thought of as a nice extra (the dinner party to which you invite family or friends on a night when no one has anything else to do) or as a component of a business school curriculum (the hospitality industry, meaning hotels and restaurants, where if you have money they will sell you a room or a meal). It has no particular moral resonance; it is just something you do, or not. But in the culture of ancient Israel, hospitality was among the moral pillars of society.[6] Israel was a wandering stranger, and God took her in and fed her and clothed her and housed her. In response, Israel was to care for the alien and stranger in her midst. Practically speaking, this meant (among other things) that when hungry people came to your door, you fed them. That is what Abraham and Sarah did for the three strangers who came to their tent by the oaks of Mamre, and it turned out that they fed God. It is what Martha did for Jesus the day he came to her house; it turns out she fed God, too. (It thus completely misses the point to say, as does one commentator on Luke 10:38-42,[7] that Martha's error was to rush around offering food to Jesus, since the "one thing needful" in hospitality is personal attention, and anything beyond that is an optional frill. No, no, no. You might just as well try to have faith without works. Show me your hospitality without food, and I by my food will show you my hospitality.)

So what is going on in the story of Mary and Martha? I think one way to approach this passage is to read it in its context in Luke 10. In verse 25, a lawyer tests Jesus, saying, "What must I do to inherit eternal life?" Jesus turns the question back on him: What does the law say? The lawyer answers, "You shall love the Lord your God with all your heart, and with all your soul, and with all your strength, and with all your mind; and your neighbor as yourself." "You have given the right answer," says Jesus. "Do this, and you will live" (Lk 10:25-28). We all know what the lawyer says next: "And who is my neighbor?" The parable of the Good Samaritan follows. Which of the three, the priest, the Levite or the Samaritan, proved a neighbor to the man who fell among thieves? The one who showed mercy on him. "Go and do likewise," says Jesus (Lk 10:37). And the next thing that happens is that Jesus visits Mary and Martha.

I'm inclined to see in the parable of the good Samaritan a story about just how radical and socially transforming the demands of the second commandment are. And I'm inclined to see in the story of Mary and Martha an illustration of just how puzzlingly paradoxical the demands of the first commandment are. Martha, it seems to me, is someone who has gone and done likewise—she has responded hospitably to a needy person who has entered her home. And then Jesus goes and commends Mary's service above hers. Even

---

[6]For a discussion of this, see Christine Pohl, *Making Room: Recovering Hospitality as a Christian Tradition* (Grand Rapids: Eerdmans, 1999), pp. 3-15 and throughout.

[7]Johnson, *Gospel of Luke*, p. 175.

something so sacred as hospitality, it appears, takes second place relative to listening to Jesus' teaching—just as something so sacred as burial takes second place relative to following Jesus.

And yet, it is not possible to follow Jesus, or to love God, or to be led by the Holy Spirit, without loving and serving one's fellow human beings in ways commanded by God in the gospel. The two great commandments are at once complementary and in tension with one another. The view from Martha's kitchen is of a paradox that lies right at the heart of the practice of Christian life and of Christian ministry. I'm not sure, frankly, how much the story of Mary and Martha tells us about women and public ministry. But I think the story of Mary and Martha reminds us of a significant truth about human beings in general and the Christian life in general, namely, that our most heartfelt obedience is something that God welcomes and desires, but even more than that, he welcomes and desires us.

PART FOUR

NEW PERSPECTIVES FROM THE HUMANITIES AND SOCIAL SCIENCES

Opposite Sexes or Neighboring Sexes?

What Do the Social Sciences Really Tell Us?

Mary Stewart Van Leeuwen

THE BROCHURE ADVERTISING THE CONFERENCE on which this collection of essays is based announced that its goals were twofold: (1) "to find fresh perspectives and lines of thought on the conversation concerning women in public ministry, . . . [moving] the conversation beyond the reflex answers routinely offered on all sides of this debate," and (2) to call "upon everyone to rethink their understanding of the meaning and nature of, not only gender, but also public Christian ministry itself, in light of the gospel." The aims of this chapter are congruent with parts of both these goals. With regard to the first (moving the conversation beyond reflex answers) let me warn that I am going to pronounce "a plague on all your houses." More specifically, I will argue that *both* gender egalitarians and gender hierarchicalists have misused the social scientific literature on gender in a misguided attempt to essentialize certain ideas about "gender complementarity" which, in turn, have mistakenly been read back into Scripture. Whether this is the result (by either side or both) of misunderstanding, of calculated ideological grandstanding or a combination of the two, I will leave for others to decide. With regard to the original conference's second aim (rethinking the understanding of the meaning of gender) I will be happy if we can learn to think about *gender* more as a *verb* than a *noun*—"gendering" as something we are responsibly and flexibly called to *do* more than to *be*. This is a position that I will argue is more in keeping with the biblical drama of creation, Fall, redemption and future hope *and* with the accumulated social science literature on gender.

COMPLEMENTARITY ANXIETY: A NEUROSIS SHARED BY BOTH SIDES

In the American evangelical context, the debate between gender hierarchicalists and gender egalitarians finds its most public representation in two parachurch organizations: the gender-hierarchicalist[1] Council on Biblical Manhood and Womanhood (CBMW) and the gender-egalitarian Christians for Biblical Equality (CBE). Each of these has a loyal group of followers, a sophisticated website and an acknowledged handbook—a large, multidisciplinary volume that challenges the other side's position and defends its own position on gender, and the applications that flow from it, as being both "more biblical" and "more scientific."[2] However, it is to the credit of both groups that each recognizes (and publicly affirms) that the issue of male headship versus gender

---

[1]Although the Council on Biblical Manhood and Womanhood prefer to be called "gender complementarians" rather than "gender hierarchicalists," I am using the latter designation because it is the concept of "gender complementarity" that I am subjecting to criticism, regardless of which side uses the term. Moreover, biblical scholar Kevin Giles has rightly argued in *The Trinity and Subordinationism: The Doctrine of God and the Contemporary Gender Debate* (Downers Grove, Ill.: InterVarsity Press, 2002) that it is highly questionable for CBMW adherents to substitute the milder term "complementarity" for "male headship" in family and church settings on the grounds that the "roles" of headship for men and submission for women imply nothing about the relative intrinsic worth of each sex. As Giles notes, "In [the CBMW] case, because a woman is a woman, and for no other reason, she is locked into a *permanent* subordinate role, no matter what her abilities or training might be. . . . The [originally-subordinate army] private can assume higher responsibilities, but a woman [on the CBMW account] can never become a leader in the church and can never assume equal responsibility with her husband in the home, simply because she is a woman. Once we ask why this is so, we must infer some permanent inability in women. . . . Introducing the sociological term *role* in this argument for the *permanent functional* subordination of women does not negate the fact that women because they are women, and for no other reason, are subordinated. Against its usual connotation [viz., role as something that is socially assigned and can be changed] the word *role* is recast [by CBMW adherents] in essential terms. Cleverly worded phraseology cannot avoid this fact. If a woman's role is not essential to her nature or being, then it can change. If it cannot change because it is basic to her nature or being as a woman, then it is not just a role she performs. Thus this novel [CBMW] case for the permanent role subordination of women is at best incoherent and at worst disingenuous. The assertion of [women's] equality remains just that—as assertion. It has no cash value. Construed in this way there is no way to meaningfully maintain the claim that women are created equal. The traditional exegesis [of the church throughout history, which consistently claimed women's essential inferiority to men] was at least forthright and logically consistent on this count" (p. 82, his emphases).

[2]The Council on Biblical Manhood and Womanhood (2825 Lexington Rd., Louisville KY 40280) has a website at <www.cbmw.org>. The organization's original handbook is Piper and Grudem, *RBMW.* Christians for Biblical Equality has a website at <www.cbeinternational.org>, and a handbook in Pierce and Groothuis, *DBE.*

equality is *not* a confessional issue—that is, one which can be used as a litmus test to separate orthodox from heterodox Christians. Each group recognizes, in the words of CBMW's founding statement, "the genuine evangelical standing of many who do not agree with all of [its] convictions."[3]

But more to the point, despite their other differences followers of these two positions are often joined at the hip in a common desire to defend the concept of "gender complementarity": roughly, the notion that "men and women are different." This gets expressed in different ways—most crudely by some who insist that men and women have completely dichotomous and fixed psychological traits. (Call this, if you will, the "Men are from Mars, women are from Venus" stance—with or without the planetary terminology.)[4] More common, but only slightly more nuanced, is the acknowledgment by some in both camps that male-female personality and behavioral differences (e.g., in aggression, in relational skills) are "general" or "average" differences only, not absolute differences. This, however, is still seen to count as "gender complementarity." (Call this, if you will, the "*Most* men are from Mars and *most* women are from Venus *most* of the time" stance.)

Interestingly, in both its absolute and average versions, the idea of gender complementarity is used to defend *both* gender hierarchy *and* gender equality in church and family. For gender hierarchicalists, the supposed gender differences combine with a patriarchal reading of certain biblical texts to support different church and family "roles"[5] for women and men and to support male headship in both spheres.[6] The same language of gender complementarity is also used by gender hierarchicalists to challenge the liberal feminist endorsement of androgyny and its resulting slippery slope into a presumed tolerance of homosexuality. By contrast, for many gender egalitarians, gender comple-

---

[3]"The Danvers Statement" (1989; prepared at a Council of Biblical Manhood and Womanhood meeting in Danvers, Mass., December 1987) available on the CBMW website <www.cbmw.org/about/danvers/php>.

[4]The reference is to John Gray's best-selling, but badly researched, *Men Are from Mars, Women Are from Venus* (New York: HarperCollins, 1992).

[5]See n. 1 for a critique of this use of the term *role*.

[6]Thus CBMW asserts, "Women are weaker in some ways and men are weaker in some ways; women are smarter in some ways and men are smarter in some ways. . . . God intends for all the 'weaknesses' that characteristically belong to men to call forth and highlight woman's strengths. And God intends for all the 'weaknesses' that characteristically belong to woman to call forth and highlight man's strengths." Answer 29 from John Piper and Wayne Grudem, *Fifty Crucial Questions,* posted on CBMW website under "Fifty Common Questions About Gender" (2005) <http://www.cmbw.org.questions/29.php>.

mentarity, in either its absolute or (more frequently) average rendering, means that women and men have different but equally beneficial strengths, and different but equally worrisome weaknesses, making it normative—both biblically and psychologically—for them to share church and home leadership roles equally.[7] In addition, by defending gender complementarity, even while denying that it underwrites male headship in church and family, gender egalitarians hope to defend themselves against possible accusations of being headed toward an "unbiblical" tolerance of homosexual relationships.

However, as an academic psychologist and gender studies scholar who did not contribute to the flagship volume of either organization, I am now going to try to explain why using the language of gender complementarity in either its "absolute" or "average" version is a misguided exercise. My basic points are as follows:

1. Research in neither the biological nor the social sciences can resolve the nature/nurture debate regarding gendered psychological traits or behaviors in humans, let alone pronounce on whether any of these should be *retained* or *rejected*. In a fallen world—however good it remains creationally—we cannot move from *is* to *ought* on the basis of science alone.

2. There are very few consistent sex differences in psychological traits and behaviors. When these are found, they are always *average*—not absolute—differences, and for the vast majority of them the small, average—and often decreasing—difference *between* the sexes is greatly exceeded by the amount of variability on that trait *within* members of each sex. Most of the bell curves for women and men (showing the distribution of a given psychological trait or behavior) overlap almost completely. So it is naïve at best—and deceptive at worst—to make absolute (or even average) pronouncements about the psychology of either sex when there is much more variability *within* than *between* the sexes on almost all of the trait and

---

[7]Thus William Webb writes in *DBE* (p. 402 n. 1): "the egalitarian claim that status differences between men and women are a cultural construct and not inherent in the sexual distinction hardly constitutes a move toward a wholesale rejection of male-female complementarity. . . . God's design . . . includes not only undisputed differences in sexual and reproductive function . . . but also the general psychological differences that can be discerned in studies comparing groups of men and groups of women. One might well argue that the best way to celebrate these general differences is the inclusion of women in leadership positions, since women can bring a focus that complements that of men. In an integrative sense egalitarians are stronger advocates of complementarity than hierarchical complementarians!"

behavior measures for which we have abundant data.

3. To adapt one of Freud's famous dictums, we cannot assume that anatomy is destiny until we have controlled for opportunity. Thus, even when appeals are made to large *crosscultural* studies that have found "consistent" sex differences, we cannot assume universality for those conclusions until we have controlled for the existence of differing opportunities by gender across the various cultures.

Let me now address these three points in more detail, after which I will make some modest proposals about how the social sciences might more reasonably be expected to be helpful to *both* sides in the egalitarian/hierarchicalist debate.

1. Research in neither the biological nor the social sciences can resolve the nature/nurture controversy regarding gendered psychological traits and behaviors in humans.

The crucial terms here are the words "human" and "psychological traits and behaviors." First of all, we should not be surprised that, given our creational overlap with all other living organisms (strikingly shown in the various genome projects that are underway) much can be learned about the structure, function and healing of the human body from animal research models. But without doubt the most salient *biological* feature of human beings is the plasticity of our brains. The legacy of a large cerebral cortex puts us on a much looser behavioral leash than other animals, with the result that, more than any other species, we are created for continuous learning: for passing on what we have produced culturally, not just what we have been programmed to do genetically. We are, as it were, hard-wired for behavioral flexibility.[8] Indeed, how could humans carry out the cultural mandate to "subdue the earth" (Gen 1:28) as God's accountable regents if this were not so? And at the other end of the biblical drama, how could we "bring the honor and glory of nations," however suitably cleansed, before God (Rev 21:26) if all the people of all the nations had no more freedom within their common biological form than that which exists in even our closest primate neighbors? And in between, what would be the point of reading and taking to heart Jesus' parable of the talents (Mt 25:14-30)?

---

[8]See for example Mary Stewart Van Leeuwen, "Of Hoggamus and Hogwash: Evolutionary Psychology and Gender Relations," *Journal of Psychology and Theology* 30, no. 2 (2002): 101-11, and *My Brother's Keeper: What the Social Science Do (and Don't) Tell Us About Masculinity* (Downers Grove, Ill.: InterVarsity Press, 2002), chap. 7.

Ah yes, but haven't the biological and social sciences shown us that men and women have clearly *different* talents, and that these are rooted in biology? Well, let us ask what we have to be able to do in order to conclude that biological sex *clearly causes* even a small, average behavioral or psychological difference between *human* males and females. First, we would have to be able to manipulate sex as an independent, experimental variable, that is, *randomly* assign people to be born with an XX or an XY pair of chromosomes apart from all the other genetic baggage they come with. Clearly we cannot do this: babies come to us as genetic package deals. Well then, perhaps we could take advantage of that marvelous natural experiment known as identical twins, each pair of whom have the same genes, have shared the same uterus, and have been shown to stay pretty similar on many behavioral and psychological measures even when raised in different environments. Surely that says something about the power of biology? Yes, it does—though not as much as you might think[9]— but it can say nothing about the origins of *gender* differences, simply because identical twins are always of the *same sex*.

Well then (descending more to the level of science fiction) perhaps we could randomly assign members of a mixed-sex group of infants to be raised as boys or as girls *after* they're born, and see just how much they remain stubbornly "masculine" or "feminine" despite being raised as members of the other sex. But aside from the fact that this comes close to the sort of "science" that was done in Nazi Germany but is repudiated (so far) in our own society, it wouldn't even begin to approximate a double-blind experiment—of the sort we use, for example, to test the effectiveness of new medicines—because the cat would be out of the bag (so to speak) as soon as the babies' caretakers began changing their diapers.[10] Finally, even if we *could* find a sure-fire method to ascertain that boys (for example) are hard-wired to be violent or girls are hard-wired to be catty gossips, this would obviously tell us nothing about the *desirability* of either state of affairs. In a fallen world, we cannot automatically

---

[9]For example, even among identical twins raised together, if one twin develops schizophrenia, the chances of the other twin developing it are a little less than one in two. This risk, while definitely higher than among pairs of progressively more distant biological relatedness, is hardly in the same category as the 100-percent likelihood that identical twins will share the same eye color or blood type. The predispositional vulnerability is greatly magnified (or reduced) by environmental factors.

[10]A "blind" experiment requires that *neither* the participants getting the experimental (or control) treatment *nor* the people administering the treatment *nor* the persons assessing the results at the end of the experiment know who was randomly assigned to either treatment group to begin with.

assume that what is "natural" is thereby desirable by the standards of God's kingdom.

So it is impossible to disentangle biological sex from the other genetic and environmental forces in which it always remains embedded and with which it constantly interacts. This means that the two essential conditions for inferring cause and effect—the manipulation of one factor (sex) and the control of other factors (both biological *and* environmental)—cannot be met. Consequently, "all data on sex differences, no matter what research method is use, are *correlational* data,"[11] and as every introductory social science student learns, you cannot draw conclusions about causality from merely correlational data. "[I]n that sense, it is more accurate to speak of 'sex-related' differences than of sex[-caused] differences."[12] So let us be very clear. When we read about a study—using *any* methodology—that describes an obtained, average sex difference of such-and-such a magnitude, that's all it is: a description of the results of a study done in one particular place and time with a particular sample of persons, but quite unable to disentangle nature from nurture. It is a *description,* not an *explanation* about the origins of obtained sex differences. Any resulting conclusions about male and female "essences," biological or metaphysical, are purely speculative.[13]

2. On almost all behavioral and psychological measures that have been studied, the distributions (bell curves) for women and men overlap almost completely.

---

[11]Hilary M. Lips, *Sex and Gender: An Introduction,* 5th ed. (New York: McGraw Hill, 2005), p. 109.

[12]Ibid., p. 109.

[13]Longitudinal studies—which are rare, because they are so costly and time-consuming—can get us a little closer to separating nature from nurture. Perhaps the most famous longitudinal study in psychology has been Lewis Terman's more than half-century tracking of over 1000 gifted boys and girls (all with I.Q. scores of over 140) starting in 1922. In this study, therefore, I.Q. was deliberately controlled for: participants of both sexes were unusually bright. In spite of this, high childhood I.Q. score was a better predictor of adult public achievement *and* adult I.Q. scores for the males than for the females: more than two-thirds of the girls with I.Q.s over 170 became homemakers or office workers in adulthood, with a parallel tendency for I.Q. scores to decrease. By contrast, occupation—not gender—accounted best for I.Q. stability over the participants' lifespans: those (fewer) women and (more) men who channeled their intelligence and education into publicly demanding careers (whatever else they did) were much more likely to display stability of I.Q. test scores from childhood through adulthood. Environment was thus a better predictor than gender per se of adult test scores. A later (but more modest) longitudinal study by Eleanor Maccoby and her colleagues of three cohorts of (normal-range) children from birth through preschool years, using a variety of biological, psychological and relational measures, found that for many variables, birth order accounted for as much or more of the variability in scores as did gender, again underscoring the importance of environmental both as a main effect and one that interacts with biology. For further details of these studies, see Lips, *Sex and Gender,* chap. 4.

Ah yes, some will say, but look how large and consistent those sex differences are—in aggression, nurturance, verbal skills, spatial abilities and so on. Surely this strongly suggests (even if it can't absolutely *prove*) that women and men have innately different talents, "beneficial differences," in the language of adherents on both sides of the debate. Everybody knows that men are from Mars and women are from Venus, at least on average. Really? Just how large and consistent *are* such differences, after a century of measuring them in domains such as aggression, nurturance, verbal skills and so on? In other words, just how much do (or don't) those bell curves overlap for women and men? Because there is so much bad science journalism floating around about these matters (written by people of every political and religious stripe), some more comments on social science methodology are in order.

I begin with what is known among social scientists as the "file drawer effect." Since the time that psychology journals began publishing over a century ago, there has been a heavy bias against accepting studies on males and females that find *no* statistically significant sex differences. In this kind of research, it appears that no news is bad news for your career because studies finding no effect for sex are likely to remain unpublished (thus ending up in the author's file drawer). You can see what this means: even when we do a literature review of many sex-comparative studies (concerning any of the usual suspects: verbal or spatial skills, aggression, empathy, activity levels, moral reasoning styles, etc.) done over many years, our conclusions—at least by the reigning statistical criteria—will be selectively tilted toward finding more rather than fewer sex differences because of the publishing bias I have just described.[14]

My second, and more important, point has to do with the misunderstanding that continues to surround the term "statistically significant." Another basic methodological caveat is this: a research result that is statistically significant is not necessarily of practical significance. According to the most common tests of significance, if an obtained, average difference between two groups (e.g., women and men doing a math test, volunteer subjects taking an experimental drug versus those taking a placebo, etc.) could have occurred fewer than five times out of a hundred "by chance," then it is deemed a "significant" difference. However,

---

[14]There now exist both print and online media aimed at reducing the "file drawer" effect, including *The Journal of Articles in Support of the Null Hypothesis* <www.jasnh.com> and the Index of Null Effects and Replication Failures <www.jasnh.com/m9.htm>.

with large enough samples and a small enough variability among scores, even a tiny average difference between two groups—i.e., groups whose bell-curve scores overlap almost completely—may be "significant" in this statistical sense, whereas (because of the file drawer effect) a much larger average difference that just misses being statistically significant will not likely see publication, even though its potentially practical significance may be much greater.[15]

As a result of such criticisms, a statistical technique called meta-analysis was developed in the 1970s for use in all areas of social science, including re-search on gender. As its name implies, this refers to a "super-analysis": one that can combine the results of many (e.g., several dozen, sometimes even several hundred) studies on sex differences in a given domain: aggression, verbal abil-ity or whatever. This technique differs from earlier ways of reviewing the liter-ature, which simply gave equal weight to all studies examined, did a tally of how many did or did not show statistically significant sex differences, and came to an "eyeball" or intuitive judgment as to whether reliable sex differ-ences existed in a given domain.[16] Instead, meta-analysis converts the findings of a large sample of studies into a common metric known as the average effect size across those studies. This is done not just by averaging all the average sex differences across the studies but also by taking into account the size of each sample and the variability of the scores found in each.[17] Consequently, meta-analysis allows us to ask, across many studies of sex differences of a certain trait or behavior, just how large that difference (known as d) is, or how far

---

[15]Thus the file drawer effect can work either way: it can mask large differences that just fail to attain statistical significance, as well as differences that that are neither statistically nor practically signifi-cant. Most journals in the psychological sciences only publish about 5 percent of the studies that fail to meet traditional levels of statistical significance, the rest ending up in the file drawers of their re-searchers. For an accessible discussion of these issues, see Christopher Shea, "Psychologists Debate Accuracy of 'Significance Test,'" *The Chronicle of Higher Education,* August 16, 1996, pp. 12, 17.

[16]An example of the use of this earlier method would be the Eleanor E. Maccoby and Carol N. Jacklin's *The Psychology of Sex Differences* (Stanford Calif.: Stanford University Press, 1974). As well as predat-ing the use of meta-analysis, the Maccoby and Jacklin review concentrated almost entirely on studies involving preadolescent (and especially preschool) children, as those were the most available mea-sures at the time. In spite of these limitations, the chapter on biology in *RBMW* treats this (and no other) literature review of gender differences as a "landmark" study (p. 281). For an excellent and very understandable introduction to the meta-analytic literature as it applies to the psychology of gender (none of which is acknowledged in *RBMW*) see Janet Shibley Hyde, "The Gender Similarities Hypothesis," *American Psychologist* 61, no. 5 (2005): 581-92.

[17]Pictorially, the variability of scores refers to how "fat" or "skinny" the bell curves of the scores are for the groups in any study. It's important to take account of because, other things being equal, the skin-nier the bell curves, the less likely it is that an average difference between the groups in the study is due to chance.

apart the tops of the two bell curves are—the tops representing the place where the male and female mean scores are.[18] In other words, across many such studies, just how much do the male and female bell curves (or distributions of scores) overlap?[19]

As you can see from appendix A, even when an average effect size (or d) is 1.00 (as was found, for example, in a meta-analysis of studies comparing self-reported empathy in men and women)[20] the range of scores within each sex is much greater than the average difference between the sexes. But in the many meta-analyses of gender differences that have been done since the 1970s, an effect size, d, even as large as 1.00 is almost unheard of. Most are in the range from 0.0 (no detectable difference) to .35 (a small difference)—and even the latter means that less than 5 percent of the variability of *all* the scores can be accounted for by the sex of the participants.[21] This underlines my previous assertion: it is naive at best, and deceptive at worst, to make essentialist pronouncements about either sex when the range of scores within each sex is, for almost all traits and behaviors measured, much greater than the difference between the sexes. (See appendix B for representative meta-analyses of studies of gender differences.)

It gets worse, dear reader: meta-analysis is full of embarrassments for gender essentialists, but also for "gender influentialists" who think that even small

---

[18]Note that meta-analysts, unlike those using more standard techniques, do not simply ask, Did the average difference between the groups, however large or small, manage to make the <.05 cutoff for statistical significance?

[19]This is another way of asking whether the differences between the male and females scores are bigger or smaller than the amount of variability within each sex group, or asking how much of the variance in the scores can be explained by the sex of the participants in the study. The best meta-analyses will include as many unpublished studies as possible (to reduce the file drawer effect), and also have clear methodological standards for which studies are included, e.g., only studies whose measures have demonstrated construct validity, only studies in which participants are randomly assigned to conditions, etc.

[20]A d of 1.00 would mean that, after meta-analysis has been done, the average gap between men's and women's scores is a full standard deviation in size. By convention, all bell curves or distributions of scores are divided across the curve into eight equal standard-deviation units.

[21]By convention, effect sizes, d's, of 0.0–.35 are considered small; those from .36–.65 are considered medium, and those above .65 are considered large. It is worth noting that, according to one review, 60 percent of the effect sizes found in the psychology of gender literature are in the small range, as compared to 36 percent in all other areas of psychology where meta-analyses have been done. See Janet S. Hyde and Marcia C. Linn, *The Psychology of Gender: Advances Through Meta-analysis* (Baltimore: Johns Hopkins University Press, 1986), and Janet S. Hyde and Elizabeth Ashby Plant, "Magnitude of Psychological Gender Differences: Another Side to the Story," *American Psychologist* 50, no. 3 (1995): 159-61.

average sex differences are pregnant with interpersonal, ecclesiastical and social policy implications.[22] For example, as previously noted, the meta-analytic
d for women's versus men's empathy scores based on self-report measures is
around 1.00, in the direction of women being more empathetic than men.
This is already a very small difference, and one which (like virtually all behavioral difference between the sexes) shows a wider distribution of scores within
each sex than the tiny, average difference between the sexes. But when based
on unobtrusive measures (i.e., studies where people do not know they are being measured for empathy), the meta-analytic *d* shrinks to an almost nonex-
istent .05. You don't have to be a rocket scientist to guess what that contrast
suggests: men and women can (and do) behave quite differently depending on
how obvious the external social pressures are to behave in a "gendered" fashion. A similar difference is found in meta-analytic analyses of women's and
men's stated interest in babies: when asked in front of an audience men are apt
(though not nearly as apt as gender stereotypes require) to say that they are
not interested in babies. When asked privately, they express, on average, pretty
much the same level of interest as women.

Meta-analyses can also be divided according to the particular era in which
the studies were done. For example, a meta-analysis of studies of gender differences in verbal fluency done prior to 1973 (when gender roles were more
rigidly dichotomized) found an overall, small effect size (*d*) of .23, in the direction of women scoring higher than men. A similar meta-analysis of studies
done after 1973 (once the second wave of feminism had begun to loosen gender stereotypes for both sexes) found an effect size of .11, less than half the
size of the earlier one. You do not have to be a professional social scientist to
know that sudden genetic mutations in men and/or women since 1973 are unlikely to have caused such a shift. Genes in humans just don't mutate and
spread that fast. Over half a century ago, lay theologian Dorothy Sayers wondered why women and men were called "opposite sexes" rather than "neighboring sexes."[23] Fifty years and many meta-analytic studies later, it seems that
women and men are very close neighbors indeed.

---

[22] Good introductions to meta-analytic research can also be found in *Lips, Sex and Gender*, chaps. 3 and
4, and Vicki S. Hegelson, *The Psychology of Gender* (Upper Saddle River, N.J.: Prentice Hall, 2002),
chap. 3.
[23] Dorothy Sayers, "The Human-Not-Quite-Human," reprinted in Sayers, *Are Women Human?* (Downers
Grove, Ill.: InterVarsity Press, 1971), pp. 37-47.

ATTEMPTS TO EVADE THESE FINDINGS

What do convinced gender essentialists (along with careless science journalists and trendy Mars-Venus advice book writers) do with such findings? The most common strategy is simply to ignore or distort them: to pretend that small, shifting tendencies are absolute gender dichotomies, or something close to it, or to assume that statistical significance is always the same as practical significance. All too many people yearn for simple black-and-white explanations of complex relations, including those involving men and women. (And as one of my gender studies students memorably observed, "Tendencies don't sell books.") A less-common strategy nowadays is to pathologize the findings: to claim that, however much those gendered bell curves do or can overlap, we have to pull them apart as far as possible, in order to approximate God's—or nature's or optimal society's—"true" purposes for males and females. This was, in effect, the approach taken by philosopher Jean-Jacques Rousseau in his eighteenth-century educational treatise *Emile*. Rousseau was convinced that "rational, active man" and "emotional, passive woman" were perfect complements for each other. Thus, though he freely conceded that men's and women's natural capacities were not rigidly dichotomous, he insisted that if they were not trained to become "opposite sexes" there was no way they would be attracted to each other and be able to pair-bond for life.[24] Two centuries later, this kind of theory was repackaged as sociological functionalism, whose adherents maintained that a division of labor by sex—whether or not the corresponding tendencies were enshrined in the genes—was "functional" for the preservation of societies, both past and present, and so should be tampered with only cautiously, if at all.[25]

It is not unheard of for theologians to have taken a similar stance. Abraham Kuyper did so in the early twentieth century, claiming (quite ahistori-

---

[24]Jean-Jacques Rousseau, *Emile*, trans. Allan Bloom (New York: Basic Books, 1979). Rousseau's idea that the sexes should be "opposite" was one of the first modern departures from the longer-standing Aristotelian notion that women and men were in all ways alike—except that women were "lesser" than men in all their human capacities, for rationality, autonomy, artistry, friendship, etc. For Aristotle women were—in Dorothy Sayers's memorable phrase—"The Human-Not-Quite-Human." See Sayers, *Are Women Human?* pp. 37-47.

[25]For example, Talcott Parsons and Robert F. Bales, *Family, Socialization and Interaction Process* (New York: Free Press, 1955). For a critical assessment of functionalism as it applies to gender, see Michael S. Kimmel, *The Gendered Society*, 2nd ed. (New York: Oxford University Press, 2004), especially chap. 3.

cally and with no clear exegetical warrant) that however much men's and women's capacities "naturally" overlapped, God had ordained, once and for all, that women's activities be limited almost completely to the domestic sphere, and men's to the public arenas of the academy, the church, the marketplace and the political forum.[26] "The woman can lend herself to study [of medicine and law] as well as the man," Kuyper conceded in 1914. But, he added, because women's (but not men's) "position of honor" was by divine definition in the home, "whoever has man take his place at the cradle and woman at the lectern makes life *unnatural.*"[27] So far, this doctrine of separate spheres is not an official affirmation of gender hierarchicalists, aside from its application to certain church offices.[28] But to the extent that gender-hierarchicalist rhetoric overlaps with romantic Mars-Venus rhetoric, as it does on the shelves of many Christian bookstores, it is a force to be reckoned with in evangelical circles.[29] And to the extent that the doctrine of separate spheres, combined with the doctrine of male headship, produces systematic social and economic disempowerment of women (as it has in both preindus-

---

[26]See Mary Stewart Van Leeuwen, "Abraham Kuyper and the Cult of True Womanhood," *Calvin Theological Journal* 31, no. 1 (1996): 97-124; and "'The Carrot and the Stick,' Abraham Kuyper on Gender, Family and Class," in *Religion, Pluralism and Public Life: Abraham Kuyper's Legacy for the 21st Century,* ed. Luis Lugo (Grand Rapids: Eerdmans, 2000), pp. 59-84.

[27]Abraham Kuyper, "De Eerepositie der Vrouw (The Woman's Position of Honor)," (Kampen: Kok, 1932), trans. Irene Konyndyk (Calvin College, 1992), pp. 11 and 13 (Kuyper's emphasis).

[28]Although he may not have been speaking officially for CBMW, one of its adherents, in a formal discussion of CBE's just-published *Discovering Biblical Equality* at the 2004 Evangelical Theological Society meetings (San Antonio, Tex.) frankly admitted that he *did* believe it was biblically defensible that men should be in permanent authority over women in *all* spheres of life (not just church and family), but that for strategic reasons he limited his defense of male headship to the spheres of church and family, since it seemed unlikely that anything more universal would gain acceptance even in the most conservative Christian circles today. This admission was (to me, to whom it was originally directed) quite startling: can one imagine serious Christians during World War II (for example) arguing that they should not protect Jews from the Nazis on the grounds that their position, however biblical, was "unstrategic"? Surely if one is prophetically convinced of the biblical warrant of a particular position, one should be prepared to defend it regardless of its social or political popularity, within or outside the church.

[29]See for example sociologist John P. Bartkowsi's analysis of patriarchal vs. egalitarian themes in contemporary evangelical marriage manuals: "Debating Patriarchy: Discursive Disputes over Spousal Authority Among Evangelical Family Commentators," *Journal for the Scientific Study of Religion* 36, no. 3 (1997): 393-410. For accounts of how evangelical and fundamentalist Christian women both contest and cooperate with church-defined gender roles and gender hierarchy, see Brenda E. Brasher, *Godly Women: Fundamentalism and Female Power* (New Brunswick, N.J.: Rutgers University Press, 1998); R. Marie Griffith, *God's Daughters: Evangelical Women and the Power of Submission* (Berkeley: University of California Press, 1997); and Christel Manning, *God Gave Us the Right: Conservative Catholic, Evangelical Protestant and Orthodox Jewish Women Grapple with Feminism* (New Brunswick, N.J.: Rutgers University Press, 1999).

trial and industrialized cultures) it hardly comports with biblical notions of justice.[30]

This points to a third strategy for rescuing "gender complementarity," one more frequently invoked in the recent past. Some gender essentialists have reluctantly recognized that neither the Bible nor the natural or social sciences can come definitively to their rescue. Consequently, they take refuge in biblically and empirically questionable Jungian gender archetypes, and their precursors in Greek mythology and Eastern religions.[31] For example, Elisabeth Elliot, in her 1982 book *Let Me Be a Woman,* warned female Christian readers that Eve, in taking the initiative to eat the apple, was trying to be like the "ultimately-masculine" God—as if God were somehow metaphysically gendered. She also appealed to the ancient Chinese concept of yin and yang to buttress her "Christian" argument for gender essentialism and gender hierarchy.[32] Her brother Thomas Howard, in a 1978 article titled "A Note from Antiquity on the Question of Women's Ordination," frankly acknowledged that the Bible does not supply enough resources to justify talking about God or humans in terms of metaphysical, eternal gender archetypes. Undeterred by this, he invited his readers to consider the abundance of sexual imagery in pagan myths, and came to the conclusion that "a Christian would tend to attach some weight to this." Really? Why?[33]

---

[30]For a further discussion of gender justice in the context of support for the Kuyperian concept of sphere sovereignty (including the sovereign rights of families as one creational sphere of human cultural activity), see Mary Stewart Van Leeuwen, "Faith, Feminism and the Family in an Age of Globalization," in *Religion and the Powers of the Common Life,* ed. Max L. Stackhouse and Peter J. Paris (Harrisburg, Penn.: Trinity Press International, 2000), pp. 184-230.

[31]Faith Martin, "Mystical Masculinity: The New Questions Facing Women," *Priscilla Papers* 12, no. 1 (winter 1998): 6-12.

[32]Elisabeth Elliot, *Let Me Be a Woman* (Wheaton, Ill.: Tyndale, 1982).

[33]Thomas Howard, "A Note from Antiquity on the Question of Women's Ordination," *The Churchman: A Journal of Anglican Theology* 92, no. 4 (1978): 323. Howard is in part following C. S. Lewis's notion that certain themes in pagan myths (e.g., the dying and rising god) are foreshadowings of the "myth made flesh" in Jesus Christ. But even Lewis realized that such myths are only "a starting point from which *one* road leads home and a thousand roads lead into the wilderness." *The Pilgrim's Regress: An Allegorical Apology for Christianity, Reason and Romanticism* (London: J.M. Dent, 1933), p. 153 (Lewis's emphases). In other words, just because pagan myths were pointing in a Christian direction with regard to their intuitions about dying and rising gods does not make them proto-Christian when they talk about male sky gods and female earth mothers. Lewis himself, however, was clearly inconsistent on this point, embracing as part of "mere" (i.e., basic) Christianity all kinds of assumptions about the "masculinity" of God and essential, metaphysical character differences between women and men. See Candice Fredrick and Sam McBride, *Women Among the Inklings: Gender, C.S. Lewis, J.R.R. Tolkien and Charles Williams* (Westport, Conn.: Greenwood Press, 2001), and Mary Stewart Van Leeuwen, "A Sword Between the Sexes: C. S. Lewis's Long Journey to Gender Equality," *Christian Scholars Review,* in press.

Joan Burgess Winfrey is thus right to express concern that "the church may once again opt for a Venus-Mars gender rubbish in the interest of cementing roles and putting up divider walls."[34] Even if Mars-Venus rhetoric is used only to cement different gender styles rather than roles it gets virtually no support from the meta-analytic literature which, as we have seen, show almost complete overlap in the gendered distribution of traits such as nurturance, empathy, verbal skills, spatial skills and even aggressiveness. Moreover, the romanticizing and/or rank-ordering of gender archetypes is biblically questionable, whether it is done by gender-role traditionalists, by cultural feminists who reverse the hierarchy by valorizing the stereotypically feminine or by evangelical writers who baptize the trendy Mars-Venus rhetoric with a thin, Christian-sounding veneer. More in keeping with both the biblical creation accounts of humankind and the overall findings of the social sciences is the bumper sticker which reads "Men are from Earth, Women are from Earth: Get used to it!"

Perhaps the most cautious way of responding to the meta-analytic literature on gender comes from behavioral biologists, who (arguing largely from animal research) suggest that both sexes are capable of the full range of human behaviors, but that the thresholds for various behaviors may vary by gender.[35] This would mean, for example, that men and women are both capable of (even violent) aggression, but men would tend to yield to such impulses more readily than women. This would help explain why meta-analyzed gender differences tend to be smaller for laboratory studies than for ones done out in the real world. Laboratory settings are deliberately shielded from a host of real-world social influences (including ones that elicit gender stereotypes), and so may allow for possible behaviors to trump more or less probable ones in both sexes. But in the end, this distinction about thresholds doesn't help gender essentialists much, because even in the animal research on which it is based, the thresholds themselves are variable within male and female subject groups, and the resulting distributions overlap greatly, just as they do for actual behaviors. Moreover, as I noted previously, it is always risky to generalize from animal to human behavior, because human brains are structured for much more behavioral flexibility than those of even their closest primate neighbors.

---

[34]*DBE*, p. 446.
[35]For example, Perry Treadwell, "Biologic Influences on Masculinity," in *The Making of Masculinities: The New Men's Studies*, ed. Harry Brod (Boston: Allen & Unwin, 1989), pp. 259-85.

3. We cannot assume that anatomy is destiny until we have controlled for opportunity.

In a final attempt to rescue gender essentialism some scholars—Christian
and otherwise—claim that if a certain gender difference holds up *crosscultur-
ally*, that is, across many different learning environments, we can more safely
conclude that it is "natural" and "fixed," for better or for worse. But this conclusion is also too simple. An oft-quoted study of this sort is the thirty-seven-
nation survey of mate-selection standards by Texas psychologist David Buss,
which found a supposedly universal tendency for men (more than women)
to rank youth and beauty high as mate-selection criteria, and for women
(more than men) to rank wealth and power highly in potential mates. Buss,
appealing to theories from evolutionary psychology, suggested his findings
meant that men everywhere are genetically predisposed for reproductive reasons to look for youth and beauty in a prospective mate, while women are
more predisposed to look for ambition and wealth in the men they seek to
marry.[36] However, Buss's study made no attempt to control for the differing
opportunities that face women and men in many cultures. That powerful,
older men marry gorgeous younger women more than the opposite scenario
is certainly the case in many cultures. But as *New York Times* science journalist
Natalie Angier once wryly observed, "If some women continue to worry that
they need a man's money because the playing field remains about as level as
Mars—or Venus if you prefer—then we can't conclude anything about innate
preferences."[37]

More recently, two social psychologists (and meta-analytic specialists),
Alice Eagly and Wendy Wood, did control for varying opportunities by sex.[38]
They took the thirty-seven countries of Buss's study and rank-ordered them
according to two indices of gender equality devised by the United Nations Development Program. One is the Gender-Related Development Index (GDI),
which rates each nation on the degree to which its female citizens do not equal
their male counterparts in life span, education and basic income (which is still
the case, though to varying degrees, in all nations). The other is the Gender
Empowerment Measure (GEM), which rates nations on the degree to which

[36]David Buss, *The Evolution of Desire* (New York: Basic Books, 1994).

[37]Natalie Angier, *Women: An Intimate Geography* (Boston: Houghton Mifflin, 1999), p. 331.

[38]Alice H. Eagly and Wendy Wood, "The Origins of Sex Differences in Human Behavior: Evolved Dis-
positions Versus Social Roles," *American Psychologist* 54, no. 6 (1999): 184-230.

women, in comparison to men, have entered the public arena as local and national politicians, and as technicians, professionals and managers.[39] Using these two measures, they found that as gender equality in Buss's thirty-seven-nation list increased, the tendency for either sex to choose mates according to Buss's so-called evolutionary sex-selection criteria decreased. Eagly and Wood concluded from this that sex differences in mate-selection criteria are less the result of evolved biological strategies than of the historically constructed sexual division of labor, which makes women dependent on men's material wealth and men dependent on women's domestic skills. As this wall of separation breaks down—a process nicely traced by the two U.N. measures—both sexes revert to more generically human (and might we add, biblical?) criteria to judge potential mates, criteria such as kindness, dependability and a pleasant personality.[40]

MAKING RELATIONSHIPS THE UNIT OF ANALYSIS: HOW THE SOCIAL SCIENCES *CAN* HELP

So far I have tried to show that the odds are not good for using social science research to define the content of gender complementarity—if by that we mean showing how men and women essentially, or even generally, differ for all times and places. Nor should that surprise us. A responsible reading of Scripture indicates that God has built a lot of flexibility into what we call gender, which is why I always prefer to talk about gender *relations* rather than using the more static term gender *roles*. Biological sex is something we share with other, lower creatures. But gender is a part of the cultural mandate.[41] If, for example, we compare Genesis 1:20-22, with Genesis 1:26-28, we see that God first speaks to both animals and humans in exactly the same terms: "Be fruitful and multiply and fill [the seas, the earth]." What differs is that in the latter text the primal human pair are given an additional mandate: to subdue the earth. Reformed theologians have taken this to mean that all humans beings—whether

---

[39]For further explanation of the development and use of these measures, see *Human Development Report of the United Nations Development Program* (New York: Oxford University Press, 1995).

[40]Even in Buss's own study, when asked what qualities are most important in a mate, both sexes, on average, ranked love, dependability, emotional stability and a pleasing personality as the highest four. Only in the average fifth rankings did the differences predicted by Buss's evolutionary hypothesis emerge. And, as Eagly and Wood showed, those already low-ranking differences were ranked lower and lower as gender equality increased.

[41]See also Miroslav Volf, *Exclusion and Embrace: A Theological Exploration of Identity, Otherness, and Reconciliation* (Nashville: Abingdon, 1996), especially chap. 4.

or not they acknowledge the divine source of this mandate—are called to unfold the potential in creation in ways that flexibly express the image of God, while staying within the limits of God's creation norms. Note well: it is not the case in Genesis.1:28 that Eve is told to "be fruitful and multiply" and Adam is told to "subdue the earth"; both mandates are given to both members of the primal pair. What Christians have too often done instead, under the influence of pagan and Greek thought and the doctrine of separate spheres, is to assign men to subdue the earth while telling women to be fruitful and multiply, then cavalierly read this back into Scripture.

This seems to me to get it quite backward. While the cultural mandate does not require a blanket endorsement of androgyny (another example of rigid, ahistoric thinking), it does suggests that any construction of gender relations requiring an exaggerated, permanent separation of activities and/or virtues by sex is eventually going to run into trouble (as it has within the last century and more) because such exaggeration is creationally distorted and thus potentially unjust toward both sexes. Sexual dimorphism is indeed part of our creational framework, but gender is something to be responsibly and justly negotiated and renegotiated throughout the successive acts of the biblical drama. Gender is not a mystical, rigid, archetypal given. Rather, we need to think of gender as much in terms of a verb as a noun: "doing gender" is a responsible cultural activity whose mixed outcomes need to be critically examined in the context of the continuing biblical drama in which we are all actors. For people with a low tolerance for ambiguity, this can be very upsetting. Many of us would rather be like the "wicked and lazy slave" in the parable of the talents (Mt 25:14-30), keeping our assets buried in the cold ground of gender stereotypes and a Fall-based gender hierarchy, instead of flexibly multiplying them in the service of God and neighbor.

By contrast, in chapter twenty-six of *Discovering Biblical Equality,* Jack and Judith Balswick (a sociologist and marriage and family therapist) have perceptively developed just such a relational approach to gender in the service of just and flourishing marriages. In such marriages, they write, "The locus of authority is placed in the relationship, not in one spouse or the other," and both independence and interdependence are crucial:

> Behind the "two are better than one" Scripture is the idea that two independent persons [note: persons, not genders] have unique strengths to offer each other and the relationship. Without two separate identities, interdependence is not

possible. Some hold to the notion that dependency or fusion is the ideal . . . [but] two overly dependent persons, hanging on to each other for dear life, have . no solid ground on which to stand when things get difficult or an unexpected stress hits.[42]

According to the gender hierarchicalist model, they note, the risk of unequal partnership is "that husbands carry the burden of having to know everything and always be right, while wives pretend not to know or suppress what they know is right."[43] In contrast to both these distortions, the Balswicks' four marital relationship principles—covenant, grace, mutual empowerment and intimacy—focus less on prescribed roles (which are seen to be flexible and negotiable throughout the family life cycle) and more on processes needed for the ongoing flourishing of couples and families. These include that "partners hold equal status; accommodation in the relationship is mutual; attention to the other in the relationship is mutual; and there is mutual well-being of the partners."[44]

Does it matter for these processes that the "partners" are male and female, or does this relations-without-roles lead to "soft androgyny" and from there to the endorsement of nonheterosexual unions? Clearly not for the Balswicks, since they have included a thoughtful section in their chapter on the demonstrated benefits, for both sons and daughters, of coparenting by fathers and mothers. However, even these gendered and generational dynamics are not as simple as was once thought. Freudian and functionalist theorists believed that boys, for example, needed to have lots of interaction with their fathers in order to cement "essential" masculine attitudes, behaviors and roles. But there is a wealth of research, both in industrialized and pre-industrial cultures, showing that the more nurturantly involved fathers are with their sons, the more secure those sons are in their gender identity (which is simply the sense of feeling happy and adequate as a male). At the same time, nurturantly fathered sons are less likely to engage in stereotypical "hypermasculine" behavior, such as antisocial aggression, the sexual exploitation of girls or misogynist attitudes and actions.[45]

---

[42]Judith K. Balswick and Jack O. Balswick, in *DBE*, pp. 454-55.

[43]Ibid., p. 461.

[44]Ibid., p. 454.

[45]For reviews of this literature, see Scott Coltrane, *Family Man: Fatherhood, Housework, and Gender Equity* (New York: Oxford University Press, 1996), and Van Leeuwen, *My Brother's Keeper,* chaps. 6, 8 and 10.

Similar benefits accrue to nurturantly fathered girls, who are more likely to show independent achievement and less likely to engage in premature sexual and reproductive activity. Why is this so? In cultures and subcultures where fathers are absent or uninvolved in hands-on parenting, boys tend to define themselves in opposition to their mothers and other female caretakers, and to engage in misogynist, hypermasculine behaviors as a way to shore up a fragile gender identity.[46] And girls who are not sufficiently affirmed as persons by available and nurturing fathers are at risk of becoming developmentally "stuck" in a mindset that sees their sexuality and reproductive potential as the only criteria of feminine success.[47] The bottom line appears to be this: children of both sexes need to grow up with stable, nurturant and appropriately authoritative role models of both sexes to help develop a secure gender identity. But strong coparenting also allows growing children to relate to each other primarily as human beings, rather than as reduced, gender-role caricatures. Those who are most concerned to display rigidly stereotypical masculinity and femininity are apt to have the least secure gender identities. I have come to call this "the paradox of nurturant coparenting."[48]

Clearly this does not require that children's role models always and only be their biological parents.[49] But it strongly suggests there are limits to the diversity of family forms we should encourage around a core norm of heterosexual, role-flexible coparenting. As Genesis 1 reminds us, sex is indeed something that we share with the lower animals, and as such it is irrelevant to the image of God in humans. At the same time, lifelong cooperation between the sexes is part and parcel—indeed the climax—of the Genesis 2 creation account, in

---

[46]This might be grounds for worrying not only about the development of misogyny in boys raised in lesbian households, but boys in conservative Christian home-schooling households, given that almost all such home-schooling is done by mothers. For a sociological analysis of the home-schooling movement in America, see Mitchell Stevens, *Kingdom of Children: Culture and Controversy in the Home-schooling Movement* (Princeton: Princeton University Press, 2001).

[47]Scott Coltrane's analysis of almost a hundred preindustrial societies (n. 42) shows that nurturant fathering of children also correlates strongly with reduced abuse of women and greater empowerment and voice for women in the cultures where involved fathering takes place.

[48]For a more extended discussion of this, see Van Leeuwen, *My Brother's Keeper*, chaps. 5 and 6.

[49]In fact, given that the metaphor of adoption is such a central one in the overall biblical narrative, I am surprised that neither *RBMW* nor *DBE* has a chapter on its significance for the organization of family and church life. See for example Jeanne Stevenson-Moessner, *The Spirit of Adoption: At Home in God's Family* (Louisville, Ky.: Westminster John Knox, 2003), and Timothy P. Jackson, ed., *The Morality of Adoption: Social-Psychological, Theological and Legal Perspectives* (Grand Rapids: Eerdmans, 2005).

a way that is not required of other animals: "Therefore a man leaves his father and his mother and clings to his wife, and they become one flesh" (Gen 2:24). Sociologist David Fraser notes that this verse holds in tension three essential aspects of marriage: public wedlock ("leaving"), sexual union ("one flesh") and lifelong covenant ("cleaving"). Yet he significantly notes, "In this passage the couple is complete without children."[50] Thus heterosexual pair-bonding is not (as evolutionary psychologists suggest) simply a convenient way to have children—although children are indeed part of Gods' promised blessing in creation. It is based on the deeper creational truth that women and men are both created in the image of God, derive equal dignity and respect from that image, and are called to be God's earthly regents, not separately, nor hierarchically, nor in competition with each other, but cooperatively. This does not mean that all men and women must marry: the New Testament is very clear on the value of singleness. But it does suggest that attempts to form permanent, single-sex communities (or to impose a rigid doctrine of separate spheres within families and/or churches) as a way of avoiding the challenges of heterosexual cooperation and gender justice are something less than creationally normative and will eventually be shown to be so by their empirical results. In other words, if we do not, in a given era—or even across large swaths of history—accurately interpret special revelation (the Scriptures), then general revelation (empirical reality) will eventually start teaching us.how to do better.

AN AGENDA FOR THE IMMEDIATE FUTURE

It's somewhat ironic that neither of the two flagship books central to the debate about male headship versus gender mutuality (*Recovering Biblical Manhood and Womanhood* and *Discovering Biblical Equality*) says much about an area of social science research that is vital to this discussion. I refer to the forty-year accumulation of data on the steady rise of divorce and its effects on both children and their parents. America is (at least according to surveys of church membership and attendance) the most "Christian" of the Western industrialized democracies. It also has the highest percentage of people (35%) who have been divorced, and born-again Christians are no less likely to divorce than are non-Christians. A slight majority of born-again American respondents in George

---

[50]David A. Fraser, "Focus on the Biblical Family: Sociological and Normative Considerations," in *The Gospel with Extra Salt*, ed. Joseph B. Modica (Valley Forge, Penn.: Judson Press, 2000), pp. 1-29 (quotation p. 18).

Barna's 2004 national poll even denied that divorce in the absence of adultery should be considered a sin.[51] Regardless of one's take on Matthew 19:8-9,[52] it is obvious that Scripture pays clear and frequent attention to the importance of the marriage covenant, in contrast to less frequent and less clear pronouncements about the organization of church and family. This being the case, it would seem that many Christians in the gender-hierarchicalist camp are straining at gnats and swallowing camels. The social science consensus on the negative effects of divorce and the positive possibilities of well-validated marriage education and enrichment programs now cuts across all religious and political allegiances.[53] Yet many Christians in the gender-hierarchicalist camp are ambivalent about any programs based on "secular" social science, preferring to believe that the only (or main) experts on marriage are conservative male pastors, theologians and biblical scholars.[54]

Persons and groups on both sides of this debate would thus do well to follow the lead of evangelical journalist Michael McManus, who for the past twenty years has been promoting "Community Marriage Policies" (CMPs) whereby all clergy in a given area agree than none of them will marry any couple who has not gone through a several-month period of marriage preparation using a research-based training program, combined with a mentoring relationship with a more experienced married couple who have also been trained for

---

[51]"Born-Again Christians Just as Likely to Divorce as Are Non-Christians," *The Barna Update,* September 8, 2004 <www.barna.org/FlxPage.aspx?PageCMD>. Barna notes in this article that many non-Christian adults cohabit, thus effectively side-stepping marriage and divorce altogether. But he also points out that if this latter group married at the same rate as Christians, their divorce statistic would be roughly 38%, still not much higher than the 35% rate that characterizes born-again Americans. He also notes that most divorces among the born-again take place after, not before, their conversion, and that almost a quarter of born-agains have been through two or more divorces.

[52]The passage reads: "Jesus replied, 'Moses permitted you to divorce your wives because your hearts were hard. But it was not this way from the beginning. I tell you that anyone who divorces his wife, except for marital unfaithfulness, and marries another woman commits adultery'" (NIV).

[53]Part of this consensus is that divorce may be the lesser of two evils in the case of high-conflict marriages; however, in the U.S.A. fully two-thirds of divorces occur in low-conflict marriages, many of which could be prevented with good, researched-based marital preparation programs or salvaged with appropriate counseling. For a good review of the relevant literature see John Wall, Don Browning, William J. Doherty and Stephen Post, eds., *Marriage, Health and the Professions: If Marriage Is Good for You, What Does This Mean for Law, Medicine, Ministry, Therapy and Business?* (Grand Rapids: Eerdmans, 2002). See also David P. Gushee, *Getting Marriage Right: Realistic Counsel for Saving and Strengthening Relationships* (Grand Rapids: Baker, 2004), and Tim Stafford, "Can This Institution Be Saved?" *Christianity Today* 48, no. 11 (November 2004): 52-59.

[54]See, for example, William J. Doherty and Jason S. Carroll, "Health and the Ethics of Marital Therapy and Education," in Wall et al., *Marriage, Health and the Professions,* pp. 208-32.

their mentoring tasks. Since the first such policy was adopted by Modesto, California, pastors in 1986, almost 200 communities in forty American states (as well in Canada and England) have followed suit. And although the divorce rate is starting to decline somewhat in the United States as a whole, a recent study has shown that the rate over the past seven years has fallen twice as fast in CMP counties (almost 18%) than in non-CMP counties (only 9%), even when county pairs are matched on demographic indices such as population density, poverty and rural versus urban location.[55] It should be uncontroversial to those on both sides of this debate that prevention is better than cure when it comes to dealing with the high rate of divorce, both inside and outside the churches. And it should be uncontroversial that, through common grace, God can get God's work done through whomever God wishes, including careful and concerned social scientists of whatever (or even no) stated religious affiliation. As Abraham Kuyper once wryly observed, sometimes the world does better than expected, and the church does worse.[56]

Finally, a few words are in order regarding another topic little dealt with in the flagship volumes of either side in the debate. I refer to the possible contribution of male headship ideology to domestic violence and other forms of religious abuse, such as male church leaders sexually exploiting women and children over whom they exercise authority. Christians for Biblical Equality has sponsored conferences and books on the topic of abuse in the church,[57] and the Council on Biblical Manhood and Womanhood is clearly anxious to show that headship and submission (as they define these terms) do not contribute to "the epidemic of wife abuse."[58] But to properly test such a hypothesis, we would need to do what George Barna did to show the relationship between conservative religiosity and divorce, that is, mount

---

[55]Stanley Weed, Paul Birch and Joseph A. Olsen's study of the impact of Community Marriage Policies on divorce rates in 114 pairs of matched American counties, *Family Relations,* in press. The lower divorce rate in CMP counties translates into about 31,000 saved marriages over seven years. An excellent resource for marriage education information is the electronic database maintained by social worker Diane Sollee at <www.smartmarriages.com>.

[56]In this respect, it is ironic to note that in Barna's 2004 survey (see n. 51), the lowest rate of divorce was in the most highly secularized northeastern seaboard region of the U.S.A.

[57]Catherine Clark Kroeger and James Beck, eds. *Healing the Hurt: Giving Hope and Help to Abused Women* (Grand Rapids: Baker, 1998); Catherine Clark Kroeger and Nancy Nason-Clark, *No Place for Abuse: Biblical & Practical Resources to Counteract Domestic Violence* (Downers Grove, Ill.: InterVarsity Press, 2001).

[58]CBMW website, "Fifty Common Questions" <http://www.cbmw.org/questions>, especially questions 5, 8 and 9.

a large, representative survey of the entire nation that included very specific questions about both the respondents' religious practices and beliefs—including those having to do with gender relations—and their experiences with various forms of abuse within church and family settings, as both survivors and perpetrators. To my knowledge such a comprehensive study has yet to be done, though there is one random-sample survey of adults in a conservative denomination (one which did not ordain women at the time of the survey) showing that prevalence rates of physical, sexual and emotional abuse were no lower—but also no higher—within the denomination than in the American population at large.[59]

University of Virginia sociologist Bradford Wilcox has shown that conservative Protestant fathers are more likely to report using corporal punishment than other groups, but also (in keeping with a "soft patriarchal" ideology) more likely to praise and hug their children and less likely to yell at them than other groups, both churched and unaffiliated. He concludes that

> conservative Protestant fathers' neotraditional parenting style seems to be closer to the authoritative style—characterized by moderately high levels of parental control and high levels of parental supportiveness—that has been linked to positive outcomes among children and adolescents. In any case, the accusations about authoritarian and abusive parenting by conservative Protestants appear overdrawn. The findings paint a more complex portrait of conservative Protestant fathering that reveals a hybrid of strict, puritanical and progressive, child-centered approaches to child rearing—all in keeping with the logic of "expressive traditionalism" guiding this subculture.[60]

However, using data from the National Survey of Families and Households (1992-1994) Wilcox also found that a little bit of conservative religion—like a little bit of knowledge—is a dangerous thing.

> Some of the worst fathers and husbands are men who are nominal evangelicals. These are men who have, say, a Southern Baptist affiliation, but who rarely darken the door of a church. They have . . . the highest rates of domestic violence of any group in the United States. They also have high divorce rates. But evangelical *and* mainline Protestant men who attend church regularly are

---

[59]Committee to Study Physical, Emotional and Sexual Abuse: Report 30, *Agenda for Synod of the Christian Reformed Church in North America* (Grand Rapids: C.R.C. Publications, 1992), pp. 313-58.

[60]W. Bradford Wilcox, *Soft Patriarchs, New Men: How Christianity Shapes Fathers and Husbands* (Chicago: University of Chicago Press, 2004), p. 129.

. . . much less likely to divorce than married men who do not attend church regularly.[61]

And conservative Protestant husbands and fathers (including those who espouse, among other things, a traditionalist ideology of gender relations) are—provided they attend church regularly—the group that is actually *least* likely to commit domestic violence.[62]

The upshot is that we have no evidence so far that a gender-traditionalist ideology—at least of the soft patriarchal variety—is a strong predictor of domestic physical abuse. Gender hierarchicalist males—at least those who have frequent and active church involvement—turn out, on average, to be better men than their theories: more often than not, they are functional egalitarians, and the rhetoric of male headship may actually be functioning as a covert plea for greater male responsibility and nurturant involvement on the home front. This I am only too happy to endorse, especially since (as I have noted above) the more nurturant the father, the less likely the son is to grow up endorsing hierarchical attitudes toward women. If so, then male headship rhetoric may be withering on the generational vine even as it is still being broadcast in articles, books and websites. Stay tuned.

About the relationship of gender-hierarchical rhetoric to various forms of abuse (sexual, emotional or physical) in Protestant church (as opposed to family) settings, we know very little at this point. But at the very least, on issues such as combating domestic violence and lowering divorce rates, might not gender hierarchicalists and gender egalitarians be able to forge strategic bonds of cooperation? In theory, yes; I would not want to discourage moves in that direction. Still, there are reasons why I remain skeptical of such an undertaking as a Christian academic. Among gender hierarichicalists, there is much casuistry and hair-splitting about questions of gender as these relate to biblical exegesis, but very little responsible appropriation of best practices and findings in either social science research or its applications. It's as if these folks really don't believe in common grace—or do so only when its results fit their

---

[61]Douglas LeBlanc, "Affectionate Patriarchs: An Interview with W. Bradford Wilcox," *Christianity Today* 48, no. 8 (August 2004): 44-46.

[62]Wilcox, *Soft Patriarchs*, chap. 3. The NSFH 1992-94 study found that just over 7% of nominally Protestant husbands committed domestic violence, compared with just under 3% of active conservative Protestants. Other groups' percentages (e.g., nominal and active mainline Protestants, unaffiliated respondents) ranged between these two.

preconceived ideas. Moreover, as Gordon Fee notes in chapter twenty-one of *Discovering Biblical Equality*,

> In order to uphold male rule in today's households [and churches] patriarchalists are regularly faced with the necessity of fine-tuning various rules and restrictions regarding "biblical gender roles." In the end, the gospel of grace and Spirit is turned into a form of the law, which gives rise to the pharisaic problem of needing to put a hedge around the law, deciding what is or is not "allowable" within its framework.
>
> Peter's very pharisaic question, "How many times must I forgive?" is now turned into "What constitutes [womanly] submission?" . . . One wonders whether Paul would laugh or cry. The gospel of grace and gifting leads to a different set of questions: How does one best serve the interest of the other? How does one encourage [not predefine] the Spirit's gifting in the other? Questions like these cross all gender boundaries.[63]

For these reasons, in spite of affirming that this debate is not about a confessional issue and that each side must continue to affirm the genuine evangelical standing of those on the other side who disagree, I conclude that for the moment both sides will—and should—continue to go their separate ways.

---

[63]Gordon D. Fee, "Hermeneutics and the Gender Debate," *DBE*, p. 379. CBMW's accumulation of more and more "hedges around the law" is particularly evident in its answers to "Fifty Crucial Questions" <www.cbmw.org/questions>.

APPENDIX A

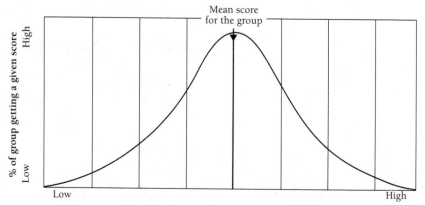

Trait or behavior measured

A normal (bell curve) distribution:
It is divided into eight standard deviations in order to
measure the spread or variability of scores.

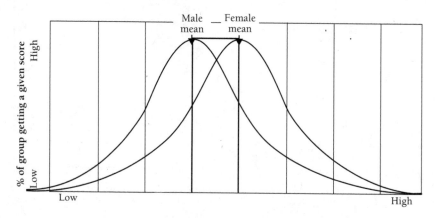

Self-report measures of empathy

Two overlapping distributions (male and female scores)
showing an effect size (*d*) of 1.000

Notice that the average difference *between* the two groups is much
smaller than the spread (or variability) of scores *within* each group.

APPENDIX B

*Some Effect Sizes (Average d's) from Various
Meta-analyses of Studies of Sex Differences.*

TRAIT OR BEHAVIORAL MEASURE	EFFECT SIZE (average *d*)	WHICH SEX SCORES HIGHER
Height (U.S. & U.K.)	2.00	M
Throwing Velocity	2.18	M
Empathy		
a. Self-Reported	1.00	F
b. Behaviorally Observed	.05	F
Helping Behavior	.34	M
Spatial Rotation		
a. Children	.38	M
b. Adults	.54	M
Interpersonal Distance	.54	F
Desires Many Sex Partners	.87	M
Math Computation		
a. Children	.22	F
b. Adults	.00	Neither
Mathy Problem Solving	.32	M
Reading Skills		
a. 5-6 years of age	.31	F
b. 11-19 years of age	.02	F
Verbal Analogies	.16	M
Verbal Fluency		
a. Studies prior to 1973	.23	F
b. Studies after 1973	.11	F

Aggression		
a. Children	.58	M
b. Adults	.27	M
Rough-and-Tumble Play	.45	M
Moral Reasoning		
a. "Care" Orientation	.28	F
b. "Justice" Orientation	.19	M

9

Holy Boldness, Holy Women

Agents of the Gospel

Cheryl J. Sanders

THE HOLINESS MOVEMENT OF THE LATE NINETEENTH century was initiated by a Methodist laywoman, Phoebe Palmer. The emergent tradition encouraged believers to testify of their experience, and these testimonies were freely received from anyone with the boldness to speak. Dr. Susie Stanley, a Church of God historian, has documented the contributions of Holiness women preachers in her recent text *Holy Boldness*.[1] Throughout our 125-year history, the Church of God has commissioned and ordained women ministers, although the proportion of women pastors waxed and waned over the course of the twentieth century. As is the case with most Holiness churches, the rationale for acceptance of women as ministers is the doctrine of the Holy Spirit, who gifts, equips and positions persons for ministry without regard to race, sex or class.

Women in the Church of God have not been immune from the factors that restrict and discourage women from doing ministry in other churches. In fact, there is evidence that today many of our congregations are not open to considering women candidates for leadership positions, notwithstanding our stance of endorsing women in ministry. Dr. Randal Huber has written a book, *Called, Equipped and No Place to Go*, which addresses this dilemma faced by women ministers in the Church of God.[2] In my book *Ministry at the Margins* I

---

[1]Susie Stanley, *Holy Boldness* (Knoxville: University of Tennessee Press, 2002).
[2]Randal Huber, *Called, Equipped and No Place to Go* (Anderson, Ind.: Warner Press, 2003).

explored the biblical foundations of the prophetic mission of women, youth and the poor in the church and society. The epilogue is an oral history collected from Rev. Hattie Downer, a Church of God minister in Brooklyn, New York, who embodies and exemplifies the notion that God chooses and uses women to bring good news to the poor.[3]

In this chapter I will address the marginalization and subordination of women's leadership in the church from the perspective of racism, sexism and other forms of elitism. From this vantage point I will assess "holy boldness" as a virtue that empowers holy women to do prophetic ministry in the face of opposition based on the deep conviction that they are indeed speaking for God. First I will profile three noteworthy women ministers from the Holiness tradition in the late nineteenth and early twentieth centuries. Next I will give an overview of some of the challenges faced by women ministers and pastors in the Church of God (Anderson, Indiana). I will conclude with an autobiographical note and a brief comment on women preaching Holiness in the twenty-first century.

HOLINESS WOMEN PREACHERS: PROFILES IN COURAGE

I have spent the past two years working with a group of religious scholars on a collection of African American sermons titled *I Can Feel My Help: African American Preaching 1645-2002: A Norton Anthology,* slated for publication within the next year or so. My specific area of focus as a contributor has been to compile and analyze African American preaching in the Holiness movement and Pentecostalism from 1860 to the present. Instead of making hard and fast distinctions between "Holiness" and "Pentecostal," I tend to follow the lead of anthropologist Zora Neale Hurston and others who prefer the designation "Sanctified Church" to encompass both traditions, especially among African Americans. Among the dozen sermons I gathered for publication are three preached by Sanctified Church women who made an impact within the urban context, namely Amanda Berry Smith, Rosa Horn and Bishop Ida B. Robinson.

Amanda Berry Smith (1837-1915). Many of the details of Amanda Berry Smith's life are narrated in the autobiography she published in 1893, *An Autobiography: The Story of the Lord's Dealings with Mrs. Amanda Smith the Colored Evangelist; Containing an Account of Her Life Work of Faith, and Her Travels in*

---

[3]Cheryl J. Sanders, *Ministry at the Margins* (Downers Grove, Ill.: InterVarsity Press, 1997), pp. 105-42.

America, England, Ireland, Scotland, India, and Africa, as an Independent Mission-
ary. She was born on a farm near Baltimore, Maryland, on January 23, 1837.
Her parents, Samuel and Mariam Berry, were slaves who lived on adjoining
farms. Her father purchased freedom for himself, his wife and children by sell-
ing the brooms and mats he made by working extra hours at night, aided by
the deathbed request of Mariam's sympathetic young slave mistress. While she
was still very young the family moved to a farm near York, Pennsylvania. Their
home became one of the main stations of the Underground Railroad, and her
family had numerous encounters with runaway slaves and the brutal men who
pursued them.

Amanda received a total of three months of formal schooling, but was
taught to read at home under the tutelage of her parents. In 1854, at the age
of sixteen, she married Calvin Devine, and they had two children, one of
whom lived to adulthood. The next year Amanda became seriously ill, and her
conversion and call to ministry were set in motion by her vision of herself being rescued from death by an angel and then preaching to thousands at a great
camp meeting:

> In the afternoon of the next day after the doctor had given me up, I fell asleep
> about two o'clock, or I seemed to go into a kind of trance or vision, and I saw
> on the foot of my bed a most beautiful angel. It stood on one foot, with wings
> spread, looking me in the face and motioning me with the hand; it said "Go
> back," three times, "Go back. Go back, Go back."
>
> Then, it seemed, I went to a great Camp Meeting and there seemed to be
> thousands of people, . . . I was on this platform with a large Bible opened and I
> was preaching from these words:—"And I if I be lifted up will draw all men unto
> me." O, how I preached, and the people were slain right and left. I suppose I
> was in this vision about two hours. When I came out of it I was decidedly better.
> When the doctor called in and looked at me he was astonished, but so glad. In
> a few days I was able to sit up, and in about a week or ten days to walk about.
> Then I made up my mind to pray and lead a Christian life. I thought God had
> spared me for a purpose.[4]

Amanda's first husband never returned from his service in the Civil War and
was presumed dead. She married a second husband, James Smith, an ordained

---

[4]Amanda Berry Smith, *An Autobiography: The Story of the Lord's Dealings with Mrs. Amanda Smith the Colored Evangelist* (Chicago: Meyer & Bros., 1893), pp. 42-43. This edition can also be found online at
<http://docsouth.unc.edu/neh/smitham/menu.html>.

deacon in the African Methodist Episcopal Church, and gave birth to more children. She worked in domestic service doing laundry and ironing. Her sanctification occurred in September of 1868 at a meeting with whites at Green Street Church in New York, and her testimony includes the experience of liberation from racial intimidation:

> "Oh!" I said, "I see it." And somehow I seemed to sink down out of sight of my-self, and then rise; it was all in a moment. I seemed to go two ways at once, down and up. Just then such a wave came over me, and such a welling up in my heart, and these words rang through me like a bell: "God in you, God in you," and I thought doing what? Ruling every ambition and desire, and bringing every thought unto captivity and obedience to His will. How I have lived through it I cannot tell, but the blessedness of the love and the peace and power I can never describe. O, what glory filled my soul! The great vacuum in my soul began to fill up; it was like a pleasant draught of cool water, and I felt it. I wanted to shout Glory to Jesus! but Satan said, "Now, if you make a noise they will put you out." I was the only colored person there and I had a very keen sense of propriety; I had been taught so, and Satan knew it. . . . Somehow I always had a fear of white people—that is, I was not afraid of them in the sense of doing me harm, or any-thing of that kind— but a kind of fear because they were white, and were there, and I was black and was here! But that morning on Green Street, as I stood on my feet trembling, I heard these words distinctly. They seemed to come from the northeast corner of the church, slowly, but clearly: "There is neither Jew nor Greek, there is neither bond nor free, there is neither male nor female, for ye are all one in Christ Jesus." (Galatians 3:28.) I never understood that text before. But now the Holy Ghost had made it clear to me. And as I looked at white people that I had always seemed to be afraid of, now they looked so small. The great mountain had become a mole-hill. "Therefore, if the Son shall make you free, then are you free, indeed." All praise to my victorious Christ![5]

After the death of her second husband in November 1869, Smith began preaching regularly in churches in New York and New Jersey, beginning with the meeting at Salem, New Jersey. She preached in African Methodist Episco-pal churches, to gatherings of Methodists and at "holiness" meetings through-out the eastern and midwestern parts of the United States. Smith made singing a significant part of her evangelistic outreach: "her simple, Quaker-like dress and bonnet, with her rich contralto voice with which she would break into

[5]Ibid., pp. 76-80.

song when inspired, made her a compelling figure."[6]

Smith remained engaged in full-time evangelism for more than twenty years, traveling abroad and conducting evangelistic meetings in Great Britain, India, Liberia and Sierra Leone. In 1890 she returned to the United States and became a national evangelist for the Women's Christian Temperance Union. Eventually she settled in Chicago, Illinois. With the proceeds from her 1893 autobiography, other income from her ministry, and support from British temperance groups and African American women's clubs, she opened a home for African American orphans in Harvey, Illinois. Ida B. Wells Barnett was one of several African American club women who served on the board of the orphanage.

In 1912, when she retired to Florida, the orphanage was taken over by the state of Illinois and chartered as the Amanda Smith Industrial School for Girls. Smith died in Sebring, Florida, on February 24, 1915. Her remains were returned to Chicago for one of the largest funerals ever held in the African American community. At the time of her death in 1915, the Chicago Defender called Amanda Berry Smith, "the greatest woman that this race has ever given to the world."[7]

Rosa A. Horn (1880-1976). Rosa A. Horn was born on December 2, 1880, in Sumter, South Carolina. She was one of ten children, all of whom were sent to private school by their mother, Sarah Baker. Horn lived in Augusta, Georgia, for eight years with her husband, William Artimus, and her two children, Jessie and William Jr. She joined the Methodist church in Augusta, and later joined the Fire Baptized Holiness Church, where she became an evangelist. After the death of her husband she moved to Illinois and later to Indiana. She was ordained to the ministry by the popular Holiness-Pentecostal evangelist Maria Woodworth-Etter. Horn married William Horn and moved to Evanston, Illinois. She established the Pentecostal Faith Church in Harlem in 1926. Bettye Collier-Thomas notes that she came to be known as Mother Horn by her followers and also as the "Pray for Me Priestess," "having a powerful presence, being an extremely effective speaker, and possessing great charisma."[8] A cultured and educated preacher, she was nevertheless able to attract southern

---

[6]Smith, *Autobiography.*

[7]David C. Bartlett and Larry A. McClellan, "The Final Ministry of Amanda Berry Smith: An Orphanage in Harvey, Illinois, 1895-1918," *Illinois Heritage* 1, no. 2 (winter 1998), p. 20 <www.lib.niu.edu/ipo/1998/ihwt9820.html>.

[8]Bettye Collier-Thomas, *Daughters of Thunder: Black Women Preachers and Their Sermons, 1850-1979* (San Francisco: Jossey-Bass, 1998), p. 173.

migrants and working-class blacks to her church. Like many other Pentecostals, she taught that there were three distinct stages of salvation: conversion, sanctification and baptism in the Holy Ghost.[9]

In 1933 Horn was invited to begin a radio ministry to compete with the "Happy Am I" broadcast of Elder Lightfoot Solomon Michaux. When Father Divine used illegal means to attempt to run Horn out of Harlem, the resulting controversy and lawsuit had the effect of further publicizing her broadcast and quadrupling her listening audience. Her church was the first in Upper Manhattan to be wired for radio broadcasting. Horn's radio ministry lasted for thirty years. According to bibliographer Charles E. Jones, the Mount Calvary Assembly Hall of the Pentecostal Faith, which she established as her headquarters in 1930, displays a neon sign outside that reads, "Church of the Air. Jesus Pray for Me."[10]

Horn moved to Baltimore, Maryland, in 1959, where she died on May 11, 1976. The Directory of African American Religious Bodies (1991) cites the Mount Calvary Pentecostal Faith Church, Inc., in Baltimore as a group founded in New York City by Bishop Rosa Artimus Horn in 1932, and states that she was succeeded by her daughter, Jessie, as bishop.[11]

Ida B. Robinson (1891-1946). Bishop Ida B. Robinson was born on August 3, 1891, in Hazelhurst, Georgia, but spent most of her childhood in Pensacola, Florida. As a teenager she worked as a cook to help support her family. She was converted at a Pentecostal street meeting and joined the Church of God in 1908. Soon thereafter she started her ministry of prayer and preaching in private homes. At the invitation of her sister, she and her husband, Oliver, migrated north to Philadelphia in 1917 to seek opportunities for employment.

Upon her arrival in Philadelphia she joined a Holiness mission in the heart of the black section. As her popularity as a preacher and singer increased within the congregation pastored by Benjamin Smith, she made a decision to leave. She was ordained an elder in the United Holy Church of America and was appointed pastor of Mount Olive Holy Church in 1919. In a recent article,

---

[9]Ibid., p. 179.

[10]Charles Edwin Jones, *Black Holiness: A Guide to the Study of Black Participation in Wesleyan Perfectionist and Glossolalic Pentecostal Movements*, ATLA Bibliography 18 (Metuchen, N.J.: Scarecrow Press, 1987), p. 204.

[11]Wardell J. Payne. ed., *Directory of African American Religious Bodies* (Washington, D.C.: Howard University Press, 1991), p. 106.

Harold Dean Trulear has noted, "this was no small appointment, for the next year Mount Olive was part of the founding Holy Convocation of the Northern District of the United Holy Church of America, . . . and by 1922 there were 35 ministers listed under the heading Mount Olive Holy Church, Philadelphia, Pa."[12] Robinson began to gain prominence in the denomination, often accompanying the United Holy Church leaders in evangelistic campaigns. Eventually she was led to establish the Mount Sinai Holy Church of America:

> Ida B. Robinson was in a period of prayer and fasting. She reported pains within her body as if she were in labor. During this time, God spoke to her and told her to "Come out on Mt. Sinai" and "loose the women." She interpreted this as a sign that God would have her begin a church movement, not a denomination in the strictest sense, but a confederation of churches that would provide opportunities for women to exercise leadership.[13]

When the first holy convocation of Mount Sinai was convened on September 23, 1925, the church already was chartered as a legal entity, and with 17 churches participating the meeting was held in a newly purchased building. Robinson was elected bishop. She "birthed" new churches instead of building them, with the emphasis on the creation of a new family, as opposed to the development of an institution or structure. Mount Sinai became one of the largest Pentecostal organizations, expanding to Cuba, British Guiana (now Guyana) and South America. With respect to women's leadership, Robinson ordained women throughout the United States, and the church's ministers, elders and administrators were predominantly female.[14]

Robinson taught that both holy living and tongues-speaking are evidence of the power of the Holy Spirit in the life of the believer. The holiness standard of Mount Sinai included restrictions on consumption of alcohol, use of tobacco and narcotics, and attendance at dances and movies. Women could not wear jewelry or braid their hair, and their heads were always covered in church. They wore long black dresses with white lace cuffs and collar. A corresponding standard was established for the men, who were forbidden to wear neckties, a practice which continued into the 1980s. She instructed her mem-

---

[12]Harold Dean Trulear, "Ida B. Robinson: The Mother as Symbolic Presence," in *Portraits of a Generation: Early Pentecostal Leaders*, ed. James R. Goff Jr. and Grant Wacker (Fayetteville: University of Arkansas Press, 2002), p. 313.

[13]Ibid., p. 313.

[14]Bettye Collier-Thomas, *Daughters of Thunder* (San Francisco: Jossey-Bass, 1998), p. 194.

bers not to accept induction into the Armed Forces as conscientious objectors who did not submit to bearing arms. She died on April 20, 1946, in Winter Haven, Florida, while conducting an evangelistic campaign in the South.[15]

HOLINESS WOMEN IN MINISTRY: THE CHURCH OF GOD (ANDERSON, INDIANA)

In the Church of God, the lifestyle concerns that flow from holiness teachings include personal considerations like abstinence from addictive substances such as alcohol, nicotine and narcotics; strict observance of the marriage covenant as the exclusive context for sexual fulfillment; rejection of forms of entertainment that glorify lust and ungodliness; and modesty in dress. However, the biblical holiness traditions centers upon ethical standards such as love, truth, justice and mercy that illumine the "setting apart" of people for partnership with God and with each other in the work of reconciliation and redemption. In this regard, holiness is more than personal piety or quiet asceticism; it is a bold and aggressive witness to the world, energized by a prophetic zeal for righteousness and enabled by the power of the Holy Spirit.

The privileged status of the white male in the Church of God must be seriously called into question in view of the ethics of holiness and unity. If holiness is our method and unity is our goal, then our ethical practices ought to be governed by the fruitfulness, love, truthfulness, righteousness, compassion and forgiveness that set us apart as holy people of a holy God. A system that reserves the vast majority of pastoral and administrative leadership positions in the church for white men not only deviates from the principles of holiness and unity but also reveals a stubborn allegiance to sexism and racism. Such a system perpetuates itself by providing role models and support networks for white men who desire to serve, in effect excluding and discouraging those who are not white or male from aspiring to be trained and employed as leaders.

The sexist and racist practices within the Church of God have not only been in evidence in the pulpits and agency offices, but in the pews as well. Most of our congregations are segregated by race and effectively proscribe the roles and influence of female members. To "reach our hands in fellowship to every bloodwashed one" is our song and our theme but not our practice, because we prefer to embrace those who are of our same race and class. While women may

---

[15]Trulear, "Ida B. Robinson," pp. 316-18.

be gladly received into the fellowship, their ministries are often regarded as subordinate and auxiliary to the ministries of males.

The extent to which Church of God people have assimilated the destructive racist and sexist ideas of the society is alarming, especially in view of the fact that we claim to serve a holy and just God. Instead of modeling for the world a community of faith whose witness is enriched and expanded by openness to all the people whom God has called and equipped for service, the Church of God sometimes mirrors the blasphemous duplicity of a society that proclaims that all are created equal, but excludes certain groups from access to justice and economic opportunity. This state of affairs is blasphemous insofar as it is grounded in the belief that God favors the white male, who alone bears God's image.

The Church of God Reformation Movement has not always embraced and practiced the racist and sexist biases of American culture. The nineteenth-century pioneers, zealous in their advocacy of holiness and unity, largely welcomed the full participation of women and blacks in the body of Christ during a time when racial and sexual discrimination was legally sanctioned and widely practiced in all sectors of the society. Their vision that the Spirit calls and equips the saints without respect to racial, sexual or sectarian boundaries enabled them to reject both racial segregation and sexual subordination as inappropriate practices for God's church. With the rise of Jim Crow segregation in the South, however, and the demise of progressive evangelical feminism in other regions of the nation, Church of God leaders began to accommodate themselves to these shifting currents of social sentiment against blacks and women. The process of accommodation to the prevailing racial and sexual norms of American culture set the stage for the founding of the National Association of the Church of God, a fellowship of predominantly black pastors and congregations, and the gradual retrenchment of women from the ranks of ordained ministry and pastoral leadership.

Blacks organized separate camp meetings and congregations because white racism essentially forced them out of fellowship with whites. The experience of women has been somewhat different, given the fact that they were excluded from leadership and not from fellowship. Instead of forming separate contexts for ministry and worship, women tended to accept subordinate status within the church, and women leaders were sometimes relegated to roles as missionaries and teachers. Ironically, black women have been subjected to dual discrimination within the Church of God—as women, they have not had equal opportunity to assume leadership positions in black congregations or within the National Association; as blacks, they have been prejudged as unfit for fellowship and service in white congregations and agency offices. In ethical and historical perspective, then, the Church of God has retreated over time from a progressive vision or unity and equality in the body of Christ to a reactionary conformity to the discriminatory divisiveness of the society.

The hurts experienced by women and so-called minorities who have been denied full partnership within the body of Christ will remain unhealed as long as the Church of God and other churches continue to embrace racism and sexism. Sanctification is more than pious adherence to a select list of dos and don'ts—it is covenantal empowerment to serve God. The doctrine of sanctification proclaims that by the grace of God we can live free from sin. Our understanding of the sin from which we have been freed, however, tends to be much too narrow, as measured by the degree of segregation and discrimination that exists within our congregations and national organizations. Since sin is manifested in both personal and social matters, so our sanctification from sin has both personal and social effects. To attend to personal concerns such as sexuality and dress without at the same time acknowledging our responsibility to overcome sin in the social order (for example, racism, sexism and economic exploitation) is to assume the same dubious moral posture as the scribes and Pharisees whom Jesus rebuked: "You give a tenth of your spices—mint, dill and cumin. But you have neglected the more important matters of the law— justice, mercy and faithfulness. You should have practiced the latter, without neglecting the former" (Mt 23:23 NIV).

When more individuals and congregations within the Church of God begin to take seriously the relationship between sanctification and social change, then the barriers of sexual and racial division can be dismantled, the needed healing and reconciliation can take place, and exciting new applications of the doctrines of holiness and unity to the divine task of offering a united ministry to a divided world can emerge.

AN AUTOBIOGRAPHICAL NOTE

I am a "lifer" in the Third Street Church of God in Washington, D.C.[16] By "lifer"

---

[16]Adapted from Cheryl Sanders, "Women in Ministry," *OneVoice* 1, no. 6 (2005): 8.

I mean that I was born and raised in the church because my parents were devout church members who brought me there to be dedicated as an infant and
enrolled in Sunday school. As a teenager I was active in the youth group, attended youth camps and conventions, and was baptized while in high school.
It was during my college years that I sensed my call to ministry, and after my
graduation from college I returned to my home church to participate fully in
its ministries as a Sunday school teacher and youth leader. I left again to attend
seminary and graduate school, and upon my return I resumed a high level of
involvement in Christian education and leadership development. I served as
associate pastor under Dr. Samuel G. Hines, and two years after his death in
1995 the church called me to succeed him as senior pastor, the position I have
held from 1997 to the present.

I do not recall ever questioning the role of women in ministry while growing up in the Church of God. I always knew strong and capable women leaders
whose influence overshadowed any doubts that might emerge to challenge
their authority. Dr. Pansy M. Brown was a highly respected Christian educator
in the Church of God at large, and at Third Street Church she inspired and motivated me early on to get involved in Christian education. Her mother, Reverend Annie Anderson, was a pastor and evangelist in the Church of God. Reverend Letitia Jones was pastor of a nearby congregation in Arlington, Virginia,
and she encouraged me to attend seminary to better prepare myself to serve
the church as a minister. It was my privilege to be supported by both women
and men in the ministry as I pursued my calling. My own pastor, Dr. Hines,
shepherded me through the credentialing process. Elder Robert Key in Washington and Reverend James Scott in Baltimore, Maryland, were among the first
pastors who invited me to preach at their churches when I was just getting
started in ministry.

I did not become fully aware of the widespread sentiment against women
in ministry until I entered seminary and encountered students of other denominations who discriminated against women based upon their traditions of
biblical interpretation and their perceptions of the subordinate roles of women
in general. I was shocked and appalled on the rare occasions when I heard
negative views of women and their roles in church and society expressed by
visiting preachers at my home church and at the Church of God congregation
I attended in Boston, Massachusetts. It was clear to me that a biblical view of
women's roles in ministry ought to take into account the entire Scripture, and

not just a verse or two referring to women being silenced. I question any biblical interpretation that would invoke 1 Corinthians 14:33-34 and 1 Timothy 2:11-12 to silence Miriam, Deborah, Huldah, Mary, Mary Magdalene, Priscilla, Phoebe and all the other women in the Bible whom God anointed and authorized to preach and prophesy.

In 1989 I participated with a group of Church of God women ministers in the production of the book *Called to Minister, Empowered to Serve*, edited by Juanita Leonard and published by Warner Press.[17] This book was an amazing collection of writings about the experiences of women as pastors, professors and missionaries in the church. We compiled the book to serve as a resource for the National Consultation on Women in Ministry and Mission convened that same year in Anderson, Indiana. As far as I know, no other group or denomination has produced anything like it, and it has been a useful text for the study of the roles of women in ministry. Unfortunately, the book was not promoted very effectively by our own church and publishing house, and to this day I feel the Church of God missed a great opportunity to advance the cause of women in leadership by failing to market the book more broadly.

From 1900 to 1920, when women won the right to vote in the United States, women pastors flourished in the Church of God, as in other groups with an emphasis on the preaching of salvation and the doctrine of the Holy Spirit. After 1920 there began a decline in the number of women pastors in the church, as if the Church of God were quietly aligning our views and vision of women's leadership with the denominations that excluded women altogether from the ministry. After the 1970s, when the mainline Protestant denominations began ordaining and calling women as pastors, the numbers of women pastors in the Church of God continued to lag behind. Some of the most gifted women in our church have sought opportunities for full-time ministry in other denominations and as chaplains in other institutional settings and in the military.

FUTURE PROSPECTS FOR HOLINESS WOMEN IN MINISTRY

The challenge remains for the church to educate congregations about giving serious attention and fair consideration to women candidates who are qualified and equipped to serve as pastors. As a pastor of a church with a significant staff

---

[17]Juanita Leonard, ed., *Called to Minister, Empowered to Serve* (Anderson, Ind.: Warner Press, 1989).

of credentialed men and women in ministry, I am disgusted with congregations in our area who call upon women ministers from our congregation to supply their pulpits while they search exclusively for men to call as their pastors.

On our Church of God campuses and at our national conventions and conferences I see women emerging and equipping themselves for ministry and leadership in the body of Christ. Holiness and Pentecostal women are preaching the gospel on television, radio and in the pulpits of some of the nation's fastest-growing congregations. I am committed to finding ways to convince Church of God congregations to be more accepting of our own women as pastors and leaders. I strongly encourage pastors, lay leaders, search committees and credentials committees everywhere to give careful consideration to the roles and opportunities we provide for women in our own church. We all will falter in our efforts to advance the gospel and grow congregations in the twenty-first century if we continue to disregard the women God has raised up, like Esther, "for such a time as this."

10

Women in Public Ministry

A Historic Evangelical Distinctive

Timothy Larsen

WOMEN IN PUBLIC CHRISTIAN MINISTRY IS A historic distinctive of evangelicalism. It is historic because evangelical women have been fulfilling their callings in public ministry from the founding generation of evangelicalism to the present day and in every period in between. It is a distinctive because no other large branch of the Christian family has demonstrated as long and deep a commitment to affirming the public ministries of women—not theologically liberal traditions, not Roman Catholicism or Eastern Orthodox traditions, not Anglicanism or other mainline Protestant traditions. I am defining "public ministry" as Christian service to adult believers—including men—that takes one or more of the following forms: preaching, teaching, pastoring, administering the sacraments and giving spiritual oversight.

A Distinctive in the First Generation of Evangelicals

Evangelicalism is a Christian movement that began in the 1730s.[1] A strong argument could be made that John Wesley is the founder of the evangelical tra-

---

[1]See D. W. Bebbington, *Evangelicalism in Modern Britain: A History from the 1730s to the 1980s* (London: Routledge, 1993). Two formidably brilliant colleagues of mine, Steve Spencer and Dan Treier, have allowed themselves to fall into the hitherto thankless habit of reading most everything I write and making astute comments on it. They are often unsuccessful at reining in my cavalier tendencies, but nevertheless do save me a multitude of errors, and I am deeply grateful for their efforts and friendship.

dition, but if that is too contentious a point one may at least say that he holds a place of prominence among the handful of key leaders from the founding generation of the movement. As a young man, Wesley's churchmanship was marked by a strong sense of propriety—indeed, one might say by a rather fastidious understanding of ecclesiastical respectability. After his evangelical conversion, however, he learned to curb this natural tendency as his commitment to the Bible and to the gospel took precedence over such personal preferences. For example, Wesley had to suppress his tendency to assume that it was only fitting to preach in a consecrated church building:

> I could scarce reconcile myself at first to this strange way of preaching in the fields, of which he [George Whitefield] set me an example on Sunday; having been all my life (till very lately) so tenacious of every point relating to decency and order, that I should have thought the saving of souls almost a sin, if it had not been done in a church.[2]

His sense of what was proper meant that he naturally disliked the idea of women preaching—an entirely conventional aversion in his day. His contemporary, Dr. Samuel Johnson (1709-1784), who was not an evangelical (or indeed a particularly devout man), famously quipped, "Sir, a woman preaching is like a dog's walking on his hind legs. It is not done well; but you are surprised to find it done at all."[3] Wesley's initial instinct, therefore, was to lay down the rule: "The Methodists do not allow women Preachers."[4]

Nevertheless, John Wesley found that his evangelical commitment to the gospel led him to abandon this position just as he had abandoned his prejudice against field preaching. His interim position was to concede to women whose ministries he respected: "Even in public, you may properly enough intermix short exhortations with prayer."[5] In the end, however, the priority of the gospel led him on to accepting the preaching ministries of gifted women. Although I do not wish to misrepresent Wesley as some sort of feminist, it is fascinating to note that he affirmed the ministries of these women in explicitly egalitarian language as of the exact same order as that of the men who had not received Anglican ordination

---

[2]Journal entry for April 29, 1739, in John Wesley, *The Works of John Wesley*, 3rd ed. (Grand Rapids: Baker, 1984-2002; vol. 1 reprint of the 1872 ed.), 1:185.

[3]James Boswell, *The Life of Samuel Johnson, LL.D.*, vol. 1 (Boston: W. Andrews, 1807), p. 361. Johnson made this comment in 1763.

[4]Letter to Sarah Crosby, February 14, 1761, in Wesley, *Works*, 12:353.

[5]Letter to Sarah Crosby, March 18, 1769, in Wesley, *Works*, 12:355.

whose public ministries he was also affirming. He wrote to one of his women preachers, Sarah Crosby: "I think the strength of the cause rests there; on your having an extraordinary call. So I am persuaded has every one of our lay Preachers: Otherwise, I could not countenance his preaching at all."[6] Incidentally, the Calvinist, George Whitefield, also affirmed Crosby's public ministry.

Other women whose public ministries John Wesley recognized included Hannah Harrison, Ann Cutler and Grace Walton. Perhaps most striking of all is the case of Mary Fletcher (1739-1815) née Bosanquet. Wesley recognized her preaching ministry when she was still a single woman. She went on to marry John Fletcher, who was not only an ordained Anglican priest but also such a prominent minister in his Methodist movement that Wesley had named Fletcher as his own successor to lead it. Once married, John and Mary Fletcher pursued a joint public ministry. When John Fletcher died in 1785, Mary continued as the senior minister, giving oversight to the church in Madeley that they had served together. If Wesley had not become an evangelical he would have never countenanced the notion of women preachers. There was a thriving liberal wing of Anglicanism in Wesley's day, known then as Latitudinarianism. Nevertheless, no nonevangelical Anglican priest or bishop in Wesley's day—or for a long time thereafter—ever approved of women preachers. In the eighteenth century, affirming women in public ministry was a distinctive of the evangelical wing of Anglicanism.

One sometimes hears it said, "Of course, there have been women in ministry in the Methodist-Holiness-Pentecostal world," as a way of quarantining these examples as irrelevant to evangelicals in other traditions. To this it might be replied: First, the Methodist-Holiness-Pentecostal stream is a rather large and important segment of evangelicalism that ought not to be dismissed as marginal. Second, if these streams have affirmed women in ministry for evangelical reasons then it would behoove the whole evangelical community to pay attention to their efforts and arguments. Third, it is simply inaccurate to imagine that other evangelical traditions have not also sometimes affirmed women in public ministry in various ways.

Indeed, the first Calvinist denomination to arise from the evangelical revival was led by a woman, Selina, Countess of Huntingdon (1707-1791). The great evangelist George Whitefield, who was also a Calvinist, declared that Lady

---

[6]Letter to Sarah Crosby, June 13, 1771, in Wesley, *Works*, 12:356.

Huntingdon had a divine call to give leadership to the Calvinist Methodists: "A leader is wanting. This honour hath been put upon your Ladyship by the great head of the church."[7] Like Wesley, it was Lady Huntingdon's intention to keep her movement in the Anglican camp, but she also ended up founding a new denomination. She had her own group of preachers. George Whitefield himself joyfully submitted to her spiritual leadership. She also set up her own theological college at Trevecca from which would emerge "Lady Huntingdon's Preachers." She was in full control of the college, personally serving as its principal, hiring and firing teachers as she saw fit, exercising final authority over all decisions, and personally overseeing its theological purity and the progress of its students. Lady Huntingdon also had complete control over a network of congregations, the ministers that served them and the buildings that were built for them. She only allowed ministers to serve in her churches who preached "the true Calvinist Doctrine."[8] Lady Huntingdon became the first Methodist leader to break away from the Church of England. In 1738, six of the students at Trevecca were ordained as ministers of the Countess of Huntingdon's Connexion. At the end of her life, there were sixty-four churches in her denomination. The denomination still exists today and still has as its official name "the Countess of Huntingdon's Connexion." It is a member of the Evangelical Alliance.[9] Calvinist evangelicals have the distinction of having a denomination that is named after a female founder. Had she not had an evangelical conversion and an ongoing evangelical identity, of course, Lady Huntingdon would never have had such a public ministry of church leadership.

The Gospel vs. Social Respectability

Throughout their history, when evangelicals have cared more about the Bible and the gospel than they did about being perceived as respectable by the wider society, these commitments have often led them to affirm women in public ministry. When, however, a preoccupation with social respectability has entered in, women have been repeatedly pushed out. After Wesley's death, Wesleyan Methodism quickly went in the direction of pursuing pub-

---

[7]Boyd Stanley Schlenther, *Queen of the Methodists: The Countess of Huntingdon and the Eighteenth-Century Crisis of Faith and Society* (Durham: Durham Academic Press, 1997), p. 39.
[8]Ibid., p. 109.
[9]For the Countess of Huntingdon's Connexion today, see its website, "Connexions": <www.cofh connexion.org.uk>.

lic buildings and public ministers that could be viewed as the equal of those in the Church of England. Traditions such as emotionally charged camp meetings and female preachers were thus suppressed. This in turn provoked Methodist renewal movements that wished to pursue evangelical distinctives even if they were deemed countercultural. This impulse produced two new, large denominations in the early nineteenth century, the Primitive Methodists and the Bible Christians. Both of these began as protests against the way that bureaucratic and snobbish policies in the Wesleyan denomination were hindering the free ministry of the gospel—and both denominations reaffirmed women in public ministry in defiance of the restrictive turn that the Wesleyan body had taken. Selina Llewellyn, for example, was a salaried, full-time Primitive Methodist preacher in the mid-Victorian era. The very name "Bible Christians" bears witness to the desire of these believers to take the Bible more seriously, not less; to make following God's word in Scripture foundational to their entire identity. The Bible Christians became an evangelical denomination that formally set people apart to the calling of being a preacher, and it recognized them irrespective of whether they happened to be male or female.

Mary Ann Werry (1800-1825) founded the Bible Christian work on the Isles of Scilly. Many people were converted through her preaching, and she formed them into a congregation before moving on to other regions untouched by the fire of the Bible Christian movement. Likewise Mary Toms (1795-1871), as a single woman, pioneered the Bible Christian work on the Isle of Wight. When her ministry there was blessed, the denomination sent two more female preachers to aid her. These women are particularly honored for their pioneering work, but numerous women served as preachers in the settled and established Bible Christian circuits. Nevertheless, the Bible Christians eventually opted for respectability as well. Having lost their countercultural edge, they began to seek union with more refined Methodists. When a merger with the Methodist New Connexion seemed probable in 1869, the more high-brow denomination was reassured that something as uncouth as women preaching would not be a long-term nuisance: "It was stated to the Committee that this usage was gradually passing away."[10] There is no hint that

---

[10]Timothy Larsen, *Contested Christianity: The Political and Social Contexts of Victorian Theology* (Waco, Tex.: Baylor University Press, 2004), p. 140.

they had been persuaded that women preachers were unbiblical; they had merely begun to internalize the assumption that they were not in keeping with a more cultured level of church life.

On the other hand, in this same decade when the Bible Christians were seeking to join the more refined Methodist New Connexion, the husband and wife ministry team, William Booth (1829-1912) and Catherine Booth (1829-1890)—who burned with evangelistic fire—were leaving that denomination precisely because it was prioritizing bureaucracy and cultural ascendancy over the spread of the gospel. Already in 1861, Catherine Booth had written the first version of her classic work, *Female Ministry; or, Woman's Right to Preach the Gospel*. While she spent the bulk of this book sifting the biblical evidence, Catherine was accurately reflecting her context in Victorian England with its "cult of respectability" when she began that work with the words: "The first and most common objection urged against the public exercises of women, is that they are unnatural and unfeminine."[11] The Salvation Army, the new denomination that the Booths had gone on to found, was thoroughly egalitarian on the issue of gender and ministry from its inception, and has been ever since. Their daughter, Evangeline Booth (1865-1950), eventually became the General, Salvation Army parlance for the president of the denomination. Evangeline Booth was so well respected by American evangelicals that when she visited Chicago in 1913, Moody Bible Institute served as her headquarters and she preached two sermons at Moody Church.[12]

As far as the Salvation Army was concerned, the women in public ministry in their midst were simply a reflection of the fact that their movement was more committed to the work of God and the spread of the gospel than to worldly notions of propriety. Salvationists were not afraid to go to the most dangerous sections of town, to the filthiest rooms, to the most notorious sinners. They were not afraid to be laughed at, to be pelted with rubbish, to be assaulted. Even many Christians were embarrassed by the Salvationists' sheer disregard for the conventions of polite society in their single-minded determi-

---

[11]Catherine Booth, *Female Ministry; or, Woman's Right to Preach the Gospel* (London: Morgan & Chase, 1859), p. 3. For the Victorians and respectability, see Geoffrey Best, *Mid-Victorian Britain 1851-75* (London: Fontana, 1979), pp. 279-86.

[12]Janette Hassey, *No Time for Silence: Evangelical Women in Public Ministry Around the Turn of the Century* (Grand Rapids: Zondervan, 1986), p. 40. (In this passage, Hassey's text mistakenly has written "Catherine" Booth, who had been dead for a couple decades by 1913, rather than Evangeline.)

nation to bring the light of Christ into "darkest England."[13]

In short, despite the declension of women in public ministry among groups such as the Bible Christians, the torch was not dying out but instead was being passed on to other evangelicals, notably in the Holiness movement. The hallmark of this renewal impulse within evangelicalism was its radical determination to eradicate completely willful acts of sin from the lives of believers. Far from being a movement that wished to take God's Word and standards less seriously, it called for a meticulous alignment between God's will as revealed in Scripture and the behavior of believers. Even actions that seemed innocent or trivial to other evangelicals such as wearing jewelry or going to the theater were intolerable to many in the Holiness movement. These Bible-believing evangelicals also generally accepted women in public ministry without any qualms. One of the key spokespeople for the movement, Phoebe Palmer (1807-1874), was also one of the most famous preachers of the nineteenth century. Indeed, it is not hard to name a whole series of popular evangelical female preachers from the nineteenth century, but it is much more difficult to think of a well-known woman preacher from that era who was not an evangelical. Women preachers were an evangelical distinctive. Far from being some imagined man-hating feminist, Palmer found that the greatest obstacle to complete holiness in her own personal life was the temptation to love her husband more than God. Phoebe Palmer expounded on the biblical and theological case for women in public ministry in her book *The Promise of the Father*, 1859.[14]

Numerous evangelical denominations that received the public ministry gifts of women were founded through the impetus of the Holiness movement. I recently went to a church history conference and ended up sitting at a dinner table next to a church historian who taught at Kentucky Mountain Bible College, an institution that serves the Holiness denomination, the Kentucky Mountain Holiness Association. The very name of the institution was enough to fill me with a presumed sense of superiority, and this un-Christian smug-

---

[13]An excellent academic study has recently explored the encounter between the Salvationists and plebeian culture, Pamela J. Walker, *Pulling the Devil's Kingdom Down: The Salvation Army in Victorian Britain* (Berkeley: University of California Press, 2001). "Darkest England" comes from the title of an influential book written by William Booth, *In Darkest England and the Way Out*, 1890.

[14]For book-length studies of Palmer, see H. E. Raser, *Phoebe Palmer, Her Life and Thought* (New York: Edwin Mellen, 1987); C. E. White, *The Beauty of Holiness: Phoebe Palmer as Theologian, Feminist, and Humanitarian* (Grand Rapids: Zondervan, 1986).

ness only grew as he began to recount for me the seemingly endless litany of quaint and exacting rules and standards of personal behavior that students at this institution are required to meet. This was holiness in its most prescribed form. Nevertheless, I was taken aback when he went on to talk without embarrassment about the woman who was the founder and first president of their denomination, the Reverend Lela G. McConnell (1884-1970). After studying at Asbury College, McConnell had been ordained to the office of deacon in the Methodist Episcopal Church. She then went on to carve out her own sphere of public ministry in regions beyond. Jennifer Woodruff Tait has observed, "McConnell supervised a network of pastors—of whom at times more than half were women."[15] Far from imagining that the apostle Paul would have disapproved of her ministry, McConnell was convinced that he would have recognized her as someone called to the same work. Thus one of her autobiographical works was tellingly titled, *The Pauline Ministry in the Kentucky Mountains; or a brief account of the Kentucky Mountain Holiness Association*, 1940.

While there would be diminishing returns in continuing to chronicle female ministers in the Holiness movement, it is worth mentioning that women were frequently ordained in the Church of the Nazarene, where one could hear the quip, "Some of our best men are women."[16] Or to take another example in the Holiness denomination, the Church of God (Anderson, Indiana), one-quarter of its leaders were women in 1902.[17] Moreover, the first woman to be ordained to the office of bishop was not in some theologically liberal or mainline context, but rather was Alma White (1862-1946) in the radical Holiness denomination, the Pillar of Fire.[18]

EDUCATING WOMEN AND WOMEN TEACHERS, PREACHERS AND PASTORS

Nineteenth-century evangelicals were also often leading movements to gain greater equality for women in society and public life in general. Oberlin, founded as an evangelical college in 1833, was the first American institution

---

[15]Jennifer Woodruff Tait, "'I Received My Commission from Him Brother': How Women Built Up the Holiness Movement," *Christian History* 23, no. 2 (spring 2004): 38.

[16]Rebecca Laird, *Ordained Women in the Church of the Nazarene* (Kansas City, Mo.: Nazarene Publishing House, 1993).

[17]Hassey, *No Time for Silence*, pp. 52-53.

[18]Tait, "I Received My Commission," p. 37.

of higher education to accept women students. The first woman to receive a bachelor's degree in America graduated from Oberlin in 1841. Oberlin could also boast that it had America's greatest evangelist of his generation on its faculty, and later as its president. The Presbyterian minister Charles Finney (1792-1875) was an advocate for greater roles for women both in society and in public church ministry. Jonathan Blanchard (1811-1982) and Charles Finney cooperated with one another as evangelical social reformers. When Blanchard founded Wheaton College, Wheaton, Illinois, in 1860, it became the first college in America to have an entirely unisex curriculum with all courses and programs being open to the women students as well. By way of contrast, Harvard University did not admit women students on a coeducational basis until 1943, and only then due to pragmatic pressures caused by World War II.

One of these early students at Wheaton College was Frances E. Townsley (1849-c.1913), who began her studies in 1867.[19] As far as I can tell, no scholar has ever even referred to Townsley in print, let alone told her story. Townsley had a dramatic evangelical conversion experience that enabled her to point with confidence to the very hour at which she was saved. She knew that God wanted to use her and she came to Wheaton as preparation for that work. Once at Wheaton, Townsley put herself forward for church membership at College Church. She had, however, also come to reject infant baptism in favor of believer's baptism. Jonathan Blanchard tried to talk her out of this view, but he quickly discovered that she was a formidable opponent in theological debate and gave up. She thereby became the first person to become a member at College Church while asserting this position. The practice that College Church maintains to this day of accepting as full members those with baptistic convictions comes directly from the pioneering efforts of Townsley. Moreover, there were women faculty members at Wheaton even in its first decade. Townsley was particularly influenced by Helen S. Norton, who taught her Latin. (Again, Harvard University hired its first tenure-track woman faculty member in 1947 at the earliest—and that is to count someone whose main assignment was to teach women-only courses.) Townsley gave a paper at Wheaton College's Aelionian Society that was so moving that it prompted Blanchard not only to

---

[19]The information on Townsley given below is derived from her autobiography, Frances E. Townsley, *A Pilgrim Maid: The Self-Told Story of Frances E. Townsley* (Butler, Ind.: L. H. Highley, 1908).

weep openly, but also to give her a semester of free tuition!

Townsley became a school teacher after her Wheaton days, but she subsequently received a call to ministry. She had already been teaching men in an adult Sunday school class for years. Her first Sunday morning sermon was at Lincoln Park Congregational Church, Chicago. She then began to preach regularly in Congregational and Baptist churches. One minister, who subsequently came to endorse her ministry, approached their first meeting with suspicion and hostility. He protested that men who desired to preach first went to college. Recalling that almost no colleges accepted women at this time, he was considerably disconcerted to learn that she had already fulfilled that requirement. He next protested that the men study courses directly related to the work of public ministry such as theology and homiletics. The astounding reply was that so had she. Again, Wheaton was probably the only college in America at that time where a woman could take a homiletics class. He then proceeded to test the mettle of her theological education by asking if she had read Walker's *The Philosophy of the Plan of Salvation*, the leading evangelical work in the field of apologetics at that time. She was able to reply that not only had she read it, but she had been taught by the author (who was a member of the Wheaton faculty) personally, and that he had written to her to confirm and endorse her call to public ministry!

In the mid-1870s, Frances Townsley became a full-time preacher and evangelist. She received a license to preach from the Shelburne Falls Baptist Church, Massachusetts. When she moved back to the Midwest, her license was reendorsed by the Oak Park Baptist Church, Chicago. Its influential minister, R. N. Van Doren, D.D., was a major supporter of Townsley's ministry. Numerous people were converted through her preaching. She specialized in reviving dying churches. This led on to serving as interim pastor for a succession of Baptist churches in need of a minister. In the late 1880s, she was called to be the settled pastor of the Fairfield Baptist Church in Nebraska. She refused to administer Communion, however, as she was not ordained. Townsley observed that Baptist men who were aspiring to ministry but had not yet been ordained often presumed to officiate at the Lord's Supper at that time, but she "was a stickler for church order."[20] Her Baptist church therefore unanimously voted that she should be ordained. Following

---

[20]Ibid., p. 276.

Baptist custom at that time, she was examined as a candidate for ordination by a council that included the ministers and other representatives from no less than fourteen Baptist churches from the surrounding area—a far larger and more representative council than was the norm. This Baptist council again voted unanimously that she was a suitable candidate for ordination. Here is a portion of its official report:

> Then came before it [the council] this cultured, Christian lady with an experience that made all feel that she had seen Jesus. Then came her call to the ministry, which was so clearly defined and beautifully and simply explained, as to make every minister present feel that she, too, had been led over his own pathway. Her views of Bible doctrine were so clearly defined, and orthodox, exhibited such an amount of careful reading and study, as would have done honor to any graduate of our theological schools.[21]

This decision was praised in the *National Baptist* newspaper (published in Philadelphia), which added, "There is not a pulpit in the land she would not grace."[22] Townsley—who never married but undertook every phase of her ministry as a single woman—was duly ordained and went on to serve as the senior minister of that church and then other churches, including officiating at the Communion service, baptisms, weddings and funerals. Despite being in a sparsely populated area, seventy-six new members were added to the Fairfield Baptist Church in her first two years of ministry there.

Townsley, of course, had sporadically received opposition to her ministry from some Christians on the grounds that she was a woman. She was fully cognizant of the fact that some believed that the Bible barred women from public ministry. Her own response to this issue included pointing to the public ministries of women mentioned in Paul's epistles such as Phoebe and Junia. As to apparently restrictive statements on women speaking, teaching and exercising authority in 1 Corinthians and 1 Timothy, Townsley argued that these were an expression, not of an eternal principle, but rather of the reality on the ground at that time. The churches the apostle Paul was addressing were situated in cultural contexts where women were not educated and where they had been raised in paganism: "In Paul's day, not a woman convert from heathenism *could* 'teach' or lead in the thought and application of the gospel messages with au-

---

[21]Ibid., p. 278.
[22]Ibid., p. 282.

thority. She simply *could not* if she would!"[23] A woman brought up in the church and in a godly family with a good Wheaton education, however, was an entirely different matter.

It must be emphasized that Townsley was an evangelical from beginning to end. She was very effective at giving appeals for people to respond to the gospel at the end of her sermons, and a passion to see souls won for Christ was at the heart of her ministry. Moreover, she was profoundly committed to being fully obedient to the word of God. A whole chapter of her autobiography is taken up with the internal struggle and external opposition she experienced while coming to the conviction that the Bible taught believer's baptism. Another entire chapter is given over to her discovering and then learning to submit to biblical teaching on tithing. Indeed, it was precisely because she was an evangelical committed to the gospel and to God's Word that the Reverend Frances E. Townsley had such a passion to proclaim it. Townsley's story has not been told because it is far from unique: she was simply one of numerous evangelical Baptist women who were ordained and served as senior ministers in the late nineteenth and early twentieth centuries. Janette Hassey lists the names of fifty Baptist women who were ordained between 1902 and 1928.[24]

Indeed, Hassey, in her pioneering work *No Time for Silence: Evangelical Women in Public Ministry Around the Turn of the Century*, has documented in numerous ways the remarkable openness to women in public ministry in conservative evangelicalism and fundamentalism in the late nineteenth century and early twentieth century. Hassey demonstrates, for example, that women were trained for public ministry by the theologically conservative Bible colleges. Moreover, women faculty members at these institutions taught Bible and theology. The flagship of them all, Moody Bible Institute, was even founded by a woman, Emma Dryer, who became, in effect, its first dean. D. L. Moody (1837-1899) supported Frances E. Willard (1839-1898) in her efforts to secure votes for women, and he so believed in her public Christian ministry that he invited her to join him in his itinerant work as a fellow preacher. Willard wrote her own defense of women ministers, *Woman in the Pulpit*, 1888. Official Moody Bible Institute publications proudly boasted about women graduates who went on to ordained ministry and to full-time, senior pastorates.[25]

---

[23]Ibid., p. 281.
[24]Hassey, *No Time for Silence,* appendix 12.
[25]Ibid., appendix 8.

A similar story can be told about Northwestern Bible School, an institution run by W. B. Riley (1861-1947), a towering fundamentalist leader in Minnesota. In 1923, Indianapolis Bible Institute had a faculty that was entirely comprised of women. Occasionally people wonder if Wheaton College "now" allows women to teach in the Bible department, not realizing that the *first* full-time Bible teacher that Wheaton ever employed was a woman, Edith C. Torrey, who taught Bible at Wheaton College from 1919 to 1958. Similarly—again, just to give a random example as many other such cases could be named—the Baptist Esther Sabel taught Bible at Bethel Seminary from 1924 to 1958. Once again, this is a reflection of an evangelical distinctive: these institutions were the ones that were the most uncompromising in their affirmation of the inerrancy of Scripture and the power of the gospel to convert sinners. By way of contrast, Harvard Divinity School, a bastion of theological liberalism, did not even admit women students until 1955, let alone women faculty members.

Many of the most prominent male leaders of evangelicalism in the late nineteenth and early twentieth centuries were vocal champions of women in public ministry. Fredrik Franson (1852-1908), a pioneering Swedish minister in America, for example, defended this practice in a work he wrote in the late nineteenth century, *Prophesying Daughters*. A denomination arising from the Swedish community, the Evangelical Free Church of America, not only welcomed women into public ministry, but also went out of its way to make this explicit by using gender-inclusive statements in its constitution. For example, the rules for ordination that the Evangelical Free Church of America adopted in 1925 stated: "a candidate for ordination shall request a reference from the church of which he or she is a member."[26] This denomination was so resolutely evangelical, of course, that it incorporated the word into its very name. A prominent Baptist minister, A. J. Gordon (1836-1895), whose name is perpetuated through Gordon College and Gordon-Conwell Theological Seminary, was an advocate of both votes for women and women ministers. The latter cause he articulated in his book, *The Ministry of Women*, 1894.

Another champion of women in public ministry was the powerful minister of Calvary Baptist Church, New York, John Roach Straton (1875-1929). Straton, a graduate of Southern Baptist Theological Seminary and the editor of the *Fundamentalist* newspaper, has been dubbed "the pope of fundamentalism."

---

[26]Ibid., p. 92.

He regularly relinquished his pulpit to women ministers on Sunday mornings, writing his own defense of this practice, *Does the Bible Forbid Women to Preach and Pray in Public?* 1926. In contrast, one might recall that women were explicitly forbidden to preach in Anglican churches at that time: Straton—archenemy of theological liberalism—was simply reflecting a historic evangelical distinctive. Perhaps most curiously of all, A. T. Pierson (1837-1911)—an ordained Presbyterian minister, one of the editors of the *Scofield Reference Bible*, and a contributor to *The Fundamentals*—wrote an entire book in praise of the preaching ministry of the medieval prophet and mystic, Catherine of Siena. Another evangelical leader who was in favor of women in public ministry was A. B. Simpson (1843-1919), the founder of the Christian and Missionary Alliance denomination.

My own introduction to this theme came through researching the public ministry of Christabel Pankhurst (1880-1958) in fundamentalist circles in Britain, Canada and America.[27] Pankhurst led the campaign for votes for women in Britain. She was so militant that she was jailed and eventually went into exile in France. She was a strong advocate of civil disobedience in service to the cause of women's rights, including the destruction of property. Nevertheless, once votes for women were achieved, she spent the rest of her life as a high-profile evangelical preacher and teacher, while telling her fundamentalist followers that she was still as committed as ever to gender equality. *How could fundamentalism have accepted such an in-your-face, militant feminist,* I wondered? The answer, I discovered, was that many conservative evangelical and fundamentalist leaders were more committed to gender equality than was society in general in the late nineteenth century and early twentieth.

When Viola D. Romans spoke from the main platform at Winona Lake Bible Conference in 1914, she took it for granted that the majority of her hearers—in contrast to the majority of Americans—were in favor of votes of women. Far from being embarrassed by Pankhurst's past work as a militant feminist campaigner, the *Moody Bible Institute Monthly* spoke of her proudly as "the great apostle of woman suffrage." Major fundamentalist leaders who campaigned for votes for women included, for example, William Jennings Bryan (1862-1935)—the famous antievolution voice of the Scopes Trial—and the evangelist Billy Sunday

---

[27]For a book-length treatment of her ministry, see Timothy Larsen, *Christabel Pankhurst: Fundamentalism and Feminism in Coalition* (Woodbridge, Suffolk: Boydell, 2002).

(1862-1935). Moreover, as I have already demonstrated, many major fundamentalist leaders were also already supporters of women in public ministry. In
short, when Pankhurst arrived, these fundamentalist leaders did not need to
change in order to accept a woman with a call to public ministry who was also
a champion of women's rights in society because they had already been endorsing both causes for some time. This was the case, for example, with Pankhurst's
main advocate in Britain, the leading Baptist minister and devotional author
F. B. Meyer (1847-1929). It was also true, as we have seen, of John Roach Straton, who was delighted to have Pankhurst deliver Sunday morning sermons to
his large fundamentalist Baptist congregation.

Christabel Pankhurst preached her first sermon one Sunday morning at one
of the largest and most powerful evangelical churches in Canada, Knox Presbyterian Church, Toronto. She was invited to do so through the advocacy of its
minister-at-large, A. B. Winchester (1858-1943), a fundamentalist Presbyterian
minister who, during those same years, was also helping to found Dallas Theological Seminary. Pankhurst went on to deliver Sunday morning sermons, including the Communion address, at Knox repeatedly over the years. Pankhurst
preached widely across the fundamentalist world. In addition to innumerable
evangelical local churches, she taught at Moody Bible Institute, Biola, the Christian Fellowship Bible Conference (organized by Westmont College), the Fundamentalist Rally and Prophetic Conference, the Bible Testimony Fellowship
and the Adventist Testimony Movement. When she spoke from the main platform at the Winona Lake Bible Conference in 1941, the other plenary speakers
included W. B. Riley, H. A. Ironside (pastor of Moody Memorial Church, Chicago), Lewis Sperry Chafer (president of Dallas Theological Seminary) and Bob
Jones Jr. In 1931, Pankhurst was even a primetime, keynote speaker at the pre-
mier national fundamentalist gathering, the World's Christian Fundamentals
Association's annual conference. On that occasion, other keynote speakers included not only, once again, Riley, Ironside and Chafer, but also J. Oliver
Buswell Jr. (president of Wheaton College) and the popular dispensationalist
teacher, A. C. Gaebelein. Moreover, Christabel Pankhurst was not usually the
only woman preacher on the main platform at these major fundamentalist gatherings and Bible conferences. Her past was more spectacular than that of the
other women teachers, but her Christian ministry was comparable to that of
numerous other evangelical women at that time.

At the start of the twentieth century, another major branch of evangelicalism emerged, the Pentecostal movement. Women in public ministry has also been a historic distinctive within this form of evangelicalism. A famous example of a woman Pentecostal minister is Aimee Semple McPherson (1890-1944).[28] She founded Angelus Temple, a large church in Los Angeles, serving herself as its senior pastor. This led on to founding her own Pentecostal denomination, the International Church of the Foursquare Gospel, and serving as its president. Numerous local pastors submitted to her spiritual leadership. McPherson had 344 affiliated churches in her denomination by 1934. She also founded her own Bible school, LIFE, famous graduates of which include Chuck Smith and Jack Hayford. Today the denomination that McPherson founded and led has over 4.1 million members worshiping in 38,217 churches in 138 countries around the world.[29]

An example from the African-American community is Ida Robinson (1891-1946). Robinson founded her own Pentecostal denomination, Mount Sinai Holy Church of America, and served as its first bishop. Moreover, she also ensured that her denomination would be committed to full gender egalitarianism in all offices of public ministry thereafter. Robinson engaged in all aspects of public Christian ministry, including administering Communion. The charismatic movement has also made room for women in public ministry, a notable example being the popular preacher and healing evangelist Kathryn Kuhlman (1907-1976), who had a widely received itinerant ministry and who also served as the senior minister of several large charismatic churches.[30]

Evangelical women have written many of the most frequently sung hymns, and it is easy to forget both how revolutionary this is and how profound an affirmation it is of the fittingness of women engaging in public ministry. It is revolutionary because for most of the history of the Christian church, congregations would have recited, sung and heard words that were written only by men. It is radical because few ideas go deeper into the thinking of a congregation than those that they habitually sing. A woman hymn writer thus becomes a teacher of doctrine in season and out of season from one generation to another, an authoritative teaching office with much more pervasive and lasting

---

[28]For a book-length treatment of her life, see Edith Blumhofer, *Aimee Semple McPherson: Everybody's Sister* (Grand Rapids: Eerdmans, 1993).

[29]The International Church of the Foursquare Gospel, <www.foursquare.org/index.cfm?cat=about &subcat=info> (accessed November 16, 2004).

[30]For a popular account of her life, see Wayne E. Marner, *Kathryn Kuhlman: The Woman Behind the Miracles* (Ann Arbor, Mich.: Servant Publications, 1993).

influence than simply delivering some sermons or lectures. Fanny Crosby (1820-1915), for example, was one of the most popular hymn writers for evangelicals in her own day and beyond.[31] Moreover, Billy Graham's standard hymn for his evangelistic appeals, "Just as I Am," was written by a woman, Charlotte Elliott (1789-1871).

It is well known that evangelical women have often engaged in public ministry on the mission field. It has frequently been claimed that over half of missionaries have been women, many of them single. Jeffrey Cox, for example, in a study of Punjab and Northwest India, tabulated that in 1931 there were 188 male missionaries, 141 married female missionaries, and 293 single female missionaries serving in that region.[32] Evangelical women missionaries have fulfilled all the duties of ministers: they have evangelized, preached, taught, pastored, administered the sacraments, planted churches and given oversight to churches and other ministers. The Scottish Presbyterian Mary Slessor (1848-1915) preached, taught and led churches and church services as part of her work in what is today Nigeria. She even officiated at weddings. To the argument that the African people "were not likely to be helped by a woman," she replied, "In measuring the woman's power, you have evidently forgotten to take into account the woman's God."[33] An African American example figure is Eliza Davis George (1879-1980). She served as a Southern Baptist missionary to Liberia. When her denomination insisted that she retire at the standard age of sixty-five, she struck out on her own. By the 1960s, she was overseeing her own denomination of twenty-seven churches, the Eliza George Baptist Association.[34]

It is, of course, a well-known fact that when these women went on furlough, often the very churches that paid for them to minister abroad would not let them do so at home. The reason for this is quite simple: on the mission field the priority clearly had to be the gospel; at home, however, things were less urgent and therefore notions of decorum and respectability could be al-

---

[31]Edith L. Blumhofer, *Her Heart Can See: The Life and Hymns of Fanny J. Crosby* (Grand Rapids: Eerdmans, 2005).

[32]Jeffrey Cox, *Imperial Fault Lines: Christianity and Colonial Power in India, 1818-1940* (Stanford, Calif.: Stanford University Press, 2002), p. 154.

[33]W. P. Livingstone, *Mary Slessor of Calabar: Pioneer Missionary* (London: Hodder & Stoughton, 1923), p. 108.

[34]Gerald H. Anderson, ed., *Biographical Dictionary of Christian Missions* (Grand Rapids: Eerdmans, 1998), p. 239; Ruth A Tucker, *Daughters of the Church: Women and Ministry from New Testament Times to the Present* (Grand Rapids: Zondervan, 1987), p. 319.

lowed to dictate what did and did not happen. The mission field is another example of the principle that when evangelicals have prioritized God's Word and the gospel it has often led to women in public ministry.

It is worth underlining the fact that this historic commitment of many evangelicals to women in ministry was profoundly countercultural. The public ministries of women in nineteenth-century England, for example, should be contrasted with the starkly private and unequal place that they had in society in general at that time. Women were not allowed to go to university or to vote in political elections. Women could not be lawyers. Indeed, virtually the only traditional profession open to them was the Christian ministry. If you wanted to hear a woman speak in public, you would not go to the universities, or the courts, or to the Houses of Parliament, but rather to an evangelical church. If a woman wanted to vote, she could do so as a member of a Baptist church, but not as a citizen of the nation.[35] Moreover, the largest portion of the Christian world that was open to women in ministry was the evangelical movement. By contrast, well into the twentieth century women could never preach in Anglican churches. The first woman priest in the Church of England was not ordained until 1994—more than one hundred years on from when Frances Townsley had been ordained as an evangelical Baptist minister with all the rights and privileges thereof.[36]

Women in public ministry has not been a historic commitment of those branches of Christianity marked by theological liberalism. In the eighteenth century one must look to Wesley rather than Schleiermacher for a champion of women in public ministry; in the nineteenth century, to Finney, Moody and company, rather than Ritschl, Harnack etcetera. While some evangelicals would come to point to Mary Magdalene's commission by the risen Christ to preach the gospel to men as biblical warrant for women in public ministry, one of the most famous liberal theologians of the nineteenth century, D. F. Strauss, argued that the resurrection of Christ was not a historic event on the grounds that the primary testimony to it came from women, and we all know how gullible, hysterical and unreliable they are. In the first half of the twentieth century, women were being trained for public ministry at Moody Bible Institute while being excluded altogether from Harvard Divinity School. Women in

---

[35]See Larsen, *Contested Christianity*, chap. 1.
[36]For women in the Church of England, see Sean Gill, *Women and the Church of England, From the Eighteenth Century to the Present* (London: SPCK, 1994).

public ministry is a historic distinctive of the evangelical movement, and this is precisely because of its commitment to the Bible and the gospel.

THE CHANGE IN THE LAST SIXTY YEARS

Nevertheless, the story I have been telling in this chapter so far might not seem to fit with the evangelicalism that you have experienced. While there have always been evangelicals who have rejected women in public ministry, something has changed in more recent decades that has made many evangelicals believe that this more restrictive position is the only evangelical one. What has happened in the last sixty years that has inclined so many conservative evangelicals toward assuming that those who affirm women in public ministry are departing from a commitment to Scripture and an evangelical position? In this concluding section of this chapter, I will explore some possible answers to that question.

First, it is well established in studies of American culture generally that the 1950s was a decade in which there were strong social and cultural pressures to restrict the roles of women. The decades prior to World War II were ones that could make space for women who wanted to achieve in a wide variety of areas. A notable example figure for this is the heroic pilot Amelia Earhart (1897-1937). Likewise, the war itself led to women working in numerous occupations. Men came back from the war, however, wanting to set up what they deemed to be an "ideal" domestic life—one with a full-time housewife. Postwar prosperity allowed for this vision to be realized for many. The "baby boom" synchronized a whole generation of married women as mothers of young children. A general culture mood was created in which women belonged in the private sphere. The churches were also subjected to this social pressure. Moreover, fundamentalism and conservative evangelicalism were by then well-established movements. It was no longer good enough to train people for ministry at Bible schools, but theological seminaries were now desirable, and like the older mainline and liberal seminaries that they aspired to imitate, evangelical seminaries would often exclude women. Many longed for the evangelical Christian ministry to be seen as just as much a respectable profession as the mainline ministry, and women were deemed to undercut this professional image. The fact that, once again, cultural pressures and issues of respectability were at work is confirmed, for example, by the fact that women in ministry also went into sharp decline in the Church of the Nazarene even though that denomination continued to affirm that there was no biblical or theological impediment to such ministries.

Second, evangelicals in general have rightly been appalled by one version of feminism that emerged in the 1960s and 1970s, which took positions in direct opposition to historic evangelical teaching on issues such as sexuality and the sanctity of life and marriage. For many evangelicals, the word *feminism* and the very notion of "women's rights" became so associated with this version of it, that it was rejected in toto. This has led to amnesia about the historic ways that evangelicalism itself has championed the rights of women. For example, the evangelical writer Elisabeth Elliot stated in 1990, "For years I have noted with growing disquiet the pollution of many Christians' minds by the doctrine of feminism. I believe it is a far more dangerous pollution than most have realized."[37] This is arguably an evangelical reaction to one form of feminism rather than all forms—or possibly a reaction against all forms because of alarm at one form. Indeed, Christabel Pankhurst was one of the most prominent feminist leaders of her generation. Far from being perceived as polluting Christian minds, however, Pankhurst was strongly supported by Elisabeth Elliot's fundamentalist father, Philip E. Howard Jr., and great-uncle, Charles G. Trumbull. At the invitation of Howard patriarchs, Elisabeth Elliot, when she was a girl, even heard Christabel Pankhurst preach in her own childhood home church, Moorestown Bible Protestant Church, in Moorestown, New Jersey.[38]

Likewise, Pankhurst taught for an entire week at Philpott Tabernacle, Hamilton, Ontario, the base church of the Associated Gospel Churches, a denomination that now has a statement saying that women are not allowed to teach.[39] Not unlike Elisabeth Elliot, James Dobson became very concerned in the late 1960s and the 1970s about cultural trends that were undermining the traditional family, leading to his founding of "Focus on the Family" in 1977. An enemy he has identified in this struggle is "feminist ideology."[40] Neverthe-

---

[37]Elisabeth Elliot, foreword to John Piper, *What's the Difference? Manhood and Womanhood Defined According to the Bible* (Westchester, Ill.: Crossway, 1990), p. ix.

[38]David Howard, interview by author, Wheaton College, Wheaton, Ill., November 1, 2001.

[39]This is not a point that I mentioned in my book on Pankhurst. Her teaching at Philpott Tabernacle is recorded in the *Sunday School Times,* November 30, 1929, p. 689. For their current position, see Associated Gospel Churches, "Policy on Women in Ministry" <www.agcofcanada.com/lit/agcwom.htm> (page last updated January 12, 2001, accessed November 20, 2001).

[40]See, for example, Dr. James Dobson's comments in a 2004 newsletter article: "Radical Feminism Shortchanges Boys," <www.family.org/docstudy/newsletters/a0032398.cfm> (labeled November 2004 newsletter, though apparently a June newsletter; accessed November 18, 2004).

less, Dobson's own spiritual heritage is part of the historic evangelical affirmation of women in ministry: both a great-grandmother and a grandmother of his were ordained ministers in the Church of the Nazarene.[41] Therefore, it is deeply misguided to imagine, as many conservative Protestants do today, that recognition of women in ministry is a product of the antievangelical camp in, to use Dobson's parlance, the "culture wars" of recent decades. L. E. Maxwell (1895-1984), founder and president of the Prairie Bible Institute in Alberta, Canada, raised some eyebrows when he wrote a book in favor of women in public ministry in 1982. When it was republished after his death, the foreword explained this seemingly surprising liberal stance from such an old-guard conservative evangelical by arguing that Maxwell was "a man ahead of his times."[42] It would be truer to say, however, that he was one of the last living links to the old acceptance of women in public ministry from the fundamentalist Bible school culture of the first half of the twentieth century.

Third and finally, there has been a significant shift since the nineteenth century in how the biblical evidence is weighed. Evangelicalism has always contained two hermeneutical traditions on this subject: one that affirms and one that restricts women in public ministry. While numerous scriptural passages are seen as germane by both sides in this discussion, each side has had a couple key passages that have been viewed as the most decisive. Evangelicals who have been opposed to women in public ministry have always located their biblical case primarily in two passages: 1 Timothy 2:11-14 and 1 Corinthians 14:34-36. Throughout history, evangelicals who have affirmed women in public ministry have argued that those verses did not express a general prohibition against all women at all times engaging in public ministry because, if they did, that would mean that they were incompatible with the evidence of other passages of Scripture. In other words, their interpretation of these passages as not offering a general prohibition has been guided by an evangelical commitment to the inerrancy and unity of Scripture. Central to this argument have been those passages that speak of female prophets and women prophesying. Most of all, Acts 2:17-18 was frequently cited as demonstrating that, far from being

---

[41]Rebecca Laird, "Women's Ordination: What Has Gender Got to Do with It?" *Christianity Today,* September 4, 2000, p. 107.

[42]L. E. Maxwell, *Women in Ministry: A Historical and Biblical Look at the Role of Women in Christian Leadership* (Wheaton, Ill.: Victor Books, 1987), p. 7. For a sketch of Maxwell's life, see Timothy Larsen, ed., *Biographical Dictionary of Evangelicals* (Downers Grove, Ill.: InterVarsity Press, 2003), pp. 417-19.

unbiblical, women in public ministry was actually a positive sign of the work of the Holy Spirit as God's plan is reaching its glorious culmination in these last days:

> And it shall come to pass in the last days, saith God, I will pour out of my Spirit upon all flesh; and your sons and your daughters shall prophesy, and your young men shall see visions, and your old men shall dream dreams: And on my servants and on my handmaidens I will pour out in those days of my Spirit; and they shall prophesy. (KJV)

This Pentecostal outpouring is the promise of the Father that gave Phoebe Palmer the title of her book. It is the text that Catherine Booth put on the title page of her work. It is the text that gave Fredrick Franson his title, *Prophesying Daughters*. It is the text that launched the "pope of fundamentalism," John Roach Straton, into his biblical defense of women preachers. And so one could go on and on.

I believe that the rise of the Pentecostal movement in the twentieth century caused noncharismatic evangelicals to shy away from contemporary applications of all texts about prophets and prophesying. An older noncharismatic evangelical hermeneutic stretching back through the Puritans to the Reformed wing of the Protestant Reformation was quite willing to apply verses about prophesying to preaching. Even those who did not believe that verses regarding prophesying could be directly applied to preaching still often reasoned that if women were used by God to prophesy—that is to speak authoritatively his Word in his name—then there can be no bar on their preaching which is, if anything, a less authoritative form of ministry. These texts about women prophesying, however, now became quarantined as not directly applicable at all. For some, evangelical hermeneutics narrowed so that, in practice, only the epistles of Paul could be used to establish normative practice in church life. The book of Acts was deemed merely descriptive, not prescriptive. Even Paul's clear affirmation in 1 Corinthians that women are free to prophesy to the whole congregation assembled for worship became irrelevant to contemporary church life. (Incidentally, this has arguably also caused evangelicals who affirm women in public ministry to place much more weight on another historic key passage for their position that seems suitably prescriptive and Pauline, Galatians 3:28.)

Nevertheless, for some, what had been a biblical conversation with many texts that affirmed women in public ministry was transformed into one in which 1 Timothy 2 was seen as the trump card of the germane evidence of Scripture on the matter. I am not arguing that a reading of Scripture that excludes women from public ministry is merely the result of these reactionary factors: a restrictive position had been articulated prior to these influences and it has been advanced since then by scholars and ministers whose work cannot be dismissed as the product of such forces. I am merely arguing that it is wrong to assume that restricting women from public ministry is the only conclusion that a robust and unclouded commitment to submission to Scripture has rendered. In fact, throughout the history of evangelicalism, there have been Christians whose belief in the full authority of Scripture has been resolute and unwavering who have conscientiously read the biblical evidence as affirming women in public ministry.

This chapter has sought to remind the evangelical community of its own exceptionally substantial and sustained history of affirming women in public ministry. In the eighteenth and nineteenth centuries, when all of the cultural and social pressure of the wider society pushed toward restricting women, major evangelical leaders and communities again and again read the Bible counterculturally as allowing women to be preachers, teachers, pastors, ministers and Christian leaders.[43] This is not the historic stance of theological liberalism or of mainline denominations, but of Bible-believing, gospel-spreading evangelicals. Often when women have been excluded from ministry in evangelical churches it has been as a result of aspirations toward worldly respectability and other cultural factors. On the other hand, from the first generation of evangelicalism and from generation to generation thereafter, when evangelicals have prioritized the gospel and the Bible, this has often led them to affirm women in public ministry.

---

[43]For an exploration of this in a particular time period in an American context, see Catherine A. Brekus, *Strangers and Pilgrims: Female Preaching in America, 1740-1845* (Chapel Hill: University of North Carolina Press, 1998).

PART FIVE

BEYOND THE IMPASSE

Toward New Paradigms

11

WOMEN, MINISTRY AND THE GOSPEL
Hints for a New Paradigm?

Henri Blocher

SHOULD WE SEARCH FOR A NEW PARADIGM? Not as seekers after novelty for novelty's sake! Not as despising our predecessors' work, their learning, their intelligence, their godly concern for the cause of God and respect for his Word—
this we try to emulate. Yet, the impression which is mine, as an onlooker from
abroad, is that the confrontation of older paradigms on the ministry of women
has led American evangelicals into a deadlock; my timid hope is that an exotic
contribution, through some providential alchemy, may help to find or to build
a new, more dialogical paradigm.

Sympathies, even ties, I have on both sides reinforce my motivation. On the
one hand, I am proud that my grandmother, Madeleine Blocher née Saillens,
was the first woman pastor in France. Though the two of us discussed her
views at length and I could not adopt many of them, I do believe that our
church, the Paris Tabernacle Church, was led of God in the recognition of her
ministry, which lasted about twenty years.[1] Since then, our church, in whose

---

[1]Special circumstances facilitated the bold move at that time (1930): the sudden death of my grandfa-
ther, Arthur Blocher, who was the pastor of the church and in whose ministry Madeleine had fully
participated; the independent status of the church, which had separated from the denomination after
the model of Spurgeon's Tabernacle (and then had taken on the "Tabernacle" name); the presence,
still, of Madeleine's father, Ruben Saillens, who had founded the church (1888) and remained its
"honorary" pastor. Madeleine, Mme A. Blocher-Saillens, set forth her feminist case in her book
Libérées par Christ pour son service (Paris: Bons Semeurs, 1961).

life I have had a fair share of responsibilities for several decades, has regularly opened its pulpit to women preaching. On the other hand, I cannot responsibly approve the way many so-called egalitarians handle biblical texts—on the part of some, it sounds indeed like *Hexegese*, according to the German pun (*Hexe* meaning "witch")[2]—or revisit the metaphor of headship; nor can I subscribe to their hermeneutics, when they identify what the biblical statements meant and conclude that it should mean something vastly different today. I feel bound, by the word of Scripture, to affirm a nonsymmetrical pattern.

Some, I guess, would call me a mild, or soft, or weak, "complementarian." I don't object to being called mild or soft or weak; but I am ill at ease with "complementarian," and this choice of words is the first topic I am now addressing.

Starting with Words: Unease with *Complementarian*

Complementarian is not the only term in current circulation that appears to be unhelpful: *egalitarian* itself is not so felicitous, and *gender* could be the target of several criticisms. But one word at a time! *Complementarian* tends, I submit, to obscure and slightly to distort the nonsymmetrical model I find in Scripture.

I realize how foolhardy it is for *me* to complain about contemporary English parlance! But, precisely, I have nothing to lose! I also acknowledge that in linguistic matters, common usage is sovereign, that forms of expression born of manifest error may, in due time, be established as the only correct ones. My objections are sand bulwarks that a child on the beach has built against the tide. There is a short time, however, when fighting the rear-guard fight is still possible, and a matter of dignity. More germane to our task: linguistic choices are not value-free, and words carry with them subtle suggestions; a critical look at them introduces us to what they partially veil; it gives us food for thought and sharpens our discernment of the issues themselves.

Complementarian implies that man and woman are viewed as complements of one another and, I suspect, woman more insistently the complement of man. I can understand the angry reaction of many feminists—for example, the Dutch theologian Catharina Halkes.[3] This apparently harmless, even gener-

---

[2] Quoted by Lutz von Padberg, *Feminismus—eine ideologische und theologische Herausforderung*, Evangelium und Gesellschaft B. 5 (Wuppertal: Verlag und Schriftmission der Evangelischen Gesellschaft, 1985), p. 142 (the pun comes from the feminists themselves, who boast of their enchanting spins).

[3] As quoted by Elisabeth Parmentier, *Les Filles prodigues: Défis des théologies féministes*, Lieux théologiques 32 (Geneva: Labor & Fides, 1999), p. 88.

ous, kind of talk covers up a structure of exploitation! A gentle-sounding term is used to perpetuate unjust and restrictive arrangements! The complementarity of pulpit and kitchen is another case of the complementarity of masters and servants. This criticism cannot be brushed off so easily.

More decisively, is the scheme that comes to mind with the word *complement* true to fact, to Bible fact? Calvin comes very close to affirming it: the French version of his Genesis commentary, on Genesis 2:18, uses the word *complément,* but the Latin has *accessio,*[4] which may be weaker or vaguer; as to Genesis 1:27c, he suggests it is equivalent to saying that "the male is only half a human person" *(ne si virum dixisset esse dimidium hominem);*[5] his main intention, in context, being to extol the institution of marriage. But the contrary judgment of Erwin Metzke is worth noticing:

> Talking of a complementarity of the sexes is a fountainhead of error. For man is not for woman (nor woman for man) a simple complement. . . . The notion of complementarity . . . always arouses a false representation, the implication of which is that the problem is how to harmonize two separate elements that together make one whole. Actually, one must understand the beginning of the relationship between man and woman in the following way: being made originally the one for the other, they collide into each other and they experience how alien and unlike they are, but, as each one accepts the other in that other's personal being, they originate a history—the history of two beings who are responsible for each other.[6]

When one considers the early chapters in Genesis (and the rest of Scripture), one hardly finds the faintest trace of the "complement" idea. The word "helper" in Genesis 2:18 does not require it. Calvin drew it from Genesis 1:27 because he took *'ādām* as a name for the individual person (though he avoided the deeply unbiblical myth of the androgyne[7]), but we may not follow him here: *'ādām* is humankind. The only possible suggestion of complementarity could be found in the words for "male" and "female," but this is not obvious.[8] Though the fundamental status of the distinction between the sexes, as

---

[4]*Calvini Opera* 23.46.

[5]Ibid., p. 28.

[6]"Anthropologie des sexes: Remarques philosophiques sur l'état de la question," *Lumière et Vie* 8, no. 43 (July-August 1959): 50 (my translation, the French version being itself from a German original).

[7]Criticized with due vigor by von Padberg, *Feminismus,* p. 156.

[8]*něqēbâ* means *perforata,* and *zākār* could mean *perforans,* as some associate its etymology to the idea of sharpness (according to some dictionaries, the cognate word designates the *phallos* in Arabic).

taught by Genesis 1:27, surely implies that humankind is not complete without both (when there is man only, the situation is "not good"), the human person of either sex is considered whole throughout Scripture: hence the value of the gift of celibacy (1 Cor 7!), which Jewish and Protestant emphatic and unilateral praise of marriage may have obscured. The union of man and woman is no fusion but one person facing, *neged,* the other person (Gen 2:18); they become "one flesh" but not "one soul" in any strict sense—to borrow William Congreve's way of putting it: "Though marriage makes man and wife one flesh, it leaves 'em still two fools."

The emphasis in the biblical text is not on complementarity but on similarity and commonality: man and woman are both created in God's image, and Calvin rightly drew the consequence: "it follows that whatever is said in the creation of man also belongs to the female sex," and one should speak of *equality.*[9] The "helper," in contradistinction with all animal species, is the man's own flesh and bones, and is given a name, *'iššā,* that corresponds most closely to his, *'iš* (Gen 2:23). In this respect, Dorothy Sayers strikes the true biblical note: "But the fundamental thing is that women are more like men than anything else in the world. They are human beings."[10] In the light of such data, complementarity should not become the key concept in any doctrine of the man-woman relationship.

Probing the Difference: The "Callings" of Man and Woman

The affirmation, first, of common humanity does not preclude interest in the difference of the sexes. It is an important focus in the first two chapters of the Bible. The prohibition of transvestitism (Deut 22:5) illustrates the constant concern that it be acknowledged and consequently honored. But how is the difference understood? The striking fact is the contrast between the traditional discourse in this regard and the emphases of Scripture. Both popular and erudite accounts, whether in coarse or refined language, have majored on supposedly natural characteristics, strengths and weaknesses, bents and abilities, of male and female constitutions: women are this and that, men are so and so.

---

[9]*Calvini Opera* 23.46: "*unde sequitur, quod in creatione viri dictum fuit, ad sexum muliebrem pertinere*"; "*aliquid aequabile notare voluit Moses.*"

[10]Dorothy Sayers, *Are Women Human?* (Grand Rapids: Eerdmans, 1992), p. 37. She seems to lose the right balance, however, when she minimizes the sexual difference: "A difference of age is as fundamental as a difference of sex; and so is a difference of nationality" (p. 34); "the brain, that great and sole true Androgyne" (p. 44).

Roles in society have been assigned on the basis of those natural features. *One finds almost nothing of the kind in Scripture.*

I am not suggesting that all differences are social constructs, cultural effects. I am not reducing, as Simone de Beauvoir tried to do, natural differences to a bare anatomical minimum. I have been convinced that the male-female distinction affects, beyond biology and independently of culture, the psychological and mental make-up of men and women: I would refer, for instance, to the objective scientific method of *le Fait féminin*, a remarkable symposium under the responsibility of Evelyne Sullerot (a highly respected figure, who was a pioneer of feminism in France), and to the rich phenomenology of F. J. J. Buytendijk, *la Femme, ses modes d'être, de paraître et d'exister.* Presumably, "obstinate" factual differences that are thus identified reflect some creational purpose, which the Proto-Gnostics in the Ephesus area (as we may guess from the Pastoral Epistles) wished to deny; they take on, thereby, some theological significance. Expressly in Scripture, it is possible that the mention of the "weaker sex *[skeuos]*" (1 Pet 3:7) refers to a natural disposition, though it might be conditioned by the socio-historical situation.[11] The privileged dimensions of the woman's and the man's lives in the Lord God's verdict, according to Genesis 3:16-19—the relationship to the man, and motherhood, for her, the relationship to the ground for him—do correspond to their constitution in the preceding chapter. Yet obviously this is not the primary emphasis.

How, then, are the different roles established? Precisely as roles! The best analogy seems to be that of the theater. On the stage of the world, the stage of God's glory (Calvin loved the metaphor), the Director has assigned different roles to man and woman. They are to *represent: she* the beloved partner of God's Covenant, his chosen people, the race under grace, and *he* the generous Lord in his dealings with humankind. Likely, they are gifted with natural characteristics that fit the roles, but the decisive element, as the divine *Commedia* unfolds, is the order decided by the Director, from whom and for whom the whole thing is taking place.

The biblical warrant for such an interpretation is overwhelmingly abundant: the use in the Psalms and the Prophets, in the Gospels, the Epistles and

---

[11]One sometimes meets the idea, in connection with 1 Tim 2:14, that the woman is more vulnerable to temptation, especially demonic temptation: so von Padberg, *Feminismus*, p. 163. I favor another reading of the passage in 1 Tim 2.

Revelation of the man-woman relationship as the figure appropriate for YHWH and Israel, for the Lord Christ and his church. It is central in the two "difficult" passages, 1 Corinthians 11:2-16 and Ephesians 5:22-33. His christological concentration enabled Karl Barth—and Charlotte von Kirschbaum, his secretary (and much more)—to perceive that biblical key of the man-woman relationship; on this topic, I treasure their insight and I definitely follow their lead. Charlotte von Kirschbaum even suggests that, paradoxically, the "privileged situation" is the woman's because her representative role is in line with her human nature: "what may appear a disadvantage in the eyes of the world here becomes an essential advantage."[12] Thus is the order grounded, the nonsymmetrical pattern established, and the predominantly masculine language for a nonsexual God, in Scripture, explained.[13]

The suspicion that his representative role makes man into a god ("the male is God") and justifies the oppression of women—who are called to restore the worship of the Goddess—is not supported by factual evidence. Elisabeth Parmentier marshals several weighty arguments against "the presupposition that there is a direct link between symbolic representations and social order,"[14] and Edith M. Humphrey notes: "We have no evidence that cultures in which the Mother Goddess was worshipped gave special privilege to women."[15] Susanne Heine offers the most perceptive insight as she discerns that the transcendent model of the Divine Father and Bridegroom limits and humbles the pretensions of his earthly representatives[16]—in the same way the kingship of YHWH prevented the kings of Judah and Israel, even the bad ones, from exalting themselves beyond measure.

---

[12]*Découverte de la femme: Les bases bibliques et théologiques d'une éthique réformée de la femme* (Geneva: Centre Protestant d'Études/Section féminine, 1951), p. 21 (my translation from the French version). See pp. 21, 50, 63, 67, 75 (quoting Kierkegaard to the same effect) for the theme of representation.

[13]This interpretation also wards off the seductive and deeply pagan absolutization of the sexual polarity when it is expanded to divine and cosmic dimensions: the Way of harmony of the *yin* and the *yang*. One can see the influence of this dualism in the otherwise helpful replies of Suzanne Lilar to Simone de Beauvoir, *Le Couple* (Paris: Bernard Grasset, 1963) and *Le Malentendu du deuxième sexe* (Paris: Presses Universitaires de France, 1970). Christian theology may be affected. The Orthodox thinker Elisabeth Behr-Siegel has come to see the danger of such speculation, as found, e.g., in the work of Paul Evdokimov (in Parmentier, *Les Filles prodigues*, pp. 236-37). Christian Duquoc, *Le Femme, le clerc et le laïc: Œcuménisme et ministère*, Entrée libre 4 (Geneva: Labor & Fides, 1989), esp. p. 31, sharply criticizes the official teaching of his (Roman Catholic) church on this score.

[14]*Les Filles prodigues*, 117-19.

[15]"Why We Worship God as Father, Son and Holy Spirit," *Crux* 32, no. 1 (1996): 8.

[16]Quoted in Parmentier, *Les Filles prodigues*, p. 126.

As it is an order that God freely disposed, and not the direct expression of the male and female "natures," the differentiation of roles has no absolute character and it stays flexible. The first truth about man and woman remains that of their common human nature, with much in their activity having little reference to their sex. The roles themselves do not imply total difference. It is most significant that Paul himself should relativize the import of what he has just said, in 1 Corinthians 11:11: *and yet* . . . Lest men should misinterpret their representative role and claim absolute authority in the name of "headship," the apostle warns about the limits: *plēn* . . . If heeded, this Greek adversative will prevent many pernicious misapplications of the truth of representative order, in homes and churches.

Distinguishing Among Ministries: Prophecy and Doctrinal Responsibility

What is the bearing of the biblical pattern we have ascertained for the accession of women to the ministry of the Word? First, the essential duality of that ministry should be acknowledged: the Word of God which begets and rules the church is delivered to the church through the channel of two different "offices": those of prophet and of *didaskalos*, the dispenser of authoritative teachings. In some measure, these two ministries correspond to prophecy and priesthood in the Old Testament (priests were preeminently teachers of the *tôrâ*, e.g., Mal 2:7). There is some overlap between them, and no hard and fast separation, but their polarity is impossible to ignore. Since the Word is to govern the church, church leaders—elders, overseers—should have at least a part in the teaching of the church (1 Tim 5:17; Tit 1:9; etc.), in marked contrast to the synagogue. Specialized *didaskaloi*, of the Apollos type, seem also to have served the New Testament churches without being elders or bishops.

The prophetic ministry of New Testament churches was probably exercised under various forms.[17] The proclamation of the Word of God in existential urgency, *hic et nunc* (the nucleus of prophecy), did not involve infallibility, as it does in canonical prophecy; it called for careful sifting (1 Cor 14:29; 1 Thess 5:20-22). It was not restricted to sudden and particular revelation, as may be

---

[17]On New Testament prophecy, see the special issue of *Hokhma* 72 (1999): 134, to which I contributed, together with Water Hollenweger, Sylvain Romerowski and others.

the case in 1 Corinthians 14:24-33. According to many experts,[18] the basic form was quite similar to later homilies: the prophets expounded and applied the Scriptures to the needs of the congregation; they had to do so "according to the analogy of faith" (Rom 12:6). In that light, one may say that up to 80 or 90 percent of traditional preaching in evangelical churches should be labeled "prophetic" by New Testament standards.

Now, that conclusion is of remarkable significance for our topic. First Corinthians 11:5 makes it clear that Paul expected women, provided they observed the creation-based representative order, to prophesy in the church! Gordon Wenham grants that female prophecy took place in Corinth but feels that "the most natural reading of 14:34 is that Paul was concerned to stop it."[19] I confess I find such a reading most unnatural. It flies in the face of much biblical evidence. Already in the Old Testament (and Gal 3:28 makes it unlikely that more restrictive conditions should obtain under the New), the prophetic office is open to women as well as to men. It is an *ordinary* feature of God's dispensations that women should bring oracles in his name, from Miriam, Deborah and Huldah to the daughters of Philip, and even to that woman "Jezebel" in Thyatira (Rev 2:20) inasmuch as the existence of pseudo testifies in favor of the authentic thing it imitates, counterfeit money witnesses to genuine banknotes! The consequence is inescapable, even for the most conservative, rigid, "wooden" if you like, interpretation of the Scriptures: there is no biblical reason to bar women from the preaching role, which is "prophetic."

There is no forbidding reason, but there is a problem for understanding: does not the prophet, does not the prophetess, wield authority and represent the Lord? How does this agree with the representative order we have found? An interesting suggestion comes from the pen of G. W. Knight: prophecy fits a woman's role because it is "an activity in which the one prophesying is essentially a passive instrument through which God communicates."[20] I would not retain the word "passive"; even in the more ecstatic forms of prophetic inspi-

---

[18]See, e.g., Edouard Cothenet, "Prophétisme dans le Nouveau Testament," in *Supplément au dictionnaire de la Bible* 8 (Paris: Letouzey & Ané, 1972), cols. 1222-1337; Peter Jones, "Y a-t-il deux types de prophéties dans le Nouveau Testament? " *La Revue Réformée* 31 (1980): 303-17; André Lemaire, *Les Ministères dans l'Église*, Croire et comprendre ([Paris]: Centurion, 1974), p. 18; and the *Hokhma* issue in the preceding note.

[19]Gordon Wenham, "The Ordination of Women: Why Is It So Divisive?" *Churchman* 92, no. 4 (1978): 313.

[20]G. W. Knight, *The New Testament Teaching on the Role Relationship of Men and Women* (Grand Rapids: Baker, 1977), p. 46, as quoted (with interest) by Wenham, "Ordination of Women," p. 313.

ration, the powers, symbols, memories, of the unconscious depths of the human spirit are stirred and used by the Holy Spirit; ordinary prophecy involves the full use of intelligence and conscious faculties. But the prophets' position in the trajectory of God's Word, God speaking through them, probably means that there is no authority attached to their persons as such—whereas the teacher stands on the side, as it were, in his own person (the Holy Spirit leads the teacher to share a thoughtful digestion of what God *has* said). Being the "mouthpieces" of God, prophets fulfill a self-effacing office, in accordance with the words we sing, "And let them forget the channel, seeing only Him."

ALLOWING FOR FLEXIBILITY: ORDINARY AND EXTRAORDINARY

There is, then, no problem with the pulpit, but what about authoritative teaching, leadership, eldership? Are women excluded from such roles in the ·church? This is the sentiment, among so many others, of Lutz von Padberg. Referring to women in the pastoral ministry, he writes: "What we find in the Bible speaks clearly and without ambiguity against such a practice."[21] Is this so clear in the whole of Scripture?

The disturbing feature of Padberg's understanding is that it confers an absolute and rigid character to the order the Bible reveals for man and woman—whereas we found indications of flexibility. Actually, it turns a pattern that comes second among the truths of human life, a beauty for the stage of God's glory, into an article of law: an article that absolutely prohibits female leadership. Isn't this a *metabasis eis allo genos*? One passage *only* might suggest such a legal angle: 1 Timothy 2. Undoubtedly the order between the sexes as taught in those verses, buttressed by a condensed midrash on Genesis 2 and 3, is a teaching independent of the situation; but the tenseness of Paul's diction, the harsher tone of his voice, as he tells his amanuensis what to write in chapter two, may be accounted for by the special problems in the Ephesus churches—and the impression that Paul was laying down a canon law pronouncement precisely comes from this diction and tone.

Focussing on order (*ordo*) makes it possible to distinguish between *ordinary* and *extraordinary,* both of them allowable. After he has established an order that pleases him—an order that remains flexible, with a limited import—God remains perfectly free to raise extraordinary ministries! Why should we forbid

---

[21]*Feminismus*, p. 176.

an extraordinary ministry of teaching and leadership conferred upon a woman? The notions of ordinary and extraordinary do not refer to habits or to statistics: it is a matter of status, as with the time-honored distinction between ordinary and extraordinary ambassadors, or ordinary and extraordinary professors (the *ordinarius* in this or that university). The distinction, regarding man and woman, embodies respect for the wise and beneficial order God has chosen, but not as a code of law. I suggest that women can be ordinary prophets (preachers) and extraordinary *didaskaloi* and *hēgoumenai*.

By use of the ordinary/extraordinary distinction one can reconcile otherwise conflicting data of the New Testament. First Timothy 2 is not the only relevant passage. There are also indications that some women were recognized as leaders in the apostolic church. Paul's female coworkers were not confined to the kitchen; Phoebe, the "Bright One," receives the titles of *diakonos* (probably "minister") and *prostatis*, titles of honor and influence;[22] and Priscilla—what a key figure in early Christianity![23] Just as the "egalitarian" handling of some passages fails to convince me, the way "prohibitionists" minimize Priscilla's role, or use the anachronistic distinction of "private" and "public" teaching, resemble efforts to skirt the natural textual suggestions. Other considerations on the changes in the notion and practice of teaching, since the time of the apostles, its multiple modes today, would also be relevant if a full systematic discussion were possible; but the ordinary/extraordinary distinction is enough to justify the acceptance of, and call for, modern extraordinary Priscillas.

How is an extraordinary vocation discerned? Since it depends on God's sovereign freedom, just as his election of individuals to all services in the church, the way of discernment is no different: apart from special revelation, the sign that God has chosen someone for a specific ministry, whether ordinary or extraordinary, is the presence of the required gifts (varieties of gifts correspond to varieties of service, 1 Cor 12:4-5). If I see in a Christian sister the gifts of prophecy or the gifts of teaching, I will gladly and gratefully acknowledge God's decision to entrust her with an ordinary or extraordinary ministry of the

---

[22]Lemaire, *Ministères dans l'Église*, p. 40; Thierry Maertens, *La Promotion de la femme dans la Bible: Ses applications au mariage et au ministère*, Points de repère (Tournai: Casterman, 1967), pp. 172-73.

[23]Harnack's bold hypothesis that she was the writer to the Hebrews conflicts with the author's use of the masculine pronoun for himself in Heb 11:32 (*diēgoumenon*); but I confess I find it still attractive enough to mention it.

Word, and align myself with it. I have not perceived any warrant for another attitude.

I am not too much of a dreamer. I realize that the distinction ordinary/extraordinary will entail, in practice, that churches may require more conspicuous evidence of gifts in the case of women. It reminds me of a quotation from Charlotte Whitton, with which I close: "Whatever she does, a woman must do it twice better than a man to get equal recognition. Fortunately, it's not difficult."

12

Forging a Middle Way Between Complementarians and Egalitarians

Sarah Sumner

I ENTERED THIS DEBATE BY COMPULSION. LEFT TO my own volition, I would rather have kept a distance from this controversy. But through a series of events, I was gently guided by the providence of God to participate in the public discussion. Since the inception of my involvement, my primary conviction has been to attempt to draw attention, not to the matter of order (as complementarians tend to do) and not to the matter of justice (as egalitarians tend to do), but rather to the matter of integrity. My concern lies with the integrity—that is, the moral character and honesty—of the church, especially among conservative evangelicals.[1]

Prophetically speaking, I believe it grieves the Spirit of God for us, as evangelicals, to be divided in the way that we are on the issue of women in ministry. No doubt, for us to debate is good ("As iron sharpens iron, so one

---

[1]Since the word *evangelical* is itself under fire, it's especially important to define what I mean by the term "conservative evangelicals." By "conservative evangelicals," I mean those orthodox Christians who read the Bible as God's own Word, and who live out a personal trust in and love for Jesus Christ as the world's only Lord and Savior, and who see themselves as sinners saved by grace, and who are committed to disciple-making according to the Great Commission. See J. I. Packer and Thomas Oden, *One Faith* (Downers Grove, Ill.: InterVarsity Press, 2004), p. 19. Whereas Packer and Oden say "evangelicals," I am using the term "conservative evangelicals" for the purpose of making clear that I am not referring to nominal evangelicals who explicitly disavow one or more of the convictions listed above.

man sharpens another" Prov 27:17 NIV). But for us to equivocate, that is, to say one thing and yet do another (contra James 1:22, "But be doers of the word"), is unacceptable. For example, it is an act of equivocation when we *say* that the Golden Rule should be applied by every Christian comprehensively, yet fail to *behave* as though loving people as ourselves is relevant to the way that the discussion about women in ministry is played out. Far too many Christians who are involved in this debate stand at odds with one another, strained relationally, too distanced to gather in fellowship, and too guarded to unravel the grave misunderstandings that are caused by conflicting points of view.

As conservative evangelicals, it may even be our tendency to deny that our viewpoints are our viewpoints. In other words, our confidence in the Bible and its measure of perspicuity may occasionally spill over into the confidence that we place in ourselves, particularly in our ability to echo the objective truth of God.[2] Since God inspired the Bible, many fervent evangelicals are eager to conclude that an authentically conservative opinion is, by virtue of association, likewise objectively true. Consequently, in our fervor to uphold a high view of Scripture, we may fall into the trap of forgetting our own human subjectivity.[3] It is not a hidden fact that conservative evangelicals on a popular level are often taught to believe that a conservative point of view is a *biblical* point of view, and thus one free of subjectivity.[4]

On a practical level, then, the notion of a "conservative opinion" can amount to nothing more than an oxymoron. Perhaps that is why we, as conservatives, have been known to confuse the theology of our favorite theolo-

---

[2]Though some might argue that all Scripture is equally perspicuous, I affirm instead the more sensible assertion of British scholar Richard Briggs, who writes, "The clarity of Scripture was designed to safeguard the insight that Scripture is *clear enough*. It is available to all. It offers guidance to allow us to live. . . . If we unleash the doctrine of the clarity of Scripture from these carefully defined moorings, and try to turn it into the claim that all things in Scripture should be understandable by everyone, then we actually move away from the traditional Christian view of the matter." See Richard Briggs, *Reading the Bible Wisely* (Grand Rapids: Baker, 2003), p. 66.

[3]Mark Noll and David Wells speak to this issue when jointly they say, "The doing of theology requires an acknowledgement of fallibility and inherent waywardness." See Mark Noll and David Wells, *Christian Faith and Practice in the Modern World* (Grand Rapids: Eerdmans, 1988), p. 16.

[4]The highly influential comments of W. G. T. Shedd here come to mind. Defending the Westminster Confession of Faith in 1893, he wrote: "The infallible Word of God is expounded by the fallible mind of man, and hence the variety of expositions embodied in the denominational creeds. But every interpreter claims to have understood the Scriptures correctly, and consequently, claims that his creed is Scriptural, and if so, that it is the infallible truth of God." See W. G. T. Shedd, *Calvinism: Pure and Mixed* (Carlisle: Banner of Truth, 1999), pp. 145-46.

gians with divine revelation itself.[5]

Despite our Protestant identity and fierce rejection of papal authority, we still have our gurus. Of course, if asked point-blank to answer which outranks the other—the theology of a faithful conservative or the Bible itself—we would say, without exception, that the Bible is superior and unique. But if asked within the context of a discussion to distill the subjectivity of our favorite Bible teacher from the actual words of Scripture, some of us might argue that there's nothing of significance to distill. Hence, we are left with a slight propensity to neglect the hard work of distinguishing the various assumptions (that we impose inadvertently into our reading of the text) from the meaning of the text itself.[6] As Justo González has astutely pointed out,

> The notion that we read the New Testament [or in this case, the whole Bible] exactly as the early Christians did, without any weight of tradition coloring our interpretation, is an illusion. It is also a dangerous illusion, for it tends to absolutize our interpretation, confusing it with the Word of God.[7]

To be clear, I am not at all suggesting that we are stuck with nothing more than our opinions. It is possible for people to have knowledge.[8] But a few things need to be said about what it means to have knowledge and what it means to have an opinion. To begin with, there is no such thing as a "conflict of knowledges," yet there are conflicts of opinions. Moreover, it is improper to speak of a "consensus of knowledge," yet we do say properly that there is a consensus of opinion. In addition, we refer to expert and inexpert opinions, but we do not refer to expert and inexpert knowledge.[9] Furthermore, while an opinion may be right or wrong, knowledge cannot be right or wrong. There is no such thing as "right knowledge" (obviously a term of redundancy) because

---

[5]Again, the counsel of Noll and Wells is helpful. They write, "[For] the Christian theologian is never merely a spokesperson for God. To do theology is to realize the depths of one's own need as well as to proclaim the provision of God for others. By its nature, therefore, evangelical theology is a theology of humility" (*Christian Faith and Practice,* p. 18).

[6]We also may forget the complexity of Scripture. Richard Briggs is right to say, "Scripture is happy to remain difficult in many, many ways, without compromising the clarity of the gospel, even if the same could not be said of certain translations." See Briggs, *Reading the Bible Wisely,* p. 66.

[7]Justo González, *The Story of Christianity,* vol. 1 (San Francisco: HarperSanFrancisco, 1984), p. xvii.

[8]Since people are made in the image of God, we are endowed with rational faculties that enable us to be knowing subjects. Even so, our knowing involves a personal commitment to take responsibility for that which we are willing to know. See Lesslie Newbigin, *Truth to Tell* (Grand Rapids: Eerdmans, 1991), p. 35.

[9]I am indebted to Mortimer Adler for the aforementioned insights. See Mortimer J. Adler, *The Great Ideas,* ed. Max Weismann (Chicago: Open Court, 2000), pp. 1-17.

the phrase implies a validation of an implausible opposite. There is no such thing as "wrong knowledge" because knowledge, by definition, rightly accords with the truth.

To *know* something is to apprehend the truth about it and also to properly understand it. To *have an opinion* is to have a personal appraisal of something, or even a professional appraisal of something as with a legal opinion or a medical opinion. According to the philosopher Mortimer Adler, an opinion, whether based on truth or not, lacks the understanding that comes with knowledge.[10]

So, for example, we have knowledge about the life of Jesus Christ: we know who he was, where he was born, many things he said and did, specifically how he died and so forth. But we do *not* have knowledge of how God became human in the first place. On the basis of Scripture, we know that the Word became flesh (Jn 1:14), but we do not understand how he did so. Curiously, we do not have knowledge about a miracle that we know by faith to be true.[11]

But we can hold opinions about it. We may either hold a right opinion or a wrong opinion. A right opinion lacks proper understanding, yet it is still reflective of the truth. A wrong opinion, by contrast, is reflective of error, though that error is mistaken as truth. Similarly, we can have either a right interpretation or a wrong interpretation of Scripture. A right interpretation discovers the right meaning of the text by honoring critical factors such as the genre, structure, grammar, original language and historical contexts surrounding the text. A wrong interpretation, by contrast, finds meaning in the text that is not there.

Thanks to the tools of critical analysis, we are well equipped to interpret the Scriptures rightly, though not equally so in every specific case. If in a given pericope, either the genre, structure or grammar seems ambiguous, or the language obscure, or the historical contexts unclear, or the plain and literal reading absurd, then we must humble ourselves by refusing to convey the same measure of certainty to our readers as we would with a passage less freighted with complications and complexities.

Sadly, some conservatives have not been careful to do this. Some have enshrined their own interpretations,[12] even to the point of pejoratively labeling

---

[10]See ibid., pp. 14-24.

[11]Incidentally, C. S. Lewis calls the incarnation the "central miracle." See C. S. Lewis, *Miracles* (New York: Macmillan, 1947), p. 108.

[12]Briggs puts it this way: "We all just know that the way we see it is the way it is, but we do not all see it the same way." Briggs, *Reading the Bible Wisely*, p. 66.

their fellow-conservatives as being "liberal." (The word *liberal,* in this context, refers to a person who denies the truthfulness and trustworthiness of Scripture.) Consequently, many *nonacademic* conservatives are led by the power of rhetoric to forget that the Bible is "profitable for correction," even with regard to the very most conservative teacher (2 Tim 3:16-17).

As a result of that forgetfulness, some of us degenerate imperceptibly into audience-like fans who feverishly cheer for fallible theologians. Caught up in the competitiveness of rooting for what we deem to be "the conservative side," we are swept into a political kind of hype that prevents us from noticing that a plethora of self-contradictory, or rather, mutually exclusive views (each one deemed as "*the* biblical point of view") are being heralded from the likes of us (both complementarians and egalitarians), even while we claim, as theological conservatives, that "the biblical view" cannot possibly be self-contradictory. Ironically then, in our quest to champion truth, some aggrandize dim-sightedness instead.[13]

What trips us up is important to point out, for our problem does not tend to be conscious defiance or doubt. Our problem has to do with our eagerness to believe the right thing. We want to feel righteous. We want to feel as though we have aligned ourselves with Scripture. But in our pursuit of that feeling, too often we forget to examine our logic and ensure that it is both biblical and coherent. If knowledge is the sum of truth plus a proper understanding, and a proper understanding ineluctably excludes self-contradictory claims, then we must discipline ourselves *not* to claim that we have knowledge until our arguments are free from inconsistencies.[14]

In other words, as genuinely conservative evangelicals, we must complement our eagerness to align ourselves with Scripture with a willingness also to be patient. Patience is required in this debate. We need patience to work laboriously in the effort to discover what Francis Schaeffer called "true truth," that

---

[13]Nathan Hatch says that intellectuals, in particular, "very easily cross the fine line and begin affirming their own intellectual self-sufficiency, trusting in their own wisdom rather than submitting the mind humbly to the truths of holy Scripture. Given their well-honed intellectual skills, academics are always prone to move in the direction of unwarrantably high opinion of human natural powers." See Nathan O. Hatch, "Evangelical Colleges and the Challenge of Christian Thinking," in *Making Higher Education Christian: The History and Mission of Evangelical Colleges in America,* ed. Joel A. Carpenter and Kenneth W. Shipps (Grand Rapids: Eerdmans, 1987), p. 167.

[14]A quote from Ralph McInerney here seems apropos. He says, "Inconsistency is the tribute that confusion pays to reality." See Ralph McInerny, *Characters in Search of Their Author,* The Gifford Lectures, 1999-2000 (South Bend, Ind.: University of Notre Dame Press, 2001), p. 91.

is, truth that makes sense biblically, theologically and practically from the vantage point of orthodox faith.

Of course, some people in this current postmodern milieu aver that truth itself is unknowable and that truths (in the plural) are all that we can hope to ascertain.[15] Echoing the arguments of skeptics in the past, present-day postmoderns commonly purport that it's impossible to know the truth about anything objectively. I would argue instead—in defense of truth's knowability—that *everyone* knows what truth is because everybody knows how to lie. Mere common sense makes that self-evident. Every honest person knows intuitively that it takes both knowledge as well as a grasp of objective truth for anyone to be able to lie. Conversely, it takes both knowledge and a grasp of objective truth for anyone to be able to tell the truth.

According to the Scriptures, "The sum of your [God's] word is truth" (Ps 119:160). The Bible itself reveals the truth of God, and yet the Bible must be rightly interpreted in order to be rightly understood. Consequently, in our pursuit to gain biblical knowledge, that is, (in Mortimer Adler's language) to gain *truth plus understanding,* we must discipline ourselves *intellectually* in order to let the truth of God's Word speak for itself, and discipline ourselves *spiritually* to the point of being able to admit it when, in reality, we are holding opinions rather than knowledge.

All of this is to say that in the case of the debate on women's place in the church, there is a great clash of *opinions* going on.[16] Despite the fact that some people (on both sides of the debate) present themselves as being knowledge-full and opinion-free, none of us have reached the level of understanding that comes with knowledge.[17] None of us have weeded out completely the internal contradictions in our viewpoints on this subject. None of us evenhandedly champion every verse in Scripture that is relevant to this debate.

And now here I stand before you as part of the problem. I say this not so as to convert a scholarly presentation into a personal time of confession, but

---

[15]See Alistair McGrath, *A Passion for Truth* (Downers Grove, Ill.: InterVarsity Press, 1996).

[16]George Marsden's insight is particularly helpful to recall at this juncture: "Whereas evangelicals appeal to the 'Bible alone' for authority, they lack the adequate mechanisms for settling differences on how the Bible is to be understood." As Marsden observes, "Debates among evangelicals therefore are often resolved, not by appealing to recognized authorities, but rather by appealing to popular opinion." As quoted in D. G. Hart, *Deconstructing Evangelicalism* (Grand Rapids: Baker, 2004), p. 148.

[17]Certainly there are many who, when espousing their opinions, *claim* to know what it means. But there's a difference between having knowledge and having an opinion.

rather to articulate a reminder that there are very important differences between these three things: opinions, interpretations of Scripture and biblical
truth itself.

Opinions are subjective: whenever an opinion is a *wrong* one, it typically
defies the rules of logic; if an opinion is *right*, then in the realm of theology, it
is regarded as orthodox. (The word *orthodoxy* literally means "right opinion.")
By contrast, interpretations of Scripture are potentially *less* subjective insofar
as they are guided—and guarded—by the tools of historical and literary analysis. And yet, as with opinions, interpretations can either be right or wrong,
or at least better or worse. A *wrong* interpretation is a misunderstanding of the
text. A *right* interpretation is an accurate understanding of the text. (Thus, as
it turns out, having a right interpretation appears to be the same as having
knowledge of the text.) Although right interpretations of Scripture are not
themselves inspired, they are nonetheless Spirit-led insofar as God alone can
unveil the interpreter's mind (2 Cor 4:3). I would, however, emphatically add
that right interpretations of Scripture do not, and cannot, contradict biblical
truth which, of course, is inherently reliable and inherently authoritative since
it is inspired by God.

Again, if I may speak prophetically, I believe it pleases God when Christian
scholars come together for the purpose of strengthening our relationships and
collectively attempting to discover the truth in dialogue and debate. Hence, I
would like to propose a cursory sketch of a four-part strategy for forging a
middle way (i.e., a consensus) between complementarians and egalitarians.
Actually, I have been trying to do that all along, though admittedly, that hasn't
always been evident, especially to my critics. Hopefully at this point I am able
to offer a bit more clarity on what a consensus realistically might look like. The
strategy I propose requires us to do four things:

1. Strengthen our relationships.

2. Reframe the debate.

3. Distinguish between divine and human choices.

4. Work together as a team.

1. STRENGTHEN OUR RELATIONSHIPS

What *is* the real problem in this debate? Is it strictly the egalitarians? Or is it strictly the complementarians? Or is it all of us collectively somehow?

A number of evangelicals may be thoroughly convinced that the problem is not collective. Some may argue that the problem resides with right-wing complementarians since they are the ones who claim that maleness itself is the main prerequisite for leaders and teachers in the church. Others, by contrast, may argue that the problem stems from left-wing egalitarians since they are the ones who insist on political equality, proclaiming that leadership roles in the church should be equally open to men and women as long as they are appropriately gifted.

If I may take the liberty, I would like to suggest, at least for a moment, that arguments such as these be set aside. For if ever we are to build a consensus, it doesn't make sense to expend our precious energy and invest our precious time blaming one another rather than sharpening one another. Besides, the truth of the matter is that all of us have contributed to the defensiveness and rancor that characterize this heated debate. All of us are complicit in having reached a point of gridlock. Whether by passivity, aggression, insensitivity, hypersensitivity or sheer prayerlessness, together we have caused this problem. Indeed, we *are* the problem. Thus we are also the solution.

Perhaps we can agree without extended conversation that the first obstacle that prevents us from working toward consensus is relational.[18] We, as conservative evangelicals, are not doing our scholarship in the context of Christian community. We are not in any structured way praying together, worshiping together or sharing meals together. Some of us have never even met in person. Some have even expressed an unwillingness to meet together personally. What does that say about us?

As comembers of the body of Christ, it is our responsibility to study the Bible corporately and in unity so that the world will know we're Christians "by our love." Yet it is our custom, generally speaking, to work separately and independently from each other. Thus we lack consideration in our writing, whether that be in book reviews written by nonacademics, or in footnotes written by scholars, or in articles written by pastors in Christian magazines. Sometimes, perhaps especially in unguarded conversations, we—and here I mean everyone—become sarcastic and impatient and

---

[18]Though I am pinpointing the first problem as being a lack of unity in the church, I am not promoting Richard Rorty's pragmatic idea that social solidarity matters more than truth. See Richard Rorty, *Philosophy and the Mirror of Nature* (Princeton: Princeton University Press, 1979).

self-righteously judgmental. Positioning ourselves against one another, we disable ourselves from obeying the top two commandments in Scripture. It is hardly a surprise that it is practically unheard of for seminaries or churches or parachurch ministries to solicit from within proponents from both sides of the debate and commission them jointly to craft a statement of consensus on this issue.

Even if the process was arduous—and it *would* be—the tone of the debate most likely would change insofar as the overall focus of it would shift temporarily from an emphasis on speaking to an emphasis on listening. That is not to say that we should call off the debate. On the contrary, I'm suggesting that we purify the debate.

This debate would be much more focused and much more fruitful if every self-identified conservative evangelical would honor a higher standard of Christian etiquette. If, in our publishing as well as in our arguing, we would hold each other accountable to speak charitably, attacking ideas not persons, and to speak fairly, so that the general readership would no longer be misled to think that a fellow believer is pushing for an agenda that he or she isn't truly pushing for, this debate would be set up to move forward.[19]

Furthermore, if we would mount a collective effort to tackle the problem of in-fighting by establishing teams composed of *unlike*-minded people all committed to the common purpose of approaching this issue from the context of Christian fellowship and making it a priority to articulate a meaningful statement that would take into account the full counsel of God, I predict that at least one of those teams would experience a significant breakthrough. But as long as we remain structurally divided, having complementarians in one camp and egalitarians in another, the gridlock will continue to grind.

To put it more succinctly, I believe that we are structurally set up for failure. Too few working relationships have been forged between complementarians and egalitarians. Too few venues for building trust between the two groups have been set up. There is simply not enough interdependence between those who invite and those who prohibit Christian women from exercising ecclesial authority. Thus I am suggesting that together we make efforts to change that.

---

[19]Perhaps those of us involved in the debate on women in ministry can learn from Kevin Vanhoozer, whose critique of I. Howard Marshall's method of biblical interpretation is uncompromised, yet collegial and respectful. See Kevin J. Vanhoozer, "Into the Great 'Beyond': A Theologian's Response to the Marshall Plan," in I. Howard Marshall, *Beyond the Bible* (Grand Rapids: Baker, 2004), pp. 81-95.

2. REFRAME THE DEBATE

Another major factor that contributes to the gridlock between complementarians and egalitarians is the way that the debate rhetorically has been framed. Generally speaking, Christians in conservative churches are taught to believe that complementarians are biblical and egalitarians are not. Hence, the title of Wayne Grudem's most recent publication: *Evangelical Feminism and Biblical Truth*. Though certainly not all complementarians affirm everything that Grudem teaches, it still can be said that at least on a popular level, many Christians are taught that the choice is really *not* between a complementarian reading of Scripture or an egalitarian reading of Scripture, but rather between egalitarianism (i.e., evangelical feminism) and biblical truth itself.

To illustrate this anecdotally, two years ago I attended a national pastors' conference that included an open microphone Q&A time for people to pose their questions to a small panel of keynote speakers. When someone in the crowd asked about women participating in ministry leadership, the three-person male panel fell silent—until one of them abruptly leaned forward, heaved his arms and shoulders across the table, and announced with passionate resolve, "I am complementarian *to the death!*" With less histrionics, he explained to the pastors that *the* defining difference between complementarians and egalitarians is that complementarians alone acknowledge the authority of Scripture.

This juncture, by the way, is precisely where the discussion gets derailed. The discussion falls off track because it collapses artificially—through rhetoric and misguided perceptions—into the battlefield of an earlier debate, namely, the inerrancy debate that was waged between conservatives and liberals.[20] If ever a middle way is to be forged between complementarians and egalitarians, then it must be understood that this debate is an altogether different debate. It is not a debate between conservatives and liberals. It's a debate between conservatives and *conservatives*. Those who are *not* conservative typically have never even heard of the conservative in-house terms of *complementarian* and *egalitarian*.

Two particular claims need to be addressed in order for the debate to be reframed: one that needs to be discarded and one that needs to be forwarded.

---

[20]For a comprehensive description of this debate, see George Marsden, *Fundamentalism and American Culture* (Oxford: Oxford University Press, 1980); Gary Dorrien, *The Remaking of Evangelical Theology* (Louisville, Ky.: Westminster John Knox, 1998); Hart, *Deconstructing Evangelicalism,* pp. 131-51.

First is the exaggerated claim that all egalitarians, by definition, are either incipient liberals or full-fledged liberals who disregard the authority of the Bible.[21] This accusation distorts the discussion in such a counterproductive way that it ought to be discarded by people on both sides of the debate. To frame the debate that way is to divert people's attention from the real issues, scaring them (with the dreaded word *liberal*) rather than equipping them (with even-handed biblical arguments). Besides, it is only fair to give the benefit of the doubt to people who acknowledge the authority of Scripture—whether they consider the Bible to be inspired and/or infallible and/or inerrant. For without good faith, it's impossible to dialogue meaningfully.

In addition, I would say that affirming Christian women who themselves uphold the doctrine of inerrancy is hardly a "liberal" thing to do. By and large, liberals are not supportive of evangelicals, much less of staunchly conservative evangelicals who affirm the Chicago Statement on inerrancy. Besides that, established conservatives such as John Stott, Millard Erickson, Grant Osborne and Roger Nicole are not disestablished, much less made into liberals, by their advocacy for women in ministry leadership.

Thus it is flagrantly misrepresentative to say that those who see Deborah as a viable example of a God-ordained spiritual leader are denying the authority of Scripture. It's rhetorically irresponsible to lead people to believe that those who recognize Junia, Priscilla and Phoebe as leaders in the New Testament church thereby advance the cause of liberalism.

Granted, if someone blatantly says, "This passage is not part of the canon," then that person can fairly be critiqued for denying the legitimacy of a portion of God's Word. But when fellow evangelicals who, by confession, embrace the full canon as being divinely inspired by God are labeled as being "liberals," the very notion of biblical authority is thereby taken captive by those who would tacitly redefine it in terms of male authority. To put it more concisely, biblical authority and male authority are not synonymous.

Second, the main point that needs to be forwarded in order for the debate to be reframed is this: that both sides of the debate are revising church tradition. Complementarians and egalitarians alike are saying something fresh whenever we contend that men and women are equal and that neither is su-

---

[21]The critiques, of course, run both ways. A well-known evangelical feminist once told me face to face that "if a person is not a feminist, that person is not a Christian."

perior to the other. Any glance at the writings of church leaders from Tertullian to Ambrose to Augustine to Aquinas to Luther to Calvin to Jonathan Edwards to Charles Hodge will show that the concept of gender equality was neither self-evident to them nor made evident to them in their reading of the Scriptures. Yet today positive statements are put forth, even by the strictest of complementarians. Consider, for instance, the following excerpt from a recent publication by Wayne Grudem:

> Every time we talk to each other as men and women, we should remember that the person we are talking to is a creature of God who is *more like God than anything else in the universe*, and men and women share that status equally. Therefore we should treat men and women with equal dignity and we should think of men and women as having equal value. We are *both* in the image of God, and we have been so since the very first day that God created us. "In the image of God he created him; *male and female he created them*" (Gen 1:27). Nowhere does the Bible say that men are more in God's image than women.[22]

In a footnote, Grudem clarifies that Paul's statement in 1 Corinthians 11:7, "For a man ought not to cover his head, since he is the image . . . of God" should in no way be understood to mean that men are more like God than women are.

What I would like to highlight is perhaps an unnoticed fact: Grudem doesn't have to do much explaining to his readers. Complementarians, far from being vexed by the complexity of Paul's argument in 1 Corinthians 11:7, are generally underwhelmed by the contrasting biblical statements that while man *is* "the image of God," the book of Genesis says that male and female were created *in* "the image of God" (Gen 1:27). To twenty-first-century Western Christians, it's "obvious" that men and women are equally human and equally reflective of God's image.

Though complementarians do tend to challenge egalitarian claims, they do not tend to press their fellow complementarians to explain hard questions such as how it can be true that women equally reflect the image of God, when in fact God incarnate was male. Hebrews 1:3 says that the Son is "the exact representation" of God's nature. If the Son is the exact representation of God's nature, and the Son walked on earth as a male, does that mean that God—like Jesus—is male? Is God the Father male? (Many evangelicals mistakenly think

---

[22]Wayne Grudem, *Evangelical Feminism and Biblical Truth* (Portland, Ore.: Multnomah, 2004), p. 26.

he is.) Does that explain why Paul says that "man," not woman, "is" the image of God?

Again, my point is that Grudem doesn't grapple with these questions.[23] His followers do not ask him to give a biblical account of how it can be factually said that men and women are "equally in the image of God."[24] Grudem's readers don't urge him to explain why Augustine's view and Luther's view dramatically differ from his. Most evangelicals have no idea of what Christians have believed in the past. Thus it doesn't occur to us that Grudem's view of women's equality might stand out with respect to church history. Since Grudem is not a feminist, we mistakenly assume that Grudem's commentary mirrors church tradition, even though it does not.

Again to reiterate the point, I believe it's critical for biblically minded Christians to be made aware that the idea of men and women being equally valuable is a relatively novel idea. It's not new (in the sense that it is grounded in Scripture). It is new, however, in the sense of being recognized as a fundamental biblical principle. Because most Western Christians think it's "obvious" that men and women are equal, we don't question the scriptural basis of that belief. Nor do we appreciate the movement of God's Spirit that has guided the church to see an age-old scriptural truth.

In summary, what I'm saying is that it needs to be publicized, that is, effectively communicated across the evangelical spectrum, that while complementarians vie for one thing and egalitarians another, *both* sides are attempting to revise church tradition by honoring the biblical truth that men and women share equal dignity since both are created in the image of the God.

---

[23]Grudem does include a footnote that states that 1 Corinthians 11:7 does "not" mean that it's better to be a man than a woman. See Grudem, *EFBT*, p. 26. But Grudem provides no theological commentary, only a stark assertion with reference to the fact that Paul says men and women are interdependent. Sadly, Grudem does not explain how male and female interdependence *disproves* Leon Podles's claim that masculinity is better than femininity—since God, Podles believes, is male. Nor does Grudem explain what the apostle Paul means when he says that man "is" the image of God in contrast to Gen 1:26, which says that male and female were made "in" the image of God. I believe that Grudem could contribute greatly to the debate by correcting other complementarians such as Leon Podles, author of *The Church Impotent: The Feminization* (Dallas: Spence Publishing, 1999), a book endorsed by CBMW and CBMW writers such as Stuart W. Scott. It's critical for people to know that it's heretical to believe that God is literally male. I also believe that egalitarians can serve by critiquing and correcting their fellow egalitarians who declare that God is Mother. To hear a theological explanation of how we know that God is not male, and that God is not to be called "Mother," see my book, *Men & Women in the Church* (Downers Grove, Ill.: InterVarsity Press, 2003), pp. 113-22. See also Stuart W. Scott, "Profiling Christian Masculinity," *JBMW* 9, no. 2 (Fall 2004): 10-17.

[24]See Grudem, *EFBT*, p. 27.

3. DISTINGUISH BETWEEN DIVINE AND HUMAN CHOICES

The third step I propose in this four-part strategy, if I may put it metaphorically, is for evangelicals to draw a wide circle around ourselves and not draw lines between us. Just as we have learned to be unified as a movement comprised of people who hold differing viewpoints on baptism, speaking in tongues, predestination and freewill, high church, low church and so on, so we can do the same regarding women's place in ministry leadership. Again, I'm not suggesting that we discontinue the dialogue or cancel the ongoing debate. Rather, I'm proposing that we, as evangelicals, covenant to support one another, even as we continue to study the Scriptures and share our disagreements and insights.

But how can we manage to achieve such unity? Practically speaking, women must either be included or excluded from church leadership. The existing strife in local churches, therefore, cannot be easily resolved. For if women are included, then they are not excluded. If they're excluded, then they are not included. There is no in-between to be discovered, or so we say. There is no consensus to be found—at least so far.

Perhaps that is so in a comprehensive sense, and yet a critical mass of evangelicals may be able in good conscience to redefine the boundaries of the debate. What if, for instance, evangelicals were to unify around one verse and diversify on another? Realistically, we could formally do this because so many local churches are informally doing it already. Specifically, what I mean is this: we could commit to unify around Ephesians 4:11, "He [Christ] gave some as apostles, and some as prophets, and some as evangelists, and some as pastors and teachers" (NASB). Echoing Scripture, together we could confess that whoever among us has been given as a pastor or teacher—has already been "given" by Christ himself. Since Christ decides who will be given as pastors and teachers, it seems reasonable for us to concede that some of those he gave are men and some are women.

Informally many evangelical churches already are acknowledging that some women have been given as pastors and teachers.[25] It is relatively common for certain women to be invited to minister to mixed groups of men and women. Thus it doesn't seem a far stretch for us to acknowledge more openly and col-

---

[25]Even the most conservative among us agree that Christ has given some women as prophetesses (such as Deborah and Philip's daughter) and evangelists (such as the women who told Peter that Jesus has risen from the dead).

lectively that Ephesians 4:11 refers both to men and women.

Here it is important to recognize that the Bible does *not* say that Christ has given some to be elders. Unlike pastors and teachers, elders are not directly appointed by God; they are appointed by people.[26] In Titus 1:5, Paul instructed Titus to "appoint elders in every town." What if, then, we as evangelicals were to diversify on this verse? What if we were to narrow the debate to the question of whether or not there is biblical warrant for women to serve as elders in the church?

I believe far fewer churches would split if all of us would distinguish between the *divine* choice of Christ, the head of the church—to have given some men and some women as pastors and teachers for the purpose of equipping his body—and the *human* choice of Christians to select biblically qualified elders on the basis of their most honest exegesis.

4. WORK TOGETHER AS A TEAM

Fourth, I believe that God would rejoice if complementarians and egalitarians as well as those participants such as myself, who see themselves standing somewhere in between, would work in tandem together as a team. In theory we could plausibly do this because of our shared commitment to accept the whole canon as the infallible and inspired Word of God. In practice, however, it would require a willingness on everyone's part to subject our preferred theological conclusions to the most rigorous and responsible critiques. We would each have to face the anomalies in our given paradigms and vulnerably confront them in community. We would each have to commit to listen to each other's perspectives with unprecedented openness and empathy. Once we had, to each other's satisfaction, articulated *each other's* best understanding of the biblical texts, then we would at last be ready to put our minds together and jointly with much prayer offer a compendium of tempered writing from scholars who had applied the Golden Rule to our research.

Following this procedure, the whole church could talk more freely. Together we could marvel that while Jesus chose twelve men, not twelve women, as his apostles, he also chose a woman, not a man, to be the first evangelist to

---

[26]Granted, some see the biblical words "pastors" and "elders" as synonymous. But since the Greek words are different, e.g., Ephesians 4:11 says that he has given some as "pastors," *poimenas*, and Tit 1:5 says to "appoint elders," *presbyterous*, it's reasonable to distinguish the two in practical church life today.

proclaim the good news that he had risen. Likewise, without feeling threatened, we could say that God created Adam before he created Eve, and that Adam was not created to be Eve's helper. Moreover, we could admit, without being defensive, that Paul prohibited women in the church in first-century Ephesus from doing something akin to teaching doctrine and exercising authority over men, while yet affirming that Priscilla doctrinally corrected Apollos, even in the city of Ephesus. At the same time, we could also freely say that God himself chose Deborah to be Israel's religio-political leader for forty years (Judges 4–5).

Such a procedure, if steadily applied, would push us toward building a consensus. If we were honest, it would at least force us to admit that Paul's prohibition of women in Ephesus has not lost its relevance since all Scripture is profitable for Christians today (2 Tim 3:16-17). It would also require us logically to admit that it can't be correct to think that Adam's prior existence to Eve's necessarily conveys that it's wrong for "a woman" to teach "a man" since Priscilla taught Apollos the real truth.

The only way for us to hold truths such as these in tension, with the aim of attaining a viable consensus, is by strengthening the integrity of the church. Together we must renounce equivocation. Together we must insist on having our practice match our words. Together we must take responsibility for confessing and repenting from our sins. Every day it starts with me. Every day building that consensus starts with you. Here at this esteemed theological conference, it starts with us.

CONCLUSION

In summary, I believe that we, as conservative evangelicals, can transcend the gridlock of the current debate by acknowledging that our opinions are *opinions;* by taking pains to represent one another fairly; by listening not only to the words, but also to the spirit of what each other is trying to say; and by following through with some kind of plan that would set us up structurally for success. Again, in my assessment, the greatest need in the evangelical movement with regard to the issue of women's place in ministry is for all of us, as scholars and pastors and leaders, to relate to one another personally with Christ's love and more genuine respect. In this chapter, I have thus proposed a four-part strategy that might forward us closer to that end.

13

EGALITARIANS AND COMPLEMENTARIANS TOGETHER?

A Modest Proposal

Timothy George

WHY AM I WRITING THIS? PERHAPS YOU HAVE heard the story of the Texas rancher who threw a big party—everything's big in Texas—and filled his swimming pool with human-eating sharks as a form of entertainment for his guests. When they had all gathered, he announced that he would give to any guest who successfully swam the length of the pool the choice of either fifty million dollars or the deed to his whole ranch. Before he could finish speaking, he saw someone swimming furiously across the pool. When the disheveled swimmer arrived successfully on the other side, the rancher said: "I'm astounded; I didn't think anyone would try that, much less do it! But I am true to my word. Now tell me what you want: the fifty million dollars, or the deed to the ranch?" "What do you mean?" the swimmer exclaimed, "I want the guy who pushed me into the pool!"

While I shall not accuse anyone of pushing me into this pool, I confess that I am writing this somewhat reluctantly. I am not a card-carrying member of either party in what has been called an emerging civil war within evangelicalism. Further, I have no special expertise in this issue; I have read widely but not deeply in the enormous literature it has generated. Apart from a brief excursus, "Was Paul a Feminist?" in a commentary on Galatians I published some ten years ago, and a few paragraphs in an essay published even earlier than that, I have written nothing on this subject, whereas many of our colleagues have spent years, even decades, exploring this theme at various levels.[1]

I have no new interpretation of 1 Timothy 2 to offer. Nor do I have any new lexical or grammatical insights into the meaning of *kephalē* or *hypotassō*. If I bring anything at all to this theme, it is by way of a reflection on the conversation itself: on how it sounds to a participant-observer within the evangelical family, one who recognizes that something crucial is involved in this discussion but who also hopes for a way beyond the polarization it has produced. The question mark at the end of my title and the adjective "modest" in the subtitle are both to be given their full force. The mood of this essay is interrogative or at least subjunctive, certainly not indicative, much less imperative! What I have to say is perhaps more a sermon than a lecture, its tone more exhortative than analytical, its *modus loquendi* more pastoral and theological than exegetical or polemical.

With this in mind, I want to do four things. First, I need to declare, as one does when going through customs, what it is I am bringing with me into this new territory, my baggage, as we say. In other words, I need to say something about my own tradition and its location within the academic and ecclesiological space in which this conversation is taking place. Second, I want to say something about the wider context that frames the egalitarian-complementarian divide within the evangelical family. This is a vast topic, of course, and I shall touch only on a few selective items to emphasize more clearly the underlying unities between egalitarians and complementarians against extreme positions unacceptable to both sides. Third, borrowing some ideas from my friend Roger Nicole, I want to review a few principles that might possibly help us learn better how to be better theologians of controversy, how to do polemics without being so polemical. And, finally, drawing on some of my experience in the Evangelicals and Catholics Together project, I want to suggest some possible, tentative steps forward for what, conceivably, in God's providence, might be a new ECT—Egalitarians and Complementarians Together: Not forgetting the question mark.

Before we get started, just a brief word about labels. I am well aware that labels can be libels. *Communist, redneck, egghead, liberal, fundamentalist, Calvinist,*

---

[1]See Timothy George, *Galatians*, New American Commentary 30 (Nashville: Broadman & Holman, 1994), pp. 286-93; and "Conflict and Identity in the SBC: The Quest for a New Consensus," in *Beyond the Impasse? Scripture, Interpretation, and Theology in Baptist Life*, ed. Robinson B. James and David S. Dockery (Nashville: Broadman & Holman, 1992), pp. 195-214.

Arminian—all of these terms carry negative connotations and can become labels with which fellow Christians attack and reproach one another. "He's a Calvinist!" might mean that he is a mean-spirited, pigheaded, hard-nosed bully who never has any fun and doesn't want anybody else to. Conversely, "She's an Arminian!" might mean she is a weak-kneed, lily-livered, mushy-minded pushover who has no convictions and won't stand up for what is right. The gender debate is filled with its own libelous labels. When you look at the literature over the last three decades, it is clear that there has been a significant shift in the preferred terms of self-designation. "Christian feminists" have become biblical egalitarians, though the former term is still used by some. Likewise, patriachialists, hierarchialists and traditionalists have become complementarians. There is a sense, of course, in which all complementarians are also egalitarians for, as far as I know, no one in the current debate denies that men and women are equally created in the image of God and share an equal access to salvation in Christ. Likewise, there is a sense in which all egalitarians are also complementarians for they seek a form of gender reconciliation that implies distinction as well as similarities between men and women, a position aptly summarized in the subtitle of a recent book: *Discovering Biblical Equality: Complementarity Without Hierarchy.* In other words, we have become all things to all people so that we might confuse everybody! It is well beyond my ken to sort all of this out. It is my general rule of thumb to refer to anyone by whatever nomenclature or designation they usually employ to refer to themselves. This is a matter of courtesy, not ideology, and I mean nothing more or less by it in this essay.

THE BAGGAGE I BRING

If anything I have said thus far should lead anyone to think that I approach this issue from a neutral epistemological platform with no *Vorverständnis* or precommitment, let me say at once that I belong to a congregation affiliated with the Southern Baptist Convention which in the year 2000 revised our denomination-wide confession of faith to include a new article declaring that while both men and women are gifted for service in the life of the church, the office of senior pastor should be reserved for men. (Nothing is said about ordination in this document.) This new addition to the Baptist Faith and Message, as we call our confession of faith, has had the effect of aligning the Southern Baptist Convention, the largest Protestant denomination in North America, with a complementarian view of women in ministry. The acceptance of this view has since become the norm for missionary appointment, faculty selection at our six Southern Baptist seminaries and employment within any of our denominational agencies. Baptists, however, are fiercely congregationalist in our church polity and this denomination-wide decision has no official bearing on local church decision-making. In theory, any Baptist congregation is free to call and ordain any person to any office of ministry regardless of gender, age, educational background or other criteria. In reality, however, this recent—and novel—denominational ruling at the SBC level has had little practical effect on local congregational practice. In effect, it merely confirmed and codified what was the already-existing practice of a vast majority of SBC churches anyway. In Alabama, where I live, there are more than 4,000 local Baptist churches affiliated with the Southern Baptist Convention, several African American Baptist denominations, as well as a number of Independent Baptist churches. To my knowledge, only two of these more than 4,000 Baptist congregations have women who currently serve as pastors. Although Alabama may be considered a very conservative state, this pattern would not vary significantly in other parts of the country among churches affiliated with these denominations, including so-called moderate Baptist churches. The congregation to which I belong has never elected, nor even considered, a female candidate for pastor or deacon, the two Scriptural offices we recognize in the congregation. At the same time, many women are deeply involved in the life of our church; at present, six very competent, compassionate and well-qualified women serve on our full-time professional ministry staff in various leadership roles.

Part of the ambiguity I feel about this issue, however, stems from the fact that I work at a theological school. Samford University's Beeson Divinity School is an evangelical, interdenominational theological school that has female faculty members and welcomes female students in all degree programs. Soon after Beeson was founded in 1988, I received a call from a somewhat suspicious pastor who said, "I understand you have women students over at Beeson." "Yes," I said, "we do." "Well, you don't let them take preaching, do you?" I thought for a moment, and then said, "No, we don't. We *make* them take preaching." It is not an option in our master of divinity track. Preaching, like the study of Hebrew and Greek, is a discipline we think all students need to study regardless of the ministry trajectory they may eventually pursue.

At the same time, Beeson does not serve as an advocacy base for either a restrictive or open view on women in ministry. Evangelical theological schools tend to fall into one of three camps on this issue. Some are unequivocally egalitarian and would not likely hire a faculty member who did not share this commitment. Fuller, North Park, Ashland, Palmer Theological Seminary (formerly Eastern) and Church of God School of Theology are among the seminaries who hold this view. On the other hand, other theological institutions, either by confession or theological conviction, have a more restrictive understanding. Westminster, Dallas, Covenant and, more recently, the six SBC seminaries fall into this group. My school, Beeson, belongs to another group of theological schools who do not make this matter a test of fellowship, but as we serve constituencies with differing polities and differing views of the role of women in ministry, we welcome both faculty and students who hold different convictions on this matter. Some of our peer institutions in this regard would be Trinity, Gordon-Conwell, Denver, Regent College, Vancouver and, although it is not a seminary, Wheaton College as well.

CONTEXT

I want to turn now to a brief consideration of the wider context against which the complementarian-egalitarian debate has been framed within the evangelical church. In reading through much of the literature on this subject, it is easy to get lost in the maze of exegetical minutia, the thrust and counterthrust of theological arguments, and to suppose that this debate among evangelicals had developed in a vacuum unaffected by the wider social, political and ideological forces in the environing culture. But this would be a serious mistake. To show the fallacy of this ahistorical approach, I want to look in very generalized terms at two polar extremes that complementarians and egalitarians find objectionable today, almost without exception. The first of these polar views I am going to call "the ugly face of androcentric sexism." I say "androcentic" because sexism, like racism, is not uni-directional despite the claims of liberationist ideologues to the contrary. At the same time, it is important to realize, as one complementarian leader has written recently, "For more cultures through most of history the most serious deviation from biblical standards regarding men and women has not been feminism, but harsh and oppressive male chauvinism. It still exists today, not only in some families in the United States, but also in a number of cultures throughout the world."[2]

---

[2]*EFBT,* p. 524.

Church history, of course, is virtually littered with evidence to support this statement whether we think of Tertullian's notorious statement that every woman was an Eve, the devil's gateway, the unsealer of the forbidden tree, whose sin destroyed God's image, man, and because of whom even the Son of God had to die; or Thomas Aquinas's definition of woman as a "misshapen man," following Aristotle; or the grim picture of women presented in the late medieval *Malleus Maleficarum* ("The Hammer of Witches") as carnally insatiable creatures who formed pacts with the devil in hopes of sexual gratification. One of the most embarrassing examples of such misogyny in the era of the Reformation came from the pen of that irascible Protestant John Knox. From the safety of Calvin's Geneva, the most perfect school of Christ on earth since the apostles, he called it, he wrote his "First Blast of the Trumpet Against the Monstrous Regiment of Women" declaring that women by nature are "weak, frail, impatient, feeble and foolish; and experience hath declared them to be unconstant, variable, cruel and lacking the spirit of counsel and regiment"—appealing to Genesis 3:16, 1 Timothy 2 and 1 Corinthians 14. Knox's comments were directed against Mary Tudor, "the Jezebel of England," "Bloody Mary," whose reversion to Catholicism had seemed to put the English Reformation into reverse. However, by the time Knox's "First Blast" had made it through the press, Mary was dead and her half-sister, Elizabeth, not the Jezebel but the Deborah of the Reformation, had ascended to the throne. She took great umbrage at Knox's generic denunciation of female governance. When Knox tried to return to England from the Continent, Elizabeth refused him entry into the country, whereupon he took his hot gospel north of the border and began the agitation which led to the Scottish Reformation.

Such views, invariably supported by an appeal to Scripture, led to a pattern of male dominance that accrued to the detriment of women in the new American Republic. Even the enlightened Thomas Jefferson held that girls were unfit in brains and character for serious study and forbade them entrance to his University of Virginia.[3] In 1848, at the famous Women's Rights Convention held in Seneca Falls, New York, agitation was undertaken to secure for women in this country the right to own property, to retain their own earnings, to share legal custody of their children, to pursue higher education and to vote in na-

---

[3]Robert L. Saucy and Judith TenElshof, eds., *Women and Men in Ministry: A Complementary Perspective* (Chicago: Moody Press, 2001), p. 37.

tional elections. Suffrage in the United States, of course, only came with the passage of the Nineteenth Amendment, allowing women to vote for the first time in 1920, a right denied to women in France until 1944, and in Switzerland until the 1960s.

Four years after the Seneca Falls meeting, Frances Dana Gage, a reformist dynamo from Ohio, peered into the future in her poem entitled "One Hundred Years Hence."

> One hundred year hence, what a change will be made,
> In politics, morals, religion, trade,
> In statesmen who wrangle or ride on the fence,
> These things will be altered a hundred years hence.
>
> All cheating and fraud will be laid on the shelf,
> Men will not get drunk, nor be bound up in self,
> But all live together, good neighbors and friends,
> As Christian folks ought to, a hundred years hence.
>
> Then woman, man's partner, man's equal shall stand,
> While beauty and harmony govern the land,
> To think for oneself will be no offense,
> The world will be thinking, a hundred years hence.
>
> Oppression and war will be heard of no more,
> Nor blood of a slave leave his print on our shore,
> Conventions will then be a useless expense,
> For we'll go free suffrage a hundred years hence.
>
> Instead of speechmaking to satisfy wrong,
> We'll all join the chorus to sing Freedom's song,
> And if the Millennium is not a pretense,
> We'll all be good brothers/neighbors a hundred years hence.[4]

Well, Emily Dickinson she is not. But it is interesting to note, more than one hundred fifty years later, how her concerns for not only the social role of women, but also racism, militarism and penal reform have remained live issues in our society, however fatuous her postmillennial utopianism has turned out to be.

---

[4]Frances Dana Gage, "One Hundred Years Hence" [1852], in Linda A. Moody, *Women Encounter God* (New York: Orbis, 1974), pp. 140-41.

As Timothy Smith and many other scholars have pointed out, evangelicals, both men and women, often motivated through spiritual awakenings and revival movements, led the way to bring about moral reform of society through abolition, temperance, suffrage and the like. Within the evangelical church however, despite and alongside of the history of evangelical women in ministry, chauvinistic and traditionalist views of women continued to prevail, sometimes in muted tones, sometimes in more virulent fashion.

An example of the latter is a book published in the city of Wheaton in 1941 by a Baptist evangelist from the South, John R. Rice. Rice had just moved to Wheaton with his wife and six daughters, who were ages four to nineteen in 1941. Rice was not a stranger to the North, having been a graduate student at the University of Chicago when he responded to the call to be an evangelist after leading a man to Christ at the Pacific Garden Mission in 1921. His famous book, *Bobbed Hair, Bossy Wives, and Women Preachers,* grew out of Sunday afternoon seminars he put on in Chicago area churches following his evangelistic meetings. Basing his teaching on Paul's advice about head coverings for women (1 Cor 11:2-16), Rice claimed that his sermons had had a visible effect on female coiffure in the area. He could point to literally hundreds of women who "now have long hair as a result of hearing me teach and preach what God's Word says on that subject." Bobbed hair invariably led to bobbed character in women, Rice said. Wives, he argued, should strictly obey their husbands "in everything," as the Bible literally says. Women are not so much created in the image of God, Rice declared, but rather in the image of their husbands. Women should not even go to church if forbidden to do so by their husband. "But what if my husband instructs me to do something sinful like visiting the tavern, going to the picture show or even having my hair bobbed?" Don't be concerned with such "imaginary cases," Rice advised. If you demonstrate a meek, submissive spirit your husband will not think of making such outrageous demands, but as 1 Peter says, will be won by example of your witness. (Rice's theology could have been greatly helped at this point by a good dose of the Calvinist doctrine of total depravity!)

Rice told of one woman in Oklahoma who had sent him a gift of six dollars for his radio ministry asking him to say nothing about it over the air as she had done this without her husband's knowledge. Rice sent the money back saying he could not accept such gifts for to do so would make him a party to her disobedience to her husband in this matter. "God is not pleased with rebellion, even though it be, ostensibly, because of love for him. God wanted a meek and quiet spirit in the heart of that Christian woman, wanted her to be subject to her husband, more than he wanted six dollars for a Gospel radio program."[5]

Rice based his views on 1 Corinthians 11, 1 Corinthians 14 and Ephesians 5, texts that still undergird complementarian views of male headship today, but I know of no complementarians in the current discussion who would draw the same conclusions from these passages as Rice did. Although complementarian arguments today are usually directed against egalitarian readings of these biblical texts, I suspect that most complementarians would find Rice's reasoning and application as morally repulsive as would their interlocutors on the other side of the debate.

But this issue is framed not only by misogynist examples from the past, the ugly face of androcentric sexism, but also by its polar opposite, the ugly face of radical feminism. I am aware that feminism covers a wide variety of viewpoints and nuanced positions including liberation theologians, mystics, eco-feminists, goddess feminists, women-identified feminists, post-Christian feminists, as well as diverse ethnic feminists who virulently criticize other feminists as white, middle-class American or Western co-conspirators in the oppression of their sisters. What all of these views share in common, however, in addition to a severe critique of male domination, is the rejection of the authority and truthfulness of Holy Scripture.

The rise of contemporary feminist hermeneutics can be traced back to *The Woman's Bible,* a revisionist rendering of the Scriptures edited by Elizabeth Cady Staton and published in the 1890s. The purpose of this project was to present the Bible as a weapon in the struggle for women's liberation. In order to accomplish this goal it was necessary to "deconstruct" the text of Scripture, which was seen as a product of an ancient patriarchal culture and androcentric religion inimical to the higher aspirations of women. Thus, Elizabeth Staton boasted, *The Woman's Bible* would reveal to the modern woman that "the good Lord did not write the book; that the garden scene is a fable; that she is in no way responsible for the laws of the universe. . . . Take the snake, the fruit tree and the woman from the tableau, and we have no fall, no frowning Judge, no inferno, no everlasting punishment—hence no need of a Savior. Thus the bot-

---

[5]John R. Rice, *Bobbed Hair, Bossy Wives and Women Preachers: Significant Questions for Honest Christian Women Settled by the Word of God* (Murfreesboro, Tenn.: Sword of the Lord Publishers, 1941).

tom falls out of the whole Christian theology."[6]

Feminist hermeneutics has come a long way since Staton, and Carolyn Osiek has offered the following classification of hermeneutical alternatives employed by feminist theologians: (1) *rejectionists* (rejecting the Bible as authoritative or useful while retaining aspects of the religious tradition it represents), (2) *loyalists* (accepting, but not uncritically, the biblical traditions as the Word of God), (3) *revisionists* (attempting to separate the content from the patriarchal mold of Scripture—a new version of the old husk and kernel paradigm), (4) *sublimationists* (searching for the eternal feminine in biblical and extra biblical symbolism and imagery) and (5) *liberationists* (using a revised understanding of biblical eschatology as the interpretive principle with which to judge the revelatory character of biblical texts).[7]

The second of these alternatives, the loyalist perspective, might conceivably with some qualifications embrace the biblical egalitarian viewpoint. The other positions, however, move beyond what anyone in the current discussion would regard as an evangelical view of Scripture. In its most basic concerns, radical feminism moves beyond the pale of anything recognizably Christian, as its clearest, most consistent theologians such as Mary Dally and Daphne Hampson have long since realized. In 1971 Mary Dally delivered her famous Exodus Sermon at Harvard's Memorial Church declaring her intention and setting forth her rationale for leaving the Christian faith.

> We cannot really belong to institutional religion as it exists. It isn't good enough to be token preachers. It isn't good enough to have our energies drained and co-opted. Singing sexist hymns, praying to a male God breaks our spirit, makes us less than human. The crushing weight of this tradition, of this power structure tells us that *we do not even exist.*[8]

The fundamental question for radical feminists is not whether God should be called Father, but whether women can be redeemed by a male savior. Thus the move from Christ to Christa and the oft-quoted statement by Delores Williams, "We don't need folks hanging on crosses and blood dripping and all that weird stuff."

Rusty Reno has written an important essay in which he describes the

---

[6]A. S. Kraditor, ed., *Up from the Pedestal: Landmark Writings in the American Women's Struggle for Equality* (Chicago: Quadrangle, 1968), p. 119.

[7]See Francis Martin, *The Feminist Question* (Grand Rapids: Eerdmans, 1994), p. 162.

[8]Quoted, Elaine Storkey, *Origins of Difference* (Grand Rapids: Baker Academic, 2001), p. 118.

project of feminist theology as an essentially modern, post-Kantian undertaking, despite postmodernist and ultramodernist gyrations here and there. It was Kant, after all, who observed that in order to interpret the Bible according to the inner essence of religion, one may do with the text what one likes. Such disdain for the concrete integrity of what one encounters in the Bible, and the Christian tradition that lies behind it, supports the iconoclasm of radical feminism, that is to say, its violence against the trinitarian and christological particularity of orthodox, biblical faith.[9]

If Kant is the true father of feminism, despite his own patriarchialist views, then its godfather is Ludwig Feuerbach. It was Feuerbach, anticipating Freud, who extended Kant's constructivist depiction of theology to define religion itself as a projection of human consciousness. We construct an idealized version of our own longings, aspirations and desires (including our own unconscious desires according to Freud) and project these outward onto an imagined deity whom we might call Father, or Mother, or the Force, or Sophia, or any number of other possibilities for the name of such a deity as protean as its reality, grounded in nothing deeper, for there is nothing deeper, than the abyss of human imagining. What this produces, to quote the title of a book published by feminist scholar Patricia Lynn Reilly, is *A God Who Looks Like Me*.[10] Elaine Storkey, an evangelical who fully appreciates the profound and valid critique feminism has brought to our culture, identifies precisely the basic problem with this approach:

> Radical feminism wants the fruit of love, but denies the Source. For in the end the stance of independence is independence from God also and an assertion of human (feminine) autonomy. Many of their diagnoses are correct. Much of what they have to say about patriarchy needs to be listened to. But at the deepest level is this problem. Their stance is a fundamentally religious one, and their faith is in themselves.[11]

I have talked about radical feminism and androcentric sexism not in order to construct a straw woman and a straw man just to knock them down, but because the contemporary evangelical debate between egalitarians and complementarians is carried on against the backdrop of these stereotypical ex-

---

[9]Alvin F. Kimel Jr., ed., *This Is My Name Forever* (Downers Grove, Ill.: InterVarsity Press, 2001), p. 188.
[10]Patricia Lynn Reilly, *A God Who Looks Like Me: Discovering a Woman-Affirming Spirituality* (New York: Ballantine, 1995).
[11]Elaine Storkey, *What's Right with Feminism* (Grand Rapids: Eerdmans, 1985), p. 109.

tremes. Many complementarians believe that the inevitable logic of the egalitarian view leads directly to radical feminism, and they oppose it, not only because of what it teaches about the role of women in the home and in the church, but also because of what they fear its ultimate trajectory might be. Likewise, many egalitarians see the complementarian position as merely a slightly updated version of the old chauvinism, an effort to suppress the full exercise of women's God-given gifts based not really on biblical truths but on a cultural captivity that borders on, if it does not finally end up in, idolatry. Both fears are motivated by legitimate concerns, and we will not move forward until such concerns on both sides are fully heard, appreciated and made a part of our dialogue with one another.

CAN WE TALK?

Many people are surprised to learn that my good friend Roger Nicole is a biblical egalitarian. He is perhaps better known for other commitments—as an unreconstructed Calvinist who has defended the Westminster standards and the Canons of Dort against Arminian detractors of all sorts; as an unflinching inerrantist who helped to found the Evangelical Theological Society in 1949; and, more recently, as one who has sounded the alarm bell against that form of semi-process theism commonly known as openness of God theology. Those who know Roger well will know that he is a person possessed of a great good humor and a very irenic spirit despite the fact that he has become entangled in numerous theological fights throughout his long and distinguished career. This has led him to reflect, perhaps more than most other theologians, on how to deal with those who differ from us. Karl Barth once said that there can be no dogmatics without polemics, and I think he is right, for Christianity makes certain claims about not only "what is true for me," but also about how things really are. Its God-talk is not only the personal love language of a private prayer group or spiritual club, it is also directed outward to the public square, the marketplace of ideas, to the human community at large, the world for which Christ died. Roger has studied the modalities of polemical theology and he poses three questions for those engaged in the kind of discussion we are considering here.[12]

---

[12]The following section is based on Roger Nicole's essay, "Polemic Theology: How to Deal with Those Who Differ From Us," in *Standing Forth: Collected Writings of Roger Nicole* (Ross-shire, U.K.: Christian Focus Publishers, Mentor, 2002), p. 10.

1. What do I owe to the person who differs from me? The point is this: we have obligations to people who differ from us. We are obliged to deal with them as we ourselves would like to be dealt with or treated, Roger says. We owe them *love*. We do not owe them agreement, but we should make every effort to understand what our interlocutor means by what he or she says, and this requires us to be good listeners as well as good talkers. We also need to understand the aims of those with whom we differ. What are they seeking to accomplish in this dispute? What are they responding to or reacting against? In almost any theological position we encounter, even in those that have been deemed manifestly heretical by the wisdom of the church, we should always ask, Is there any validity in the position of my opponent? In the second century, for example, Marcion had a legitimate concern: he wanted to uphold the radical newness of the message of Jesus against certain theologies of continuity that obscured this gospel insight. That was a legitimate concern over against the Ebionites and others. However, Marcion pursued this concern to a complete rejection of the entire Old Testament, and much of the New, which resulted in a horrible heresy the effects of which are with us still. All the same, we owe those who differ from us, including radical feminists and unreconstructed traditionalists, an effort to listen to and understand their deepest concerns.

2. What can I learn from those who differ from me? Here is what Roger says:

> The first thing that I should be prepared to learn is that I may be wrong and that the other person may be right. Obviously, this is not applied to certain basic truths of the faith like the deity of Christ for salvation by grace. The whole structure of the Christian faith is at stake here, and it would be instability rather than broad-mindedness to allow these to be eroded by doubts. Yet, apart from issues where God himself has spoken so that doubt and hesitancy are really not permissible, there are numerous areas where we are temperamentally inclined to be very assertive and in which we can quite possibly be in error. When we are unwilling to acknowledge our fallibility, we reveal that we are more interested in winning a discussion and safeguarding our reputation than in the discovery and triumph of truth.[13]

William Webb's book, *Slaves, Women & Homosexuals* contains a chapter

---

[13]Ibid., p. 15.

titled "What If I Am Wrong?"[14] However one evaluates Webb's "redemptive movement hermeneutic" set forth in this volume, his heuristic strategy is on target. To ask this kind of question is not to relapse into a kind of wishy-washy relativism or loss of conviction. It is simply to proceed in a spirit of humility believing, as Pastor John Robinson said to the departing Pilgrims, "The Lord hath yet more truth and light to break forth out of his Holy Word."[15]

3. How can I cope with those who differ from me? At this point in his essay, Roger deals with various strategic arguments from Scripture, reason, history and tradition. He presents good advice on how to construct a theological argument, but he also notes that the word *cope* carries an interpersonal connotation. If we are believers in Christ, not to say evangelicals, we will recognize that our theological opponent—our "enemy" if you will—is also our brother and sister in the Lord. Just as in evangelism, where we can win an argument and lose a soul, so also in church polemics; we can squash an adversary and damage the cause for which we are striving. Our goal is not to pommel our interlocutor into the ground, like a boxer demolishing his opponent in the ring, but rather to win him or her over to a new and, we trust, better understanding. So, as Paul says, "the Lord's servant must not quarrel but must be kind to everyone, able to teach, not resentful. Opponents must be gently instructed, in the hope that God will grant them repentance leading them to a knowledge of the truth" (2 Tim 2:24-26 TNIV).

In surveying the recent literature on both sides of this issue, I have found in both camps two motifs held together in uneasy equipoise. On the one hand, there is a tendency to be tenacious, unyielding and unrelenting in the critique of the other side. In a recent anthology of egalitarian essays, the editors state this clearly: "Though we speak strongly in favor of unity, points of agreement and dialogue, it must be noted that we see no middle ground on this question."[16] In an earlier essay from the same perspective, another writer, an outstanding New Testament scholar, urges that the teaching of a genuine mutuality and equality in Christ should be pursued actively, even aggressively, to the point of declaring that this commitment is constitutive of the gospel. Just as

---

[14]William J. Webb, *Slaves, Women & Homosexuals* (Downers Grove, Ill.: InterVarsity Press, 2001).

[15]Robinson's famous "Farewell Address" was quoted by Edward Winslow in *Hypocrisie Unmasked* (London, 1646), pp. 97-98. See the discussion in Timothy George, *John Robinson and the English Separatist Tradition* (Macon, Ga.: Mercer University Press, 1982), pp. 91-92.

[16]*DBE*, p. 17.

some Christians saw the former system of apartheid in South Africa as not only a moral failure but also a theological heresy, a perversion of the gospel, should not those who deny that all avenues of ministry and leadership are open to women as well as men be placed in the same category? This scholar comes right up to the edge of anathematizing his complementarian colleagues, but then (wisely, I think) backs away from such a pronouncement:

> I am fearful of placing myself in the position of judging others without humility or sensitivity; that I do not want to do. In other words, I will call no one a heretic, but I would call an expression of the Gospel that excludes women in any way or sense from equality with men in Christ in status, response, action and ministry a misguided form of the Gospel as presented in the New Testament.[17]

Statements like this indicate that a great deal is at stake for those deeply committed to the egalitarian view.

But these statements can be matched, with equal if not greater severity, by those on the other side. For some complementarians, what is at stake is nothing less than the authority of the Bible itself. If I'm not mistaken, and I may well be, this position represents a hardening of the earlier complementarian recognition of egalitarians as sharing with them a common commitment to the inspiration and authority of Holy Scripture while differing exegetically and hermeneutically on key biblical texts. This has prompted one egalitarian scholar to protest: "I hope those who disagree will challenge my interpretation, not my commitment to the authority of Scripture."[18] Complementarians also fear that if the egalitarian position prevails, its principles will be broadened to other areas of concern, such as homosexuality, so that eventually "no moral command of Scripture will be safe from its destructive procedures."[19] For those who share this analysis, this is no tempest in a teacup but a struggle for the very soul and life of the church.

So perhaps a new ECT is doomed from the outset, and I have set out on a fool's errand. Perhaps. But there is another note in both literatures that is sounded with what I take to be true conviction and integrity, and this gives me some basis to think—and hope—that we are not quite yet at a total impasse. For both sides speak clearly of shared values, mutual recognition and

---

[17]Catherine Clark Kroeger and James R. Beck, eds., *Woman, Abuse and the Bible* (Grand Rapids: Baker, 1996), p. 51.
[18]*DBE*, p. 158.
[19]*EFBT*, p. 377.

patterns of cooperation. Here, for example, is such a statement from the egalitarian side:

> Evangelicals who promote biblical equality can affirm the core values of fellow Christians who disagree with us on gender equality. What we have in common as Christians far outweighs our disagreements. We must, therefore, rehearse our shared values frequently and clearly. We must regularly reiterate our support of family values and the responsibility of parents for their children. . . . by pointing to our commitment to the authority of Scripture, the sacredness of the family and the centrality of evangelism and missions, we connect to the core values of those who are otherwise apprehensive of biblical equality. By carefully establishing the enormous ground we have in common, we build sturdy bridges to those who are unsure of our message.[20]

Perhaps the clearest expression of a similar openness from a complementarian side is in the essay "Charity, Clarity, and Hope: The Controversy and the Cause of Christ," first published in *Recovering Biblical Manhood and Womanhood* in 1991. "We are sure," say the authors,

> that neither the Council on Biblical Manhood and Womanhood nor the Council for Biblical Equality flatters itself by thinking that it speaks for evangelicalism, let alone for the church as a whole. We do not know whether history will attach any significance to our statements. . . . This issue has important implications for marriage, singleness, and ministry, and thus for all of life and mission. Yet we sense a kinship far closer with the founders of CBE than with those who seem to put their feminist commitments above Scripture. . . .
>
> In profound ways we share a common passion with egalitarians: a passion to be obedient to biblical truth about manhood and womanhood; a passion to see men and women affirm the awesome reality of equal personhood in the image of God; a passion to see marriages whole and lasting and freeing and happy for both husband and wife; the passion to resist the moral collapse of our culture in all manner of tolerated abuses and addictions and perversions; a passion to be a winsome, countercultural, outcropping of Kingdom beauty and truth; a passion to equip all men and women for ministry according to their gifts with none throwing life away in trivial pursuits; a passion to magnify Christ—crucified, risen, and reigning—to a perishing society; and a passion to mobilize the whole church—men and women—to complete the Great Commission, penetrate all the unreached peoples of the world, and hasten the day of God. . . . We long for

---

[20]*DBE*, pp. 487-88.

a common mind for the cause of Christ. . . . our aim is to carry on the debate
with clarity and charity.[21]

As this document has been reprinted without change several times, I assume
that its authors still accept and are committed to what they wrote nearly one
and a half decades ago.

A NEW ECT?

Now comes the modest proposal I promised in the subtitle. Perhaps the time
is right for egalitarians and complementarians to come together, to work together, to stand together precisely for the reasons stated clearly by both groups
in their advocacy literatures—to further the cause of Christ and to advance the
gospel of life in a culture increasingly marked by violence, decay and death.
Shortly after the release of the first Evangelicals and Catholics Together (ECT)
statement in 1994, I wrote an editorial in *Christianity Today* in which I described this new initiative as "an ecumenism of the trenches."[22] It was clear
that Catholics and evangelicals had come together not as proponents of a kind
of armchair ecumenism seeking to rehearse and unravel the deep divides of
the Reformation, but rather as cobelligerents in a shared struggle against a
common enemy. Catholics and evangelicals found one another as allies working together on behalf of the sanctity of human life, the sacredness of marriage
and family life, as advocates for justice and peace in a conflicted world that
desperately needs to hear a word of reconciliation, a word that sounds far
more credible when spoken by Catholics and evangelicals together rather than
in isolation from one another.

I am not here to defend the ECT project, and I am well aware that not all
evangelicals think that what we have attempted to do is such a great thing. But
perhaps there are some strategic lessons gleaned from that experience that can
inform the issue before us. Both the Catholic and evangelical participants in
ECT have been determined to pursue an ecumenism of conviction, not of accommodation. We do not seek a placid *via media*, nor a sweeping under the
rug of trenchant, clear-cut differences. Both sides in our dialogue are passion-
ately committed to an unfettered search for truth, and this strategy requires the

---

[21]*RBMW,* pp. 404, 406.
[22]Timothy George, "Catholics and Evangelicals in the Trenches," *Christianity Today,* May 16, 1994,
   p. 16.

honest confrontation of ideas and truth claims as well as a conciliatory spirit that is open to convergence and reconciliation. This same kind of commitment, I believe, must mark any genuine progress in the quest for mutual understanding by egalitarians and complementarians. These words by Simone Weil could well serve as a guidepost on this journey: "Christ likes us to prefer truth to him because, before being Christ, he is Truth. If one turns aside from him to go toward the truth, one will not go far before falling into his arms."[23]

With that in mind, I want to suggest a tentative agenda—nine general themes or areas of concern—that I believe could be helpfully pursued by persons of goodwill and high moral imagination from both the complementarian and egalitarian communities. I have given no thought to the practicalities of such a process—the Evangelical Theological Society which welcomes both egalitarians and complementarians in its membership could play a role, as could Christian colleges and seminaries, local congregations and denominations, and parachurch ministries of various kinds. Some of these suggestions have already been acted upon and are underway in various places, and where that is the case I encourage an intensification of such efforts.

1. Let's study the Bible together. This has been our primary strategy in Evangelicals and Catholics Together. We have come together with open Bibles and open hearts and have learned a great deal from such personal explorations of the Word of God. Evangelicals and complementarians have, of course, been studying the Bible on this issue overtime—no doubt there are many empty forests as a result of their published labors on this subject! But apart from the several multiple-views books on this theme, much of this work stands as discrete silos of scholarship that lack the dynamism and cross-fertilization of a live interactive approach.

Perhaps a good text with which to begin such a study would be 1 Corinthians 7:29-31, Paul's comment about the time *(kairos)* being shortened, so that "those who have wives should live as if they had none; those who mourn, as if they did not; those who are happy, as if they were not; those who buy something, as if it were not theirs to keep; those who use the things of the world, as if not engrossed in them. For this world in its present form is passing away" (NIV). Admittedly, this is not one of the famous purple passages about women in ministry, but it is nonetheless one of the most pertinent pericopes

---

[23]Simone Weil, *Waiting for God* (San Francisco: Harper & Row, 1973), p. 69.

in the New Testament for getting our priorities in order. It challenges us to a life of costly obedience as those "on whom the fulfillment of the ages has come" as Paul refers to this present dispensation (1 Cor 10:11). These verses are embedded in a passage dealing with the messy matters of sexuality, celibacy, divorce, marriage and sexual purity. It would be interesting to see what a committed cadre of competent complementarian and egalitarian biblical scholars would say *together* about a passage like this. Perhaps it could even shed some new light on 1 Corinthians 11 and 14, not to say Ephesians 5 and 1 Timothy 2.

In any event, if we're evangelicals, there is no way around the exegetical task. Roman Catholics and Eastern Orthodox Christians—from whom we have much to learn in this matter, I believe—have a very different rationale for their insistence that only males can be admitted to the priesthood. It is a rationale based on a decidedly sacramental understanding of ministerial orders in which the priest, especially at the Eucharistic offering, is required to be not only a representative, but also a representation, literally a re-presentation of Christ: *sacedos est alter Christus.* This concept corresponds to an ecclesiology that sees the church itself as the extension of the incarnation. This rationale does not work for evangelicals for whom apostolic continuity is not represented in an unbroken succession of duly ordained priests and Roman Catholics in fellowship with a bishop who is in fellowship with a bishop of Rome. For evangelicals, that church is apostolic which honors the succession of apostolic proclamation in the inscripturated witness of the Bible. This, I take it, is common ground for egalitarians and complementarians, and indeed for all good Protestants, and so we have to wrestle with what in the world Paul means by the *hapax legomenon* in 1 Timothy 2:12, *authenteō,* and how this relates to the overarching storyline of biblical revelation.

2. Celebrate together the consensus of the Great Tradition. Evangelicalism at its heart is a renewal movement within historic Christian orthodoxy. This is a commitment we share with many other Christians, to be sure, but it is also at the heart of our own appropriation of the Reformation legacy and the Spirit-inspired movements of the Awakening. Egalitarians and complementarians stand together on one solid foundation, the only foundation that can be laid, Paul says: Jesus Christ (1 Cor 3:11). Let me quote again from the complementarian document I cited earlier:

The things that unite egalitarians and complementarians are inexpressibly magnificent and infinitely valuable. We serve the same omnipotent God, and there is none like him. Do we not share the faith that the earth is the Lord's and everything in it—that he made everything and everyone? Do we not share the faith that in these last days God has spoken to us by a Son, Jesus Christ, whom he appointed the heir of all things and through whom he made the world? Do we not believe that this great and glorious Son of God became flesh and dwelt among us, that he gave his life a ransom for many, that he rose from the dead never to die again? Do we not share the faith that anyone and everyone who turns from sin and calls upon the name of the Lord will be saved? Do we not believe that Christ is coming again to establish his Kingdom of righteousness and peace?[24]

Yes, yes, yes, yes, yes, yes, yes! These are not trivial theological ideas, but the very heart of the gospel message itself, that which Paul declared in 1 Corinthians 15:3 to be "of first importance," indeed, the message by which we are saved, if we hold fast to these things. This is not to say that the differences between egalitarians and complementarians are trivial or unimportant—far from it—but it is to plead that such differences be placed in the context of the underlying unities which form the basis of a common witness of love and service to the world.

3. Testimonies of mutual conversion. It is a fact of life that people change their mind from time to time. It would be interesting to take a poll of evangelical leaders and ask how many had changed their mind about the role of women in ministry. I would like to hear more testimonies of those who have undergone such a change of mind and heart on this issue. Such testimonies, of course, cannot settle the issue for us exegetically or theologically, but they can help us to understand why certain things are persuasive to us at different moments in our lives. They can prompt us to ask where we sense the Holy Spirit may be leading us at any given moment. I would like to hear a discussion, for example, between Craig Keener, an egalitarian scholar who used to be a complementarian, and Father Patrick Reardon, an Antiochian Orthodox priest who used to be an Episcopalian egalitarian. Why did they change their minds on this issue? This kind of conversation, I believe, could lead to greater mutual understanding on both sides.

4. The naming of God. I would like to encourage a symposium of com-

---

[24]*RBMW,* pp. 420-24.

plementarian and egalitarian scholars, liturgists and theologians on the issue of gender-inclusive language for God. Whatever one may think about gender-inclusive language for humans, the use of feminine appellatives for God seems to be of a very different order. While no complementarians, to my knowledge, would countenance gender-inclusive language for God, the best arguments against this practice have been put forth by egalitarians, including the late Elizabeth Achtemeier, Roland Frye, Robert Jenson, Geoffrey Wainwright, Elizabeth Morelli, Donald Bloesch, Tom Oden and, most recently and most thoroughly, John W. Cooper. Cooper also gives full weight to feminine imagery for God in the Bible, as well as the notion of "kenotic masculinity of God" implied in the title Abba, and he calls for Christians to find biblically faithful ways to talk about "the motherly touch of our heavenly Father," as he calls it, without revising the biblical and historic Christian orthodox Trinitarian language of Father, Son and Holy Spirit.[25] This is the kind of topic that could well benefit from the sort of careful exegetical study that both complementarian and egalitarian scholars have shown themselves capable of doing.

    5. The sanctity of life. In a culture of death, can egalitarians and complementarians stand and work together on behalf of the sanctity of human life to oppose abortion on demand? On this issue, I take it, egalitarians stand together with complementarians over against mainstream feminism, with the exception of the tiny Feminists for Life group.

    6. Defend marriage and family integrity. While demonstrating the Christian and neighborly approach to all persons, including homosexual persons, can egalitarians and complementarians agree that homosexual activity is not a God-ordained lifestyle that should be approved and recognized within the Christian community? Can evangelicals and complementarians agree to be welcoming of homosexual persons but not affirming of homosexual practices and different lifestyles as accepted norms of church and family life? And without entering into the political debate over the proposed amendment to the federal constitution, can we agree to support the understanding of marriage as the God-ordained union of one man and one woman?

    7. Sexual abuse. Running throughout the literatures of both communities

---

[25]John W. Cooper, *Our Father in Heaven: Christian Faith and Inclusive Language for God* (Grand Rapids: Baker, 1998), pp. 265-94.

is a debate about whether one of these views, or the other, contributes to the sexual abuse of women. Charges and countercharges are made on both sides about this, but every person I have read in the current discussion is strongly opposed to such horrible abuse and believes Christians should never countenance sexual abuse in any form. Surely here is a topic where the stated agreement between complementarians and egalitarians far outweighs their backwater differences about what motivates and contributes to such practices. Why not form a joint complementarian-egalitarian task force to study this issue, propose a concrete action plan for pastors and congregations to use in dealing with sexual abuse cases? Why not develop a joint literature and curriculum for churches, colleges and seminaries to use in raising the consciousness of the evangelical community on this matter?

8. *Concerts of prayer.* In a lecture presented at Regent College several years ago, Mary Stewart Van Leeuwen challenged her audience to remember that the issues raised in gender discussions could not be resolved by arguments, organization and church political strategies alone, that such matters required a serious, prayerful engagement.[26] What about a round of prayer meetings in which representatives of both communities meet together to pray for one another, to seek the illumination of the Holy Spirit in our study of the Scriptures, in our joint projects on behalf of the least, the last and the lost all around us, and in our efforts to be both faithful to our conscientious convictions and also agents of reconciliation within the evangelical family?

9. *Evangelism and missions.* Can egalitarians and complementarians agree that Jesus Christ is the only way of salvation for all persons everywhere? We do! Can we find ways of working together to support the world Christian mission, giving special attention to our brothers and sisters in Christ who struggle in various parts of the world against persecution, harassment, poverty and isolation from other believers? If we could see the world through the eyes of the Savior's love and see ourselves perhaps through the eyes of such brothers and sisters who do so much with so little, perhaps we would see our own intraevangelical debates, including this one, in a different light.

Well, that is the end of the sermon, or almost. I want to close with a prayer. It's a prayer from a nineteenth-century Christian woman, Christina Rossetti, a

---

[26]See Mary Stewart Van Leeuwen, "Principalities, Powers, and Gender Relations: Some Reflections for Patient Revolutionaries," *Crux* 31 (September 1995).

prayer that takes us to the heart of Jesus' own life and ministry and his embracing invitation to us all:

> Jesus, who didst touch the leper, deliver us from antipathies; who didst eat with them who washed not before meat, deliver us from fastidiousness; who didst condone inhospitality, deliver us from affront-taking; who wouldst not promise the right or the left, deliver us from favoritism; who, having called didst recall Peter, deliver us from soreness; who didst love active Martha and contemplative Mary, deliver us from respect of persons. Deliver us while it is called today. Thou who givest today, and promisest not tomorrow.[27]

---

[27]Christina Rossetti, in *Prayers of Women*, ed. Lisa Sergio (New York: Harper & Row, 1965), p. 93.

CONTRIBUTORS

Henri D. Blocher is the Knoedler Professor of Theology at Wheaton College and professor of systematic theology at the Faculté Libre de Théologie Evangélique in Vaux-sur-Seine, outside Paris. He has authored six books, including *Original Sin: Illuminating the Riddle* and *In the Beginning: The Opening Chapters of Genesis*. In addition, he has recently assumed the presidency of the Fellowship of European Evangelical Theologians.

Lynn H. Cohick is associate professor of New Testament at Wheaton College. She taught for three years at Nairobi Evangelical Graduate School of Theology in Nairobi, Kenya, and is the author of *The Peri Pascha Attributed to Melito of Sardis: Setting, Purpose and Sources*, and coauthor of *The New Testament in the World of Antiquity*.

Timothy George is founding dean and professor of divinity at Beeson Divinity School. He is a remarkable evangelical statesman, serving as executive editor *for Christianity Today* along with serving on the editorial advisory boards *of The Harvard Theological Review, Christian History* and *Books & Culture*. He has written more than twenty books, including *Theology of the Reformers*.

James M. Hamilton is assistant professor of biblical studies at Southwestern Seminary's Havard School for Theological Studies in Houston, and the author of *God's Indwelling Presence: The Holy Spirit in the Old And New Testaments*. He has published articles in *Scottish Bulletin of Evangelical Theology, Themelios, Trinity Journal, The Journal for Biblical Manhood and Womanhood* and *Westminster Theological Journal*.

Mark Husbands was recently appointed the Leonard and Marjorie Maas Associate Professor of Reformed Theology at Hope College. He has completed the monograph *Barth's Ethics of Prayer*, and has edited six books, including *The Community of the Word, Justification: What's at Stake in the Current Debates* and *Essays Catholic and Critical*.

Rebecca G. S. Idestrom is associate professor of Old Testament at Tyndale Seminary. She is the author of *From Biblical Theology to Biblical Criticism: Old Testament Scholarship at Uppsala University, 1866-1922*. She has published articles and reviews in *Journal of Pentecostal Theology, Didaskalia, Studies in Religion/Sciences Religieuses, Journal for the Study of the Old Testmament, The Pentecostal Testimony, Themelios* and *Hebrew Studies*.

Timothy Larsen was recently appointed McManis Professor of Christian Thought, Wheaton College, Illinois. He is currently also a Visiting Fellow, Trinity College, Cambridge University. He is the editor of several works, including the *Biographical Dictionary of Evangelicals*. His books include *Christabel Pankhurst: Fundamentalism and Feminism in Coalition* and *Crisis of Doubt: Honest Faith in Nineteenth-Century England*.

Mary Stewart Van Leeuwen is professor of psychology and philosophy at Eastern University. She has published over forty articles, three edited books, and is the author of *My Brother's Keeper: What the Social Sciences Do (and Don't) Tell Us About Masculinity*, *Gender and Grace: Love, Work and Parenting in a Changing World* and *After Eden: Facing the Challenge of Gender Reconciliation*.

Fredrick J. Long is director of Biblical Studies Program and assistant professor of New Testament at Bethel College. He is the author of *Ancient Rhetoric and Paul's Apology: The Compositional Unity of 2 Corinthians*, and is senior editor of *Reflections: A Publication of the Missionary Church Historical Society*.

I. Howard Marshall is Emeritus Professor of New Testament Exegesis and Honorary Research Professor, and the author of *A Critical and Exegetical Commentary on the Pastoral Epistles* and the recently published volumes *New Testament Theology: Many Witnesses, One Gospel* and *Beyond the Bible: Moving from Scripture to Theology*.

Margaret Kim Peterson is theologian in residence at the First Presbyterian Church at Norristown and associate professor of theology at Eastern University. She has published articles in *Christian Century, First Things* and *Theology Today*, and is author of *Sing Me to Heaven: The Story of a Marriage* and the recently published volume *Keeping House: The Litany of Everyday Life*.

Sarah Sumner is professor of theology and ministry for the Haggard School of Theology at Azusa Pacific University. She has published articles in *Leadership Journal* and *Christianity Today* and is the author of *Men and Women in the Church: Building Consensus on Christian Leadership* and the recent volume *Leadership Above the Line*.

Cheryl J. Sanders is senior pastor of the Third Street Church of God in Washington, D.C., and professor of Christian ethics at the Howard University School of Divinity. She is the author of over fifty articles and several books, including *Ministry at the Margins, Saints in Exile, The Holiness-Pentecostal Experience in African American Religion and Culture, Empowerment Ethics for a Liberated People*, and is the editor of *Living the Intersection*.

Name Index

Achtemeier, Elizabeth, 286

Ackerman, Susan, 28n

Adler, Mortimer, 252n, 253, 255

Anderson, Annie, 210

Angier, Natalie, 186

Aristotle, 88n, 182n, 271

Arlandson, James M., 106, 108-9, 111n

Artemus, Rosa, 205

Artemus, William, 204

Balch, David, 112

Balswick, Jack and Judith, 188-89

Balthasar, Hans Urs von, 131

Barth, Karl, 132n, 244, 277

Bartkowsi, John P., 183n

Beale, G. K., 48n

Beauvoir, Simone de, 82n, 243, 244n

Behr-Siegel, Elisabeth, 244

Belleville, Linda L., 29n, 40n, 41, 42n, 62n, 68n, 92n

Berry, Samuel and Mariam, 202

Blanchard, Jonathan, 221

Blocher, Henri, 10, 239

Blocher, Madeleine, 239

Block, Daniel I., 21-22, 25, 27

Bloesch, Donald, 286

Bonhoeffer, Dietrich, 128, 140, 146

Booth, Catharine, 218, 234

Booth, Evangeline, 218

Booth, William, 218, 219n

Brasher, Brenda E., 183n

Briggs, Richard, 251-53n

Brown, Cheryl, 24n

Brown, Pansy M., 210

Bruce, F. F., 85, 104n

Brunner, Emil, 139

Bucer, Martin, 156

Buss, David, 186-87

Buswell, J. Oliver, Jr., 227

Buytendijk, F. J .J., 243

Calvin, John, 156-57, 241-43, 261, 271

Camp, Claudia V., 29n

Capper, Brian J., 59n

Carson, D. A., 39n, 47n

Catherine of Siena, 226

Chafer, Lewis Sperry, 227

Cohick, Lynn H., 81

Coltrane, Scott, 189-90n

Congreve, William, 242

Cooper, John W., 286

Cowan, Ruth Schwartz, 153

Cox, Jeffrey, 229

Craigie, P. C., 28n

Cromwell, Oliver, 78

Crosby, Fanny, 229

Crosby, Sarah, 214n-15

Cutler, Ann, 215

Dally, Mary, 275

Devine, Calvin, 202

Dobson, James, 232-33

Doren, R. N. Van, 222

Downer, Hattie, 201

Dryer, Emma, 224

Eagly, Alice, 186-87

Earhart, Amelia, 231

Elizabeth I, 271

Elliot, Elisabeth, 184, 232

Elliott, Charlotte, 229

Ellis, E. Earle, 43n, 98n-99n, 103-4

Erickson, Millard, 260

Eves, Ailish Ferguson, 22

Exum, Cheryl J., 25, 29

Farrow, Douglas, 133

Fee, Gordon D., 35n, 37n, 93n, 99n, 196

Feuerbach, Ludwig, 276

Finney, Charles, 221

Fletcher, John, 215

Fletcher, Mary, 215

France, R. T., 76

Franson, Fredrik, 225, 234

Fraser, David, 191

Freud, Sigmund, 175, 276

Frye, Northrop, 286

Gaebelein, A. C., 227

Gage, Frances Dana, 272

George, Eliza Davis, 229

George, Timothy, 9, 52, 266-67n, 279n, 282n

Giles, Kevin, 72, 85, 172n

Goldingay, John, 17, 20n-21n

González, Justo, 252

Gordon, A. J., 225

Griffith, Marie R., 183

Grudem, Wayne, 43n, 46n, 54n-56n, 62n-63n, 66, 67n-69n, 70, 73-75, 76n, 77, 78n, 172n-73n, 259, 261-62

Gundry-Volf, Judith M., 43, 94n

Halkes, Catharina, 240

Hamilton, James M., Jr., 10, 32

Hampson, Daphne, 275

Harnack, Adolf von, 230, 248n

Harrison, Hannah, 215

Hassey, Janette, 218n, 220n, 224

Hatch, Nathan, 254n
Hauser, Alan J., 23n
Hayford, Jack, 228
Hays, Richard, 90, 99n
Heine, Susanne, 244
Hess, Richard, 50
Hines, Samuel G., 210
Horn, Rosa A., 201, 204-5
Horn, William, 204
Howard, Philip E., Jr., 232
Howard, Thomas, 184
Huber, Randal, 200
Humphrey, Edith M., 244
Hurston, Zora Neale, 201
Husbands, Mark, 127
Idestrom, Rebecca G. S.,
   11, 17
Irenaeus, 132-33
Ironside, H. A., 227
Jefferson, Thomas, 271
Jenson, Robert, 286
Johnson, Luke Timothy,
   42, 43n, 47, 49n, 56,
   151n, 166n
Johnson, Samuel, 214
Jones, Bob, Jr., 227
Jones, Letitia, 210
Kant, Immanuel, 276
Keener, Craig S., 39-40,
   47n, 285
Key, Robert, 210
King, Karen, 92n
Kirschbaum, Charlotte
   von, 135-37, 244
Klein, Lillian R., 27n
Kloppenborg, John S.,
   111n-12n, 113, 116n
Knight, G. W., 246
Knox, John, 271
Köstenberger, Andreas J.,
   40n-41n, 62n, 66, 70n,
   71-72, 83
Kraemer, Ross, 82n, 111n

Kuhlman, Kathryn, 228
Kuyper, Abraham, 182-83,
   184n, 193
Larsen, Timothy, 129,
   140n, 213, 217n, 226n,
   230n, 233n
Leonard, Juanita, 211
Lewis, C. S., 184n, 253n
Liefeld, Walter L., 56, 68n,
   75n, 77n
Llewellyn, Selina, 217
Long, Fredrick J., 11, 98,
   114n
MacMullen, Ramsay, 110
Manning, Christel, 183n
Marcion, 278
Marsden, George, 255
Marshall, I. Howard, 44n-
   45n, 53, 54n, 56n, 64n,
   87n, 114, 140, 258n
Martin, Dale, 84, 88-97
Maxwell, L. E., 233
Metzke, Erwin, 241
McCann, Clinton J., 19n,
   31n
McConnell, Lela G., 220
McInerney, Ralph, 254n
McPherson, Aimee Semple,
   228
Meyer, F. B., 227
Moo, Douglas, 41n, 50
Moody, D. L., 224, 230
Morelli, Elizabeth, 286
Mounce, William D., 40-
   41n, 44n, 49-50n, 56, 66
Mount, Christopher, 89n
Neyrey, Jerome H., 59n
Ng, Esther Yue L., 69n
Nicole, Roger, 260, 277
Noll, Mark, 251n-52n
Norton, Helen S., 221
Oden, Tom, 250n, 286
O'Donovan, Oliver, 130

Olson, Dennis, 20n, 26n-
   28n, 29-30, 31n
O'Neill, Mary Aquin, 83
Ortner, Sherry, 82
Osborne, Grant, 260
Padberg, Lutz von, 240n-
   41n, 243n, 347
Palmer, Phoebe, 200, 219,
   234
Pankhurst, Christabel,
   226-27, 232
Parmentier, Elisabeth,
   240n, 244
Peskowitz, Miriam, 82n
Peterson, Margaret Kim,
   11, 148
Pierson, A. T., 226
Piper, John, 138, 173n,
   232n
Reardon, Patrick, 285
Reilly, Patricia Lynn,
   276
Reno, Rusty, 275
Rice, John R., 273-74
Riley, W. B., 225, 227
Ritschl, Albrecht, 230
Robbins, Vernon K., 110
Robinson, Ida B., 201,
   205-6, 207n, 228
Romans, Viola D., 226
Rorty, Richard, 257
Rossetti, Christina, 287,
   288n
Rousseau, Jean-Jacques,
   182
Sabel, Esther, 225
Sakenfeld, Katharine Doob,
   28n, 30n
Sanders, Cheryl J., 140n,
   200-201n, 209
Sayers, Dorothy, 181-82n,
   242
Schaeffer, Francis, 254

Schleiermacher, Friedrich, 230

Scholer, David M., 100n

Schreiner, Thomas R., 37n-38n, 40n-41n, 45n, 49n-51n, 61n, 66-67, 69-71, 73, 83n

Schultz, Richard, 22n

Scott, James, 210

Seim, Turid K., 101n, 102, 105n

Selina, Countess of Huntington, 215

Shedd, W. G. T., 251n

Simpson, A. B., 226

Slessor, Mary, 229

Smith, Amanda Berry, 201-2n, 203-4

Smith, Chuck, 228

Smith, James, 202

Stanley, Susie, 200

Staton, Elizabeth Cady, 274-75

Stendahl, Krister, 85

Storkey, Elaine, 275n, 276

Stott, John, 260

Straton, John Roach, 225-27, 234

Strauss, D. F., 230

Sullerot, Evelyne, 243

Summers, Larry, 32-33n

Sumner, Sarah, 10, 52, 250

Tait, Jennifer Woodruff, 220

Taylor, Glen J., 28n

Tertullian, 89, 261, 271

Thiselton, Anthony, 83, 93-94, 96, 118-19, 122

Thomas Aquinas, 261, 271

Toms, Mary, 217

Torrey, Edith C., 225

Towner, Philip H., 57n, 59n, 74n

Trulear, Harold Dean, 206, 207n

Trumbull, Charles G., 232

Tudor, Mary, 271

Van Leeuwen, Mary Stewart, 10, 171, 175n, 183n-84n, 189n-90n, 287

Vanhoozer, Kevin, 87, 97, 258n

Wainwright, Geoffrey, 286

Walton, Grace, 215

Waters, Kenneth L., Sr., 71n

Webb, William J., 46n, 76n, 83-84, 87, 96-97, 174n, 278-79

Weil, Simone, 283

Wells, David, 251n-52n

Wenham, Gordon, 246

Werry, Mary Ann, 217

Wesley, John, 213-16, 230

Whitefield, George, 214-16

Whitton, Charlotte, 249

Wilcox, Bradford, 194-195n

Willard, Frances E., 224

Williams, Delores, 275

Winchester, A. B., 227

Winfrey, Joan Burgess, 185

Winter, Bruce, 51n, 57-58n, 68n-69, 83-84n, 85-88, 98n, 184n, 204n, 207

Wire, Antoinette, 84, 92, 95, 112n

Witherington, Ben, 101n, 103n, 107-8, 113

Wood, Wendy, 186

Woodworth-Etter, Maria, 204

Wright, N. T., 143

Yee, Gale A., 27n

Subject Index

Abraham, 103, 109, 141-43, 166
action, 127, 130, 143
 human, 30, 127
Adam, 46, 48, 57n, 60, 63-64, 70-71, 99, 132-37, 188, 265
 Christ as true, 132-33
 superiority over Eve, 60, 63, 134, 137
Adventist Testimony Movement, 227
African Americans, 140n, 201, 204-5, 229
Alexandria, 164
Angelus Temple, 228
Anglicanism, 213, 215
anthropology, 46, 83, 134, 141
 biblical, 46
 theological, 141
Antioch, 164
Apollos, 37, 69, 75, 93, 107-8, 110, 119, 245, 265
apologetics, 113, 222
apostle, apostolate, 62, 115, 117, 120, 123n, 131, 263-4
Aquila, 37, 69, 75, 107-8
Ashland, 270
Associated Gospel Churches, 232
atonement, 141
 substitutionary, 141
authority, 36, 38n, 39, 40-51, 54-56, 58-59, 61-62, 64-65, 67-68, 71-72, 74-78, 81, 89, 92, 94, 99-100, 103-4, 106, 113, 128, 136, 146, 158, 162,

183n, 188, 193, 210, 216, 223, 235, 245-47, 252, 255n, 258-60, 265, 274, 280-81
 authenteō, 67n, 68, 68n, 284
 authoritative leaders, 45
 Roman, 113
baptism, 43, 84, 95-96, 119n, 122n, 129-30, 141-45, 158, 205, 221, 223-24, 263
Barak, 22-23, 25-26, 28, 30-31n
Beeson Divinity School, 9, 269
behavior, 175, 197-98
 misogynist, 190
being, 172n
 -in-encounter, 129, 132, 134, 137, 145-46
Bethel Seminary, 225
Bible, 33, 36-37, 42-45, 51, 54, 81, 83, 87, 241-42, 247, 251-52, 254-57, 260-61, 264, 273-76, 280, 283-84, 286
Bible Testimony Fellowship, 227
Biola, 227
biology, 176, 177n, 179n, 243
boundaries, 32-33, 36, 44-45, 51, 105-6, 165, 196, 208, 263
Bucer, 156
Calvin, 156-57, 261, 271
Calvinist Methodists, 216
Chalcedon, Council of, 164

charismatic, 25n, 131, 228, 234
 charism, 131
 movement, 228
 office, 131
child, children, 35, 36n-37n, 44, 49n-50n, 57n, 60-61, 63, 67, 71, 73, 76-77, 102, 110, 143, 156-57, 160, 177n, 179n, 190-91, 193-94, 198-99, 202-3, 231, 271, 281
Christ, 12-13, 44, 46, 50, 61, 79, 81, 83-84, 87, 91, 93-97, 100, 116, 118n-19, 121, 127, 130-33, 141-47, 164, 203, 208-9, 219, 224, 230, 244, 250n, 263-64, 271, 273, 275, 277-80, 282-85, 287
 body of, 79, 81, 91, 121
 lordship of, 44, 50
 new life in, 84
Christian and Missionary Alliance, 226
Christian, Christianity, 12, 17, 29-30, 33-34, 36, 41, 43, 45, 50, 53, 54, 56n, 58n-60, 62-63, 71n, 74n-75, 77, 82n, 92n, 95, 98-101, 103-4, 106-7, 110-14, 120-22, 127, 129-32, 141-45, 148-49, 155-63, 167, 171-73, 183-86, 188, 190n-93, 195, 202, 210, 213, 218-19, 223-24, 227-8, 230-32, 235, 244n, 248, 250n-52, 256-62, 264-65, 268, 272, 274-78, 280-81,

283-84, 286-87
  Brethren, 53
  fellowship, 227, 258
  Gentile, 111, 141-43
  life, 130, 159, 167, 202
  Pauline, 111
Christian education, directors of, 157
Christian Fellowship Bible Conference, 227
Christians for Biblical Equality, 10, 172, 193
Christology, 160, 164, 244, 276
chromosomes, 176
church, 12-13, 34-40, 41n-42n, 43-45, 47, 50-51, 53-56n, 61-63, 65-66, 70-74n, 75-78, 81, 83, 85-87, 89-92, 94-97, 99n-101, 107-8, 111, 113-14, 116-17, 119-23n, 127-31, 133, 140-46, 156-60, 164-65, 172-74, 183, 185, 190n-96, 200-12, 214-35, 239, 244-50, 255, 257-65, 268-71, 273, 275, 277-81, 283-84, 286-87
  African Methodist Episcopal, 203
  British Methodist, 53
  ekklēsia, 98, 106, 123
  of England, 54, 216-17, 230
  German, 128, 140
  of God, 200-201, 205, 207-12, 220, 270
  of the Nazarene, 220, 231, 233
  of Scotland, 53, 78
Church of God School of Theology, 270

circumcision, 43, 130, 141-43n
College Church, 221
collegia, 110-11n
command, 35-40, 44n, 48, 51, 54n, 64, 67, 70-72, 128-29, 131, 133, 139-42, 146, 166-67, 258, 280
  of God, 129, 131, 139
Community Marriage Policies, 192-93
complementarian, 9-10, 13, 41, 50n, 56n, 63, 66, 71-78, 130, 167, 171-74, 184, 187, 240-42, 250, 254, 256-62, 264, 266-98, 270, 274, 276-77, 280-87
council, 10, 65, 106, 164, 172-73, 193, 223, 281
Council of Biblical Manhood and Womanhood, 10, 172-73, 193, 281
counseling, counselors, 65, 157, 192
covenant, covenantal, 19, 103, 122, 129-30, 137, 141-43, 145-45, 189, 191-92, 207, 209, 243, 263
  faithfulness, 142
  of grace, 130, 141, 143, 145
  lifelong, 191
Covenant Theological Seminary, 270
creation, 33, 46-50, 61, 63-65, 68, 71-71, 75n, 82, 90-91, 93-97, 99n, 129, 132-34, 136-40, 142-44, 172, 185, 188, 190-91, 242, 246

narratives, 94, 132, 134, 136-37
culture wars, 233
Dallas Theological Seminary, 227
Danvers Statement, 173
daughter, daughters, 104-5, 109, 263n
  of Philip, 104, 263n
deacon, 42-44, 107, 123n, 156-58, 203, 220, 269
Deborah, 11, 17-31, 103, 211, 246, 260, 263n, 265, 271
Delilah, 27
Denver, 270
dialogical paradigm, 239
didaskalos, 245, 248
difference, 32, 36-37, 45, 93-94, 96-97, 134, 138, 158, 161, 163, 173-81, 184n-87, 197-98, 232, 242-43, 245
Dionysius, 107, 112-13n, 120
discipleship, 116n, 132, 146
diversity, 32-33, 96, 116, 121n, 190
  and gender, 32-33
divorce, 109, 161, 191-95, 284
  culture of, 161
doctrine, 12-13, 51, 53, 55, 59, 65, 67, 70, 77, 129, 131, 133, 141, 148, 152, 156, 160, 183, 188, 191, 200, 209, 211, 216, 223, 228, 251n, 260, 265, 273
  of ministry, 131
  of Trinity, 12, 152
dogma, dogmatics, 127,

129-31, 141, 146, 277
domestic life, 62, 231
Eastern Orthodox, 213,
  284
Ebionites, 278
egalitarian, 9-10, 13, 42n-
  43, 45n, 49n, 52, 70, 76-
  77, 130, 161, 163, 165,
  171-75, 183n, 195, 214,
  218, 228, 240, 248, 250,
  254, 256-62, 264, 266-
  68, 270, 274-77, 279-87
  functional, 195
Ehud, 20
elder, 12, 36, 42, 45, 51,
  103, 156-57, 205, 245,
  247, 264
empire
  Roman, 106, 110, 112
Enlightenment, 85, 145,
  271
Ephesus, 40-41, 44n, 107,
  243, 247, 265
equality, 33, 43, 49n, 72-
  73, 87, 90, 95, 136, 138,
  141, 172-73, 186-88,
  191, 193, 196, 209, 220,
  226, 242, 257, 261-62,
  268
Esther, 103, 212
Evangelical Free Church of
  America, 225
Evangelical Theological Society, 183n, 277, 283
evangelicalism, 213, 215,
  219, 224-25, 228, 231-
  33, 235, 266, 281, 284
  historic distinctive of,
    213, 228, 231
  history of, 235, 273
  as a renewal movement,
    284
Evangelicals and Catholics

Together, 267, 282-83
Eve, 46, 48-49, 57n, 59-
  60, 63-65, 68n, 70-71n,
  99n, 134-37, 184, 188,
  265, 271
  naming of, 49
Fairfield Baptist Church,
  222-23
fall, fallen, 46, 61, 65, 138,
  140, 163, 172, 174, 176,
  274
family, 63, 77, 86, 141,
  143, 172n-73, 183n,
  188-90, 192, 194-95,
  202, 232, 281-82, 286
fellowship, 114n, 133-35,
  137, 145-46, 207-9, 251,
  258, 270, 284
female, 21n, 24, 26-27,
  31n-33, 35, 43, 45, 46n-
  48, 50n, 54, 57n, 61, 73,
  75, 81, 83-86, 88-90, 92-
  93, 95-97, 101-2, 107,
  113, 117n, 122n, 131,
  134-35, 137-38, 141,
  143, 144-45, 151-52,
  158, 173-74n, 176-78,
  180, 182, 184-86, 189-
  90, 197, 203, 206-7,
  216-20, 229, 233, 241-
  43, 245-48, 261-62n,
  269, 271, 273
  body, 84, 88-90, 95
feminist, feminine, femi-
  ninity, 38-39n, 43-44, 47,
  49-50n, 55, 74n, 76, 81-
  83, 90, 117n, 134, 161,
  173, 176, 181, 185, 190,
  208, 214, 218-19, 226,
  232, 239n-40, 243, 259-
  60n, 262, 266, 268, 270,
  274-78, 281, 286
  movement, 161

  radical, 274-78
  studies, 81
Feminists for Life, 286
freedom, 31, 45, 51, 74n,
  106, 110-11, 122, 127,
  131, 135, 141-42, 175,
  202, 248, 272
  of the gospel, 141-42
  of Roman women, 106,
    110
Fuller Theological Semi-
  nary, 270
Fundamentalist Rally and
  Prophetic Conference,
  227
gender, 12, 21, 31n-33, 35,
  37-38, 44n-51, 62, 81-
  83, 86-89n, 90-92, 95-
  103, 111, 113n, 115-18,
  121-22, 130, 134, 137-
  39, 145, 151, 153-54,
  161, 163, 171-77n, 179-
  92, 194-96, 218, 225-26,
  228, 240, 261, 268-69,
  281, 286-87
  hierarchicalist, 171-73,
    183, 189, 195
  social construct,
    82
Gender Empowerment
  Measure, 186
Gender-Related Develop-
  ment Index, 186
Genesis, 41n, 46-50, 58n-
  59, 61, 63n-64n, 65, 69-
  70, 84n, 94-95, 132, 134,
  136, 187-88, 190, 241-
  43, 247, 261, 271
  creation narratives, 94,
    132, 134, 136-37
Gentile, 95, 111, 114n,
  122, 141-43
Gideon, 20n-21

gift, giftedness, 31, 33-36,
44, 49n, 50, 66, 97-103,
105, 114-23, 133, 142,
196, 200, 219, 242-43,
248-49, 257, 268, 277,
281
  prophecy, 120
  spiritual, 34-35, 66,
    99n, 105, 122
  tongues, 36, 90, 95, 97,
    115, 119-20, 206,
    263
God's glory, 243, 247
Gordon College, 225
Gordon-Conwell Theologi-
cal Seminary, 225
gospel, 13, 58, 61, 63, 71n,
77, 90n, 94-97, 108,
116n-17n, 127-28, 130,
132, 138, 141-44, 146-
48, 150, 152, 156, 158,
160, 165, 167, 196, 200,
212, 214, 216-18, 223-
25, 229-31, 235, 239,
243, 252n, 271, 274,
278-80, 282, 285
  transgressive nature of,
    130, 144
Greco-Roman, 46, 81-82,
84, 86, 89-90, 96, 99-
101, 104-6, 110, 120,
122
  world, 82, 90
hair, 81, 88n-89n, 94, 206,
273
  covering, 81, 89n, 94,
    206
Harvard Memorial Church,
275
Harvard University, 32,
221
head covering, 37, 39n, 46-
47, 85, 92, 99n, 273

head, headship, 46-47, 49,
50, 70, 94, 96, 117, 130,
133, 161-62, 165, 172,
173-74, 183, 191, 193,
195, 240, 245, 264, 274
Hellenism, 59-60, 69, 104,
109
hermeneutics, 83-87, 96-
97, 113, 233-34, 240,
274-75, 279-80
  contemporary feminist,
    274
  evangelical, 234
hierarchy, 50n, 62, 89-94,
144, 155, 173, 183n-85,
188
holiness, 51, 60, 116, 203,
206-9, 220
Holiness Movement, 200-
201, 204-5, 207, 211-12,
215, 219
homosexual, homosexual-
ity, homosexuals, 36n,
76-77, 173-74, 280, 286
  practice, 76-77, 286
housekeeping, 148-50,
160-61
housework, 149, 151, 153-
54, 160
Huldah, 26, 29, 103, 211,
246
human, 33-34, 50, 60, 84,
88, 90, 92-93, 96-97,
102-3, 114, 127-47, 152-
53, 161, 163-67
  biological feature of, 37,
    84, 87-88, 90, 174-
    77, 179, 187, 188,
    190, 243
  flourishing, 133, 137,
    154-55, 188-89
  personhood, nature of,
    128-29, 132, 137-38,

145-46, 281
husband, 29, 37, 56-59,
63-64, 68-69, 75, 86, 99,
106, 118, 149, 162-63,
172, 218-19, 273-74,
281, 293
  as "head" of wife, 161-
    62
identity, 47, 50, 90, 127-
67, 189-90, 216-17, 252,
263
  male and female, 33,
    45-48, 84, 92, 113,
    122, 134-52, 177,
    180, 185, 189, 197,
    241-45, 261-62, 293
image of God, *imago Dei*,
33, 48, 94-96, 133, 135,
188, 190-91, 252, 261-
62, 268, 273, 281, 293
imperative, 139, 267
Indianapolis Bible Insti-
tute, 225
indicative, 139,
industrialization, 153-54,
161
inerrancy, 225, 233, 259-
60
infallibility, 245
inspiration, 29, 31, 121,
280
instruction, 37, 39, 45, 75-
76, 144, 156
International Church of the
Foursquare Gospel, 228
Israel, 18-31, 50, 90, 103,
128, 135, 166, 244, 265
Jephthah, 20-21, 27
Jesus Christ, 43, 46, 50, 61-
62, 83, 87, 90, 99, 110,
114, 116, 119, 120, 123,
127, 132-33, 141-48,
150, 152, 160, 162-67

Jezebel, 246, 271

Jim Crow, 208

Joshua, 18, 26, 102-3

Judaism, 63, 111, 113, 130, 141, 144

Judges, 17-31, 265

Junia, 62, 123, 223, 260

Kentucky Mountain Bible College, 219

Kentucky Mountain Holiness Association, 220

kephalē, 46, 94, 267

Knox Presbyterian Church, Toronto, 227

labor, 151, 153-54, 182, 187

Latitudinarianism, 215

leadership, 9, 17-31, 36, 49, 54, 56, 59, 62, 65-66, 72-75, 81-96, 103-4, 108, 111, 116, 122, 132, 138-39, 174, 200-201, 206-12, 216, 228, 247-48, 257, 259-60, 263, 269, 280

limitations, 36, 87, 105

Lincoln Park Congregational Church, 222

Lydia, 107-9, 123

male, 18, 32-33, 45-48, 50, 54, 56n, 58n, 61, 65n, 69n, 70, 71n, 72, 75, 81-97, 101-13, 122n, 131, 134-45, 149, 152, 158, 161, 172-74, 177, 180, 183-97, 207-8, 217, 225, 229, 241-45, 259-61, 262n, 270-75

Malleus Maleficarum, 271

mantle, 86

marriage, 13, 32, 44n, 53, 56n, 59-61, 69-70, 77,

86, 99n, 100n, 110, 160-63, 191-93, 207, 232, 241-42, 281-86, 293

Martha, 109, 150-52, 165, 288

Mary, 107-9, 150-51, 166-67, 211, 230

Magdalene, 109, 211

men's work, 48, 151-57, 161, 165

meta-analysis, 179-81

Methodist, 53-54, 200, 203-4, 215-18, 220

mind, nous, 91-92, 139

ministry
  fourfold pattern of, 156-57

  full participation in, 32-36, 44-45, 50, 87, 128, 130, 141, 144-46, 208

  ministerial, 11, 13, 44, 55, 152, 155-59, 165, 284

  offices, office of, 42, 107, 114, 131, 156-59, 220, 228, 246, 268-69

  "ordered," 129-32, 137, 146, 186

  prophetic, 23, 25-26, 38, 92, 101, 103-5, 109, 119-20, 127, 141, 201, 245-46

  teaching, 35-44, 47, 54-62, 64-76, 99, 107-8, 115, 131, 213, 222-23, 228

Miriam, 23, 26, 103, 211, 246

misogyny, 190, 271

monophysitism, 164

Moody Bible Institute, 218,

224, 226-27, 230

Moorestown Bible Protestant Church, 232

Moses, 18, 23-26, 102-3, 122-23, 192

Mount Sinai Holy Church of America, 206, 228

National Socialism, 128

Nestorianism, 164

Nicea, Council of, 164

Nicene Fathers, 152, 163

Nineteenth Amendment, 272

Noadiah, 26, 103

North Park Seminary, 270

Oak Park Baptist Church, 222

office
  charismatic, 131, 228
  sacramental, 131, 284

ontology
  essentialist, 134
  of grace, 129, 137
  relational, 133-34, 137, 145-46

order, creation, 46-47, 49, 49, 94, 99, 138-140, 143, 144

ordination, women, 53-55, 75-76, 184, 223, 225, 233n, 246n

overseer, 42, 51

oversight, pastoral, 65, 157, 213, 215, 229

Pacific Garden Mission, 273

Palmer Theological Seminary, 270

Paris Tabernacle Church, 239

pastor, pastoral care, 69n, 117, 156, 158-59, 205,

211, 239, 263, 268-69
patriarchy, 49, 87, 96,
  183n, 276
pattern, nonsymmetrical,
  240, 244
Pentecost, 52, 100-101,
  109, 119-20, 122
Pentecostal, Pentecostal-
  ism, 201, 204-6, 212,
  215, 228, 234
Philo, 69
Philpott Tabernacle, 232
Phoebe, 42, 112, 123n,
  211, 223, 248, 260
Prairie Bible Institute in Alberta, 233
prayer, pray, 37-40, 43-45,
  47, 52-53, 57, 76, 81, 98,
  99n, 109, 112, 114n,
  119-20, 159, 202, 204-6,
  214, 226, 257, 264, 275,
  277, 287-88
preindustrial, 154, 190n
Presbyterians, 156
priest, priestesses 30, 54n,
  99n, 112, 131, 156n,
  158-59, 166, 204, 215,
  230, 245, 284-85
Priscilla, 37, 69, 75, 107-8,
  123n, 211, 248, 260, 265
private sphere (for
  women), 105, 108, 153-
  55, 161, 165, 231
proclamation, 105, 116n,
  130-31, 142, 144, 146-
  47, 156, 245, 284
prohibition, 56n, 58-59,
  61, 63-66, 68, 72-76,
  233, 242, 248, 265
Prometheus, 120
prophecy, gift of, 120
Protestants
  conservative, 194, 233

evangelical, 159
psychology, 174-75, 177-
  81, 186
public wedlock, 191
racism, 201, 207-9, 270,
  272
reconciliation, 143-46,
  207, 209, 268, 282-83,
  287
redemption, 83n, 132,
  152, 172, 207
  history of, 128
Reformation, 156, 234,
  271, 282, 284
Regent College, 270, 287
representation, 103, 261,
  284
rhetorical analysis, 84, 95
Salvation Army, 218-19
Samson, 20n, 21, 27
Samuel, 18, 20, 23, 25-26,
  29
sanctification, 49n, 203,
  205, 209
Sarah, 103, 166, 204
science, sciences, 10-11,
  171-99
secular, 30, 32, 56n, 57,
  62-63, 73-74, 76, 85,
  151-52, 165, 192
segregation, 118, 155,
  208-9
Serapis, 120
serving, *diakoneō*, 42, 115-
  17
sexism, 201, 207, 209,
  270, 274, 276
sexual dimorphism, 188
shame/honor, 39n, 89, 91,
  94n, 96
Shelburne Falls Baptist
  Church, 222
slave, slavery, 87, 92, 95,

102, 109, 141, 143,188,
  202, 272
social respectability, 216
social science, 172, 175n,
  177-79, 187, 191-92,
  195
society
  first-century, 61n, 62,
    53, 99n, 265
  Greco-Roman, 46, 81-
    97, 99-123
Southern Baptist Conven-
  tion, 9, 268-69
Spirit, 34-35, 101-5, 114,
  142, 144-45, 234, 247,
  262, 287
  gifts, 121-23, 133, 200,
    206-8
  pneuma, 91
  spiritual practice, 148,
    150
structure of exploitation,
  241
submission, 39, 44n, 47,
  71n, 86, 99n, 140, 172n,
  193, 196
subordination, 49n, 58n,
  59, 66-69, 74, 85, 89, 93,
  155, 164, 172n, 201, 208
suffrage, 226, 272-73
teacher, 39, 69, 75n, 156,
  225-28, 247
  Sunday school, 210
tradition, 34, 103, 118-20,
  133, 157, 200-201, 260,
  262, 275, 284
Trinity, 93, 143, 152, 162,
  172n
Trinity Evangelical Divinity
  School, 270
typology, 83-92
United Nations Develop-
  ment Program, 186-87

unity, 54, 96, 128, 138,
    207-9, 257, 263
University of Chicago, 273
University of Virginia, 271
veil, 85-86, 89n, 240
voluntary association, 99n,
    100-101, 110-12, 115-
    16, 122
Westminster Theological
    Seminary, 270
Wheaton College, 221,
    225, 227, 270
wife, 68-69, 99n, 161-62,

191-93, 281
Winona Lake Bible Confer-
    ence, 226-27
women
    active participants, 119-
        20
    evangelical missionar-
        ies, 55-56, 158, 208,
        211, 228-29
    and ordination, 53-55,
        75-76, 158, 184, 223,
        225, 246n
    rights, 226-27, 230,

232, 271
    Roman freedom of, 111
    Roman views of, 86
    work, 151-55, 159,
        161, 165
Women's Christian Tem-
    perance Union, 204
Women's Rights Conven-
    tion, 271
works of mercy, 159-60
workplace, men and
    women in, 138

Scripture Index

Genesis
1—2, 47
1—3, 41, 44, 48,
   49, 50, 84
1:5, 48
1:20-22, 187
1:26, 262
1:26-28, 187
1:27, 48, 241, 242,
   261
1:28, 48, 175
1:31, 96
2, 46, 49, 50, 190,
   247
2:2-5, 49
2:4-25, 134
2:7, 48, 49
2:15, 46, 48
2:17, 48, 64
2:18, 46, 48, 135,
   136, 241, 242
2:19, 48, 49
2:20, 48
2:22, 48, 49
2:23, 48, 49, 242
2:24, 191
3, 49
3:1, 49
3:6, 49
3:8, 49
3:15, 49
3:16, 49, 271
3:16-19, 243
3:20, 49
4:1, 71
5:3, 102
20:7, 103
35:8, 22, 24

Exodus
7:1, 103
14—15, 23
15, 23

15:1-21, 23
15:20, 26, 103
18:13-16, 23, 25

Numbers
11:16-17, 103
11:16-29, 103
11:24, 103
11:25, 103
11:29, 103
12:6, 102

Deuteronomy
6:7, 37
13:1-5, 102
15:12, 37
16:18-20, 19, 23,
   25
18:15, 103
18:20-22, 26
22:5, 242
34:5, 102
34:10, 103

Joshua
24:29, 102

Judges
1:11-15, 27
2:7, 18
2:11-23, 18
2:16, 19
2:16-23, 21
3:7-11, 18, 21
3:7—5:31, 20
3:15, 20
3:31, 19
4, 27, 28
4—5, 17, 23, 29,
   30, 31, 265
4:3, 30
4:4, 21, 22, 29, 103
4:4-5, 19, 22, 23, 24

4:4-8, 22
4:5, 25
4:6-8, 28
4:7, 31
4:8, 25
4:8-9, 26
4:9, 26, 31
4:10, 28
4:13, 30
4:14, 26, 28, 31
4:15, 31
4:17-22, 27
4:23, 31
5, 23, 28
5:1, 28
5:2-3, 28
5:6, 27
5:6-7, 22
5:7, 28
5:9, 28
5:12, 28
5:15, 28
5:24, 27
5:24-27, 27
5:31, 31
6:1—10:5, 20
6:7-10, 25
6:15, 19
8:22, 19
9:22, 20
10:1, 19
10:3-5, 25
10:6—16:31,
   20
12:8-15, 25
13, 27
13:5, 19
17:6, 19, 30
21:25, 19, 30

1 Samuel
3:19-21, 25
3:20, 103

4:18, 20
7:10-11, 25
7:15-17, 20, 25
8:1-3, 20
10—15, 25
10:10-12, 103
24:11, 29

2 Samuel
20:16-19, 29
20:19, 29

1 Kings
18:22, 103
19:16, 103

2 Kings
2:12, 29
6:21, 29
10:23, 102
13:14, 29
18:12, 102
22:14, 29, 103
22:14-20, 26

Ezra
5:11, 102

Nehemiah
6:14, 26, 103

Psalms
18:1, 102
36:1, 102
72:12-14, 135
119:45, 51
119:103, 43
119:160, 255

Proverbs
3:1, 37
3:5, 37
27:17, 251

Isaiah
8:3, *26, 103*
54:17, *102*

Jeremiah
23:28, *102*

Daniel
3:26, *102*

Joel
2, *117*
2:28-32, *101, 114*
2:32, *119*
3:5, *119*

Malachi
2:7, *245*

Matthew
13:11, *52*
16:22, *37*
18:15-17, *75*
19:8-9, *192*
23:23, *209*
25:14-30, *175, 188*
25:34-40, *160*

Mark
8:32, *37*
10:45, *116*

Luke
1—2, *108*
1:2, *39*
2:25-35, *105*
2:36-38, *26, 105*
9, *151*
9:59, *151*
9:59-60, *150*
10, *151, 166*
10:7, *39, 166*
10:25-28, *166*
10:37, *166*
10:38-42, *150, 166*

11:28, *105*
24:19, *116*

John
1:1-3, *94*
1:14, *253*
12:12, *109*

Acts
1:14-15, *101*
2, *100, 101, 102, 114, 115, 119, 120, 121, 122*
2:1, *101*
2:7-11, *52*
2:13, *114*
2:16-18, *101*
2:16-21, *101, 114*
2:17-18, *233*
2:21, *119*
2:38-39, *102*
2:41-47, *114*
4:23-31, *114*
4:32-35, *114*
5:3-4, *104*
7, *114*
7:38, *116*
8:3, *122*
8:21-23, *104*
9:2, *122*
10, *114*
10:10-16, *104*
11, *114*
11:13, *114*
11:27-28, *104*
11:28, *104*
12:12, *108, 114*
13—28, *114*
13:1, *104*
15:22, *103, 104*
15:27, *104*
15:32, *104*
16:14-15, *108, 114, 123*

16:40, *108, 114, 123*
17:28, *134, 146*
18:24-25, *119*
18:25-26, *119*
18:26, *37, 43, 110*
20, *59*
20:17, *42*
20:23, *104*
20:25, *104*
20:28, *42*
20:29, *104*
21:9, *26, 105, 117*
21:10-11, *105*
21:11, *104*
22:4, *122*

Romans
1:11, *117*
1:13, *117*
3:2, *116*
5:12, *48*
6:4, *144*
8:38, *89*
9:15, *117*
9:18, *117*
9:23, *117*
10:13, *119*
11:30-32, *117*
11:31, *117*
12, *122*
12:1, *117*
12:3, *118*
12:3-8, *117*
12:4, *118*
12:5, *118*
12:6, *246*
12:6-8, *100, 101, 115*
13, *117*
14—15, *117*
15:9, *117*
15:15, *117*
15:18, *116*
15:20-23, *118*

15:24, *117*
15:28, *117*
15:30, *117*
16:1, *42, 43, 116*
16:2, *112*
16:3, *123*
16:7, *62, 117, 123*
16:17, *117*
16:25-26, *39*
16:26, *39*

1 Corinthians
1—4, *119*
1:2, *119*
1:7-8, *119*
1:11, *123*
1:12, *119*
1:18-20, *98*
1:19, *47*
1:31, *47*
2:1-4, *119*
2:1-5, *99*
2:5-8, *99*
2:9, *47*
3:4-8, *119*
3:5, *93*
3:11, *284*
3:18-23, *98*
3:19-20, *47*
3:22, *119*
3:23, *93*
4, *120*
4:6, *47*
4:8-13, *99*
5:1, *99*
5:9-13, *99*
6:1-3, *99*
6:2-3, *89*
6:9-13, *99*
6:12-20, *95*
7, *242*
7:12-16, *99*
7:17, *99*
7:20-24, *99*
7:29-31, *99, 283*

8, *99*
8:6, *94*
8:10, *99*
9, *120*
9:19-22, *114*
9:19-23, *99*
10:11, *284*
10:31, *35*
11, *37, 38, 39, 44,
  45, 46, 48, 51, 53,
  81, 97, 118, 120,
  274, 284*
11—14, *101, 119*
11:2-12, *37*
11:2-16, *37, 41, 44,
  51, 81, 82, 83, 84,
  86, 87, 88, 89, 90,
  92, 95, 96, 138,
  244, 273*
11:3, *46, 47, 49, 89,
  93, 94, 162*
11:3-4, *94*
11:3-16, *89, 118*
11:4, *38*
11:5, *37, 43, 98,
  115, 117, 120*
11:5-6, *39, 99*
11:7, *38, 45, 46, 47,
  94, 261, 262*
11:7-9, *47*
11:7-10, *92*
11:7-12, *90, 94*
11:8, *46, 47, 48, 49*
11:8-9, *45, 94*
11:9, *46, 47*
11:10, *38, 46, 89,
  99*
11:11, *87, 95, 122,
  245*
11:11-12, *46*
11:14, *38, 89*
11:17-32, *118*
11:17-34, *94*
11:23, *39*
12, *34, 121, 122*

12—14, *35, 90, 97,
  104, 118, 121*
12:1, *118*
12:2, *99, 105, 120,
  121*
12:3, *35, 119, 120*
12:4-5, *248*
12:4-6, *35, 121*
12:4-7, *33*
12:7-11, *121*
12:8-10, *33, 34,
  100, 101, 115*
12:11, *34, 123*
12:12-13, *121*
12:13, *95, 96, 99,
  122*
12:15, *34*
12:16, *34*
12:18, *35, 122*
12:21, *34*
12:23, *91*
12:24, *35*
12:25-26, *35*
12:27, *121*
12:27-31, *116*
12:28, *35, 105, 115,
  120*
12:28-30, *34, 100,
  101*
12:29, *34*
12:29-30, *115*
13, *121*
13:1-3, *101, 115*
13:1-13, *35*
14, *51, 271, 274*
14:1, *120, 121*
14:1-25, *120*
14:3, *120, 121*
14:3-5, *35*
14:5, *120, 121*
14:6, *38*
14:12, *35, 99, 121*
14:13-15, *105*
14:14-17, *91*
14:19, *35*

14:20, *105*
14:22-23, *52*
14:22-25, *98, 99*
14:24, *120, 121, 122*
14:24-25, *120*
14:24-33, *246*
14:26, *35, 120, 122*
14:27-28, *36*
14:27-40, *35*
14:29, *38, 245*
14:29-35, *51*
14:30, *38*
14:31, *121, 122*
14:32, *105*
14:33, *39*
14:33-34, *211*
14:33-36, *59*
14:33-38, *138*
14:34, *39, 40, 47,
  98*
14:34-35, *39, 41,
  44, 99, 100, 115*
14:34-36, *99,
  233*
14:35, *39, 58, 98*
14:35-36, *99*
14:37-38, *118*
14:38, *36*
14:39, *121*
15:1, *39*
15:3, *39, 285*
15:19, *99*
15:24-28, *93*
15:28, *93*
15:31-33, *99*

2 Corinthians
4:3, *256*
11:2, *100*
12:7, *89*

Galatians
3, *43*
3:1-3, *142*
3:7, *142*

3:7-14, *142*
3:9, *142*
3:27, *142*
3:27-28, *95*
3:28, *10, 33, 43, 61,
  64, 141, 143, 203,
  234, 246*
6:12, *142*
6:14, *142*
6:15, *142*

Ephesians
1:10, *101*
1:17, *116*
2:19-21, *116*
3:1-9, *116*
3:5, *117*
3:14-19, *116*
4, *122*
4:1-3, *116*
4:4, *116*
4:8, *117*
4:10-11, *101*
4:11, *101, 115, 117,
  263, 264*
4:12-15, *116*
4:13, *116, 117*
4:15, *117*
4:17, *116*
4:24, *94, 116*
4:25—5:1, *116*
5, *274, 284*
5:9, *116*
5:21, *64*
5:21-33, *41, 44, 99*
5:22-33, *244*
5:23, *117*
5:25-27, *100*
6:14, *116*

Philippians
1:1, *116*
2:5, *94*
4:2-3, *123*
4:17, *117*

Colossians
1:15-18, 94
1:16-17, 132
2:11-12, 142
3:1-3, 145
3:3, 129, 145
3:9-11, 95
3:10, 94
3:17, 116
3:18, 99
3:18-19, 41, 44, 64
4:15, 123
4:16, 40

1 Thessalonians
5:20-22, 245
5:27, 40

2 Thessalonians
2:15, 39

1 Timothy
1:4, 65
1:19-20, 70
2, 5, 9, 10, 40, 41,
  51, 53, 56, 65, 70,
  72, 73, 75, 140,
  235, 243, 247,
  267, 271, 284
2:1-2, 40, 56
2:1-8, 40
2:1—3:13, 56
2:3-7, 40
2:4, 41
2:8, 41
2:8-12, 56
2:8-15, 56
2:9, 41, 60
2:9-12, 40

2:9-15, 40, 41, 49,
  50, 57, 58, 70, 71,
  72, 83, 85
2:11, 56, 73
2:11-12, 44, 59,
  115, 211
2:11-14, 233
2:11-15, 40, 41, 50,
  68, 71, 100, 138,
  140
2:12, 40, 41, 42, 43,
  44, 48, 50, 51, 56,
  71, 99, 284
2:12-15, 99
2:13, 48, 49, 50
2:13-14, 40, 49, 50,
  99
2:13-15, 40, 41,
  48
2:14, 48, 49, 71,
  243
2:15, 49, 56, 58, 63,
  71, 99
3:1, 56
3:1-7, 42
3:1-13, 36
3:2, 42
3:2-7, 36
3:5, 42
3:8, 43
3:8-13, 42
3:15, 41
4:1, 65
4:1-3, 60
5:15, 65
5:17, 42, 245
5:18, 39
5:19-20, 70
6:20-21, 70

2 Timothy
1:5, 44, 58
1:14, 39
2:14-26, 58
2:16, 70
2:24-26, 279
2:25-26, 70
3:5, 70
3:6-7, 58, 65
3:15, 44, 58
3:16, 39, 43
3:16-17, 254, 265
4:2-3, 39

Titus
1:5, 264
1:5-9, 36, 42
1:6, 36
1:7, 42, 51
1:9, 36, 39, 42, 51,
  245
1:10-11, 70
1:10-14, 58
2:1, 39
2:1-6, 44
2:3, 58
2:3-4, 73
2:3-5, 35, 37, 44
2:5, 61
3:9, 65
3:9-11, 58
3:10-11, 70

Hebrews
1:1-3, 94
1:3, 261
2:3, 39
5:12, 116
11:32, 23, 248

James
1:22, 251

1 Peter
1:23, 116
1:25, 116
2:2, 116
3:1-7, 44, 99
3:3, 67
3:7, 64, 243
4, 122
4:10, 116
4:10-11, 101, 115
4:11, 116
5:1-2, 42
5:1-4, 36

2 Peter
1:20-21, 39
2:3, 116
3:15-16, 39

1 John
3:18, 116
5:3, 51

Jude
1:3, 39

Revelation
2:20, 246
5:6-13, 33
19:7, 100
21:2, 100
21:9, 100
21:26, 175
22:17, 100